The
Food Lover's Guide
to the
BEST
ETHNIC
EATING
in New York City

The
Food Lover's Guide
to the
BEST
ETHNIC
EATING
in New York City

REVISED AND UPDATED
EDITION

Robert Sietsema

WITH A FOREWORD BY
Calvin Trillin

ARCADE PUBLISHING • NEW YORK

FIRST ARCADE EDITION

Library of Congress Cataloging-in-Publication Data

Sietsema, Robert.
  The food lover's guide to the best ethnic eating in New York City / by
Robert Sietsema; with a foreword by Calvin Trillin.—Rev. ed.
      p. cm.
Originally published: New York : City & Company, 1994.
    ISBN 1-55970-716-X
      1. Ethnic restaurants—New York (State)—New York—Directories.
2. New York (New York)—Directories. I. Trillin, Calvin. II. Title

  TX907.3.N72N48297 2004
  647.95747'1—dc22   2003020372

Published in the United States by
Arcade Publishing, Inc., New York
Distributed by Time Warner Book Group

10 9 8 7 6 5 4 3 2 1

Visit our Web site at www.arcadepub.com

Designed by Charles Rue Woods

IMAGO

PRINTED IN CHINA

CONTENTS

Foreword by Calvin Trillin | vii
Introduction | ix
Special Features | xi

Argentinean, Chilean, and Uruguayan | 1
Brazilian, Colombian, and Venezuelan | 7
Central American | 13
Guatemalan, Honduran, Panamanian, and Salvadoran
Central Asian and Caucasian | 18
Armenian, Azerbaijani, Georgian, Tajikistani,
and Uzbekistani
Chinese | 24
Beijing and Northern Chinese, Cantonese, Chiu Chow,
Fujianese, Hong Kong, Imports and Exports,
Shanghai, Sichuan and Hunan, Taiwanese,
Uighur, and Vegetarian Chinese
Cuban, Dominican, and Puerto Rican | 45
Eastern European | 54
Albanian, Bosnian, Bulgarian, Czech,
Hungarian, Istrian, Latvian, Lithuanian, and Polish
Ecuadorian, Bolivian, and Peruvian | 64
English, Irish, and Scottish | 73
Ethiopian, Eritrean, and South African | 77
French and Belgian | 81
German, Austrian, Dutch, and Scandinavian | 92
Ghanaian and Nigerian | 98
Greek | 105
Haitian | 112
International | 117
Italian | 124
Heroes; Italian-American; Osteria, Trattoria,
and Locandi; Pasticerria and Espresso Bars;
Pizza; and Wine Bars
Jamaican, Bajan, Grenadian, and Vincentian | 155

167	**Japanese**
	Noodle Shops, Other Specialties, Restaurants, and Sushi Bars
178	**Jewish-American**
	Dairy and Meat
184	**Korean**
191	**Malaysian, Indonesian, Philippine, and Singaporean**
199	**Mexican**
212	**Middle Eastern**
	Egyptian; Israeli; Jordanian; Lebanese, Syrian, and Palestinian; and Yemeni
222	**Moroccan and Tunisian**
228	**Persian and Afghani**
232	**Regional and Vernacular American**
	Barbecue; Cajun and Creole; Hamburgers; Hot Dogs; Lunch Counters, Diners, and Ice Cream Parlors; New American; Philly Cheese Steaks; Sandwiches and Comfort Food; Seafood; Southwestern; and Tex-Mex and Burritos
250	**Russian and Ukrainian**
256	**South Asian**
	Anglo-Indian, Bangladeshi, Gujarati, Hyderabadi, Northern Indian, Pakistani, Southern Indian, Sri Lankan, and Tibetan
276	**Senegalese, Guinean, Ivory Coastal, and Malian**
283	**Soul Food**
291	**Spanish and Portuguese**
	Asturian, Basque, Catalan, Galician, Pan-Regional Spanish, Portuguese, and Tapas
298	**Thai and Burmese**
306	**Trinidadian, Guyanese, and Surinamese**
312	**Turkish**
318	**Vietnamese and Cambodian**
325	**Neighborhood Index**
341	**Restaurant Index**

FOREWORD BY CALVIN TRILLIN

I once admitted in *The New Yorker* that before I knew Robert Sietsema I used to follow his adventures in outer borough eateries the way some sedentary Victorian burghers in Manchester or Leeds must have followed the travels of Henry Stanley in Africa. Reading a review by Sietsema in *The Village Voice* or an issue of *Down the Hatch,* a newsletter he seemed to put out whenever it suited his meal schedule, I'd say something like "my man Sietsema's been eating at an Egyptian fish joint in Brooklyn" or "my man Sietsema has found the ultimate bowl of Uzbekistani lagman." That's right: I called him "my man Sietsema." I know him now, and I still call him "my man Sietsema."

In the vernacular of New York, Sietsema would be called my ethnic-food maven—maven being a Yiddish word that means someone who's depended on for his expertise in a particular field. In New York, everyone has a battery of mavens. A New Yorker wouldn't think of buying a computer without consulting his computer maven or of choosing a nursery school for his three year old without having a chat with at least one nursery-school maven. When someone calls me to ask if I know, say, where a person can get a decent pljeskavica in this town or what a savvy diner should order in a new Malaysian restaurant in the eastern reaches of Canal Street, I reply, in the prescribed New York manner, "Of course I know! You take me for some kind of farmer or something? I'll get right back to you." Then I call my ethnic-food maven, Robert Sietsema.

It was Sietsema who took me to the Malaysian restaurant in the first place. He introduced me to pljeskavica, a sort of Bosnian hamburger that's about the size of a frisbee. He also took me to the place with the ultimate bowl of lagman, which is a vegetable soup with udon noodles in it. That was in a kosher Uzbekistani restaurant called **Salut,** in Forest Hills, Queens. I predict that if you try a bowl of lagman at Salut, you will start referring to the author of this book as "my man Sietsema."

INTRODUCTION

The first edition of this book was published in 1994 with the title *Good & Cheap Ethnic Eats Under $10*. It boasted 17 ethnic categories and 94 restaurants, and seemed fairly comprehensive at the time. Nowadays those totals look positively puny. In subsequent editions, as the name of the book got longer, the list of restaurants and ethnicities lengthened, too. This new fourth edition, vastly revised and expanded, now contains 820 restaurants in a whopping 100 categories. It includes dining establishments in every corner of every borough, so that, wherever you go in the city, you need never be far from a great meal. New ethnic cuisines we welcome to this volume include Uighur Chinese, Honduran, Afro-Panamanian, Keralan and Hyderabadi Indian, Tajikistani, Lithuanian, Latvian, Bolivian, Uruguayan, Romanian, Dutch, and several more. Sadly, we lost our only Swiss restaurant in 2003 — stalwart **Roetelle A.G.** Our new lack of Swiss food notwithstanding, there has never been a more exciting time to eat in Gotham. And if you decide you really need some fondue, 32nd Street's excellent **Artisanal** awaits you. In addition, the new spate of Austrian restaurants provides a ready substitute for Swiss.

Each successive volume has added more features in an attempt to become more helpful, and this edition is no exception. Symbols added in this edition include a tomato 🍅 for vegetarian-friendly places, a fish 🐟 for places that have unusually good seafood options, a chile pepper 🌶 for places that can fulfill your jones for fiery food, and a dollar sign $ for places that are likely to cost more than $20 per person. Cheapness remains an important priority of this book, and the vast majority of restaurants reviewed can be enjoyed for less than $20, and often for way, way less. At the city's recently sprouted Northern Chinese dumpling stalls, for example, you'd be hard pressed to spend more than $5 for a very full meal.

Introduced here for the first time is a star system: ★ indicates good restaurants, ★★ great restaurants, and ★★★ amazing ones. Remember that this book represents my favorite spots out of the thousands of places I've eaten in the last decade, so that every establishment mentioned comes enthusiastically recommended. Even the one-star places are magnificent in their own unobtrusive way, so please don't neglect them because they only have a single star. On the other side of the coin, you ought to drop what you're doing right now and run to every three-star place in the book, because who knows when harsh real estate conditions may force them to close. Three-star restaurants include Flushing's **Dosa Hutt**—the city's premier purveyor of the South Indian crepes called masala dosas, and **Romano** in Brooklyn's Dyker Heights, where a batter-dipped and deep-fried sandwich of fresh mozzarella with a tomato dipping sauce is one of the best things I've eaten in the last few years. Nor does Manhattan itself lack for superlatives, with Cuban lunch counter **Margon** wowing a crowd of office workers and good-food hunters with its roast pork, Cuban sandwiches, and fricasseed chicken, and is consequently awarded three stars as our thanks.

If you become increasingly serious about ethnic food, especially about finding newly arrived examples, you will invariably find yourself orienteering in the so-called "Outer Boroughs." Like any explorer, make sure you have a good map before you set out, since complicated directions are beyond the purview of this book. I recommend the *Hagstrom 5-Boro Atlas*, available at bookstores and lots of drugstores, too. Alternately, you can go to Yahoo Maps (http://maps.yahoo.com/) and get one printed out automatically, with a big red star indicating your destination. As in the previous editions, it's also necessary to warn you that, in a city where the average restaurant exists for less than five years, a few of the places mentioned in this book will have closed before you get to them. My advice, as before, is to go anyway—you're likely to find another joint just down the block, and it might even be better.

What are the newest and hottest cuisines? Chinese continues to fascinate, and now that we have our first

Uighur restaurant, you can eat your way across the entire Silk Road without leaving the confines of the city. Indian places are exploding, too, with many new restaurants devoted to regional cuisines. Keep your eye on the new Indian strip along Hillside Avenue in Floral Park, Queens, where South Indians have been congregating at places like **Indian Coffee House**, which has all the excitement **Jackson Diner** had in its heyday. Richmond Hill in Queens has plenty of new Punjabi places, while Curry Hill on Lexington Avenue is undergoing a renaissance more profound than any in its two-decade history. While Francophone African restaurants have clearly declined since the last issue, Anglophone places from Ghana and Nigeria are on the upswing, especially in Flatbush, East Flatbush, Brownsville, and Crown Heights. Regional Mexican fare from Puebla has been commonplace in the city for the last 10 or so years, and now more recent immigrants from places like Guerrero, Michoacán, and Oaxaca have expanded the catalog of available dishes, adding new and more arcane chile combinations to the repertoire. Wherever you happen to be, you're never very far away from an exciting new dining experience.

And what I said in the first edition of this book remains true: Life is too short to have a bad meal.

SPECIAL FEATURES

★ good
★ ★ great
★ ★ ★ amazing
$ over $20 per person
spicy food available
good fish place
vegetarian-friendly

The
Food Lover's Guide
to the
BEST
ETHNIC
EATING
in New York City

Argentinean, Chilean, and Uruguayan

A 2,300-mile Andean spine separates Argentina and Chile, and this mountain range keeps culinary resemblance to a minimum. The prototypical Argentinean rides the pampas, subsisting on the semiferal cattle that also pay his salary. In addition, half of all Argentines are of Italian descent, and Argentine menus are loaded with pasta, and, especially, gnocchi. These pastas are often freighted with a sauce mixing tomatoes and cream, which can be a little on the sweet side, or skewed with spices like nutmeg and cinnamon. Chileans, on the other hand, are fishermen who depend on the Humboldt Current for the richness of their diet. The piscatory diversity is demonstrated at Elmhurst's **El Arrayan**, where one of the highlights is a plate of locos, a sea creature like an outsize abalone. In addition, Chile benefits from the inherited diet of its indigenous peoples as modified by the influence of the conquistadores, who introduced cheese, among other things. Where Argentina and Chile meet is in their love of empanadas.

An Argentine friend in Brooklyn threw a barbecue. He'd built a brick pit in his townhouse backyard, and when I arrived, the pit was being tended by his Chilean assistant, who carefully turned the churrasco and tripe and sausages, as my friend supervised. The Chilean barbecuer was also responsible for making the seafood empanadas, baked to a deep brown and displaying the braided spine that's an invariable sign of South American empanada technique. Smiling as he bit into one, my friend turned to me and exclaimed, "If I'd made them myself they would have been beef."

As the Argentine economy has tanked, immigrants to the United States have opened all sorts of new restaurants, though these invariably resemble parrillas (South American barbecues) to one extent or another. Chilean restaurants remain rare. New York's Uruguayans, meanwhile, are finally intent on distinguishing themselves from their Argentinean brethren, with whom they share many culinary similarities. But so far, Uruguayans have mainly opened bakeries.

LOOK FOR:

asado *short ribs*

bife de chorizo *porterhouselike cut*

chimichurri *Argentine parsley-and-garlic steak sauce*

churrasco *sirloin steak*

color *Chilean mixture of oil, garlic, and paprika*

dulce de leche *caramel*

empanadas *meat, cheese, or seafood turnovers*

entraña *skirt steak*

guatita *beef tripe*

humitas *Chilean sweet corn tamales*

locos *larger abalone cousin, served with thick mayo*

mariscal *Chilean ceviche*

matambre *Argentinean stuffed veal roll*

noqui *Argentine gnocchi*

parrillada *Argentine barbecue assortment*

pastel de choclo *Andean corn-and-meat casserole*

Russian salad *mayonnaisey vegetable salad*

Argentinean

ARGENTINE PAVILION ★ ★ $

32 West 46th Street, Manhattan, 212-921-0835 Rumors have been flying that this old-timer — badly outnumbered by Brazilian restaurants in this nabe — is on the verge of dissolution. Far from it, as we discovered during a meeting of the Organ Meat Society. Done on the flashy grill in the window, the chitlins and sweetbreads are still up to snuff, and the skirt steak still a glorious chunk of chewy striated meat. Even the people in the ancient dining room seem to have been sitting there for decades.

LA CABANA ★ ☺

86-07 Northern Boulevard, Queens, 718-426-5977 Overshadowed by its better-known peers like La Portena and La Fusta, this comfy Argentine steakhouse, with a particularly gracious staff, persists on a strip of Northern Boulevard known for its Colombian eateries. Its penchant for Italo-Argentine fusion is particularly notable, seen especially in the namesake wood-oven pizza, which comes draped with luscious strips of skirt steak — I've never seen anything quite like it. The parrillada for two is generous, and focused on organ meats, while the fettuccine Alfredo is one of the richer editions in town.

CHIMICHURRI GRILL ★ $

606 9th Avenue, Manhattan, 212-596-8655 Named after the zingy parsley-and-garlic sauce that Argentineans spoon on their steak, this meatery offers beef flown in daily from South America. Unaged, it's mildly flavored and well marbled with fat, and grilled medium rare with a beautiful char (although not, alas, over charcoal). If you like to fight with your meat, pick the beef short ribs; if you want butter-soft, get the filet mignon.

LA FUSTA ★ ★

80-32 Baxter Avenue, Queens, 718-429-8222 This queen of Argentine parrillas is located across the street from Elmhurst Hospital, in case you overindulge. Skip the mixed grill, unless you relish

---

KILL HUNGER

I once edited a book of 19th-century photos collected by a traveling salesman from South American junk shops. In particular, the shots of the Argentine pampas knocked me out — one depicted a rancho's fenced yard littered with mutilated carcasses, as if every time the gauchos wanted a snack they'd haunch a calf with a single machete stroke, roast it on a makeshift spit, then leave the corpse to rot. That's how passionate they were about fresh beef, and that's how available it was. One of the best starters at an Argentinean restaurant is matambre ("kill hunger"), a veal breast rolled around carrots, pimento, spinach, and boiled egg, sliced crosswise and served at room temperature. It was invented as a portable lunch for travelers crossing the vastness of the pampas, who couldn't be bothered pausing long enough to shoot a cow.

its heavy component of sweetbreads and blood sausage. Instead, order individual meats. Especially recommended are the beef short ribs, or any of the vast selection of steaks and variety meats (calf liver alone is done five different ways). Plenty of attention is paid to pastas, including splendid homemade potato noquis.

EL GAUCHITO ✫
94-60 Corona Avenue, Queens, 718-271-8198 Heart of Corona's Little Argentina, this combo parrilla and meat market produces luscious grilled skirt steaks, sweetbreads, short ribs, and homemade chorizo and blood sausage, while the overcooked kidneys and oddly fatty chitlins are less than impressive. The pickled tongue appetizer, bathed in oily chimichurri, was so good we ordered another plate.

PAMPA ✫ ✫ $
768 Amsterdam Avenue, Manhattan, 212-865-2929 Debuting on the lower lip of the Manhattan Valley a couple of years ago, this Argentinean was instantly popular among neighborhood diners, who knifed their way through outsized portions of entraña, asado, and filet mignon, grilled precisely to order. Kidneys, tripe, and blood sausage are also offered, but you may want to opt for the pastas, including homemade noquis sauced with tucco, a delicious combination of pureed tomatoes, strips of roast meat, and garlic. For starters, the fried empanadas can't be beat, or pick one of the unexpected Peruvian appetizers.

LA PORTENA ✫ ✫ ✫
74-25 37th Avenue, Queens, 718-458-8111 It's no accident that a former butcher shop is now the city's most beloved Argentine restaurant. The proprietors combine an indefatigable passion for beef with an insider's knowledge of how to acquire it. The mixed grill is too huge to be negotiated; you're better off cherry-picking the best cuts, including perfect skirt steak, well-grilled short ribs, and some of the loamiest blood sausage around. The breaded cutlet that bears the restaurant's name is a dead ringer for Texas chicken-fried steak — but bring your own gravy.

SUR ✫ $
232 Smith Street, Brooklyn, 718-875-1716 Joining the burgeoning restaurant scene along Smith Street in Carroll Gardens, this Argentine focuses exclusively on beef. The skirt steak is the most righteous, tender and richly textured, done to perfection on the gas-fired grill. The mixed grill for two includes blood and Italian sausages, skirt, sweetbreads, and dual racks of chewy short ribs, served with perfunctory bowls of salad and mashed potatoes and an appropriately zingy chimichurri sauce. But don't miss some of Brooklyn's best french fries, or the dulce de leche crepes for dessert.

EL ARRAYAN ☆ ☆ ◄━

91-06 43rd Avenue, Queens, 718-478-6245 El Arrayan occupies a handsome four-story townhouse in an Elmhurst neighborhood of curving small-town lanes. Starters include baked empanadas filled with a tasty seafood hash, and mariscal, a ceviche of clams, baby shrimp, and gooey raw mussels. Best of all is locos mayo, a Stonehenge of abalone, each specimen decorated with a pig's tail of mayonnaise. Reflecting Chile's Indian heritage, pastel de choclo casseroles ground meat, chicken, and raisins, with a topping of crushed corn and sugar. Guatita bathes tripe in the mixture of olive oil, garlic, and paprika called "color." It's one of the best renditions of cow stomach in town.

LAS GAVIOTAS ☆

63-12 Broadway, Queens, 718-639-3426 As we squeezed in the door, an elderly platinum blond in a cowboy hat and fringed vest circled the room. Trailed by a power-chording guitarist, she clutched a red carnation as she belted patriotic songs. Las Gaviotas ("the seagulls") is the least ambitious Chilean restaurant in town, a comfy Woodside bar handy to the BQE slinging South American bar food. We were delighted by a ceviche of corvina, a favorite Chilean fish sometimes called spotfin croaker as a result of the ugly noises it makes when caught. The empanadas de queso, too, were flawless — bulging half-moon pies with braided spines. Pastel de choclo, though, is a pale shadow of Pomaire's.

POMAIRE ☆ ☆ $

371 West 46th Street, Manhattan, 212-456-3055 Pomaire is a quiet Chilean village famous for its pottery, and the restaurant displays lots of it. First, the waiter brings homemade bread, flat round loaves like Moroccan bread. It can be smeared with butter or, even better, the red salsa called color. From the special menu come eight bargain entrées accompanied by salad, dessert, and coffee. I went for pastel de choclo, a crocked casserole of corn puree filled with ground beef, chicken, sliced egg, black olives, and onions with white sugar sprinkled on top. The menu excels at pricey seafood, some of it imported from South America. Carbo alert: entrées often come with both rice and deep-fried potato cubes.

SAN ANTONIO BAKERY #2 ☆ ☆ ☆

36-20 Astoria Boulevard, Queens, 718-777-8733 No one need be ashamed of eating a hot-dog meal, especially if the frank comes from this Chilean bakery, which has a seating area where you can watch planes treetop into La Guardia. The dog comes in a just-made bun heaped with chopped tomatoes, guacamole, and crema. You can also get sandwiches, empanadas, and humitas, and wash it all down with a can of the despicable yellow soda called Pap.

Uruguayan

LA ESQUINA CRIOLLA ☆ ☆ ☆

94-67 Corona Avenue, Queens, 718-699-5579 This gleaming Uruguayan outpost, anchor to a neighborhood filled with Argentinean and Uruguayan small businesses, is also one of the best cut-rate steakhouses in town, expertly grilling cuts like bife de chorizo, skirt steak, and churrasco — the thin-sliced sirloin luxuriantly flopping over the sides of the plate. Fried yuca replaces french fries as the preferred accompaniment. The decor focuses on an outsized meat saw that sees frequent use.

LA URUGUAYA Y PARAGUAYITA BAKERY ☆ ☺

68-24 Roosevelt Avenue, Queens, 718-672-1919 As you can see from the name, this cozy bakery also claims to be Paraguayan, although disentangling the two cuisines would require more expertise than I can muster, especially since the output is distinctly pan–South American. A couple of comfy tables and an espresso machine make this a convenient Starbucks substitute, and the spinach empanada, at least, is worth walking a mile for. In addition to empanadas, a line of sandwiches is also available, dressed with a thick mayonnaise that threatens to dissolve the vegetable garnish.

Brazilian, Colombian, and Venezuelan

Colombian used to dominate the dining scene in Jackson Heights, East Elmhurst, and Corona, but as the immigrants who fueled the phenomenon became better-off and moved away, Colombian places were replaced by Mexican and Ecuadorian ones, and many of the remaining Colombian cafés became dispirited and mediocre. Along Northern Boulevard in the 80s Colombian restaurants are making a last stand. Here about a dozen newish hot dog stands, cafés, and juice joints have put down roots, with the occasional Mexican, Ecuadorian, Bolivian, and Argentinean place thrown down for culinary contrast, but mainly catering to Colombians. It's a chance to see culinary fusion in the making.

LOOK FOR:

almojabana *Colombian cheese bread*

arepa *grilled corn cake*

bolinhos de bacalhau *salt-cod fritters*

caldo verde *bean and kale soup*

churrascaria *Brazilian meat assortment*

dende *bright orange palm oil*

feijoada *meat-and-black-bean gunk*

mondongo *tripe stew*

muqueca *shrimp in coconut milk*

pabellon *Venezuelan shredded beef*

pão de queijo *cheese-stuffed breadlets*

picanha *steak Brazilian-style*

reina pepiada *chicken-and-avocado salad*

sancocho *hearty pork or chicken soup*

tamale *meal in a banana leaf*

vatapá *Afro-Brazilian fish stew*

The Brazilian community in New York has continued to thrive, mainly in Astoria, Long Island City, and the East Village, though the Brazilian food served there is more often from the European side — rather than the African side — of Brazil's culinary ledger. Finally, Venezuelan food has never been much of a player in town, though I'm not sure why. Maybe it's because Venezuelan food, like Honduran, is often bland, and Venezuelan immigrants can easily get a reasonable facsimile at other Latin places. The most exciting Venezuelan restaurant ever — Woodside's **El Rincon Venezolano** — opened early in 2003, and then promptly closed, but there are two others remaining in town, if you're curious.

Brazilian

BRAZIL GRILL ☆
787 8th Avenue, Manhattan, 212-307-9449 The grilled meats were a dry disappointment, and neither did the caldo verde do much for me, salty and nearly devoid of kale. Thus it was a great surprise when the vatapá was better than any I've had in the city. This African-leaning dish from Bahia features shrimp and fish in a multifaceted orange sauce that depends on coconut milk and dende oil for richness, and garlic and chiles for sharp flavor.

CABANA CARIOCA ☆
123 West 45th Street, Manhattan, 212-581-8088 Trudge upstairs to the breathtakingly inexpensive lunchtime buffet and discover an antique tableau of Olde New York, featuring faded paintings and craggy-browed waiters with 'tude. The huge feed encompasses unlimited salad, entrées, sides, and desserts, with invariably two spectacular entrées along with eight mediocre ones: plump mussels in an oily red sauce and chewy beefsteak littered with garlic and onions were best on a recent revisit.

CANTINA DE LINA ☆ ☆
31-90 30th Street, Queens, 718-278-2801 Call ahead for daily specials at this tiny carryout-only canteen, where Queens's most beloved Brazilian cook turns out such profoundly good one-dish meals as the shrimp stew bobô de camarão, and a chicken, okra, and polenta miracle called frango com quiabo.

DELÍCIA ☆
322 West 11th Street, Manhattan, 212-242-2002 Who knows how this quiet West Village hideaway stays in business? Few baked goods attain the ecstatic heights of their pão de queijo, the golf-ball-like Brazilian cheese bread. The cook makes fine rendi-

tions of shrimp muqueca, an African-inspired concoction that finds the crustaceans swimming in coconut milk and tomato, and spice-rubbed roast pork. But foremost among the meat-bearing entrées is feijoada. In its inky depths lurk pork ribs with the meat falling off the bone, intensely smoky ham hocks, and sausages, a symphony of oink bound together by black beans. This is a dish that the devil reserves for his own dinner.

MALAGUETA ☆ ☆ 🐟

25-35 36th Avenue, Queens, 718-937-4821 This is no hash house, but an ambitious white-tablecloth bistro that offers tasty and voluminous renditions of Brazilian standards like shrimp muqueca and picanha (Cariocan churrasco), in addition to some French-leaning things like poached chicken breast in shallots and white wine.

TAPAJOS RIVER STEAK HOUSE ☆ ☆ ☆ 🐟

48 Wilson Avenue, Newark, New Jersey, 973-491-9196 Evidence of a flowering Brazilian presence in Ironbound, Tapajos is named after an Amazonian tributary, and combines the meaty excitement of the churrascaria with African-leaning seafood dishes from the Brazilian coast. In the former category are several meat assortments, usually including sirloin, chicken thighs, pork loin, and, the Brazilian fave, picanha, all cooked over real charcoal. In the latter, muqueca is a tilefish stew heaped with peppers, tomatoes, and onions, and thickened with coconut milk turned orange with palm oil.

TERRA BRASIL ☆

33-04 36th Avenue, Queens, 718-609-1367 Go at lunch or right after work to this small cafeteria, which closes early, and features a steam table with a weekly rotating schedule of nicely prepared dishes sold by weight (chicken with okra Tuesday, salt cod and potatoes Friday), along with good, cheap, prepared-to-order steaks. A favorite of Museum of the Moving Image visitors.

MEAT ORGIES

The rodizio is something of a Utopian concept, proposing that you eat your fill of as many meats as the restaurant can muster. Guys dressed as gauchos stroll by, bearing swords crammed with filet, sirloin, lamb, pork tenderloin, chicken, and — at some of the funkier spots — chicken hearts, lamb kidneys, and sweetbreads. While meat is the focus, these places also offer giant buffets to try to tempt you away from the meat. Though voluminous, the buffets are often mediocre in the extreme, featuring all sorts of fried seafood, wilting salads, and mystery raw materials gobbed with mayo.

GREEN FIELD ☆
108-01 Northern Boulevard, Queens, 718-672-5202
Founded by Korean immigrants from Rio and still patronized mainly by Asians, Green Field caused a hubbub in the 1990s, and Manhattan reviewers dutifully made pilgrimages to write about it.

MASTER GRILL ☆
34-09 College Point Boulevard, Queens, 718-762-0300 This is Green Field's even larger and more unwieldy cousin. Worth visiting just to marvel at the size.

CHURRASCARIA PLATAFORMA ☆ ☆
316 West 49th Street, Manhattan, 212-245-0505
Manhattan's best rodizio was also one of the few remaining after the fad fizzled. The meat is good, appetizers and desserts are included, and you can probably make one meal last the entire day. The exotic buffet is loaded with salads and Brazilian dishes of high quality.

GIRASSOL ☆
33-18 28th Avenue, Astoria, 718-545-8250 This is one of the Astorian Brazilian places that does churrascaria on a modest scale on the weekends, even though individual cuts of meat can be ordered separately during the week. The prices, too, are correspondingly more modest.

Colombian

COSTAL COLOMBIANA ☆
21-20 35th Avenue, Queens, 718-706-0663 This joint offers a broad selection of fish, beef, and chicken dishes, plus a pair of special stews each day. My medium order of the tripe stew called mondongo — green with cilantro, smelling intensely of garlic — contained ragged pieces of stomach and an equal number of chunks of good pork. Potatoes, peas, carrots, and rice filled out the bowl. The chorizo appetizer is also recommended, one large garlicky sausage garnished with onion, tomato, and lettuce, plus an arepa.

LA POLLERA COLORADO ✭ ✭

41-20 Greenpoint Avenue, Queens, 718-729-8586 This Colombian rotisserie makes the best beans in Queens – brown, slippery, oily, and garlicky, a meal in itself. The chicken is pretty damn good, too, with an unexpected jolt of cumin. Omnibus Colombian plates featuring ganged-up things like steak, beans, ribs, rice, plantains, sausages, and fried eggs are also offered.

RINCON COLOMBIANO ✭

106-20 Corona Avenue, Queens, 718-393-1060 For a huge, cheap meal keep your eye on the daily special soups: Sunday it's sancocho de gallina, a cilantro-accented chicken broth crammed with potatoes, yuca, and plantain, sided with an even bigger plate of fricasseed chicken, rice, and salad. Also featured are outsize Colombian tamales stuffed with meat and vegetables, shrimp in creole sauce, and, of course, arepas, the rotund white corn cakes that are a national signature. For dessert, the Lemon Ice King of Corona is just down the block.

TIERRAS COLOMBIANAS ✭ ✭

82-18 Roosevelt Avenue, Queens, 718-426-8868; 33-01 Broadway, Queens, 718-956-3012 Ensconced in a gleaming diner on bustling Roosevelt Avenue that's kept so clean you could eat off the floor, Tierras Colombianas is favored by families who chow down on meal-sized soups and omnibus platters that include – in addition to boiled and grilled cuts of meat – rice, avocado, fried plantain, well-stewed pink beans, and the delicious corn cakes called arepas. Colombian friends tell me the newer, nondiner location on Broadway is superior for both food and service.

Also see Mosaico in the International chapter.

Venezuelan

CARACAS AREPA BAR ✭ ✺

91 East 7th Street, Manhattan, 212-228-5062 For a glimpse of what the world was like before spices were discovered, when mayonnaise was the only flavoring, get your ass over to Caracas. It occupies the diminutive former home of Harry's Burritos, though the space now seems smaller. The prime business of Caracas is slitting fluffy white arepas and ruining them by piling on salads heavy with mayo (or sometimes meat and cheese). Alternately, you can get an empanada with a variety of fillings, the masa crust so grease sodden you better watch out it doesn't drip on your shoes.

FLOR'S KITCHEN ☆

149 1st Avenue, Manhattan, 212-387-8949; 170 Waverly Place, Manhattan, 212-229-9926 The original five-table joint on 1st Avenue is so narrow there's barely enough room for all the rave reviews plastered in the front window. I guess the food lives up to the notices, although Venezuelan cuisine is not exciting enough to send you running to the travel agent. Arepas are a big part of the menu — light, fluffy, and pleasingly crusty despite the paleness of the exterior. They are split in half and stuffed with fillings like reina pepiada, a chicken salad glued together with avocado. Entrées run to pabellon, a sweet version of Cuban ropa viejo, and grilled king-fish sided with salad and rice.

Central American

Guatemalan, Honduran, Panamanian, and Salvadoran

I wish I could say there were plenty of Costa Rican and Nicaraguan places in town — but there aren't. Instead, we have tons of Salvadorans — many of them excellent and cheap — and, collectively, only a handful of Honduran, Panamanian, and Guatemalan spots. Salvadorans have become the most numerous restaurateurs among Central Americans, perhaps because their cooking has the most universal appeal and they're aggressive about seeking out obscure storefronts with cheap rents. While Honduran and Guatemalan spots invite you in for a ponderous, sit-down meal, the Salvadorans furnish delicious on-the-run snacks like pupusas. One of the world's great fast foods, it's a million times better than a Whopper, and cheaper, too. Moreover, the Salvadorans have been willing to go head to head with Mexican restaurants in their own neighborhoods.

Honduras was the original banana republic. Since independence in 1821 it's been dominated by multinational fruit conglomerates through dozens of alternating coups and elections. The U.S. influence is obvious in the food, not only in the replacement of homemade hot sauce with American ketchup, but in the general blandness of the fare. Despite political troubles going back decades which might have encouraged emigration, New York has few Guatemalan restaurants. A couple of years ago we had two; now we have only one. Which is a shame, since the food represents a mind-boggling shape-shifting of Mexican fare, while displaying many of the same earthy qualities.

One of the most interesting places to open recently was the city's first Afro-Panamanian coffee shop, combining elements of African, Dominican, Salvadoran, and Jamaican cooking, and featuring plenty of snacks as well as set meals. Take a meal at **Kelso Diner**, and you'll be eating something really rare.

LOOK FOR:

atol de elote *sweet corn beverage*
carne asado *beef roasted or stewed with sofrito*
carne guisado *beef stew*
curtido *tart pink cabbage relish*
enchilada *fried tortilla with topping*
higado *Afro-Panamanian liver and onions*
hilachas *Guatemalan shredded beef with chile
     sauce*
jocon *Guatemalan chicken in tomatillo sauce*
longaniza *spicy sausage*
ojaldo *Afro-Panamanian fry bread*
pollo con crema *chicken in sour-cream sauce*
pupusa *Salvadoran stuffed masa cake*
revolcado *pork-head stew*
salpicon *beef-and-radish salad*
sofrito *paste of onions, green pepper, and garlic*
sopa de caracol *Honduran conch chowder*
sopa de res *Salvadoran oxtail soup*
taco *stuffed, rolled, and fried tortilla*
tamale de elote *Salvadoran sweet tamale
     studded with corn kernels*
yuca con chicharron *fried pork and manioc*

Guatemalan

LA XELAJU ☆ ☆ ☆
87-52 168th Street, Queens, 718-657-5407 Decorated with worry dolls and weavings, this intimate café turns out food that's tasty and somewhat unusual, if you're used to Mexican. Tacos are like flautas, enchiladas are like tostadas, and the handmade corn tortillas are half the size and twice the thickness of the usual Mexican product. Don't miss salpicon, a delicious cold salad of ground meat, radishes, and tomatoes zapped with lime juice and fresh mint, or thick stews like jocon (chicken with scallions and tomatillos) and hilachas (shredded beef in chile gravy).

Honduran

HONDURAS MAYA ☆ 🐟
587 5th Avenue, Brooklyn, 718-965-8028 The towering enchilada showcases a diminutive deep-fried tortilla topped with beef and potatoes concealed by crumbly cheese and a slice of boiled egg. Sopa de caracol is the national dish, a conch chowder with plenty of the rubbery beast interspersed with yuca, plantain, and carrots in a broth whitened with coconut milk. It's a trip to the tropics in a bowl. Sopa de jaiba substitutes three whole crabs for the conch. Breakfasts are a particularly good deal here.

LA ORQUIDEA ☆ ☆
500 East 149th Street, Bronx, 718-585-1488 This recently bloomed flower offers the usual tasty Central American fodder, including pupusas, enchiladas, and fried yuca combos, in addition to uniquely Honduran specialties like sofrito-rubbed carne asado, weekends-only conch soup, and a delicious typical breakfast of eggs with chorizo, frijoles, fried plantain, avocado, and thick homemade tortillas.

Panamanian

KELSO DINER ☆ ☆ ☆
648 Franklin Avenue, Brooklyn, 718-857-4137 Afro-Panamanian cooking displays a wild assortment of influences — the wonderful deep-fried flatbread called ojaldo points straight to Africa and India. This hopping Prospect Heights café and social club features snacks and filling soups at lunch, and more ambitious sit-down meals at suppertime. The searing yellow hot sauce might be Haitian or Trinidadian, while the tortillas mimic Colombian arepas, only coarser and oilier. Higado reprises the kind of liver and onions that parents sometimes have to force their children to eat, only the tender strips have been zapped with Jamaican-style curry powder, improving the dish 1,000 percent.

Salvadoran

LA CABANA SALVADOREÑA ☆
4384 Broadway, Manhattan, 212-928-7872 Perhaps unsure of its Salvadoran constituency, this Upper Broadway establishment with a very handsome dining room features a menu adding Mexican and Dominican stuff to the Central American repertoire. While I've never liked the soups much, standards like yuca con chicharron

15

and homemade pupusas — the latter available in a rarely encountered rice version — are impressive.

LOS CHORROS ☆

46 5th Avenue, Brooklyn, 718-230-5365 This serviceable Salvadoran on the frontier of Park Slope offers the usual Central American specialties: cheese or bean-stuffed papusas, satisfying soups crammed with vegetables and laced with spaghetti, and comida tipico entrées of roast chicken, liver and onions, and pepper steak. The most satisfying snack is a chicken enchilada that looks like a Mexican tostada. Fridays only there's atol de elote, a sweet puree of fresh corn described on the menu as "oatmeal of corn."

EL COMAL ☆ ☆ ☆

148-62 Hillside Avenue, Queens, 718-657-1929 This boxy lunch counter creates its pupusas to order from a heap of masa right by the griddle, and you can't get any fresher than that. The hairnetted counter gal flings a pair on the griddle as you order, and with a great show of dexterity, flips them again and again, patting them with the spatula after every flip. The curtido also has an extemporaneous quality: the spice-bearing component is squeezed on at the last moment, and the plastic container given a mighty shake. The delicious sopa de res comes in a white bowl and contains oxtail, yuca, chayote, green beans, red peppers, zucchini, and potatoes in a light broth redolent of onions, green peppers, and garlic.

IZALCO ☆ ☆ ☆

64-05 Roosevelt Avenue, Queens, 718-533-8373 Named after an active volcano, the city's premier Salvadoran is more than your typical pupuseria. Culinary triumphs include elote tamales — husk-wrapped, studded with corn kernels, and light as soufflés. The best of the corn-based snacks is the towering Salvadoran enchilada, showcasing a diminutive tortilla deep-fried and topped with beef and potatoes concealed by a light snowfall of queso seco and a slice of boiled egg. Don't miss salpicon, a salad of cold shredded beef, or the ambitious selection of stuffed vegetables, if only to answer the question, How the hell do you stuff a green bean?

EL PULGARCITO DE AMERICA ☆ ☆ ⏱

3133 Fulton Street, Brooklyn, 718-647-7762 Barely within Brooklyn borders, this Cypress Hills Salvadoran has endeared itself to vegetarians with a plethora of nonmeat pupusas, including spinach, zucchini, and cheese with loroco flowers. Meatwise, the tripe and cow foot soup verges on the astonishing, with a gluey and flavorsome amber broth. The moniker means "little thumb of America," El Salvador's nickname.

EL REFUGIO ★ ★ ⏾

114-11 Rockaway Beach Boulevard, Queens, 718-634-5097 The Rockaway peninsula can be a bitch when it comes to finding a decent place to eat. Luckily, this "refuge" makes wonderful pupusas in multiple varieties. One cheese rendition comes flecked with loroco flowers, which taste like a cross between thyme and oregano, while another exploits the zucchini skin's leathery properties. The huevos rancheros accompanied by a porcupiney rice-and-refried-black-bean admixture is also not to be missed.

EL SALVADOR ★

1544 Myrtle Avenue, Brooklyn, 718-628-0606 Twin maps of Guatemala and El Salvador adorn the wall of this humble lunch counter a few steps south of the Queens frontier in Bushwick. The carne guisado (beef stew) is tasty, but is almost overshadowed by the moist, chile-flecked rice that comes alongside. Among the hand-patted pupusas, the rare spinach and cheese combo won us over immediately.

TIERRAS SALVADOREÑAS ★

94-16 37th Avenue, Queens, 718-672-0853 This East Elmhurst carryout is something of a national home for homesick Salvadorans, who run in and out all evening for pupusas, served with a copious quantity of excellent curtido and a red sauce you should throw away. The dining room next door offers a complete Salvadoran menu.

USULUTECO ★

4017 5th Avenue, Brooklyn, 718-436-8025 Stuffed with cheese or pork, hand-patted, then cooked to speckled brownness on the griddle, pupusas get their name from a Nahuatl Indian expression meaning "swollen tortilla." At Usuluteco, queso is best, oozing ropes of white cheese flecked with green loroco flowers, rescued from mellowness by curtido, a zany cabbage relish tinted beet-juice pink. Heap it on top or, as real aficionados do, slit the pupusa and insert the slaw. Bet you can't eat just one. The salpicon and chicken soup are both highly recommended at this mellow Sunset Park Salvadoran, though the main courses tend to be ho-hum.

Central Asian and Caucasian

Armenian, Azerbaijani, Georgian, Tajikistani, and Uzbekistani

The appearance of Uzbeki, Georgian, and Azerbaijani restaurants was one of the big food stories of the last decade. Always good cheap places to score shish kebabs, usually grilled over charcoal, each group revealed a new cuisine unfamiliar to most New Yorkers. In particular, the Georgian use of nuts and pomegranates, and their superior renditions of chicken tabaka — the world's best fried chicken — made me want to go again and again. Uzbeki places have also established themselves as some of the best kosher dining opportunities in town — just don't order the syrupy wine. Azerbaijani restaurateurs accommodatingly serve a pan-Russian menu, in addition to their own secret vices of kufta-bozbash meatballs and horseradish-heaped tongue. And, hey, there's one restaurant from Soviet Armenia mentioned here, and I leave it to your imagination to reconstruct its culinary relationship to Eastern European Armenian food. Note that specialties of these countries can also be found on the city's Russian and Ukrainian menus, including decent renditions of things like manti and khinkali at some of the new Russian dumpling joints.

Armenian

YEREVAN ☆
47-57 41st Street, Queens, 718-784-4651 Khinkali arrived ceremoniously, a huge dumpling shaped like a round coin purse with a pucker on top, made of thick dough and stuffed with ground meat. Dusted with black pepper and bathed in butter, three would

LOOK FOR:

borek *red pepper stuffed with cheese*
chakapuli *Georgian lamb casserole*
chalokhoch *lamb chop*
chicken tabaka *flattened garlic chicken*
chikhirtma *Georgian yolk-thickened chicken consommé*
damlama *Tashkent braised baby lamb ribs in broth*
golubzi Tadjiki *stuffed veggies*
hasib *rice-and-blood sausage*
khachapouri *Georgian cheese bread*
khinkali *large meat-stuffed dumpling*
Korean carrots *garlicky shredded Uzbeki salad*
kufta-bozbash *meatball soup*
lagman *lamb-and-noodle soup*
lobbio *kidney bean salad*
lula *ground lamb kebabs*
manti *giant lamb raviolis*
pelmeni *meat-stuffed tortellini*
pilaf *lamb and rice*
rassolnik *lamb-and-barley soup*
satsivi *cold Georgian chicken in walnut sauce*
sujuk *spicy sausage*
vareniki *potato pot-stickers*

make a fine entrée. Other appetizers were equally as good, especially a borek made by breading a long red pepper stuffed with feta and frying the heck out of it. The main courses featured a pair of ground-beef kebabs, light and moist, littered with onion and flat-leaf parsley. Another, charmingly titled "home specialties," included chicken, mushrooms, pickles, kashkaval cheese, and seasoned sauce. What the menu doesn't tell you is that these ingredients are, somewhat repulsively, mixed together.

Azerbaijani

SARMISH ☆
1162 Coney Island Avenue, Brooklyn, 718-421-4119 Ditmas Park boasts several cafés from the Caucasus; this one offers fare from Azerbaijan. Kebabs are succulent, charcoal flamed, and bargain priced (pick the pork). Soups like rassolnik are also dependable, combining lamb, barley, and vegetables in a dilled tomato

broth. Also enjoy standards like fist-sized lamb dumplings called manti, looks-like-it-was-run-over-by-a-truck chicken tabaka, and rounds of grilled eggplant dressed with enough garlic to blow the top of your head off. Then go elsewhere for coffee and dessert.

Georgian

PIROSMANI ☆ ☆

2222 Avenue U, Brooklyn, 718-368-3237 Pirosmani is one of three Georgian restaurants in the city that I know of, named after a celebrated 19th-century muralist whose work is replicated on every wall. The chicken tabaka is predictably superior to the Russian version — supremely salty and garlicky, flattened but still tender, and there are plenty of uniquely Caucasian dishes like pkhali — a hockey puck of herbed spinach strewn with pomegranate seeds, and khachapouri — a deliriously good flatbread oozing gooey cheese. Unfortunately, the menu is only in Russian, and little English is spoken. But if you memorize the names of the dishes mentioned above, you'll do just fine.

TBLISI ☆ ☆ ☆ ⬲ ☉

811 Kings Highway, Brooklyn, 718-382-6485 Offering the nut-stuffed, fruit-sauced, herb-rife, and grilled glories of Georgia, Tblisi's narrow room sports a wraparound mural in a quasi-Impressionist style depicting peasants toasting each other in conical fur hats. The novelty of Georgian cooking is apparent as you begin your meal with a handful of cold dishes. Satsivi smothers chicken pieces in a puree of crushed walnuts, garlic, fenugreek seed, and onions sautéed just long enough to give the sauce its golden hue. Constructed like Japanese maki, cabbage rolls are even more delicious, the pickled wrapper crisp and the ground-walnut filling amplified with loads of cilantro and raw garlic. Hot soups are also popular, including the uniquely Georgian chikhirtma, an impossibly rich broth thickened with egg yolks zapped with cilantro and garlic. Best appetizer is khachapouri, a round flat loaf of bread stuffed with white cheese and eggs beaten together. Don't miss chakapuli, a mossy casserole of lamb chunks cooked with herbs that retain an intense green color.

Tajikistani

TADJIKISTAN ☆

102-03A Queens Boulevard, Queens, 718-830-0744 Admirers of Central Asian fare will find much that's already familiar at the city's only kosher Tajiki restaurant, including a Korean-style shredded carrot salad showered with garlic and chile flakes, dill-laced soups like shurba and lagman, and a selection of kebabs cooked over charcoal, including lamb rib, turkey, cow heart, and ground-meat lula. More surprising is a winningly sweet salad of eggplant and red bell peppers, and golubzi, an assortment of meat-stuffed vine leaves and summer squash. But skip the bland and overcooked chicken tabaka and the truly awful coffee.

Uzbekistani

CAFE SHISH-KEBAB ☆
414 Brighton Beach Avenue, Brooklyn, 718-368-0966 The rapid multiplication of Uzbeki cafés in Brighton Beach is making my head spin! Here's the newest, with food not quite as good as Chio Pio, but with a much broader menu. Included are Middle Eastern vegetarian fare, and a kebab list heavy on the organ meats like chicken heart, sweetbreads, and lamb testicles. French fries are killer, baba ghanoush is above average, and the chicken tabaka damned good.

CHEBURECHNAYA ☆ ☆ ☆ ⟳
92-09 63 Drive, Queens, 718-897-9080 This new restaurant immediately leaped to prominence due not only to its modern attitude toward running a restaurant — young waitresses in beguiling outfits, no less — but also because of the length of its charcoal-grilled kebab list, which runs to 20 varieties, including ram's testicles, skirt steak, and the supremely decadent "lamb fat." The cospecialty is the triangular Tartar turnover chebureka, of which the lamb and cabbage varieties are the best. Also don't miss the parabolic cracker bread called non-toki.

CHIO PIO ☆
3087 Brighton 4th Street, Brooklyn, 718-615-9221 Floor-to-ceiling murals of swaying palms make this seem like a Jamaican joint, while the name evokes Peruvian somersaulting rotisserie chickens. Unexpectedly, the food comes from Uzbekistan, but with a Muslim Tashkent bent, rather than Jewish Bukharan. In addition to the usual plov and lamb kebabs, enjoy unique specialties like Tashkent salad, a cold toss of julienne lamb and shredded radish in a vinegary dressing, and a kebab assortment — featuring pork, chicken, beef, and, best of all, the ground-lamb lula — called (what else?) Tashkent. Another unique specialty is damlama, a braise of baby lamb rib with winter vegetables seasoned with cumin, bay leaf, dill, and garlic, presented swimming in an irresistible broth.

EASTERN FEAST ☆
1001 Brighton Beach Avenue, Brooklyn, 718-934-9608 Like the parasite in *Alien*, Eastern Feast insinuated itself in the belly of Mrs. Stahl's Knishes, where they cooked and dealt kebabs — pork,

TANDOOR

In 1996, the first Uzbeki joint appeared in Queens, possessing the admirably direct name of Uzbekistan Tandoori Bread (since changed to Uzbekistan Community Center), located among the Tudor facades of Kew Gardens. The nucleus of this establishment was an amazing tandoori oven, and if your idea of tandoori comes from Indian places, you've got the wrong idea. This was an oven you could crawl into. It was made of mud with hair sticking out. It turns out horse hair is an ineluctable component of Uzbeki ovens. As you sat in the dining room, you could see the oven through the open door, and there were never less than four guys gyrating around it. A baker would grab a dough ball and pitch it into the oven like a baseball so that it stuck to the interior clay surface. Then he'd grab a stick with a metal basket on the end that looked something like a bundt pan. Singeing his eyebrows, he'd lean into the oven and press the bundt against the dough ball, shaping it into a loaf about the size of a whoopee cushion, and stamping a design into the center. Nigella and sesame seeds were also somehow strewn across the top as it baked. When the lepeshka emerged, it was well browned and fragrant, and possessed a thin and crackling center with the texture of a pretzel. These loaves were borne to the table piping hot, hence the name Uzbekistan Tandoori Bread and the principal appeal of this restaurant, then as now.

lamb, beef, chile-rubbed chicken, and, if you were lucky, sweetbreads — out of a musty corner. A couple of years ago, they moved next door and increased the prices by a dollar or two. A gas hob was installed, and promptly abandoned as they reverted to the irregular charcoal beloved of all Uzbekis.

GAN EDEN ★ ☆
74 West 47th Street, Manhattan, 212-869-8946 Trudge up to the third floor, past lofts where Sikhs and Hasidim peddle jewelry, through the flimsy door and — poof! — you're in Uzbekistan. Smoke from the charcoal fire curls up under the ceiling, perfuming the air. The bill of fare includes the usual plov, a carrot-laced lamb pilaf, as well as meaty soups like lagman and shurba (called "chick pea soup" on the menu), and composed salads featuring beets, cabbage, and potatoes. The kebabs are perfectly cooked and way

smoky, and there are other dishes from Russia and Israel on the menu at this amazing glatt kosher establishment.

REGISTAN ☆

65-37 99th Street, Queens, 718-459-1638 The short menu at Registan, whose staff comes from Bukhara, is bizarrely inexpensive: soups, served in big bowls, easily make a complete lunch. Add one of the huge salads to make dinner. Pelmeni is a wonton soup with a lighter broth and even more vegetables than lagman — almost health food. When I say vegetables, you can automatically assume I principally mean carrots, which are soul food in Uzbekistan. Half the dishes on the menu feature them in one form or another. The rest of the menu consists of kebabs (kefta, or ground meat, lamb, chicken, beef, liver, and sweetbreads) and french fries. Most of the patrons eat with their fingers.

SALUT ☆ ☆ ☆

63-42 108th Street, Queens, 718-275-6860 Salut is a kosher café offering food from Uzbekistan, where the ancient cities of Bukhara, Samarkand, and Tashkent harbored communities of Jewish (and ethnically Persian) silk traders for a millennium. Ensconced in a former diner, Salut sculpts the city's best baba ghanoush, then furnishes you with an incredibly fresh turban-shaped loaf for dipping. Kebabs are also exceptional and exceptionally cheap (pick lamb rib or "chicken with bone"), as is lagman, the soup that probably introduced Marco Polo to pasta, here made with wonderful homemade noodles. Don't miss some of the city's finest french fries, heaped with garlic and parsley.

TAAM TOV ☆ ☆

46 West 47th Street, 4th floor, Manhattan, 212-768-8001 Challenging Gan Eden on the same 47th Street diamond district block, Taam Tov boasts a similar menu of plov and kebabs with plenty of Israeli and Soviet specialties thrown in for good measure. Hike up the long stairway to find chicken schwarma in a mercifully thin and flavorful gravy, a pickled vegetable salad platter that includes more selections than you can well count, and a carrot-laced and lamb-driven pilaf that would do Rego Park proud.

UZBEKISTAN COMMUNITY CENTER ☆ ☆

120-35 83rd Avenue, Queens, 718-850-3426 Sunday afternoon the Casio's pumping, the belter is belting, and those perfect, turban-shaped loaves called lepeshka are sailing from the huge clay oven. If you must kebab, pick lula and bone-in chicken, but don't forget the meat-stuffed samosa, noodley lagman soup, and steaming pot of green tea, proof of Uzbekistan's Silk Road location.

Also see Bay Shish Kebab in the Turkish chapter and Café Kashkar in the Uighur section of the Chinese chapter.

Chinese

Beijing and Northern Chinese, Cantonese, Chiu Chow, Fujianese, Hong Kong, Imports and Exports, Shanghai, Sichuan and Hunan, Taiwanese, Uighur, and Vegetarian Chinese

Chinatowns in Manhattan, Queens, and Brooklyn are booming. Not just with more restaurants and better restaurants, but with more choices than Baskin-Robbins, at a price that, unbelievably, goes as low as $2.95 for a capacious meal, and $1 for a very filling snack. Not only do we have the old-hat-by-now Sichuan, Hunan, Hong Kong, Shanghai, Taiwanese, Chiu Chow, and Cantonese — we can now boast Fujianese (aka Fuzhou) and Northern Chinese, the latter represented by a string of dumpling stalls that runs from Queens to Brooklyn to Manhattan's Chinatown, the most ancient in the city. Though we've lost our only Dai restaurant, it has been replaced by a restaurant from Xinjiang in remote northwestern China, serving authentic Uighur (pronounced "way-were") chow. For a real change of pace, check out the newest Chinatown in Brooklyn's Homecrest, a 10-block strip of restaurants and markets that threads its way along Avenue U in the shadow of the elevated D and F tracks.

Cantonese cafés used to be the cheapest feed in town, but they were eventually undersold by the Vietnamese, which, in turn, were undercut by the Malaysians. Now the Fujianese have taken over. A hearty meal of three dishes selected from the steam table over rice anywhere along Manhattan's East Broadway will set you back less than $4 in most places. Sometimes there's a free bowl of soup, too. And only the Cantonese are bigger soup fanatics. And now we have Chinese food aimed at other immigrant groups, too. Under the new heading Imports and Exports you'll find a restaurant that serves Indian-style Chinese food, but you'll have to look in the Ecuadorian, Bolivian, and Peruvian; Trinidadian, Guyanese, and Surinamese; and Korean chapters to find Chinese food adapted for those groups. Luckily, your chopsticks will work in any of these places.

LOOK FOR:

black chicken *black-skinned bird with medicinal properties*

butterfish *small fish usually braised in soy sauce*

chive box *Northern Chinese empanada*

congee *rice gruel, also called jook*

dim sum *dumplings and other snacks*

drunken crabs *ceviche of crab in wine vinegar*

fermented bean curd *Taiwanese fermented tofu*

Fuzhou soy sauce *thick and sweet*

ginger chicken *chicken braised with star anise and holy basil*

hoisin *thick sweet sauce of fermented bean paste*

holy basil *smaller and more licoracey than European variety*

hong zao *tart and gritty red Fuzhou rice-wine lees*

Horlicks *Hong-Kong Brit hot malt beverage*

hot-and-sour soup *Northern Chinese specialty*

loofah *pale green squash*

Peking duck *roasted and served with crepes, scallions, and hoisin*

rabbit foo chow *Fujianese bunny braised in hong zao*

rice cake *box-shaped rice noodles*

snow pea shoots *most prized Chinese vegetable*

Spam *potted meat product*

three precious ingredients *pork, chicken, and egg over rice*

tong shui *quasi-medicinal fruit beverages and desserts*

vegetarian duck *tofu-skin roll*

XO *fiery and fishy sauce*

yellow chives *seasonal Shanghai vegetable*

Beijing and Northern Chinese

PEKING DUCK HOUSE ☆ ☆ $
28 Mott Street, Manhattan, 212-227-1810 Relocated in new, SoHo-style digs, this old-timer continues to thrill crowds with its rendition of Peking duck. The well-browned bird is taken through a multistep cooking process that involves inflating it with air and brushing the skin with malt sugar. A white-clad chef carves yours tableside, fanning the meat and skin around a metal tray. The canvasback is served with cucumber, scallion, and a gravy boat of hoisin sauce, to be assembled and wrapped in pancakes which stand at the ready in a steamer. The duck is perfection but, alas, the pancakes are too thick and gummy. Full Chinese menu also available.

DUMPLING WARS

Six years ago Chinatown's first dumpling stall appeared on Allen Street. At **Fried Dumpling**, a dollar got you five pork-and-chive pot-stickers, four fluffy pork buns, or a bowl of hot-and-sour soup — you could dine splendidly for two bucks. Others soon followed, and the current census stands at four, with several more in Sunset Park and Flushing Chinatowns. While most Chinese eateries serve food from Shanghai and points south, these establishments — which take fine advantage of some exceedingly cramped, low-end real estate — hail from Beijing, offering snacks based on wheat rather than rice. **Dumpling House** is the best, but the others are damn good, too.

DUMPLING STALL ☆
40-52 Main Street, Queens, 718-353-6265 The potsticker dumplings are superb at this modest stall, loaded with unctuous chopped pork and little snippets of green vegetable, and the flavorful hot-and-sour soup is a forest of lily buds, bamboo, and cloud-ear mushrooms. Note: entrance around the corner on 41st Avenue.

FRIED DUMPLING ☆
99 Allen Street, Manhattan, 212-941-9975; 14 Mosco Street, Manhattan, no phone At this amazing one-dollar eatery, a Washington gets you five wonderful dumplings fried

on one side like gyoza, or four pork buns shaped like bread igloos, or a bowl of thin gruel studded with mung beans that pleads to be fortified with the chile sauce and flavored vinegars on the table.

DUMPLING HOUSE ✮ ✮ ✆

118A Eldridge Street, Manhattan, 212-625-8008 On the way out, I noticed a big jar of kim chee, and wondered how it got there. Through a translator I asked, "Was it a present from a Korean patron?" The reply: "We have Korean food in North China, too." This is my favorite dumpling stall in Chinatown, offering killer pork-and-chive pot-stickers; boiled beef sandwiches on wedges of homemade sesame bread; hot-and-sour soup rife with tofu and cloud-ear mushrooms; and the legendary chive box (ask for "chives and egg pancake") — a half-moon pie filled with scallions, vermicelli, scrambled egg, and baby shrimp. Best of all: most selections are $1, and there are bags of frozen dumplings to take home.

NORTH MAI XIANG CUN DUMPLING HOUSE ✮

775A 49th Street, Brooklyn, 718-431-9220 Brooklyn's first dumpling stall flaunts its "Northern Taste" via fried and steamed buns filled with pork and seafood. Moving in the direction of a full-service teahouse, congees and over-noodle dishes are also offered at this microscopic place.

TASTY DUMPLING ✮ ✮ ✆

54 Mulberry Street, Manhattan, 212-349-0070 In expanding its menu to the utmost limit by offering more variations on the standard formula than other places, Tasty Dumpling may have bitten off more than it can chew, because the service is confused and fumbling. Yet, they manage to turn out most of the stuff eventually. The chive box is squeezed in a sandwich press rather than fried, an interesting innovation, and it's a shame they never seem to have the wheat congee mentioned on the menu, because I'm dying to find out what it is.

Cantonese

CONGEE ✮ ✮ 🐟

98 Bowery, Manhattan, 212-965-5028 Like a new and improved version of Congee Village, Congee offers a solid Cantonese menu with great rice gruel at its heart. My faves are the lobster and sampan congees, the former plied with plenty of lobster, the latter peppered with miscellaneous ingredients and agreeably topped with roasted peanuts. Beef is also a specialty, but prepare to find it tenderized to a fare-thee-well. I can never resist the fried chicken (which one diner pegged as "duck-style chicken"), which comes in a delicious garlic sauce. Best dish: "sautéed dried squid and dried shrimp with green and yellow chives." What a mouthful!

CONGEE VILLAGE ☆ ☆
100 Allen Street, Manhattan, 212-941-1818 Though decorated like a rustic village, featuring overhanging bows, bamboo fences, and hokey peasant murals, C.V. offers a menu reflecting international sophistication. The humble porridge for which the restaurant is named avails itself of a breathtaking 28 add-ons. Rice steamed in a bamboo log is another economical one-dish meal (my fave: sizzling eel), as are the sputtering casseroles, one of which matches beef spare rib and bitter melon.

EXCELLENT DUMPLING HOUSE ☆
111 Lafayette Street, Manhattan, 212-219-2333 This small restaurant has much in its favor, especially at the cheaper end of the menu. Fresh-tasting scallion pancakes are lighter and less greasy than usual, while rice cakes turn out to be culinary wonders — fried with garlic, green onions, and a choice of meats. Another outstanding item is the forbidding-sounding sliced fish and

DIM SUM SUMMARY

This is the place where I'm supposed to give my dim sum recommendations. Were this volume written 10 years ago, there would have been a glowing account of five or six places, in Manhattan as well as Flushing. Unfortunately, the dim sum fad has fled, and though many places still offer it, the hapless consumers are too often tourists who have not yet learned to resent the miniature rubbery dog toys now passed off as dim sum. Even formerly exciting places like the sainted **Sun Hop Shing Tea House** have descended into lacklustrosity. You have two choices: get your dumplings at Taiwanese or Hong Kong places like **Sweet-N-Tart** or **Congee Village**, where, though your selection will be truncated, the little morsels will at least be fresh and hot. The second choice is to find the new dim sum frontier that should be developing any day now. Hint: Check out **Gum Fung** in Flushing.

sour cabbage, fresh hunks of cod deep-fried and then wokked with tangy strands of pickled cabbage. Avoid the high-priced "sizzling" dishes, which arrive repulsively cloaked in French dressing.

FAMILY NOODLE ☆
19 Henry Street, Manhattan, 212-571-2440 This marble miracle, on a sunny corner at the frontier of the expanded Chinatown, faithfully merchandises the same Cantonese fare that first won American hearts long ago, though the menu also makes a few faint stabs in the direction of Sichuan and Hong Kong. The combo over-rice dishes are especially well put together, including my favorite of roast pork, soy-sauce chicken, and duck lacquered to within an inch of its tender life.

FORTUNE GARDEN ☆ ➤ $
1771 Hylan Boulevard, Staten Island, 718-979-6100 Dressed in dark suits, the waiters stand stiffly at attention, then deferentially show you to a table. The somber decor is reminiscent of a funeral parlor viewing room, and your fellow diners converse in hushed tones. Shaped like a seashell, the menu unfolds to reveal the older sort of Chinese-American fare, heavy on the Cantonese and seafood. But don't be scared away — the disgraced General Tso's chicken here is the best you've ever had, while the "Fuchow" fried rice represents a refined version of that standard: rice topped with delicately gravied ham, chicken, shrimp, and fish cake.

GUM FUNG ☆ ☆ $
136-28 39th Avenue, Queens, 718-762-8821 Successor to KB Garden, the city's best dim sum parlor, this hulking banquet hall is already showing promise, and not just in the area of dim sum. Two standouts include bean curd skin generously stuffed with wild mushrooms and fried like tempura, resulting in something that looks like a plate of shaggy dogs; and an eggplant casserole — found only on the small banquet menu — flavored with dried shrimp, just the right combo of sweetness and funk.

HALAL KITCHEN ☆
187-14 Hillside Avenue, Queens, 718-217-8888 The interior has the antique quality of a chop suey house and the menu is mainly Cantonese. On offer are several halal beef dishes, no pork, and a handful of lamb specialties, a meat rarely seen in Chinese restaurants. The food is generally delicious, including a lamb and broccoli stir-fry made with miniature ribs, and a dish described as halal chicken wings that comes coated in a shiny brown sauce dotted with garlic. Although neither dish was even remotely Uighur, both hinted at Middle Eastern cookery as much as Chinese. The wings, in particular, tasted of white vinegar. The thick-skinned beef wontons, however, are a major disappointment.

29

NATURAL RESTAURANT ☆ ☆ 🐟

88 Allen Street, Manhattan, 212-966-1325 Who could resist the conch with yellow chives? Wok-frying furnishes the smoky flavor, and a fermented shrimp sauce adds salty highlights. Everything we sampled at this no-frills Chinese was fresh and perfectly seasoned, including baby octopus with black bean sauce, ostrich (like thin-sliced beef only more tender) with scallions and ginger, and chicken lo mein made with noodles firmer and thinner than usual. Best of all was the salt and pepper soft-shell crab — big, meaty, two to an order, and strewn with shredded jalapeño and orange rind.

N.Y. NOODLE TOWN ☆ ☆

28-½ Bowery, Manhattan, 212-349-0923 An enthusiastic review by Ruth Reichl catapulted this noodle shop into national prominence a few years back and there were soon lines extending around the block. Noodle Town soon began to suffer from swelled-head syndrome: though the dishes continued to be competently prepared and plenty edible, there was a certain lack of excitement to be found in the output. My favorites remain the Cantonese-style wide noodles, China's answer to Italian fettuccine. Order the seafood and vegetable version and amaze yourself with the sheer quantity of squid, cuttlefish, octopus, scallops, and shrimp. The suckling pig — as distinguished from the plain side of pig more often seen in the window — always ranks among the top 10 in the metropolis.

SUN HOP SHING TEA HOUSE ☆

21 Mott Street, Manhattan, 212-267-2729 Most people prefer to eat dim sum at restaurants where the dining rooms are as big as football fields. As the carts go 'round the room, the plates of dumplings become progressively colder and more dried out. I prefer this tiny place with 10 tables, where the distance from the kitchen to the front door is only about 30 feet. After each cart passes, the plates not purchased are stacked in a glass steam case. Fried taro is excellent here, lacy cakes of shredded root with a nutty sweetness. And don't miss the bean curd skin roll — stuffed with pork in a thin rubbery wrapper, one of the most successful bean curd disguises ever invented. In line with the general decline of dim sum in New York, Sun Hop Shing sometimes fails to impress these days, though you can't beat the coffee shop ambiance.

WIN SING ☆ 🐟

1321 Avenue U, Brooklyn, 718-998-0360 New York's newest Chinatown is devoid of tourists and curio shops. On a recent frigid evening, this place was the most popular, thronged with families enjoying dishes like paper-wrapped chicken (aluminum foil, really) that arrives steaming and studded with mushrooms; a moist barbecued duck that is one of the best in town; and a fortifying and flavorful cilantro-and-flounder soup. And the seafood wrangler was pulling live lobsters and eels out of the tanks so fast that his hands were just a blur.

WONG'S RICE AND NOODLE SHOPPE ☆ ☆

86 Mulberry Street, Manhattan, 212-233-2288 Giving N.Y. Noodletown a run for its money, the elusive Wong's slings Cantonese barbecue, congee, noodles, and simple meat-and-vegetable combos over rice. Nothing is over $5 if you stick with the coffee shop menu, where you can also search out the unusual steamed rice crepes and the dish cryptically called "any roast pork combination with fried egg," which comes with a wonderful salty scallion relish.

Chiu Chow

CHANOODLE ☆ ☆ ☆ 🐟

79 Mulberry Street, Manhattan, 212-349-1495 This new noodle shop shows amazing diversity and expertise at the humble lower end of the menu. Gold and silver fried rice — from a list of many usual fried rices — is a masterpiece of salty fish tidbits, delicate egg drops, onions, and a scatter of golden raisins, just enough to vary the terrain but not enough to be repulsive. Another favorite, and showing an obvious Chiu Chow bent, is a dish called "fried clams" that turns out to be tiny clams in their shells cooked with crunchy fried garlic and morsels of ground pork and strewn with cilantro. Yum! And don't miss the braised bird immodestly billed "King of the Roast Duck."

CHAO ZHOU ☆ ☆

40-52 Main Street, Queens, 718-353-7683 Just inside the door is an ancient Chinese knight in full regalia, but from that point on, this noodle shop is relentlessly modern. Reflecting the Chinese diaspora across Southeast Asia, the fare has been zonked with flavors from diverse corners of the East. Home-style congees come with a bewildering array of pig parts, and the menu runs to an astonishing 500 items — there's something for everyone. Dig the gigantic rice bowl with chopsticks on the roof. As Jonathan Gold boasted once in *Gourmet*, it can be seen by planes taking off and landing at La Guardia.

NEW CHAO CHOW ☆ ☆ ☆

111 Mott Street, Manhattan, 212-226-2590 This humble establishment persists right next door to the glamorous new Joe's Ginger, the latest incarnation of Joe's Shanghai. The combination of Vietnamese and Chinese writing in the window lets you know that something's up, and you'll find Thai inside, too. The display of multiple different forms of rice noodles in the window is also unusual. These noodles are most frequently served as "broth noodles," with the noodles and toppings, including lots of fresh cilantro, presented in a deep bowl. The wonderfully rich broth is offered on the side in a separate bowl. Congee, too, seems to have been deconstructed: instead of the smooth white jook we've come to expect, with a consistency close to Elmer's Glue, the rice still reads as grains of rice, not completely disintegrated into the amber broth. The favorite congee? Fish and pork, with lily bulbs and preserved vegetables floating around in addition to the usual ginger and cilantro. The crowning glory of this place is the chao chow duck, glistening a beautiful golden color in the window, with a skin moist but not crisp and a memorably mellow flavor that seems to have infused every square centimeter of flesh.

SUN GOLDEN ISLAND ☆ 🐟

1 Elizabeth Street, Manhattan, 212-274-8787 Until a few years ago, this restaurant was one of the only places in New York where you could find Chiu Chow cooking, a spicy variation on Cantonese with an emphasis on seafood-pork combos and noodle dishes. Skip the appetizers and go right to the entrées. Crab is the best deal of all. Crab with chingens sauce is a good-sized plate of four hacked-up Dungeness crabs (enough for two people) with a briny sauce of ginger and black beans. Try the house specialty, fried e-fu noodles Chiu Chow style — a nest of thin, deep-fried noodles with white sugar and wine vinegar poured on top. Unusual? You bet!

Fujianese

AMERICAN EAST FUZHOU RESTAURANT ☆ 🐟

954 East Broadway, Manhattan, 212-226-0969 Though Shanghai restaurants got the lion's share of attention a few years back, Fuzhou establishments were multiplying at an equal rate — there seemed to be a new one every month. At American, order anything with "foo chow sauce" and get dishes braised in hong zao, a red paste of rice-wine lees with a subtle and intriguing flavor and a pleasing grittiness. We ordered rabbit done this way, and the dish came larded with pieces of pork to make up for the leanness of the bunny. Sautéed snow pea shoots dotted with caramelized cloves of garlic was another favorite at our table.

EAST BROADWAY GOURMET ☆

40 East Broadway, Manhattan, 212-274-0701 Fuzhou restaurants have nearly completed their conquest of the Lower East Side, and this is the most ambitious of the dozen or so. One side of the menu features Cantonese standards, while the other offers Fujianese specialties like limpid rice dumplings of the same specific gravity as the surrounding fluid so they float up and down like lava in a lava lamp, rabbit tidbits in an intensely red sauce, and a cavalcade of duck tongue, pig intestine, and "edible frog's legs," as the menu encouragingly refers to them. Paper dragons festoon the peaked ceiling, and a beacon flashes every time a selection arrives via dumbwaiter.

88 REACH HOUSE ✭
88 Division Street, Manhattan, 212-625-8099 Fuzhou food continues to flourish up and down Eldridge Street, and this restaurant has a menu oriented toward noodle soups and over-rice dishes. From the former category comes a lamb soup with thin wheat noodles in a rich mutton broth; from the latter, an astonishing "spare ribs with cooking wine on rice" — little nuggets of taro and boneless meat lightly breaded and inundated with a tart red sauce. The upscale end of the menu includes Fuzhou favorites like tortoise, rabbit, and the quizzical "braised crucian in soy sauce." Fujianese are very proud of their thick sweet soy sauce, said to be the best in China.

FU CHOW RESTAURANT ✭
84 Eldridge Street, Manhattan, 212-343-3905 Obscurely located next to a shop that specializes in rat poison, Fu Chow has a large dining room decorated with a bas-relief of smiling babies. As I sat looking out at the tumbledown tenements across the street, restaurant employees kept sneaking up behind me and screaming in Chinese at the top of their lungs. At first I thought they were being playful, until I realized that a PVC pipe sticking out of the floor was their intercom to the basement kitchen. The standard combo (three dishes over rice is $3) is preceded by a bowl of pearly broth bobbing with mussels. As an added refinement, the three dishes are served on a separate plate from the rice. My choices: a sumptuous fried kingfish steak moistened with a chile solution, surprisingly good green peanuts braised with tiny chunks of pork, and a generous heap of chewy lotus root.

NEW BAI WEI GOURMET FOOD INC. ✭ ✭ ✭ 🐟
51 Division Street, Manhattan, 212-925-1921 This splendid new Fujianese café boasts a gleaming steam table with an amazing 33 choices stacked up in the front window, including a particularly enticing display of seafood: big fried shell-on shrimp, sautéed crabs, steamed miniature mussels, and several types of whole fish lightly breaded and hacked into sections. Also find there such Fuzhou favorites as duck cooked in bright red rice-wine lees and thin-sliced pork liver in addition to glistening baby bok choy

and other seasonal veggies. The best part: a choice of five dishes served with a plate of rice and bowl of seaweed soup is $2.75.

SPRING BOY FUZHOU FOOD ☆
81 Allen Street, Manhattan, 212-625-0001 In the Fujianese style, this microscopic lunch counter favors slow braising over stir-frying, deploying soy sauce, sugar, vinegar, and hong zao to create dishes of unexpected lightness and subtlety. Memorable selections include tortoise sautéed with vegetables, rabbit cooked in hong zao, the poetic "boneless duck hand with conch," and a supernally good platter of three butterfish braised in sweet soy sauce.

Hong Kong

BIG EAT ☆ ☆
97 Bowery, Manhattan, 212-219-9955 Don't miss "huge curry bun" at this new Hong Kong party barn, a hollowed-out loaf of sesame-seeded Italian bread overflowing with a spicy chicken curry — weird and wonderful. Nothing is quite what it seems on the menu, including a Dungeness crab that drowns in marinara, and steamer clams that come laced with Pernod. Downstairs, a hopping juice bar dispenses bubble tea and invented specialties such as a dessert of green tea ice cream and pristine fresh fruit heaped in a martini glass. Upstairs, where Mao presides in a Last Supper mural, there's more room to spread out and relax.

C & F RESTAURANT ☆ 🐟
171 Hester Street, Manhattan, 212-343-2623 Hong Kong soaked up the regional cuisines of China like a sponge, then turned to England, Southeast Asia, and the United States for further inspiration. To savor Hong Kong's complexities, start with a salad of julienne jellyfish dressed with sesame oil and tossed with Vietnamese vegetables. Next try baked salt-and-pepper shrimp — to be eaten without removing the crunchy shells — or the Malaysian-influenced pork with pickled vegetables over rice. Wake up early and check out the wacky breakfasts, like a Spam-and-egg sandwich washed down with Horlicks.

FUNKY BROOME ☆ 🐟
176 Mott Street, Manhattan, 212-941-8628 With the East Village rolling rapidly south and Chinatown plowing north, it was only a matter of time before they collided. The point of impact is Funky Broome. The waiters dress head-to-toe in black, and the decor features spindly iron chairs with zebra-striped cushions. The menu is organized according to presentation gimmicks. A series of rice dishes is shrouded in lidded bamboo logs. The ingredients are

heaped atop the rice, the gravy trickles down, and trapped steam diffuses the flavor — making the rice the best part. Every dish I've ordered this way has been good, including chicken cooked with black mushrooms, sausages combining duck liver and pork, and, most emphatically, dried duck and pickled vegetables in culinary hand-to-hand combat. Best dish: pork-stuffed lotus — a gloppy mess of cloud-ear 'shrooms, lily buds, napa cabbage, and dried tiny red dates swarming around slices of stuffed lotus root.

HOLDING UP THE MIRROR

Hong Kong rivals New York in cosmopolitan allure, and you won't be surprised when I tell you that that city boasts ethnic restaurants that specialize in American and European food, modified for Chinese tastes. Of course, many of the Hong Kong coffee shops sell a handful of American and English dishes featuring Spam and Velveeta, but **ABC American Cooking** (41-13 Kissena Boulevard, Flushing, 718-461-1313) goes for it whole-hog, with an entire menu and premises devoted to what it believes is authentic Western cooking. A few of the dishes, like escargot bourginoise [*sic*], improve on the original, but most — like pork chops with fruit sauce and tofu-stuffed trout — taste like airline food, and seem like a species of culinary revenge. The dramatic dining room features a stunning full-wall transparency of Hong Kong harbor, while the vaulted ceiling is a galaxy of tiny twinkling lights. It's worth a visit, especially if you also plan to eat somewhere else in downtown Flushing.

HONG KONG SEAFOOD ☆ 🐟 $
40-48 Main Street, Queens, 718-961-3302 You can spend a little or a lot here. Chinese barbecue over rice is available at low prices, as are soups, dim sum, and bakery products. All of the Chinese families dining around us were enjoying a bean curd appetizer, which consisted of a huge mound of fried bean curd squares with several unexpected sauces: one combines anchovies and red wine vinegar, another is mustard based, the third a fiery red chile paste. Of the higher-priced entrées, the best is squid with sour vegetables in a semisweet brown sauce with red and green bell peppers and hunks of pickled cabbage. Also recommended: stir-fried conch in salty garlic sauce.

PING'S ☆☆☆ 🐟 $

22 Mott Street, Manhattan, 212-602-9988; 83-09 Queens Boulevard, Queens, 718-396-1238 Named after its celebrity Hong Kong chef, Ping's serves innovative pan-Pacific chow out of a palatial restaurant in the heart of Manhattan's Chinatown, and in an isolated and unexpected location in Elmhurst. Presented as a collection of color snaps, the menu includes dishes from Malaysia, Japan, Thailand, and Korea, in addition to Cantonese, with the emphasis always on the aquatic. Where'd they get those amazing three-bite oysters, nearly eight inches in length? Get them steamed instead of raw, with a vaguely Malaysian concoction called XO — a smoky, incinerating relish in which bits of bacon, dried shrimp, and pickled chili are bound together with bean thread. The non-Chinese dishes can get pretty zany. Delicate Korean beef rolls came arrayed in spokes, stuffed with silky enoki mushrooms. Some of the wildest offerings are pure inventions, like seafood soup tai chi, eye-appealingly configured as a yin-yang.

SAINT'S ALP TEAHOUSE ☆ 🍑

39 3rd Avenue, Manhattan, 212-598-1890; 170 Bleecker Street, Manhattan, 212-260-5330 The menu of this Hong Kong chain mixes fruit juices, milk, teas, and coffee into an inscrutable series of hot and cold beverages, and it may take years of serious drinking to identify your favorite. The signal ingredient is a translucent black tapioca bead, featured in the Frothy Tea section. Sometimes known as "bubble teas," these drinks are accompanied by large-diameter straws to suck up the pearls. You can also have them tossed into any other beverage. In addition, there's a list of strange snacks, including peanut-butter-smeared pancakes, coconut-butter toasts, purple yam jelly, and eggs boiled in smoky tea.

X.O. KITCHEN ☆ ☆

148 Hester Street, Manhattan, 212-965-8645 With waitresses clad in gingham, and your table beside a rustic bridge, you might think you're in Kansas, but the food reflects the sort you might find in a Hong Kong diner. The formidable bill of fare runs from fortifying noodle soups, to ungreasy Hong Kong lo mein, to over-rice dishes for which spaghetti can be substituted, to Japanese teriyakis, to appetizers with a Portuguese lineage. And there's an apothecary's worth of tong shui, the healing tonics that take the form of custard or fruit shakes or tea, including the somewhat odd snow frog with milk chestnut paste. "It's only frog saliva," the waitress assured me.

Imports and Exports

HAPPY SHABU SHABU ☆ ☆ 🐟 ⏾
54 Canal Street, Manhattan, 212-226-8868 This gleeful spot represents a retooling of the Japanese beef shabu-shabu ("cook it yourself") tradition by Chinese restaurateurs. Cook servings of seafood, chicken, pork, beef, or a vegetarian assortment by swooshing morsels in a pot of broth at your own individual radiant cooking station. Invite lots of friends and have a foolproof party, as guests figure out what to do with the various ingredients. The inexpensive all-in price features a mind-bending assortment of accessory cookables, including napa cabbage, bean thread vermicelli, raw egg, watercress, fish balls, tofu, taro root, etc., etc., and a cavalcade of condiments from all over Asia.

TANGRA MASALA ☆
87-09 Grand Avenue, Queens This is the most ambitious of several restaurants offering Chinese food modified for Indian tastes, which often means stir-fries with tons of ginger and garlic. The meat is halal and the staff looks Chinese. There are Tibetan momo — a lackluster vegetarian version wrapped in wonton skins accompanied by a gonzo sweet green chile sauce (keep the sauce, toss the dumplings); Pakistani pakora; vegetarian dishes featuring both paneer and tofu; and lots of neighborhood-style Chinese dishes like beef and broccoli and chicken with oyster or black bean sauce. In a switch from the usual Chinese menu, the dishes with the stars (a third of the volume) are designated "not spicy." In other words, spiciness is one of the signifiers of Chinese food for Indian tastes.

Shanghai

JOE'S SHANGHAI ☆ ☆
9 Pell Street, Manhattan, 212-233-8888; 136-21 37th Avenue, Queens, 718-539-3838 The best seats in the house are in the back, huge green communal tables where you'll be seated with extended families, couples on dates, and singles loudly sucking soup. The compulsory first course — the waiters will prompt if you forget — is steamed buns, the celebrated soup dumplings of Shanghai. Other noteworthy starters include smoked fish noodle soup, with wonderful leathery fish redolent of star anise that tastes like it's been smoking since the Long March, and Shanghai yellow chive and shrimp wontons, much perkier and chewier than the usual article. Russia is said to have inspired the Shanghainese penchant for short cold dishes. One is vegetarian duck, braised

tofu skin layered around shiitake mushrooms — it really does look like a slice of duck breast, especially if you've had a few beers. The wildest dish on the menu is "drunken crabs," meat and orange roe marinated in an aged wine vinegar and plenty skanky.

NEW GREEN BO ☆ ☆
66 Bayard Street, Manhattan, 212-625-2359 With Shanghai restaurants more common than Cantonese these days, news that another has opened in Chinatown is likely to provoke a shrug. But this establishment, which bears a familial connection to defunct old-timer Say Eng Look, distinguishes itself by reproducing all the standards with superior delicacy: juicy buns crowned with an extra wad of crabmeat, for instance, or cold spiced beef more aromatic than usual. My favorite entrées make unusual use of tofu: pork sautéed with strips of floppy bean-curd skin, and okra with tofu puffs — clouds of spongy curd that soak up the soothing sauce. The decor will remind you of an operating room.

NO. 1 PEOPLE'S AND PEOPLE ☆
38-06 Prince Street, Queens, 718-460-8686 Lately, they've taken to pushing a charcoal grill onto the sidewalk and hawking squab, pork, and squid brochettes at this utilitarian Shanghai café, but best of all is the corn on the cob, lathered with sweet sauce and hot pepper powder. Inside, find an unusual menu which features many diverting cold selections such as jellyfish in garlic sauce, "pork hoofs" in wine sauce, and stewed mutton jelly.

SHANGHAI CUISINE ☆
89 Bayard Street, Manhattan, 212-732-8988 Another entry in the Shanghai stampede — this one looking more SoHo than Chinatown with its brick walls and antique posters. The food com-

---

SLURPIN' DUMPLINGS

In 1996, Shanghai soup dumplings were all the rage, puckered purses of noodle dough filled with pork and trace amounts of crab inundated with a greasy gravy that you have to deal with somehow before downing the dumpling. Bite into it unawares, and you'd be sprayed with molten grease — high-risk cuisine. Here's how to do it: gingerly transfer a dumpling from steamer to spoon so as not to prick the envelope and lose the soup, nip off the top, and noisily suck up the gravy inside before polishing off the pouch. Or do as a friend does, and prick the dumpling first, allowing the fluid to spill onto the lettuce leaf. And then ignore it, eating the dumpling dry.

plements places like Joe's and Shanghai Gourmet by including many unique dishes like wine-marinated hog tongue and fried turnip cake with shrimp, in addition to the predictable soup dumplings and mock duck. Be shocked by the pork shoulder — a very, very fatty mountain of meat smothered in brown gravy with a forest of steamed baby bok choy guarding its perimeter, or enjoy bean curd skin with fermented cabbage and fresh soybeans, or the knockout Shanghai fried chicken.

TEN PELL ☆
10 Pell Street, Manhattan, 212-766-2123 If you don't want to wait in line at Joe's, this across-the-street alternative will do just fine. It's an old-guard Shanghai place with Hunan and Sichuan for the tourists, but stick with some of the Shanghai dishes, like an assortment of cold appetizers including faux sliced duck made from vegetable substances, shredded garlic kelp, pickled cabbage, and spicy dried sardines. A favorite entrée was "bean curd leaf with snow vegetable and beans" — masses of flavorful greens chopped fine, interlaced with bean curd skin and dotted with fresh green soybeans — a protein powerhouse.

YANG TZE RIVER ☆ ☆ ☪
135-21 40th Road, Queens, 718-353-8500 The mighty Chang (Yangtze), third largest river in the world, originates as a trickle in the Tanggulashan Mountains of Qinghai, traverses Tibet, then meanders through six further provinces before emptying just north of Shanghai. The restaurant Yang Tze River, located on the most famous culinary cul-de-sac of Flushing's Chinatown, is mainly a Shanghai restaurant, but, like the river, it reflects a wealth of influences from other Chinese regions. On a recent evening, six friends and I stared in wonder at gluten and black mushroom, a name that might have discouraged less intrepid diners. Engulfed in a savory brown sauce were dozens of pale bulging globs of gluten, interspersed with equal-sized black mushrooms. Though gluten is what makes bagels chewy, the gluten puffs were cloudlike, generating murmurs of astonishment as the eaters demolished them.

YEAH SHANGHAI DELUXE ☆ ☆ ☆
65 Bayard Street, Manhattan, 212-566-4884 Your current best choice among Manhattan Chinatown Shanghai eateries — now numbering nearly 10 — Yeah Shanghai wows with its technical virtuosity, from the impressive-but-too-sweet chrysanthemum fish, to the tasty fresh eel with yellow chives, which the chef improves with extra sizzling oil just prior to serving. Recommended dishes include bean curd with an eggy crabmeat sauce, and, especially, "roast chicken Northern Chinese style," a haystack of pulled poultry inundated with a star anise sauce and carefully covered with pieced-together skin. Though the front room doesn't look

like much, the dining room, attained by crossing a wooden foot-bridge, is cavernous and comfortable. Warning: skip the Shanghai soup dumplings here.

Sichuan and Hunan

GRAND SICHUAN ✰ ✰ 🦐
125 Canal Street, Manhattan, 212-625-9212; 229 9th Avenue, Manhattan, 212-620-5200; 745 9th Avenue, Manhattan, 212-582-2288; 227 Lexington Avenue, Manhattan, 212-679-9770; 1049 2nd Avenue, Manhattan, 212-355-5855 One of two mighty chains that kept the Sichuan dream alive in New York, eclipsing all the ancient bad "Szechuan" joints around town, which are long on sugar, short on hot peppers, and devoid of that most important pepper of all, Sichuan peppercorn. Both chains are highly recommended, though the differences lie more in personality than in choice of dishes and care in preparation. Grand Sichuan is the wackier of the two, a fun-loving imp that also offers Hunan scarf from a menu dedicated to Chairman Mao. (Are the proprietors Maoists? you ask. Probably not. They just think that's the only Chinese name you'll recognize.) No one eats the tea-smoked duck at Grand Sichuan without bursting into raves. Other hits include beef fillets with chile sauce and — claimed to be one of Mao's favorites — monkey mushrooms with three treasures.

SICHUAN DYNASTY ✰ ✰ 🦐
135-32 40th Road, Queens, 718-961-7500 This palace of Sichuan peppercorns turns out some of the spiciest food in the city — but you've got to demand it. Hottest dish is "rabbit stew meat," which deploys spectacular quantities of dried red chiles and peppercorns that don't burn your mouth so much as anesthetize it. Pick three dishes from the family-style menu for a bargain $16.95, but also make sure to examine the carryout menu, available by the entranceway and featuring a much longer list of chef's specials. Chanubei cold noodles and ma po bean curd are two "don't miss" selections.

SPICY & TASTY ✰ ✰ ✰ 🐟 🦐
39-07 Prince Street, Queens, 718-359-1601 This is the best Sichuan restaurant in town, not stinting on the Sichuan peppercorns, nor on the fresh green chiles, crushed dried red chiles, or on the chile oil either. Once it was a low gambling den with excellent food at the rank end of Roosevelt Avenue; now it's a marble-clad luxury palace with brocade chairs. Order any combination of the room-temperature appetizing dishes displayed with great panache in the window and be rocketed to heaven. The smoked tea duck is

40

excellent, but rather crude compared to Wu Liang Ye's. Go for any dish designated "with spicy pepper," "with spicy sauce," "in red chile sauce," or "in b.b.q. sauce," and you'll leave with a mouth on fire.

WU LIANG YE ☆ ☆ ☆ 🐟

36 West 48th Street, Manhattan, 212-398-2308; 215 East 86th Street, Manhattan, 212-534-8899; 338 Lexington Avenue, Manhattan, 212-370-9648 Rumored to be partly owned by the People's Republic of China, Wu Liang Ye is the other chain that dominates the Sichuan dining universe. It is somewhat more staid, and a little higher priced than its madcap rival, and less willing to make things really hot unless you demand it. That said, the menu is a bit more focused, as seen in triumphs like prawns with citrus sauce and, that old chestnut, sesame noodles, more moist, tart, and just plain greasy (in a good way) than other versions. The 48th Street location is preferred, not because of its convenient proximity to Times Square, but because of its occupation of a townhouse, making you feel like a rich person. Still, if you want tons of Sichuan peppercorns, eschew both chains and go to Sichuan Dynasty or Spicy & Tasty.

Taiwanese

CAPTAIN KING ☆

82-39 Broadway, Queens, 718-429-2828 Choose any three main dishes from a list of 59 for $16.95 (each additional $5), and rice and soup are furnished gratis. Our faves on a brisk winter afternoon included a Taiwanese chicken pungent with basil, and preserved pork with garlic greens — the savory meat tasting like it had just emerged from the smoker. Shaped like fingers rather than pincushions, the pan-fried dumplings were memorably crisp and fresh; another "don't miss" is the chive-and-egg-stuffed fried buns.

DAVID'S TAIWANESE GOURMET ☆ ☆ ☆ 🐟

84-02 Broadway, Queens, 718-429-4818 Demonstrating the Taiwanese admiration for all things Japanese, David's affects Japanese decor, including lithographs of kimono-clad women and a rustic appliance for polishing rice that nearly blocks the front door. A special that the waitress assured us was her favorite, crab with squash, shows the culinary contrast between Taiwan and the rest of China. While mainlanders sauté the whole crab with black-bean sauce, Formosans steam the crustacean and surround it with lozenges of loofah. But the inherent lightness of Taiwanese food doesn't mean it doesn't pack a punch. Holy basil, rarely encountered in Chinese restaurants, is all over the menu, and you don't have to look very far on the menu to find the fabled "stinky bean curd."

LAIFOOD ★ ★

38-18 Prince Street, Queens, 718-321-0653 At the corner of Prince and 39th is Laifood, a Taiwanese restaurant with a handsome bilevel dining area. The bill of fare is a menu reader's delight, filled with inscrutable entries like "tasty duck tongue," "intestine, pig blood with sour mustard," and "crispy smelled bean curd" — suggesting that other noses have enjoyed it before your own. But maybe smelly is what's really meant, since the bean curd appetizer comes smothered in preserved black beans, fermented cabbage, and Vietnamese-style hot sauce, vying with each other for stinkiness. We wolfed it right down. Another amazing appetizer is rice sausage — thick slices of sausage stuffed with sticky rice studded with peanuts and dried shrimp. It comes with a bowl of oily amber dipping sauce jazzed with cilantro.

SOGO ★

11 Mott Street, Manhattan, 212-566-9888 Manhattan's first Taiwanese restaurant is a novelty in Manhattan's Chinatown. Everyone will love specialties such as a Taiwanese hamburger nestled in bao dough instead of a conventional bun; pan-fried pomfret; and chicken cooked in a casserole with ginger, basil, and wine, also known as three-cup chicken. Don't miss "meat ball Taiwanese style," entombed in a dome of quivering sweet potato

---

BLOODY ANGLE

Doyers is now an insignificant byway, but around 1900, this crooked street joined with Mott and Pell to constitute the entirety of Manhattan's Chinatown. In those days, the tongs held sway over a Chinese population estimated at less than 10,000. As the On Leongs and Hip Sings vied for supremacy in gambling, opium, and prostitution, the oblique curve in Doyers became a notorious place of ambush by tong members bizarrely clad in chain mail and wielding hatchets and pistols, earning it the sobriquet "Bloody Angle." Several underground passages led from the curve to Mott and Pell, making for the speedy escape of assassins. Nowadays, the street plays host to Vietnamese, Malaysian, and Cantonese restaurants, as well as the Chinatown post office, and the loudest noise to be heard is not the clash of hatchets, but the dropping of the mailbags from the postal trucks.

---

starch. More challenging are sautées of duck blood cake with chives, pig intestines, and anything incorporating stinky bean curd. Sogo's menu also has an extensive section devoted to Sichuan food twisted for Taiwanese tastes.

SWEET-N-TART ✭ ⏲

20 Mott Street, Manhattan, 212-964-0380; 136-11 38th Avenue, Queens, 718-661-3380; tiny original location: 76 Mott Street, Manhattan, 212-334-8088 Combining a tea shop menu with regional Chinese snacks, the raison d'être for this minichain is really tong shui — salutary fruit-based beverages, puddings, and soups with quasi-medicinal properties. The bewildering array of sweet jellies, tonics, and shakes constitutes only one of the three menus. The other two include a startling array of dim sum, from excellent Shanghai soup dumplings, to "Italian spring rolls" oozing mozzarella, to a salad of iceberg, shrimp, and diced papaya served in the hollowed-out fruit shell. Favorite bigger feeds — invariably soups, noodles, or rice dishes — include crystal fried rice, deliciously tossing shrimp, vermicelli, and rice with little clouds of egg white. Note: this is one of the few places that serve dim sum into the evening.

Uighur

CAFÉ KASHKAR ✭ ✭ ✭

1141 Brighton Beach Avenue, Brooklyn, 718-743-3832 Xinjiang is China's most remote province, a majestic land of mountains and deserts in the far northwest through which the Silk Road meanders past salt lakes and dry river beds. Most numerous in the south are the Uighurs (pronounced "way-wooers"), a Muslim Turkic group who historically served as guides along the ancient trade routes. Kashkar is New York's first Uighur eatery. It's named after Kashgar, a lush oasis with a famous Sunday market 100 miles east of the Tajikistan border. Though the interior of the restaurant makes a wan attempt to recall the lushness of the oasis with sprays of purple plastic flowers and a beer-sign waterfall, the food is much more effective in doing so. One can easily imagine soups like chuchuara being ladled from huge pots in a market stall, the little mutton dumplings dancing in the buttery broth, while, right next to it, a cauldron of mampar bubbles with beef and homemade pasta, sprigs of fresh dill and cilantro waiting to be tossed in. Not only are the celebrated homemade noodles called lagman available in soup, they're stir-fried like a Chinese lo mein in goiro lagman. Charcoal kebabs are also fab, especially lamb and the off-menu lamb rib.

Vegetarian Chinese

BUDDHA BODAI ☆ ☆ ◷

42-96 Main Street, Flushing, Queens, 718-939-1188 In Main Street's smorgasbord of Chinese restaurants, this joint is unique, offering an entirely vegetarian menu, with meatless renditions of congee, steamed dumplings, and bean curd Szechuan style. Perhaps more interesting are the dishes that mimic flesh, ranging from barbecued ribs to duck to snails, with varying results (marvel at the roast pork fabricated from rye-bread crusts — it almost works). Top of the line, and most recommended, is the whole lobster — spinach torso, asparagus legs, and tail composed of shredded tofu textured like lobster meat, though falling somewhat short on flavor.

18 AHARNS ☆ ◷

227 Centre Street, Manhattan, 212-941-8986 This combo Buddhist temple and vegetarian restaurant — the only employees, one cook and one priest — is not much bigger than your living room, and opinions vary as to the desirability of the food. It tends to be freshly prepared and a little on the dull side, substituting meat surrogates for the real thing. The faux ham succeeds admirably in fried rice, but, in general, the offerings are as greasy and sweet as those at your local Chinese carryout. The real gems at this unusual place are the fruit-flavored teas, which change by the day.

Cuban, Dominican, and Puerto Rican

Decades ago, mercantile Manhattan was littered with Cuban luncheonettes that operated only during the day and served a constituency of both Spanish-speaking laborers and gringos who admired the greasy, salty, garlicky nature of the food. As the Cubans migrated out of town, these places were taken over first by Puerto Ricans, then by Dominicans. With the decline in industrial jobs and the upscaling of restaurant properties, these luncheonettes have all but disappeared. Pride of the East Village, the tiny Cuban lunch counter **National Café**, finally bit the dust in 2003. Only a few of these places remain. Witness old-timer **Margon**, just east of Times Square, mobbed morning and afternoon with enthusiastic diners of every social stripe, fidgeting in anticipation of cheap and tasty eats.

As a group Puerto Ricans have always preferred to enjoy their national specialties at home, and even today on the island there are relatively few restaurants — making it easy prey to fast-food chains. New York has far fewer Puerto Rican restaurants than the population would indicate, but those tend to be of exceptionally high quality. By contrast, the Dominicans are natural restaurateurs, and there are zillions of Dominican restaurants around town, especially in Washington Heights, East Harlem, the Lower East Side, and the Bronx. Dominican restaurateurs, too, are prone to take over Cuban and Puerto Rican places as the original owners flee to the suburbs. One dead giveaway for a Dominican place is a glowing neon sign that says "Seafood," since Dominicans appreciate anything from the ocean in a way that Cubans and Puerto Ricans do not. Still, Cuban cuisine is one of the world's most influential, dominating the menu of many Latin-Caribbean eateries, whatever the nationality.

45

Cuban

HAVANA CENTRAL ☆
22 East 17th Street, Manhattan, 212-414-4999 The costillas Cubanas at Union Square newcomer Havana Central taste just like real barbecued ribs, rich and smoky and dripping a slightly sweet mango-habanero sauce that wouldn't be out of place in the Carolinas, Memphis, or even Texas. And the rice-and-bean sides go just as well with ribs as, say, dill pickles and Wonder Bread. The

Cuban cooking here is untraditional, but it's good anyway and the price is right. A lunchtime favorite of students and office workers.

HAVANA CHELSEA LUNCHEONETTE ☆ ☆
190 8th Avenue, Manhattan, 212-243-9421 This Cuban greasy spoon has a refrigerator case with a window on the street, so you can look in at all the great stuff: timbales of flan and coconut pudding, big ceramic bowls of octopus and salt-cod salads, and slices of pork waiting to be incorporated into the best-selling Cuban sandwich. Made on Italian loaves with layers of roast pork, boiled ham, Swiss cheese, and pickles, the sandwiches are placed into a hot press that toasts, melts, smashes, crisps, and generally anneals the sandwich to the benefit of both bread and fillings. The Cuban sandwiches here come in two sizes — mediano and grande, big and bigger. Pulpo salad is a shadow of its former self these days, so skip it. Consider the chalkboard specials, often including a meaty beef-rib stew flavored with bay leaf and green olives.

MARGON ☆ ☆ ☆
136 West 46th Street, Manhattan, 212-354-5013 This ancient and well-worn Cuban lunch counter — now reverently run by Dominicans — is an anomaly in the culinary wasteland of Times Square, and the office workers prove it by thronging the narrow space at lunch, scarfing superlative oxtails, fried kingfish, paprika-dusted chicken, Cuban sandwiches, and wonderfully oily octopus salad. The paltry number of seats fills up early, so be prepared to stand in line and carry out. Hey, just standing in line here is a pleasure — like being a member of a private club.

EL SITIO ☆
35-55 31st Street, Queens, 718-278-7694; 68-28 Roosevelt Avenue, Queens, 718-424-2369 A Cuban lunch counter in the shadows of the elevated N train, El Sitio is Long Island City's foremost pit stop for strong coffee and presses one of the city's most memorable Cuban sandwiches. It's not overstuffed, but more modestly furnished in the style of the finest examples in South Miami. A real bargain at $3.50. The branch on Roosevelt Avenue is significantly less relaxing.

SOPHIE'S ☆
96 Chambers Street, Manhattan, 212-608-9900 Something of a modern miracle, Sophie's is the first Cuban-style lunch counter created in over a decade, striking a blow against the franchises striving to dominate Chambers Street. Snacks like yuca croquettes and empanadas are displayed in the front window for carryout, or sit down for a Cuban sandwich or that Iberian throwback camarones al ajillo, shrimp in a pungent garlic sauce, made to order at this comfortable joint.

CUBAN CHINESE

Now dwindling in numbers, this unique ethnic group originated as Chinese indentured laborers brought to the Caribbean before the First World War to work in the sugarcane fields. They became Cuban in every regard but race: they spoke Spanish, dressed in guayaberas, and mastered the art of Cuban cooking. Fleeing Fidel, the Cuban Chinese hit New York in the early 1960s. Plenty of the 5,000 who came to New York opened restaurants, especially on Chelsea's 8th Avenue, on the Upper West Side of Manhattan, and along the Grand Concourse in The Bronx. The most famous was **Sam Chinita**, ensconced in a streamlined chrome diner, recently demolished. Now there are very few left, although Chinese restaurants have begun serving Latin food in some neighborhoods. However, the Latin food is often mediocre. At any real Cuban-Chinese place, such as **La Chinita Linda** (166 8th Avenue, Manhattan, 212-633-1791), ignore the Chinese side of the menu — which contains bland Cantonese fare imperfectly remembered from the 1920s — and go straight to the Cuban side, where you'll find the food that the Cuban Chinese themselves prefer to eat. These dishes are prepared with gusto, and can be judged on an equal footing with the slightly different versions found in regular Cuban restaurants.

VICTOR'S ☆ ☆ ⋙ $

236 West 52nd Street, 212-586-7714 The U.S. embargo has decimated the restaurant industry in Cuba, and there are very few places on the island that match the menu of our own Victor's in scope and variety. Skip the underseasoned appetizers and ignore the shaky and slow service. Rather, start with a glass of the complex sangria and go right to the voluminous entrées, invariably accompanied by perfect white rice and the best black beans in town. Favorites include a pair of red snapper fillets crusted with plantain and flavored with sofrito, and oxtails in an aromatic gravy configured around a sweet-potato mound.

Dominican

LAS ANTILLAS ☆

4413 4th Avenue, Brooklyn, 718-438-1994 You can't beat the sofrito-rubbed rotisserie chicken, prominently displayed in the front window, either for flavor or price (half chicken $3.25) at this Dominican lunch counter, which fills out its menu with sancocho, sopa de gallina, steak and onions, rice with pigeon peas, and traditional breakfast choices like green banana, yuca, mango with cheese, and salami and eggs.

CARIDAD ☆

18 East 33rd Street, Manhattan, 212-779-7969 The pig-inflected pink beans are fabulous, and you get them automatically with every main course. On a recent revisit they were the perfect complement to well-stewed oxtails cut into thin coins and rimmed with a delectable layer of fat. Also experience the Dominican answer to tamales: pasteles.

CARIDAD LA ORIGINAL ☆

588 Amsterdam Avenue, Manhattan, 212-595-8121 Vestige of a once-thriving Hispano-Caribbean population in these parts, this comfortable café presents Cuban food with a discrete overlayering of Dominican culinary styles. Go to the rotating menu of daily specials for real down-home cooking, like gallina guisado, a stew featuring a tough old hen marinated and then cooked into complete submission.

DOMINICAN-CHINESE FUSION

Founded by a Chinese family who lived in the Dominican Republic for many years, **Sabrosura** (1200 Castle Hill Road, Bronx, 718-597-1344) is an oddball establishment in J. Lo's old nabe that offers a unique Dominican-Chinese cuisine which has — unlike its Cuban-Chinese counterpart — lots of fusion going on. Pork egg fu young comes in an achiote-tinged sauce, the over-rice farrago called locrio will remind you of paella, and the garlicky broiled clams will leave you enthusing about them days later. Also on a menu with a dizzying array of choices are plain Dominican standards featuring the usual chicken, chorizo, and pork.

EL CIBAO ☆ ☆

172 Smith Street, Brooklyn, 718-596-1501 Named after a gorgeous and fecund Dominican valley, El Cibao has been overlooked in the listless queue of trendy restaurants along Smith Street. This well-lit old-timer tosses a formidable and fillerless bacalao (salt cod) salad dressed with onions, peppers, and vinegar, and purveys a well-seasoned pork roast in massive portions.

EL CONDE ☆ ☆

4139 Broadway, Manhattan, 212-781-4139 Columbia Presbyterian Hospital just wouldn't be the same without this excellent Dominican steakhouse. Watching the enthusiastic chef tend a skirt steak — prodding, poking, and flipping — is a cinematic treat. The roast chicken and octopus salad ain't bad, either.

LA CONQUITA ☆

236 Lafayette Street, Manhattan, 212-226-9835 The sharp smell of vinegar wafts out the door of this decrepit and unbelievably cheap SoHo carryout, so jammed at lunch you may have to wait outside. Chicken fricassee and steak with onions are particularly good. Side either with moros — the admixture of white rice and black beans admired by both Cubans and Dominicans.

DALQUIS RESTAURANT ☆

318 West 36th Street, Manhattan, 212-502-5363 The lunch counter in this storefront runs along one wall and ends in a steam table with eight or so main dishes. The steam table entrées — oxtail, pork chops, two kinds of chicken, beefsteak — are in the $6 to $8 range and include mounds of rice and beans. Try the codfish salad — salt cod, green olives, chopped tomato, green pepper, and Spanish onion dressed with vinegar and olive oil. Chicken baked with garlic and black pepper and strewn with raw onions is also fine.

EL DESPERTAR ☆

1875 Lexington Avenue, Manhattan, 212-348-4557 Don't be discouraged by the steamed-up window, which prevents you from seeing the goodies stacked therein. This Dominican fried-food stand has the meatiest chicharron de cerdo (twice-cooked pork ribs) I've ever tasted, making a perfect meal when paired with pasteles — tamales stuffed with chicken, red chiles, and onions.

EL ECONOMICO ☆ ☆

5589 Broadway, Bronx, 718-601-5577 Man, this is my kind of place: a bustling retro lunch counter located under the elevated tracks in working-class Kingsbridge, dispensing food several notches better than the premises would suggest. The roast pork is particularly moist (ask for boiled yuca with green sauce alongside), and El Economico serves superb Dominican sancocho, in this case a soothing chicken soup thickened with pumpkin.

GALICIA ☆ ☆
4083 Broadway, Manhattan, 212-568-0168 Many Dominicans trace their ancestry to the northern Spanish province of Galicia, and this fascinating institution offers food from the old country filtered through Caribbean sensibilities. Key is caldo gallego, a hopelessly rich soup bobbing with kale, white beans, pig trotters, and wine-laced sausage. It seems almost Portuguese. Dig the stuccoed Spanish-village decor.

LECHONERA SANDY ☆ ☆ 🐟
2261 2nd Avenue, Manhattan, 212-348-8654 The name of this East Harlem standby says it all — pig, pig, and more pig. Start with cuchifritos, the family of fried snacks that fester in the window at most places. Here they're incredibly fresh: codfish fritters, stuffed potatoes, blood sausage, and alcapurrias — torpedoes of mashed plantain filled with ground meat. But don't miss the signature pork roast, drenched with garlic and sided with crunchy skin, or mofongo, a fried mound of mashed plantains with the richest garlic gravy you've ever tasted. The menu at this excellent restaurant is rounded out with seafood, soups, and fruit shakes.

EL LINA ☆ 🐟
500 West 207th Street, Manhattan, no phone Determined to put this ancient Dominican lunch counter to the test, I ignored the usual steam table stuff and ordered shrimp asopao. Fifteen minutes later appeared an extravagantly good rendition: a red-tinged broth savory with vinegar, garlic, and cilantro, bobbing with shrimp and loaded with rice and cubed potatoes.

EL MALECON ☆
4141 Broadway, Manhattan, 212-927-3812 The smell of roasting chicken wafts down the block from this spacious and comfortable Dominican diner, and the bargain bird comes with a well-browned skin and an astringent lime-garlic dipping sauce. But don't let it distract you from the stewed yuca, doused with garlic oil and topped with pickled purple onions, or salcocho, an herby beef soup rife with plantain, potato, and carrot, making it a well-rounded meal. There's a mural of a malecon — a seaside road — at the end of the room, and two rows of spacious booths that are mobbed with diners from diverse backgrounds.

EL MAMBI ☆
558 West 181st Street, Manhattan, 212-568-8321 This narrow Dominican lunch counter has developed a sideline in promoting Vegas-style music extravaganzas, but still produces Washington

Heights's best Cuban sandwich, generously layered with roast pork, cheese, and good ham. Their secret: pickles and garlic sauce are applied post-pressing.

EL MUNDO FRIED CHICKEN ✫ ✫ ✫
4456 Broadway, Manhattan, 212-567-9325 You can't go wrong with the poultry at El Mundo, located on a hilly corner of Washington Heights that may remind you of San Francisco, including spice-slathered rotisserie chicken, the vinegary chicken tidbits chicharron de pollo, or even the namesake fried chicken. This Dominican also serves great soupy red beans and twice-cooked chicharron de cerdo.

NEW CAPORAL FRIED CHICKEN ✫ ✫
3772 Broadway, Manhattan, 212-862-8986 Strategically located at the southern gateway to Washington Heights, this venerable hill-country carryout does wonderful chicken and little else. The bird has been thoughtfully marinated in garlic and citrus — a variation on Cuban mojo — then deep-fried to a sienna brown. The chicken is made fresh all day long, so it's never stale and limp, and the shoestring fries are an adequate foil. Kudos to the friendly and talented staff for making a product that people drive miles to get, and who can resist the logo: a beaming chick in a cowboy outfit brandishing a six-shooter?

SPANISH AMERICAN FOOD ✫ ✫
351 East 13th Street, Manhattan, 212-475-4508 Can a restaurant name get any more plainly descriptive than that? S.A. Food is a beloved institution on 13th Street, a Dominican takeout so small you practically sit in the lap of the friendly counter gal when you order. Cuchifritos such as the wonderful chicharron de cerdo — twice-cooked ribs that were learned at the knee of French colonialists — and codfish fritters smashed flat and cooked like latkes share a menu with more ambitious soups and stews. My favorite from the former category is pig foot–pork tripe combo in a red broth thickened with tasty animal fat.

Puerto Rican

CASA ADELA ✫
66 Avenue C, Manhattan, 212-473-1882 The chicken soup may be the cheapest complete meal in the East Village: a drumstick in a clear, tomato-tinged broth jumping with cumin, green pepper, and oregano, anchored by big hunks of carrot and potato. The surprise additional component is spaghetti, generating a double-carbo blast. Other choices include pork roast and biftek encebollado, a razor-thin piece of meat quick-cooked with onion,

so the onion stays triumphantly firm, deliciously finished with a dash of vinegar that generates an impromptu gravy. Don't miss the tostones, crisp and light despite the lard component.

LA FONDITA ☆ ☆

226 Willis Avenue, Bronx, 718-401-4741 Formerly known as Cuchifritos 2000, La Fondita features irresistible bronzed pork skins in the window, as light as Styrofoam despite being saturated with lard and prodigiously rubbed with salt. This tiled and cavernous Puerto Rican restaurant also slings amazing moist lechon asado; the alcapurrias are also admirable, though a bit heavy for the cuchifrito neophyte.

LECHONERA EL COQUI ☆ ☆

1251 Castle Hill Road, Bronx, 718-892-7734 No part of the pig is neglected, including ears and tongue, at this friendly café named after the tiny Puerto Rican frog that makes annoying peeping noises while you're trying to sleep. The pork roast is fantastic, but my favorite dish is boiled yuca with purple onions doused with a powerful garlic sauce.

EL NUEVO BOHIO ☆ ☆ ☆

791 East Tremont Avenue, Bronx, 718-299-4218 The machetes flash at this authentic lechonera, pride of Puerto Rican East Tremont, as the roast pig is hacked and arrayed in the window, the moist chunks salty and garlicky, the skin well bronzed and gloriously chewy. Everything depends on this perfect mammal, including excellent morcilla (blood sausage) and made-to-order mofongo.

EL RINCON BORICUA ☆ ☆

158 East 119th Street, Manhattan, 212-534-9400 Snip, snip, snip go the scissors as the affable counter guy cuts your portion of baby pig (some fat, some lean, with crisp swatches of copper-colored skin adhering. The accompanying rice, beans, and fried plantain are so humbled by this delicacy, they seek out a separate plate. Note: the menu has been expanded in the last couple of years, and the food has come down a notch as a result.

LA TAZA DE ORO ☆ ☆

96 8th Avenue, Manhattan, 212-243-9946 Latin restaurants once dominated Chelsea's 8th Avenue, replaced one by one over the last decade by pricey bistros and trattorias. Perch at the lunch counter or relax at one of the tables at this venerable Puerto Rican greasy spoon, and enjoy sancocho — a delicious stew of chicken, chorizo, and vegetables laced with garlic and oregano — or more ample main courses like fried fish or lechon asado. Face the perennial dilemmas: Should I pick white rice or yellow, red beans or black?

Eastern European

Albanian, Bosnian, Bulgarian, Czech, Hungarian, Istrian, Latvian, Lithuanian, and Polish

Wandering around Greenpoint, Williamsburg, Sunnyside, or the East Village you're likely to stumble on a Polish café with little in the way of decor, but great prices when it comes to gravied hunks of meat and mashed potatoes. Hats off to the Poles for some of the best cheap food in the universe. Though the Poles dominate the Eastern European dining landscape, the Bosnians — mainly ethnic Albanian Muslim refugees from Sarajevo — are definitely catching up. Look carefully at the menu of your local pizza parlor, especially if you live in Astoria, Queens, or Pelham Parkway in the Bronx, and you're likely to find bureks on the menu — tire-sized phyllo pies that cook up very well in a pizza oven. Czechs continue to hold their own, while Hungarians and Bulgarians are a decidedly minor presence in the dining landscape, though our municipal complement of Hungarian restaurants recently doubled to two. Finally, we welcome the first Lithuanian restaurant to the city. All these countries were influenced by the cooking of the Ottoman and Austro-Hungarian empires, and share an admiration of paprika. Brought to Eastern Europe by Ottoman soldiers returning from India in the 18th century, paprika is really a type of chile, available in mild, medium, and hot. Since 1945 the market has sadly been dominated by a sweet form that has a sunny flavor but little heat.

Now that the *Times* and other publications have finally discovered that many Arthur Avenue Italian restaurants are being run by Albanians, the real story is that Albanian restaurateurs are coming out of the closet. Proudly festooning their awnings with hard-to-pronounce names, and replacing the Italian tricolor with the two-headed black eagle, they've begun serving their own country's food, including roast lamb, sautéed brains, vinegary composed salads, and fresh fish cooked with lemon and garlic.

LOOK FOR:

bigos *Polish hunter's stew*

bosanska tufahija *Bosnian baked apple*

burek *round phyllo pie*

cevapcici *grilled ground-lamb cylinders*

false soup *vegetarian soup*

flaczki *Polish honeycomb tripe soup*

fuzi *Istrian envelope-shaped pasta*

ivar *sweet pimento puree*

kavarma *Bulgarian pork and sweet-pepper stew*

kielbasa *garlic sausage*

kufte *ground meat kebab*

kyopolu *Bulgarian ratatouille*

liptauer *Hungarian cheese spread*

minestra *vegetable soup*

nokedli *Hungarian spaetzle*

owocowa *Polish cold fruit soup*

palacinky *dessert crepes*

pyzy *potato dumplings*

qofte *Albanian ground veal patty*

sallate turshie *pickled vegetable salad*

shav *Polish sorrel soup*

spaetzle *free-form homemade noodles*

suxhuk *wine-laced Kosovar lamb sausage*

tarator *Bulgarian cucumber-yogurt soup*

zeljanica *spinach and phyllo pastry*

Albanian

ALL STAR CAFÉ RESTAURANT ☆ ☆ ◄══

2328 Arthur Avenue, Bronx, 718-367-3917 This venerable Albanian institution took an odd turn a couple years back when it was bought by a pair of Swedish dames, who soon imparted a Scandinavian spin to the menu. Though it doesn't come with lingonberries, there's a nicely grilled salmon filet, and a pair of ethereal crumbed and butter-sautéed trout that would find a hearty welcome in both Sweden and Albania. But where All Star really distinguishes itself is in the fulfillment of the Albanian passion for variety meats. Well-cleansed kidneys come dripping with butter and garlic, while brains can be had two ways: simply grilled and drizzled with lemon, or — even better — battered, fried, and inundated with a light lemon sauce. Finally, there's a homely stew of navy beans that comes bobbing with slices of a thin sausage flagrantly named suxhuk, a Kosovar specialty with an intriguing winey aftertaste.

BUREKTORJA DUKAGJINI ☆ ☆ ♨

758 Lydig Avenue, Bronx, 718-822-8955 The simplicity of this tiny coffee shop is refreshing, with a menu limited to three kinds of bureks (cheese, spinach, and ground meat), homemade yogurt to dip them in, and the standard permutations of espresso. The contraption the bureks fly out of looks like a miniature pizza oven, and these round phyllo pies appear with clockwork regularity. Though they outwardly resemble the Bosnian bureks of Astoria, the Albanian examples are generally less greasy; the spinach version lacks cheese, but is more powerfully flavored with dill as a result; while the cheese is extracheesy and even tastes good stone cold.

GURRA CAFE ☆

2325 Arthur Avenue, Bronx, 718-220-4254 The awning grandly proclaims "Shqiptare Cuisine," though the interior resembles a Swiss chalet, with exposed beams and peeling murals of snow-capped mountains that look suspiciously like the Rockies. When asked for a menu, the owlish waiter smiles and shakes his head, offering instead, "I make assortment for you." Five minutes later he materializes with a metal tray, a landscape of meat mountains separated by meadows of pale green iceberg lettuce dotted with tomatoes and crisscrossed with picket fences of feta. The peaks are indeed awesome, formed from pounded-thin filets, short skinless sausages, and hamburger patties that glow with tallow and exude a faint odor of smoke. Pointing and beaming, the waiter boasts "All veal!"

RESTORANT SHQIPTAR ☆ 🐟

660 East 187th Street, Bronx, 718-562-4700 Taking its moniker from the Albanian name for the homeland, this bar seems to have replaced a much older Neapolitan joint. Spilling tables onto the sidewalk, the raffish hangout is populated with dudes smoking, playing cards, and nursing Buds. The menu is less complicated than it looks. The section designated "Makaronet" lists familiar Italian pastas, and the poultry section remains Italian, too. If you're looking for Albanian food, turn your attention to the sections headed Salad, Fish, and Meat. Sallate turshie is a platter of cucumbers and red peppers, pickled and pinned down with a plank of feta. Peshk zgare grills an entire sea bream till the thick skin is crisp and the yellow-tinged flesh aromatic of lemon and garlic. Also remarkable is qofte, a chef's special that features a patty of ground veal that — in a wonderful feat of food architecture — squirts sour cream when you slice into it. But blowing everything else away is qingj i pjekur, a sizable haunch of baby lamb roasted deep brown and plated elegantly with a pair of lemon wedges.

Bosnian

BASCARSIJA ☆

44-09 Broadway, Queens, 718-777-8344 To get a fresh perspective on what happened to Yugoslavia, visit this Bosnian bar in Long Island City, named after an ancient neighborhood in Sarajevo. Skip the menu, most of which is permanently "not available," and let the barkeep assemble a banquet for you. What you'll probably get — as we did on two occasions — is a sumptuous heap of grilled meats, including lamb shish kebabs, veal cutlets, and cevapcici — cylinders of savory ground meat accented with onions and cilantro. The belt-busting array is sided with tangy cabbage slaw assembled from vegetables grown in the backyard garden, pitas, cubes of mellow feta, and ivar, a sunny puree of pimentos that's the perfect dip for the meats.

BOSNA-EXPRESS ☆ ☆ ☆

791 Fairview Avenue, Queens, 718-497-7577 Trust Bosnian immigrants to give us our best hamburger. Located on a shady corner under the moribund M train, where the huddled buildings form a quaint Eastern European town square, with Bosnian, Croatian, and Polish institutions describing a circle around a patchy greensward, Bosna-Express is a carryout window that specializes in great grilled meats and homemade yogurt. Pljeskavica is a one-pound belt-busting beef-lamb patty the size of a dinner plate. It's served up on a massive roll made right on the premises, and dressed with yogurt and chopped vegetables — the perfect one-dish meal.

CEVABDZINICA SARAJEVO ☆ ☆

37-18 34th Avenue, Queens, 718-752-9528 The name translates as Sarajevo Fast Food, and this diminutive eatery dispenses delicious grilled meat platters, savory pastries, and desserts. Cevapi are skinless homemade sausages the size of a shotgun shell made of lamb and beef — oniony, rubbery, and fatty enough to absorb the smoke — and the list of grillables also includes lamb chops, trout, salmon, and variety meats like kidneys, liver, and especially delectable sweetbreads, served with freshly baked bread and chopped raw onion. But the surprise hit at our table was a special dessert called bosanska tufahija, a baked apple stuffed with walnut cream.

DJERDAN #3 ☆

221 West 38th Street, Manhattan, 212-921-1183 Sojourning to Astoria or Pelham Parkway is no longer necessary where Bosnian bureks are concerned. These fantastic flaky phyllo pies — stuffed with cheese, meat, or spinach — are now available in Manhattan's garment district. Trouble is, at this location they reheat them in the microwave, decreasing your culinary delight substantially. Either ask to have the burek served at room temperature, or carry out a wedge and find your own oven. Or go for the wonderful goulash, a heap of tender veal chunks laved in a light paprika gravy and deposited on enough rice to provision a small army.

HOUSE OF PIZZA ☆ ☆ ☆ 🍎

42-20 30th Avenue, Queens, 718-545-9455 The best Balkan bureks in town come from this unassuming Astoria pizza parlor. These rotund flaky pies — fabricated from phyllo dough and well oiled — come stuffed with a choice of ground meat, cheese, or spinach and cheese. The spinach is preferred, with cheese a close second. Order a mug of the homemade yogurt to go with it, to be poured over the top or used as a dip for pieces torn from the massive pie, which easily feeds four. Other non-Italian offerings include a sorrel-laced veal goulash, and grilled cevapi, skinless mixed-meat sausages fragrant with onion.

Bulgarian

416 B.C. ☆ ☆

416 Broadway, Manhattan, 212-625-0981 This place, spectacularly located at the crossroads of Canal and Broadway, bills itself as a mehanata, or "little tavern," a rugged country establishment that furnishes simple meals washed down with local wines. If many of the dishes seem Turkish, why not? Witness kyopolu, a fragrant puree of roast eggplant, red peppers, tomatoes, parsley, and garlic. Equally desirable is "snowhite," a dip studded with cucumbers, garlic, and walnuts. If you'd rather slurp than scoop, try tarator — a dilled and chilled cucumber-yogurt soup with a name like a Japanese superhero. "Chicken livers — country style" often contains hearts, gizzards, and other innards as well, cooked in about a stick of butter and blizzarded with paprika and garlic. Bulgarians dote on ground meat kufte and its cumin-laced cousin kebabche, both included in the generous mixed grill, which also contains a couple of pork cuts, decent fries, navy bean stew, and ajvar, a sprightly pepper paste. But more interesting is the kavarma omelet, an outsized egg crepe wrapped around a delicious pork stew sweetened with peppers and onions.

KOLIBA ☆ ☆

31-11 23rd Avenue, Queens, 718-626-0430 Koliba attracts a younger crowd, who sport hip American threads and hairstyles while chattering in their native tongue. The cod liver appetizer is particularly good, little cubes of pale pink, light as a feather and snowed with capers and chopped onions. Another surprising starter is garlic soup, an intensely odiferous broth in which a submerged egg yolk shines like the sun on a smoggy day. Also consider visiting the bar menu to begin your meal. The pair of natural-skinned franks is locked into orbit by the grainy mustard and freshly grated horseradish that come alongside. The headcheese, too, is a revelation. Offered in thick slices and wobbly with gelatin, it tastes like gourmet baloney. Following Czech custom, the entrées are divided into two opposing camps. The cheaper section consists of steam table offerings that can be devoured almost immediately: goulash, roast chicken, and smoked pork loin. Under the designation Special Orders are dishes that take a half hour to prepare. Unfortunately, not only are they more expensive, these offerings are inferior to the steam table stuff.

RESTAURANT MILAN'S ☆

710 5th Avenue, Brooklyn, 718-788-7384 This café is, according to the waiter, one of only two places in town that serves Slavic dumplings — magnificent moist loaves sliced like white bread and served with stews. The best main course to enjoy them is szeged goulash, chunks of tender pork in a beige sauce thickened with sour cream and awash in sauerkraut. It tastes a million times better than it sounds. Also good are pork chops Belehrad, deep-fried in an egg batter and sided with vinegary purple cabbage slaw. Avoid the pudding sundae, though — canned peaches smothered with chocolate pudding and whipped cream.

ZLATA PRAHA ☆

28-48 31st Street, Astoria, Queens, 718-721-6422 Zlata Praha, which means Golden Prague, recalls the glory days of pre-Nazi and presocialist Bohemia, when meat was heaped in mountains and gravy flowed like the Vltava River. Tripe soup makes a spectacular starter, with chewy hunks of honeycomb tripe foundering in a chocolate-brown broth. Alternatively, there's a refreshingly light lentil soup flecked with vegetables, known as a "false soup" in Czech cooking because the broth isn't made with meat. Most of the entrées are sided by a dumpling the size of a slow-pitch softball, dotted with caramelized onions and sliced like bread. The tastiest

is smoked pork loin, swimming in beige sauce and sided by unusually sweet sauerkraut pricked with caraway. Or pick the mid-
night-brown goulash, which struggles mightily to distance itself
from the Hungarian product and succeeds. The compulsory last
course: sugar-dusted palacinky, crepes bulging with apricot jam
and bent acutely to fit the small plate.

Hungarian

MOCCA HUNGARIAN ☆
1588 2nd Avenue, Manhattan, 718-734-6470 The tin ceiling,
tile floor, and rickety furniture time-warp you to an earlier decade,
and the average age of the diners — seemingly around 80 — will
make you feel like a kid. Of the ethnographic gewgaws on the
walls, only a well-used leather whip and pair of fur canteens make
you wonder about the staid demeanor of the patrons. The 20 main
courses present a nearly insurmountable dilemma. First eliminate
the schnitzels — though nicely cooked, they're not the kind of veal
people dream about. Also avoid the interesting sounding veal
knuckle, a flattened, breaded mass of glistening gray gelatin.
Choose instead the twin cabbage leaves stuffed with rice, pork,
and veal, smothered in sauerkraut and unexpectedly bursting with
flavor. The beef goulash is a triumph, too, the chunks resting in a
gravy as dark as Mexican mole, sharing the plate with miniature
dumplings. But the best thing on the menu is gypsy roast, a wild
ride of a dish featuring two long-boned pork chops cooked in tons
of garlic and hot paprika, and deglazed with a puckering squirt of
vinegar, a spicy kick in the pants.

A TOUCH OF HUNGARY ☆
121-17 14th Road, Queens, 718-762-3436 Though the top
entrée price of $15.95 might seem a little steep for the peasant
food of Eastern Europe served in a modest storefront so far north
in Queens it feels like Minnesota, the portions are large enough for
Paul Bunyan. The nicely browned schnitzels of chicken, pork, and
veal are toothsome, but nearly impossible to digest. Go instead for
the pork Holstein: tender medallions dipped in butter and topped
with two fried eggs, and side it with spaetzle ("nokedli").

Istrian

ISTRIA SPORTS CLUB ☆ ☆
28-09 Astoria Boulevard, Queens, 718-728-3181 Founded in
1957 by immigrants from that region of the former Yugoslavia (the
one right next to Trieste in Italy), Istria Sports Club has a dining
area that mimics a suburban rec room, the blond paneling lined

with soccer trophies and men playing card games — in this case tresete and briskula. But walk out back and you'll find the best tables on a covered terrace overlooking bocce courts and a sunny vegetable garden. There is no formal menu; the waiter recites the short list of dishes, pausing to describe them in Italian to a member of our party. The thing to get is fuzi, a homemade pasta made by taking squares of dough and folding in two opposite corners, making envelopes like miniature Danish. It's sauced with chunks of veal in a light brown gravy laced with paprika and garlic. Potato gnocchi, nearly as good, offers an agreeably earthy flavor and the same sauce. Another fine choice is cevapcici, shotgun shells of grilled beef on a bed of red onions, the meat accompanied by a zingy dipping sauce of pureed red pepper called ivar. In happier days, this was the national dish of Yugoslavia.

Latvian

KING OF LATVIA II ☆
87-18 112th Street, Queens, 718-850-9061 This well-kept grocery specializes in Latvian charcuterie, including a plethora of sausages and smoked meats that make perfect picnic fare. The cheese and yogurt selection is also diverting, and there are all sorts of Russian groceries, as well. As we stood at the counter pondering the selection of pastries, the aproned old lady who runs the place flipped a couple of pieces of smoked lard over the counter for us to sample, gratis.

Lithuanian

KREZO 2 ☆
318 Grand Street, Brooklyn, 718-388-5768 Krezo 2 claims to be the only Lithuanian restaurant in New York, and they're probably right, though it seems more like a disco than a restaurant. The food arrives in copious quantities, however, and includes all sorts of grilled meats and stuffed doughs and potato puddings, and you'll have to excuse me for not noting the names of these dishes, since there was no menu at the time, and I was somewhat plowed on the flutes of brandy brought by the somewhat sullen waiter.

Polish

HAPPY END ☆
924 Manhattan Avenue, Brooklyn, 718-383-9862 The menu board reads in Polish with a chalkboard offering English as an afterthought. On my first visit, a group of us sat for ten minutes be-

fore realizing that there is no waiter service. A woman of amazing girth is seen through the door of the tiny kitchen, swinging pots in every direction, assembling the dinners with deadly accuracy. A hunk of meat is deftly scooped from a deep container on the steam table, then slung onto a plate with mashed potatoes and paprika gravy. Next, identical mounds of two barely distinguishable salads are heaped on: cabbage salad and carrot-and-cabbage salad. The same presentation on every plate makes this one of the most single-minded dining places on earth — and one of the cheapest. And like it says on the menu, a free beverage is provided — orange Kool-Aid that you serve yourself from a reservoir on a card table. Add your own vodka or LSD if you feel like it.

LITTLE POLAND ☆

200 2nd Avenue, Manhattan, 212-777-9728 The soups, 13 in all, give B & H (see the Dairy section of the Jewish-American chapter) a run for its money. The list includes tripe, chicken noodle, dark bean with kielbasa, potato lamb, and a wonderfully tart, dense, flavorful cabbage. The homemade pierogi are also available in multiple variations, deep fried to a golden brown and served with sour cream. I especially liked the plate-eclipsing veal cutlet, much thicker than the usual Wiener schnitzel, the tender meat annealed with a stout coating of crumbs. Feeling particularly ravenous? Pick the signature combo platter, which includes four pierogi of your choice, stuffed cabbage, kielbasa, and bigos.

MONIKA ☆

643 5th Avenue, Brooklyn, 718-788-6930 If you had a Polish grandma, this is how she'd cook. Right off the bat, there's an over-the-top selection of 17 soups, running from the light and fruity owocowa to the heavy and ponderous flaczki, loaded with tripe and potatoes. But the heart of the menu are entrées like pork chops, kielbasa, ham hocks, and a goulash that comes Hungarian-style — sided with potato pancakes.

OLD POLAND BAKERY AND RESTAURANT ☆ ☆

190 Nassau Avenue, Brooklyn, 718-349-7775 This Greenpoint mainstay offers a full-course meal of entrée, gravy, two scoops of potatoes, and a selection of vegetables for as little as $3.50 (delicious sautéed chicken livers). For $4 you can enjoy a pair of pork shanks, boiled skin-on till the shreds of rich flesh attain a ruby hue, or a lake of lima bean stew dotted with bits of ham and kielbasa. And don't miss the excellent red-cabbage slaw. Other entrées sampled on several recent visits included long strips of tongue in a soothing white sauce, plate-flopping Wiener schnitzel, calf's liver with plenty of onions, and meatballs stuffed with finely diced vegetables. For a lighter meal try shav, a soup made with fresh sorrel in a light chicken stock.

THE POLISH PLACE ☆ ☆

19 Corson Avenue, Staten Island, 718-442-8909 This Polish salumeria and grocery has comfortable seating in an adjacent storefront, and a cheap and unstinting menu of soups, pierogi, blintzes, and main courses like pot roast with horseradish sauce, vegetable-and-cheese-stuffed chicken breast that looks like a small submarine, and a more than generous Wiener schnitzel. Massive sides (pick three) include fresh green beans and multiple cabbage preparations.

RAYMUND'S PLACE ☆

124 Bedford Avenue, Brooklyn, 718-388-4200 When the frigid wind knifes off the East River, pop into this Polish café for a bowl of sour grass soup, made with strong meat stock fortified with cream. The little bits of sour grass floating on the top would look like something mowed in your backyard, if you only had a backyard. A hard-boiled egg is submerged, and alongside comes a loaf-shaped mass of mashed potatoes sprinkled with plenty of crumbled-up bacon. You're supposed to dump the potatoes and bacon into the soup, which turns a light meal into something more substantial. By the way, it's delish.

TERESA'S ☆ ☆

103 1st Avenue, Manhattan, 212-228-0604 Flagship of the East Village Polish fleet, Teresa's is priced a dollar or two above par — but it's a sum well spent for bigger portions, higher-quality food, and a premises plastered with real oil paintings. The veal cutlet is the best in town, if you don't count Zum Stammtisch (see the German chapter) and Danube, and the stuffed cabbage is the definition of mellow. Note that the green beans are made from fresh and come strewn with sautéed garlic and bread crumbs.

Ecuadorian, Bolivian, and Peruvian

Ecuadorian eateries are burgeoning — in Sunset Park, Woodside, Jackson Heights, Corona, and Washington Heights. The ceviche invented by Ecuadorians (some credit Peruvians or Mexicans) is now all the rage in many of the city's fancier restaurants. Meanwhile, Peruvians have cornered the market in carryout chickens, with a mysterious spice rub that's difficult to analyze, though the Chinese presence in Peru during the last century may have something to do with it. Peruvian restaurateurs have also been fairly successful in popularizing their chow for the bistro crowd, at places like **Coco Roco** in Park Slope and **Lima's Taste** in the East Village. Bolivians are so rare in New York that there are only two that I know of, but their food presents a fascinating contrast with that of their Peruvian and Ecuadorian neighbors, embodied in an enhanced appreciation of mutton, and less emphasis, quite obviously, on seafood. The commonality of all Andean fare includes an emphasis on tuberous vegetables and meat, and an indefatigable love of corn, potatoes, and chiles in their myriad forms.

LOOK FOR:

aji de gallina *bright yellow chicken stew*
almuerzo *lunch special*
anticucho de corazon *beef heart shish kebab*
arroz con camarones *Chinese-style shrimp fried rice*
caldo de bola relleno *Ecuadorian soup with big stuffed dumpling*
chifles *plantain chips*
choclo *section of corn on the cob*
chuños *tiny freeze-dried potatoes*

---

falso conejo *Bolivian mock rabbit*
hornado *roast suckling pig*
jalea *Peruvian fried seafood assortment*
kamlu wonton *Peruvian fried wontons*
leche de tigre *Peruvian aphrodisiacal ceviche*
llapingachos *cheese-stuffed potato patties*
mazamorra morada *purple Jell-O type dessert*
mote *big white hominy kernels*
papas a la Huancaina *Peruvian potatoes with
    cheese sauce*
parihuela *Chinese-leaning Peruvian seafood stew*
pique lo macho *beef stir-fry*
seco de carne *beef stew*
seco de chivo *"dry" goat stew*
seco de gallina *old-hen stew*

Bolivian

MI BOLIVIA ★ ★
44-10 48th Avenue, Queens, 718-784-5111 Originally known as Rumi Hausi ("stone house" in Aymara), this restaurant miraculously transfers Bolivian cuisine to Sunnyside with every element intact, including tiny freeze-dried potatoes known as chuños. Sample a mutton and cabbage boiled dinner (thimpu); mock rabbit of heaped beef cutlets (falso conejo); or a combo platter named after the capital (plato paceño). There are a couple of even odder dishes, including pique lo macho ("prick to the manhood") — a stir-fry of beef strips, hot and sweet peppers, tomato wedges, white cheese, purple onions, french fries, and cocktail franks (hey, maybe that's the manhood part).

Ecuadorian

ALEX AGUINAGA — AKA FANNY ★
214 Knickerbocker Avenue, Brooklyn, 718-497-2828 While most Ecuadorians are ceviche oriented, this is one of the rare places that concentrates on highland food, including anthology platters like bandera, and stews called secos. Specialty of the house is churrasco Aguinaga, a spectacular sirloin heaped with a chunky creole sauce and topped with a pair of fried eggs like the twin suns of some remote galaxy.

FREEZE-DRIED

Who invented freeze-drying? Some scientist at Kraft or General Foods? Wrong! This seemingly high-tech endeavor was perfected millennia ago by South American Aymara Indians, who cultivated over 200 varieties of potato on the Titicaca altiplano. Newly dug tubers were left out overnight to freeze. After thawing the next morning, they were trampled by the farmer in a highland fling, squeezing out moisture and sloughing the peels. On subsequent days this was repeated, until the chalky, shrunken spuds were ready for a weeklong soak in cold water to remove any bitterness. Redried in direct sunlight till a protective white pellicle formed on the outside, they would keep for four or five years. When the conquistadores landed in South America, Indians were using freeze-dried potatoes as currency.

BRAULIO'S AND FAMILIA ☆ 🐟

39-08 63rd Street, Woodside, Queens, 718-899-3267 This Ecuadorian bar is run by a family who hails from the seaside province of Manabi, and their origin is reflected in the care taken with seafood. The ceviche puts pretentious Manhattan ceviche parlors to shame — huge bowls of citrus-saturated seafood that feel more like summer soups than solid entrées. Best are the plain fish and octopus versions, although the homeland favorite of concha negra ("black clam") is also interesting, if not the freshest thing in the fridge. Typical Ecuadorian platters are also available, such as bandera, a comestible rendition of the flag featuring yellow and white rice, shrimp ceviche, red lamb stew, and yellowish tripe in peanut sauce.

DON PEPE ☆

40-56 Junction Boulevard, Queens, 718-396-4366 Who can finish the $5 almuerzo, a fusillade of oxtail soup loaded with corn, meat, and yuca washed down with a glass of orange soda, followed by a giant plate of rice, salad, stewed lentils, and your choice of meat, poultry, or fish? On a recent afternoon I picked corvina (aka weakfish), a couple of tasty fillets crosshatched to increase the crispy surface. This home-style Ecuadorian café is located on Corona's busiest corner.

EVA RESTAURANTE ☆

551 4th Avenue, Brooklyn, 718-788-9354 The interior of Eva's is comprehensively pink, with long mirrors, rounded on top, which make you feel like you're in an arcade. A waitress brings a menu with a small section devoted to pan-Latin cuisine, including pernil and pescado frito. Another section lists the daily soups, with some days being favored with two. The largest section is devoted to Ecuadorian fare, but no roasted guinea pig or pig-blood soup. I ordered sopa de torreja, a brown broth in which peregrinate pieces of omelet made with peppers, onions, and potted meat. There are also pieces of stringy pot roast, cabbage, potatoes, and a choclo. The soup came with a dish of lime wedges and an astringent sauce of green chiles, onions, oil, and vinegar. I slurped it down as Spanish reggae throbbed in the background.

HORNADO ECUATORIANO ☆ ☆
76-18 Roosevelt Avenue, Queens, 718-205-7357 The name identifies the specialty — perfectly roasted suckling pig, carefully allocated in portions encompassing bronze skin, lean meat, rich meat, and globs of fat. The humongous platter also includes heaps of hominy, two llapingachos (cheese-laced potato patties), salad, and pickled purple onions, so you'd better fast for 24 hours beforehand. Corn tamales called humitas are also excellent, but some of the other Ecuadorian specialties — tripe in peanut sauce, goat stew, and ceviche — can't compete with the pork.

PET FEAST

For years I looked high and low in Ecuadorian eateries for the national dish of cuy, a small animal belonging to the cavey family, which comes barbecued, deep-fried, or stewed depending on what part of the country you're in. Though a relative of the guinea pig, it might be mistaken for a rat if you saw it creeping through the underbrush. In the northern highlands of Ecuador, Indian women keep them in their gardens, which are always surrounded by low walls about six inches in height. It seems that the little critters are incapable of climbing this comically low impediment, so they can't escape. Cuy is eaten by the head of the family on special occasions, so when dad wants guinea pig, mom just goes to the garden and grabs one. Cuy is also featured in the truck stops in the northern highlands region, with big signs advertising it by the side of the road.

LA PICADA AZUAYA ☆ 🐟
84-19 37th Avenue, Queens, 718-424-9797 Of the ceviches, I prefer mixto: shrimp, red snapper, purple onion, and parsley

swimming in lime juice. A few chunks of yuca have been thrown in as a culinary joke — you can't distinguish them from the fish. Forget about ordering sopas (soups) as an appetizer. These selections are meals in themselves. Choices include fish, sausage, chicken, rib, and "feet cow." As at most Ecuadorians, caldo de bola relleno is the best, floating a plantain dumpling that looks like a brown matzo ball, filled with chopped egg, meat, and raisins. The combination platters are strictly for hearty diners. The absurdly capacious picada azualaya includes deep-fried cutlets of beef, fish, and chicken strewn over a salad of avocados and tomatoes.

PIQUE Y PASE ☆ ☆ ☆

110-04 Lefferts Boulevard, Queens, 718-843-9128 Don't expect desserts, appetizers, or ceviches at this tiny Ecuadorian lunch counter — actually, just a single big table — in the middle of a kitchen where a supremely talented cook concocts secos, "dry" soups ladled over an Andean mound of yellow rice. Go for the pungent and tomato-tinged goat, or the peanut-sauced and soft-as-a-kid-glove guatita (tripe). The jolly chef interrupts his work at the stove to pull the lids off several steam table receptacles next to the front window to show what's available. Another delight is seco de gallina, traditionally made with an old hen that needs to be boiled into oblivion to be halfway tender. I suspect this version is made with supermarket chicken, because the bird is more yielding than you have any right to expect. The name means something like "thrust and parry."

SALINAS ☆

499 5th Avenue, Brooklyn, 718-788-9263 This combo Ecuadorian restaurant and ballroom doesn't really crank up till the weekend, when the menu bulges with home-style favorites like llapingachos served with fried pork, and cuy, the little furry varmint that few Ecuadorian restaurants in town dare to serve. This old favorite has lost some of its culinary dazzle since the last edition.

EL TAXISTA ECUATORIANO ☆ 🐟

206 Audubon Avenue, Manhattan, 212-543-9160 As with many Ecuadorians in Washington Heights, El Taxista is a combination café and car service. A picture of a limousine that looks like it was carved from a cake of soap adorns the top of the menu. There are gauzy red curtains at the windows, topped with black valances gathered halfway down to afford a view of the street. It being a warm day, and there being no air conditioning, most of the diners have selected tables by the open front door. Most Ecuadorians in town specialize in the earthy fare of the sierra. Rarer are those that, like El Taxista, concentrate mainly on seafood. The menu presents over two dozen types of lime-and-chile marinated ceviche, and particular pride is taken in the conch, flown in fresh from

Ecuador. Many of the ceviches incorporate potatoes and fresh corn kernels. Another specialty is bola de pescado, a mash of green plantains embedded with pieces of kingfish steamed in a banana leaf, resulting in a custardy consistency.

EL TESORO ☆ ☆ 🐟

40-15 5th Avenue, Brooklyn, 718-972-3756 Profusely decorated with neon, the city's best Ecuadorian favors seafood of the coastal lowlands, including perfect soupy ceviches littered with toasted corn nuts to remind you of the pre-Columbian origins of this dish, assembling every conceivable combo of octopus, shrimp, corvina, and the national favorite of black clam, which tints the broth a lovely shade of slate gray. As suggested by the glowing pig in the window, the hornado is also top notch.

Peruvian

COCO ROCO ☆ 🐟

392 5th Avenue, Brooklyn, 718-965-3376 When this slightly upscale, watered-down Peruvian first opened, it was in the Gowanus neighborhood. Now it's called Park Slope. The food is a good introduction to Andean fare, with decent papas a la Huancaina, grilled skirt steak with Argentine chimichurri, and a great ceviche of octopus in olive oil, but stay away from the other ceviches. Another good choice is tacu-tacu, a red snapper wrapped with sweet potato shreds and fried, showing the hand of a cooking-school-trained cook. A comfortable, popular spot, but not for the seeker of the most authentic Peruvian fare.

INCA'S ☆ $

120-20 Queens Boulevard, Queens, 718-263-6767 Sit in the wraparound dining annex, which offers splendid views of the Boulevard of Death, and enjoy the Afro-Peruvian jazz ensemble on weekend evenings. The menu of this most ambitious of Andean restaurants also features Argentine parrilladas, but stick with the ceviches and, especially, hard-to-find sierra fare: tender veal heart brochettes called anticuchos, the bread-thickened and turmeric-yellow chicken stew aji de gallina, and potatoes a la Huancaina, a cheese-sauced casserole that perfectly demonstrates the coequal contributions of Indians and conquistadores to Peruvian food.

INTI RAYMI ☆ 🦐 🐟

86-14 37th Avenue, Queens, 718-424-1938 The granddaddy of Peruvian restaurants — named after a stony-faced Incan god — marinates a damn good ceviche; best is mixto, a compelling combo of flounder, squid, octopus, clams, and conch. Aji de gallina, the bread-thickened chicken porridge sometimes said to be the national dish, is superb. Don't miss chicha morada, a delicious fruit beverage made with pineapple and lemon, flavored with cloves, and colored with purple corn.

KIKIRIKI ☆
6007 5th Avenue, Brooklyn, 718-567-2873 Sunset Park has become the rotisserie center of the world (a title Jackson Heights once treasured), and once again the Peruvians are in the driver's seat. In this case, Peruvian-Chinese, a bona fide national minority that put lo mein and other stir-fries on the South American menu. At Kikiriki, the chicken is one of the biggest and moistest I've ever seen, and comes butchered like a Chinatown duck. The homemade hot sauce is also spectacular, as are the anticuchos — grilled beef heart brochettes.

LIMA'S TASTE ☆
432 East 13th Street, Manhattan, 212-228-7900 The East Village finally has its answer to Park Slope's Coco Roco: a slightly upscale café that aims to popularize Peruvian food for the hip masses. Located on a quiet side street, the café spills a few tables onto the sidewalk; inside, pictures feature liquid-eyed peasants that could have been painted by Keane. The appetizers are especially good, including causa — a potato ball festooned with mayo-dipped chicken; a tangy fish ceviche; and, best of all, cold lemony mussels heaped with chopped onion and cilantro. Arriving tardily, the entrées lag somewhat, with a tart chicken escovitch and aji de pollo being our favorites. Skip the dry beef stew.

PERUVIAN VIAGRA

While most Peruvian ceviche is served as a damp fish salad, the exception to the rule is the soupy leche de tigre ("tiger's milk"). It's served in an elegant wineglass brimming with a marinade of lemon, coconut milk, and hot chiles. A hacked crab flails its pincers over the edge, and additional crabmeat lurks in the depths, plus a couple of substantial shrimp. Traditionally the solid parts are eaten first, then a South American brandy called pisco is added to help knock back the marinade. In most places, you must bring your own pisco. As you may have guessed, tiger's milk is one of those products aimed at erectile enhancement, hence the nickname "Viagra Peruano."

PIO PIO ☆ ☆ 🖋

62-30 Woodhaven Boulevard, Queens, 718-458-0606; 84-13 Northern Boulevard, Queens, 718-426-1010 This Peruvian chicken joint lays claim to being the first in the city, and it's still one of the best. Birds come swaddled in a sweet spice mixture, the exact composition of which is open to conjecture (I think there's some star anise in there, others claim black oregano; see Chicken a Go-Go.) The bird is obsessively watched until it reaches maximum crispness, and presented with a sauce whose thin greenness holds no hint of its powerful chile charge.

PIO RICO ☆ 🖋

109-18 Jamaica Avenue, Queens, 718-850-3769 Ever since Pio Pio sowed the seeds, a zillion Peruvian chicken places have sprouted, with little reason to prefer one over the other, other than where you happen to find yourself at a given moment. The plump chickens at Pio Rico manage to be well done — almost crusty — on the outside, while remaining succulent in the middle. That's saying a lot. Don't know if I'd touch the ceviches, though.

CHICKEN A GO-GO

Rotisserie chickens are now as common as pigeons, and it's hard to walk a block in some neighborhoods without seeing an enticing window display. It's foolproof dinner plan for harried workers trudging home — you don't even need utensils. In the last five years, Peruvians have made a bold attempt to dominate the market, by proffering a tastier bird. What's in the spice rub is a secret, but there are many theories. I think they use Chinese five-spice powder, among other things like crushed garlic and green onions, a spicing technique learned from the Chinese immigrants who arrived in Peru in the 1920s. The first was **Pio Pio** on Woodhaven Boulevard in Queens, conveniently located on a shortcut to Kennedy Airport. Buy a bird to eat on the plane. The chicken remains succulent hours later, as you devour it under the envious gaze of your fellow passengers.

LA POLLADA DE LAURA ☆ ☆ ☆ 🐟

102-03 Northern Boulevard, Queens, 718-426-7818 While Ecuadorian ceviches are soupy, Peruvian specimens are more like seafood salads, drenched in lemon juice and topped with pickled purple onions. La Pollada makes great Peruvian ceviches, including an octopus rendition that achieves brilliance via olives and olive oil, and a fish ceviche that shares a plate with a mound of fried calamari, offered with a choice of chile sauces. Fried seafood also excels, especially jalea, a humongous mound of ocean creatures atop planks of yuca, with some salad strewn here and there. Finally, there are the toothsome chicken dishes suggested by the name (La Pollada means "the brood").

RINCONCITO PERUANO ☆

803 9th Avenue, Manhattan, 212-333-5685 This metaphoric "Little Corner of Peru" makes only a fraction of the dishes on its expansive menu each day. From the list recited by the waitress we selected tamales, surprisingly crammed with chopped egg, chicken, and a half-dozen other ingredients, and papas rellenos, a pan-Latin classic of potatoes stuffed with ground meat and raisins. Don't miss the weekend breakfast combos, or the lunch specials, which include a soup, entrée, rice, and beans. The baby crawling around on the floor is your guarantee of home-style food.

EL TIO JULIO ☆ 🍖

101-02 42nd Avenue, Queens, 718-426-8686 Across the street from a mosque and a Jehovah's Witnesses temple, the carry-out right on the corner purveys some of the finest Peruvian chicken, with a thick crust loaded with earthy spices, and a miraculously damp and flavorful interior. Despite the complicated menu, which mainly pertains to the restaurant in back, pollo is about all this place does, and it's enough to draw me back.

LA UNION ☆ 🐟

90-59 Corona Avenue, Queens, 718-699-7473 Proving that food doesn't have to be good to be fascinating, this eatery is an authentic chifa – a South American Chinese restaurant – transplanted from Lima. The playful menu features a chef on the cover with a baby's head superimposed, and emphasizes seafood, including a good parihuela, a thick soup rife with crab and squid. Stick with lo mein stir-fries of duck or shrimp and you'll do fine, but avoid kamlu wonton, a smoldering heap of fried wontons smothered with canned peaches and pineapple in thick red syrup that will leave you nearly retching. Dishes are big enough to serve two or three people.

English, Irish, and Scottish

The days when you could completely write off United Kingdom food are long past. Fish and chips have regained their rightful place in the food chain, as demonstrated by a slew of new places that make it their specialty. Devotees complain, though, that the grease in which the fish is cooked is of insufficient age and rancidity to make the product taste authentic. Though Irish pubs have been a mainstay in all five boroughs for 150 years, and many of them serve food, it's beyond the scope of this book to detail or distinguish between the estimated 500 or so that still thrive. In fact, the smell of corned beef and potatoes from a steam table is still one of the signature odors of the city. Finally, places like **Café Topsy** may presage a whole new world of slightly upscale British food. On the other hand, the place may be out of business before this book sees print.

LOOK FOR:

banger *white sausage*

blood pudding *dark blood-laced sausage*

bubble and squeak *cabbage, bacon, and, sometimes, potatoes*

cock-a-leekie *leek-flavored chicken soup*

Cornish pastie *empanada of potatoes and minced meat*

haggis *oatmeal and organ meat boiled in sheep's bladder*

mash *mashed potatoes*

mushy peas *canned pea puree*

> **neeps and tatties** *mashed turnips and mashed potatoes, respectively*
>
> **Scotch eggs** *boiled eggs rolled in sausage and bread crumbs*
>
> **shepherd's pie** *minced meat topped with mashed potatoes*

English

CAFÉ TOPSY ☆ ☆ $
575 Hudson Street, Manhattan, 646-638-2900 Thought you hated English food? Topsy may change your mind, offering impressive reworked Brit standards like cottage pie, fish and chips, shepherd's pie, and a delicious dark hunk of brisket braised in Guinness, with an errant shot of balsamic providing extra flavor and sweetness. Other dishes reach across the channel for inspiration, including a singularly uninspiring rendition of pork rillettes and the vastly preferable "Topsy's coddler," a very Alsatian heap of smoked meats cooked in sauerkraut. The limited dessert menu is similarly distinguished.

CHIPSHOP ☆ 🐟
383 5th Avenue, Brooklyn, 718-832-7701 It's officially a mini-trend! Park Slope's Chipshop joins the West Village's A Salt and Battery as establishments that attempt to recreate the English fish and chips shop, with stunning success. While Chipshop doesn't have quite the range of fish offered by its Village precursor, it does provide the full complement of culinary arcana. The cod and chips is particularly recommended, a generously sized filet with good fries. Don't be fooled by the "rock salmon" — its real name is dogfish.

MYERS OF KESWICK ☆ ☆
634 Hudson Street, Manhattan, 212-691-4194 Happy is the person who arrives on Saturday as the Cornish pasties — bulging with a mellow filling of potatoes and ground meat — emerge from the oven. The impressive list of flaky pastries also includes steak and kidney pie and Scotch eggs. Named after a Lake District town in England, this well-organized grocery is stocked with an amazing array of canned goods, including many that will evoke laughter in those that are unfamiliar with them. I got a kick out of the canned bean product called All Day Dinner.

74

A SALT AND BATTERY ☆ 🐟

112 Greenwich Avenue, Manhattan, 212-691-2713; 80 2nd Avenue, Manhattan, 212-254-6610 Britannia Rules! The most recent addition to the Tea and Sympathy empire is a replica fish and chips shop that strives for perfection in every detail, even wrapping the product in English newspapers. The seafood is wonderfully fresh, with a selection that runs to whiting, halibut, cod, cod roe, squid, scallops, and — my fave — rock salmon. Numbered among the sides are curiosities like mushy peas, deep-fried beets, potato "scallops" (preferable to the limp and greasy chips), and, improbably, deep-fried candy bars. Test question: What do Tizer, Vimto, and Lucozade have in common?

TEA AND SYMPATHY ☆ ☆ 🍵

108 Greenwich Avenue, Manhattan, 212-807-8329 This English tea shop, beloved of West Villagers, specializes in afternoon tea served with scones, finger sandwiches, lemon curd, and all the usual delicacies. Bigger feeds run to various English pies, Stilton and walnut salad, and baked beans on toast. It's now part of a burgeoning empire that includes a grocery and tea store and a fish and chips shop, all on the same block. Getting a table and eating at this institution requires a complex set of behaviors I don't pretend to understand.

For English-style Indian food, also known as Balti cooking, see Brick Lane Curry House and Curry Shop in the Anglo-Indian section of the South Asian chapter.

Irish

BRENNAN & CARR ☆

3432 Nostrand Avenue, Brooklyn, 718-769-1254 Granddaddy of the roast beef joints is Brennan & Carr. Founded in 1938 when Homecrest was still crisscrossed with country lanes, it's nostalgically decorated like a Civil War stockade, with a parking lot inside chain-link battlements. The somewhat dainty sandwiches are furnished with an undrained wad of roast beef steamed to grayness, served with a decent cup of bouillon for dipping, and there's no doubt that, in addition to the name, the deplorable method of dealing with roast beef characterizes this place as Irish. The one star is mainly for its amazing ambiance — I'd eat cardboard there.

DONOVAN'S ☆

57-24 Roosevelt Avenue, Queens, 718-429-9339 Of the dozen or so big-scale Irish pubs that still linger in Woodside — even though the Irish population has mainly sauntered north to the Bronx-Yonkers border — this is the most venerated. I've got to admit the huge hamburger is quite good, but it's so obvious that they care more about beer than food — if the Guinness varies by more than one degree from the correct temperature, a collective groan goes up. The menu encompasses regular bar food as well as Irish sentimental specialties like shepherd's pie, fish and chips, and bangers and mash.

RAMBLING HOUSE ☆

4290 Katonah Avenue, Bronx, 718-798-4510 Stroll down the hill from Van Cortlandt Park's primeval forest and find the main street of a wee Irish village. There are public houses (aka pubs), bakeries, and a grocery or two. The most formidable eatery is Rambling House, a bar and dining room boasting a west-facing window that admits a golden light during Sunday afternoon brunch. Favorite dish was a shepherd's pie with masses of meat surmounted by nicely browned mashed potatoes — but just try to get them to cook a burger anything less than "medium well." A glass of Guinness at the proper temp and foaminess comes with the brunch.

Scottish

ST. ANDREWS ☆ ☆ 🐟 $

120 West 44th Street, Manhattan, 212-840-8413 New York's only Scottish restaurant, named after the course where golf was invented, looks a lot like a plush gentleman's bar, and the food is mainly steaks and salads and oysters. But look around the corners of the menu for Highland specialties like haggis — traditionally an accumulation of diced organs mixed with oatmeal and onions and stuffed into a sheep's bladder. While the original recipe usually calls for slicing, St. Andrews's has been removed from the casing, and served with the traditional accompaniment of "neeps and tatties" — mashed turnips and potatoes, which are frisbeed above and below the pile of meat. It tastes like a more delicious version of shepherd's pie. The Scottish salmon, whether served as a salad or a regular entrée, is top-notch, as are the fried oysters.

Ethiopian, Eritrean, and South African

Ethiopian immigrants must be among the nation's canniest restaurateurs. Though numbering only 33,000 nationwide, they've founded an impressive collection of restaurants in major American cities, way out of proportion to their paltry numbers: Washington boasts 17, Seattle 11, and New York 12, plus an Eritrean joint — though an upscale Eritrean in the Flatiron district closed last year, probably because it wasn't very good. Most share an assortment of predictable names like Blue Nile, Red Sea, **Queen of Sheba**, and **Meskerem** (the joyous first month of the Coptic Christian calendar), though none is part of a chain. Sadly, these places also mount nearly identical menus of brick-colored meat stews and hard-to-differentiate pulse purees.

One of the chief pleasures of Ethiopian food is eating with your pinkies, enjoying the subtlety and piquancy of the spice mixtures that the cooking depends on. Scoop bites with injera, a rubbery flatbread made from a variety of milletlike grain called tef. Now cultivated in this country, tef is fantastically rich in protein and iron, brown in color, and hosts a symbiotic yeast on its surface that causes natural fermentation, producing a pleasing sourdough. In Ethiopia, it's also made with lighter grains like barley, millet, corn, rice, and sorghum. In neither Washington nor New York will you find freshly made injera these days, though a decade ago it was fairly common. In spite of that, the food is still wonderful, and quite unlike any other kind of ethnic food, bridging the gap between African and Indian.

Eritrean fare is similar in most respects to Ethiopian, but with an overlayering of Italian and Egyptian influences, making it possible to eat foul, the Egyptian bean stew, in Eritrean restaurants and finish up with a cup of espresso. Note that none of the Ethiopian restaurants in town serve the boiled coffee that's an important part of Ethiopian culture, usually served with a convivial handful of popcorn. I'm not kidding! South African food is available only at Madiba, and it's worth a trip just for the novelty. Encompassing the broadest range of influences of any African cuisine, the food displays Malay, Dutch, Portuguese, English, and African tribal influences. Last edition, this section also included a Somalian restaurant in Harlem, but that closed two years ago. R.I.P.

LOOK FOR:

ayib *cottage cheese with cardamom butter*
azifa *tangy lentil salad*
berberé *chile powder*
biltong *Transvaal beef jerky*
bobotie *Malay–South African curried meat pie*
bunny chow *vegetable curry in hollowed bread from KwaZulu-Natal*
buticha *shallot-laced Ethiopian hummus*
dabo *semolina cake*
doro watt *spicy chicken and boiled eggs*
droewars *South African slim-jims*
foul *Eritrean fava bean stew, pronounced "fool"*
gored-gored *beef in chile butter*
injera *fermented flatbread made from tef*
kategna *buttered injera salad*
kitfo *raw minced beef with spices*
peri-peri *Angolan-Portuguese hot sauce*
poitjie *South African oxtail stew*
quanta *Ethiopian beef jerky*
tej *Ethiopian honey wine*
yebeg tibs *lamb sautéed with chile and onions*
yemsir watt *green lentils laced with berberé*

Eritrean

MASSAWA ☆ ☆ ♨
1239 Amsterdam Avenue, Manhattan, 212-663-0505 What's the difference between Ethiopian and Eritrean? Find out at Massawa and do your wallet a favor in the process. From Egypt came

foul, the delicious fava bean stew, while Italy provided baguettes and excellent espresso. Apart from that, find the usual lentil and meat-bearing stews inflected with fenugreek and ginger on a lush sour carpet of injera.

Ethiopian

AWASH ☆ 🍎

947 Amsterdam Avenue, Manhattan, 212-961-1416 Like Washington, D.C.'s Ethiopian restaurants, Awash — named after a tributary of the Nile — is furnished with the basket tables and tipsy stools that serve to put you in the mood, though if you drink too much of the honey wine called tej, you'll probably fall off and crack your skull. Despite its emphasis on mild and fiery stewed meats, Awash has more vegetarian options than most Ethiopians, including lentil-stuffed turnovers called sambusas, greens called gomen, and the usual vegetable combo platter of five or six dishes on injera.

GHENET ☆ 🍎 $

285 Mulberry Street, Manhattan, 212-343-1888 Consistent with the upscale neighborhood, Ghenet is decorated like a bistro — yellow walls, potted palms, a long bar with elephant-sized stools, and a few tasteful framed prints. The food is carefully prepared and generally delicious; the spicing and range, however, are timid by Ethiopian standards. Like the Indians, Ethiopians make much of lentils and beans, and like the West Africans, they admire green leafy vegetables. These come together in the vegetarian combo, a gorgeous food painting on the dun canvas of injera. Yemsir watt laces green lentils with berberé, the variable national spice mixture, here more reminiscent of the red chile of the American Southwest. Gomen be siga is one of the better dishes here, collard greens dotted with lamb. Perversely, kitfo — a hopelessly rich tartar of ground beef and buttery spices — arrives fully cooked when it should be raw.

MESKEREM ☆ ☆ 🍎 🌶

468 West 47th Street, Manhattan, 212-664-0520; 124 MacDougal Street, Manhattan, 212-777-8111 Head and shoulders above the other Ethiopians in town, Meskerem pads the communal dining platter with a fresher and springier injera, and heaps it with mounds of meat, poultry, and veggies in gravies more delicately spiced. The vegetarian special is particularly good, a bean and lentil museum painted with a palette of earth colors. You get six dishes, enough for two hungry diners. Two are particularly compelling: shiro features ground chickpeas in a moist toss of green onion and jalapeño pepper and looks and tastes like mom's potato salad until your mouth catches fire. Azifa, served cold, is an odd salad of brown lentils made earthier with ginger and horseradish that climb right up your nose. The national dish is doro watt, a quarter chicken with a boiled egg in thick red muck. Delicious!

QUEEN OF SHEBA ✫ ✫ ⌀

650 10th Avenue, Manhattan, 212-397-0610 While the food doesn't quite attain the dizzying heights of Meskerem, just around the corner, it provides a solid introduction to Ethiopian cooking. More important, there are several kinky things on the menu that Meskerem can't provide, including kategna, a warm salad of toasted injera fragments tossed with plenty of spiced clarified butter, which turns your fingers bright red. Even the French would find it decadent. Bozena shiro is another interesting novelty, bits of lamb suspended in a chickpea whip that's too bland as far as I'm concerned. Much better is quanta fiffir, a scalding scramble of torn injera and quanta, a beef jerky much chewier and tastier than fresh beef.

South African

MADIBA ✫ ✫ ⌀

195 DeKalb Avenue, Brooklyn, 718-855-9190 Cobbled together of salvaged wood and Quonset-hut tin, it might be a grog shop in Soweto. There's a shelf crowded with hand-woven baskets, a couple of ostrich eggs, and a row of kerosene lanterns suspended near the ceiling — as if the electricity might flicker off at any moment. First to hit the table is umgqushu stambu, a tasty porridge of crushed hominy and kidney beans that, for many cash-strapped South Africans, constitutes an entire meal. The flavors of the so-called safari platter open a window into the world of the Voortrekkers, the contentious Dutch homesteaders who invented apartheid. Included are strips of biltong, dried beef cured to an intriguing semirancidity, and crumbly sticks of droewars, which taste like slim-jims buried underground. A notably delicious dish originated in Portuguese Africa: peri-peri chicken livers, which come planted on a piece of toast that absorbs the spicy cooking oil. Sosaties are kebabs based on the Malay model, six massive meatballs redolent of onion, clove, and ginger. Another Malay contribution, bobotie is a great pie filled with curried meat and boiled eggs. Reflecting the Huguenot heritage, oxtail poitjie dumps prodigious hunks of bony meat into a red-wine gravy, engagingly served in a three-legged iron pot.

French and Belgian

Founded by the Swiss Delmonico brothers in 1831, the first fancy restaurant in the city was French, and for the ensuing 130 years French dining remained the exclusive province of the wealthy. Then the bistro arrived sometime in the 1960s, ushering in vernacular French dining of a sort the city had never seen before. The West Village was a hot spot, and a few of the original places like **La Ripaille** and **La Metairie** still remain. French bistros once again became all the rage in the East Village and Fort Greene during the 1990s and on into the new millennium, with new ones popping up on a monthly basis. Now the trend seems moribund, as trattoria and panini parlors open on every corner. Creperies looked to be every bit as popular for a while, but that fad fizzled, too, though now it seems to be making a minor resurgence. Luckily, some of the best examples of bistros and creperies remain. Love French food? Don't miss its close cousins in the fare of Haiti and the Ivory Coast (the latter in the chapter on Senegalese, Guinean, Ivory Coastal, and Malian restaurants), or its more distant relatives Vietnamese and Cajun (see Regional and Vernacular American).

Partly propelled by the popularity of pommes frites and the cult that grew around them, Belgian restaurants have expanded to become a durable, if slight, phenomenon. Both **Petite Abeille** and **Le Pain Quotidien** are now sprawling chains with sense enough to keep the quality consistent. Though rumored to be run by French people, **Cafe de Bruxelles** is the only ancient Belgian café remaining from the old days, while **Markt**, in the Village's meat district, stays afloat by attracting diners who can't get into **Pastis**. In recent memory, the Brit-Belgian chain **Belgo** tried mightily to establish a beachhead on Lafayette Street, but to no avail, so all is not completely rosy on the Walloon dining scene.

LOOK FOR:

assiette *cold combo platter of meats or cheeses*
bouillabaisse *Marseilles fish stew*
crepes *thin pancakes folded around a filling*
croque monsieur *toasted ham-and-cheese sandwich*
croque madame *croque monsieur with a fried egg*
duck confit *leg and thigh cooked in its own fat*
flammande *Belgian prune-and-beef stew*
fritessaus *mayo for fries*
garnaalkroketten *Belgian shrimp fritters*
gigot *leg of lamb*
luikdr salade *Belgian bacon, potato, and green bean salad*
moules frites *steamed mussels and french fries*
pied de cochon *compressed pig feet*
pissaladière *caramelized onion tart*
rouille *garlicky red-pepper paste*
steak frites *steak upstaged by crisp french fries*
stoemp *Belgian vegetable hash*
tartine *toasts topped with various spreads*
waterzooi *Belgian fish or chicken stew*

Belgian

MARKT ☆ 🐟 $
401 West 14th Street, Manhattan, 212-727-3314 Listing dishes in Flemish and French, handsome wood-clad Markt starts strong with an appetizer of luikdr salade/salade Liègeoise, an improvement on German potato salad combining green beans, potatoes, sautéed onions, and crumbled bacon in a vinegary dressing. Also dependable are garnaalkroketten, oblong fritters suspending North Sea gray shrimp in an oozy puree of cheese and potatoes. But good as the starters are, the menu stumbles on main courses. The very juicy steak frites turns out to be the best entrée. Sit at the bar for a very good moules frites and a glass of Duvel or Hoegaarden.

LE PAIN QUOTIDIEN ☆ ☆ ✆ $

1131 Madison Avenue, Manhattan, 212-327-4900; 100 Grand Street, Manhattan, 212-625-9009; ABC Carpet and Home, 38 East 19th Street, Manhattan, 212-673-7900; other locations This Belgian eat-in bakery is the perfect shopping pit stop, offering, on excellent bread, such sandwiches as brie with pecans, smoked salmon sprinkled with green onions and dill, and jambon de Paris sided by three pots of mustard with fantastically different flavors. The soup of the day is also worth considering, as is the creamy lemon tart with ground nuts in the crust, and the dark and rich hot cocoa.

PETITE ABEILLE ☆ ☆

134 West Broadway, Manhattan, 212-791-1360; 466 Hudson Street, Manhattan, 212-741-6479; 400 West 14th Street, Manhattan, 212-727-1506; 107 West 18th Street, Manhattan, 212-604-9350 Starting out as a sandwich shop just off the Ladies Mile shopping district, Petite Abeille ("the little bee") has morphed into a multibranch chain, still offering good sandwiches and soups, and a handful of comical-sounding Belgian specialties like stoemp and waterzooi. Though the fries are not twice-fried, they're good anyway, and the burger topped with mild cheddar, strips of pancetta, and creamy red sauce was considered tops in the 2003 edition of the *Village Voice*'s annual "Best Of" issue.

TWICE FRIED

Street-level food fads — flavored popcorn, low-fat ice cream, candy by the pound all come to mind — battle to see who can dominate the city's narrowest shop fronts. Lately, stuffed pretzels, fresh-squeezed juice, chicken wings, and wraps have been vying for attention, but for me, the most interesting micro-scaled fast food has been Belgian fries, and the regular coffee shop product won't do anymore. Here are some purveyors, each offering a range of dips for the fries. Stay away from the mayonnaisey sauces — they're often not refrigerated (**Cafe de Bruxelles** is the exception).

B. FRITES

1657 Broadway, Manhattan, 212-767-0858 This latecomer to the fad uses a creamier potato and cultivates an atmosphere like a chemistry lab. I think their fries are the best.

CAFE DE BRUXELLES
118 Greenwich Avenue, Manhattan, 212-206-1830
Sit at the bar and wash them down with overpriced, monk-made beer. The service, flavor of the fries, and excellence of the dipping mayonnaise nearly justify the price, as does the West Village view through the big windows.

LE FRITE KOTE
148 West 4th Street, Manhattan, 212-979-2616 The frites here are slightly better than Pommes Frites, the sauces slightly worse. Moules and Belgian beer have extended the formula. The upstairs dining room is a great hideout.

POMMES FRITES AUTHENTIC BELGIAN FRIES
123 2nd Avenue, Manhattan, 212-674-1234 The first and, some say, still the best of the fry stalls. A second branch near Times Square has now closed.

POMME-POMME
191 East Houston Street, Manhattan, 646-602-8140
The fries are not quite as good, but the "hot ajvar," a Turkish red-pepper dip, rocks hardest of all among exotic sauces for fries. Unfortunately, this new place has discovered that the fryers can also be used for falafel, fritters, onion rings, etc., so your fries are likely to be contaminated by phantom flavors.

French

À TABLE ☆ ☆
171 Lafayette Street, Brooklyn, 718-935-9121 How many French bistros can Fort Greene absorb? This is my favorite so far, purveyor of bistro classics with a twist, like the haricots verts glistening with vinaigrette and topped with capered chicken livers which come singed on the outside, warm and pink in the middle; or a roasted chicken breast on mashed potatoes improved with a ratatouille whose orange-colored juice makes the plate glow. We enjoyed the steak with cube fries, though the lamb with a stuffed tomato left us unimpressed.

BALTHAZAR ☆ ☆ ☆ $
80 Spring Street, Manhattan, 212-965-1414 Bleary-eyed and jet-lagged after an international flight, and famished from

skimpy airline meals, a friend and I dropped by Balthazar for breakfast. The wonderful le panier, a collection of baked goods from the patisserie next door, was enough for two, including chocolate bread, a caramel nut roll, a brioche, sourdough raisin bread, and a coffee cake topped with dried fruit and nuts. Find similar diversity among cooked selections, including eggs baked "en cocotte" in a ramekin with cream and thyme and furnished with toast fingers. A pricey bistro menu prevails during the rest of the day and long into the night.

BOUCHON ☆
41 Greenwich Avenue, Manhattan, 212-255-5972 Ignore the sometimes surly service at this West Village bistro and wine bar, and go for the solid French peasant food, such as the towering braised loin of veal with root vegetables, and the rib eye mired in hearty red-wine gravy. An exception to the culinary focus is a pair of skate wings browned to crispness and served in a delicious sauce featuring ginger, soy sauce, and two types of sesame seeds. The cozy subterranean room and profusion of reasonably priced wines makes this a great date spot.

CAFÉ DEVILLE ☆
103 3rd Avenue, Manhattan, 212-477-4500 This handsome brasserie outruns most of its East Village bistro brethren by featuring a more expansive menu of French standards, including raw bar stuff, sandwiches, and assiettes of vegetables, meats, and cheeses. About half our selections on a recent visit were memorable, especially a spectacular bowl of mussels in a broth that subtly incorporated curry, fresh herbs, and rich chicken stock. The salmon tartare, too, was top-notch, although a fish ceviche — effervescing on the tongue — was clearly over the edge, while we thought the sirloin in the steak frites too puny. There's also a diverting by-the-glass wine list.

CHEZ BRIGITTE ☆
77 Greenwich Avenue, Manhattan, 212-929-6736 Every rule has an exception, and the exception to "There's no such thing as cheap French food" is Chez Brigitte. This ancient and minuscule lunch counter serves up Gallic peasant fare unencumbered by cream or nouvelle cuisine, such as a luscious Provençale omelet flecked with fresh herbs and oozing ratatouille. Also recommended are any of the daily roasts — Monday it's leg of lamb, served with gravy, potatoes, steamed vegetables, and petits pois. Avoid the meager heroes.

CHEZ OSKAR ☆
211 DeKalb Avenue, Brooklyn, 718-852-6250 Neighborhoods don't come any cuter than Fort Greene, and this self-consciously

bohemian bistro is a good addition to the African-Cambodian-Italian-Soul Food culinary scene. Start with assiette de charcuterie, a worthy plate of sweet and hot dry sausages complemented with a firkin of duck liver pâté that goes great with the sourdough peasant bread. Then move on to the marvelous, fork-tender steak au poivre, or the poached cod under a toupee of olive puree. Portions are huge, so a light sorbet is your only option for dessert.

FADA ☆ ☆ ♿

530 Driggs Avenue, Brooklyn, 718-388-6607 Fada is a Williamsburg bistro specializing in the vegetable-intensive provender of Provence. The dining room affects a raffish air, and the menu runs from sharable combination plates, to refreshing salads, to main courses voluminous enough to stand alone as your evening meal. Recommended entrées: steak frites featuring a thin sirloin sided with mounds of glistening fries, a bouillabaisse served in the traditional manner with the solid parts as a second course, and an aioli garni of cod and homemade mayonnaise accompanied by steamed vegetables and a handful of snails. Open for breakfast.

LE GAMIN ☆

183 9th Avenue, Manhattan, 212-243-8864 A cute and comfortable French bistro from the Old School, priced below par, with fine steak frites, roast chicken, penne with basil, croque monsieur, and a salad made from mesclun and smoked duck breast that has a texture reminiscent of prosciutto. I can still taste a special appetizer of mussels steamed with saffron and shallots, the broth fortified with a dash of cream.

LE GIGOT ☆ ☆ ☆ 🐟 $

18 Cornelia Street, Manhattan, 212-627-3737 This French bistro distinguishes itself not only by its charming dining room, but with a menu more ambitious than its 20 or so West Village compatriots. Try the duck confit served on a herbed crouton that sponges up the delicious juices, sided with leek-ribboned mashed potatoes. Against all odds, Gigot also scores with an ethereal bouillabaisse — a riot of shellfish and finfish in a dense broth to which you add toasted croutons and Gruyère cheese at your discretion.

JACQUES TORRES CHOCOLATE ☆ ☆ ☆ $

66 Water Street, Brooklyn, 718-875-9772 The celebrity French chef Jacques Torres blew into Dumbo (Down Under the Manhattan Bridge Overpass) two years ago to create Jacques Torres Chocolate, flogging tiny filled chocolates for a little over a dollar apiece, which is cheaper than you can get them in Manhattan. My favorite is a semifirm caramel with a salty center. A dangerous addiction.

EAST VILLAGE BISTROS

During the last decade, you couldn't throw a rock in the East Village without breaking the window of a bistro, and some of the best remain. Depend on these places to be filled with hipsters chain-smoking in contravention of the antismoking laws, and to be open way into the wee hours of the evening. Here's brief rundown of the contenders for your hard-earned dollar:

CASIMIR ☆
103-105 Avenue B, Manhattan, 212-358-9683
Named after a jolly cartoon dinosaur. An entrée of compressed pig feet called pied de cochon will knock your socks off, and the bouillabaisse is better than you have any reason to expect.

FLEA MARKET ☆ ◄══
131 Avenue A, Manhattan, 212-358-9282 You can dine cheaply on omelets or burgers, or more dearly on leg of lamb or sautéed skate. The location across the street from Tompkins Square puts it in the center of the action.

LUCIEN ☆ ☆ $
14 1st Avenue, Manhattan, 212-260-6481 Especially appreciated are the salads, which make a nice light meal, the ample sardines grilled by the chef in full view of the patrons, and the very Gallic lapin moutarde, rabbit in mustard sauce. This is the East Village's best bistro, and priced accordingly.

RESTO LÉON ☆
351 East 12th Street, 212-375-8483 A cod pot au feu curiously paired with a marrow bone and a beef daube sided with polenta make the menu more interesting than the usual cookie-cutter bistro. Formerly my favorite East Village bistro, still with plenty of spunk.

JUBILEE ☆ ◄══
347 East 54th Street, Manhattan, 212-888-3569 The heart of the menu is Prince Edward Island mussels, offered in five variations with a choice of fries or salad. The remarkable thing, apart from the pristine freshness of the shellfish, is the quantity delivered for the price. A rough census of my bowl of "poulette" yielded

60, swamped in a cream sauce of rich chicken stock and mushrooms, perfected with a sprinkle of chives. The excellent side of lanky, well-browned fries was better for mopping the thick sauce than bread; the salad, alas, was not worth the $4 add-on.

MARQUET PATISSERIE ★ ★ ★ ⓒ

15 East 13th Street, Manhattan, 212-229-9313 This reasonably priced patisserie might have been transported from Paris, with its boatlike raspberry barquettes, airy croissants, and brittle cat's tongue cookies. They also provide excellent light meals until 6 p.m., including soups, pâtés, salads, and amazing sandwiches — my fave made with rosette de Lyon, a coarse and powerful salami, with lettuce on white peasant bread smeared with both mustard and mayo. The carryout roast chickens are also divine, their cavities stuffed with onions and fresh herbs.

MARSEILLE ★ $

630 9th Avenue, Manhattan, 212-333-2323 This Hell's Kitchen bistro has a dangerous name, evoking a romantic and tumultuous port associated with splendid seafood and international drug dealing. The pan-Mediterranean menu includes a few North African, Turkish, and Middle Eastern elements, in addition to the predictable Provençal ones. Meze are reinterpreted as little tasting platters, one including hanger steak merguez planted in vegetable puree, a puck of foie gras torchon, and miniature fingers of Fatima. At $8, it's a steal. Inevitably, there's a bouillabaisse, pleasingly rife with baby vegetables and diverse tidbits of seafood, including a fish quenelle and baby octopi.

NICE MATIN ★ ★ $

201 West 79th Street, Manhattan, 212-873-6423 Named after a French Mediterranean daily paper, this welcome addition to the Upper West Side does an estimable job of recreating the daily fare of Provence. Find it in the seemingly redundant menu sections Appetizers and Hors d'Oeuvre. From the former comes the miniature caramelized onion pizza, dotted with raisins, known as pissaladière. From the latter comes panisse, absolutely wonderful french fries made of smooshed chickpeas, fluffy and steamy in the middle, and served with a zippy garlic aioli. Also inspiring: a salade Niçoise reverently made with canned tuna and an entrée of tender beef short ribs.

PARADOU ★ ★

8 Little West 12th Street, Manhattan, 212-463-8345 I never expected to see the French ripping off the Italians. Riffing on the current wine bar craze, this closet in the meat district offers topped toasts styled "bruschetta francaise" and pressed sandwiches which run from the expected (ham and Gruyère) to the unexpected (duck rillettes and capers). The menu rounds out with crepes, salads, and combination plates of cheese and charcuterie. Though on the expensive side, everything at a recent lunch was tasty and well prepared, especially a tartine smothered in Parmesan and garlic mayonnaise. A backyard garden offers outdoor seating, but beware — the service often sucks back there.

PASTIS ☆ ☆

9 9th Avenue, Manhattan, 212-929-4844 Pastis was the most talked-about new restaurant of the 1999/2000 winter season, obsessively duplicating a certain type of Parisian establishment that has no interest in the innovations of haute cuisine, offering short dishes that make good snacks with a glass of wine, sandwiches, entrée salads, and heavy grandmotherly fare. Sure, you can blow a wad here, but some of the cheapest dishes are the best, including a transcendent croque monsieur (lunch only), and the tiny pizza called pissaladière. Burgers and herb omelets are available anytime. Open late into the evening; go at the most off-hour you can manage.

PAYARD PATISSERIE AND BISTRO ☆ ☆

1032 Lexington Avenue, Manhattan, 212-717-5252 Bravely flying its anchovy from a toothpick like a pennant, Payard's pan bagnat (takeout only) is a brilliant evocation of Provençal's favorite sandwich: a flying saucer roll split down the middle and stuffed with a salade Niçoise featuring creamy tuna salad, purple onions, lettuce, tomato, radishes, and lots of other goodies, surmounted by sliced boiled eggs. You won't walk away hungry from this bad boy.

PIGALLE ☆ ☆

790 8th Avenue, Manhattan, 212-489-2233 Many of today's most ambitious restaurants are opening in luxury hotels, and, located on the ground floor of the Days Inn, Pigalle follows the trend. I was prepared to dislike this touristy facsimile of a Parisian brasserie, until I tasted the food. The salt-cod brandade was superb: more like cod mashed potatoes, the largish cylinder was anchored in mushroom cream. The thick gazpacho served with a skewer of fresh-tasting shrimp and the cassoulet cooked with duck, pork sausage, and smoked bacon were also tastier than expected. Open 24 hours.

PROVENCE ☆ ☛ $

38 MacDougal Street, Manhattan, 212-475-7500 The perfect antidote for the winter blahs is lunch at this SoHo old-timer, where a bank of westward-facing windows fill with sunlight and turn the yellowish interior golden. Focusing on seafood, the menu dredges up the by-now-standard menu of southeastern France,

CREPES

Anyone who's wandered around Paris knows that the apex of its sidewalk food is crepes, prepared on a brace of round griddles as you watch, drooling. The fillings are usually limited to ham, Gruyère, Nutella, and a scattering of other ingredients, although if you wander into a full-blown creperie on the Left Bank you'll be bewildered by 50 or 100 choices. The Manhattan crepe revival of the 1990s has largely deflated, but a number of good stalwarts remain.

PALACINKA ☆ ⌀
28 Grand Street, Manhattan, 212-625-0362 This informal SoHo dive stands right across the street from a junkyard. Crepes come with a salad; better still are the dessert versions filled with honey, chestnut paste, or Nutella.

CREPERIE ☆ ⌀
135 Ludlow Street, Manhattan, 212-979-5543 Seeking to fulfill the fast-food needs of the hopping Ludlow/Orchard night zone, this narrow stall is part of a mini–crepe revival. The spinach and goat cheese model is quite good, and a friend and I even liked the selection that mixes pizza sauce, mediocre mozzarella, and Arabian harissa sauce — who the hell thought that up, we wondered? Open till 4 a.m. on Friday and Saturday.

CREPES TO GO ☆ ⌀
90 West 3rd Street, Manhattan, 212-982-6275 CTG is a window in the middle of the NYU campus associated with a bar named Shade that affects a rakish air. Good if you don't mind standing while eating your crepe.

RUE DES CREPES ☆ ⌀
104 8th Avenue, Manhattan, 212-242-9900 With an interior made to look like a hokey Parisian street scene, Rue des Crepes encourages you to snack or assemble a complete meal. Avoid anything featuring the white bean puree (such as the merguez sausage crepe), in favor of the dessert crepes.

including a durable if not brilliant bouillabaisse, a thick-crusted version of the onion and anchovy tart called pissaladière, and simply cooked Mediterranean daurade. The fish of the day is always worth considering — on this revisit it was a goodly hunk of boneless cod seared to crunchy brownness on both sides and served on a bed of sculpted vegetables.

LE SINGE VERT ☆

160 7th Avenue, Manhattan, 212-366-4100 This bistro, whose name means "the green monkey," was actually filled with French people one recent evening. Best starters include gazpacho served with a plate of diced vegetables, prosciutto and melon nestled in a basket of fried potatoes, and sinister black raviolis bulging with crab. The shell steak wears a delicious pat of garlicky butter on its breast, though it's difficult to get them to cook the meat beyond a slight sear on the outside.

German, Austrian, Dutch, and Swedish

Most of the German restaurants in Manhattan date from the early 20th century, when there was a major Teutonic presence in Yorkville on the Upper East Side. **Heidelberg** (1648 2nd Avenue, Manhattan, 212-628-2332) and **Rolf's** (281 3rd Avenue, Manhattan, 212-477-4750) date from that era. Neither are particularly good. Just as the German-American identity took a drubbing during two world wars, so did the fatty and starchy cuisine during the health-conscious 1980s. But German cooking has bounced back, aided by beer lovers and the runaway popularity of **Danube**, David Bouley's haute-Austrian restaurant, and the advent of modern German places like **Silver Swan** and **Hallo Berlin**. But look to Queens, Staten Island, and the Bronx for a number of establishments that still serve old-style German cooking, especially **Niederstein's**, favored by generations of Deutsch families attending funerals in the adjacent cemetery.

We lost our only Swiss restaurant in 2003, **Roetelle A.G.** Luckily, many Swiss dishes are available other places around town, including fondue in profusion at the wonderful **Artisanal** (2 Park Avenue, Manhattan, 212-725-8585). Dutch food has appeared for the first time in a New York restaurant, as far as I can tell. Which is strange in a city whose original name is New Amsterdam, where half the streets and neighborhoods seem to have Netherlandish names. What is Dutch food, anyway? Find out at **NL**.

LOOK FOR:

bauernwurst *pepper-studded beef sausage*
Berliner curry *knockwurst with curry powder*
gentleman's delight *Swedish herring salad*

jaeger schnitzel *hunter's veal cutlet with mushrooms and bacon*

Königsberge klopse *white veal meatballs*

laxpudding *Swedish potato and salmon casserole*

matjes herring *sweet pickled young herring*

rauchfleisch *German extrasmoky ham*

rijsttafel *Dutch-Indonesian smorgasbord*

sauerbraten *beef roast braised in a tart marinade*

spätzl *free-form homemade noodles*

sülze *pork headcheese*

tafelspitz *Austrian boiled beef served with horseradish*

Tiroler schnitzel *veal cutlet with wine-mushroom sauce*

Wiener schnitzel *breaded veal cutlet*

wurst *sausage*

Austrian

CAFÉ SABARSKY ☆ ☆ ☆ 🐟 ⏱ $

1048 5th Avenue, Manhattan, 212-288-0665 Ensconced inside the diverting Neue Gallerie, Café Sabarsky is a Viennese café and konditerei, an offspring of the West Village's Wallsé that easily outshines its parent. The short dishes make for perfect museum-hopping snacks, including a charcuterie platter (the most challenging feature: double-smoked raw bacon), a generous salad of jumbo asparagus in a remotely sweet lemon-dill sauce, and savory smoked trout crepes with horseradish crème fraîche. The hungrier can move on to sandwiches, to entrées like boiled-beef tafelspitz, or to pastries, of which plum crumble sided with a cloud of whipped cream was a favorite on a recent visit.

Dutch

NL ☆ ☆ 🐟 $

169 Sullivan Street, Manhattan, 212-387-8801 Having run through most of the world's cuisines, our attention turns to this faddish place offering Netherlandish cooking (hence, "NL"). Particularly enjoyable were a mustard soup that was mellow, creamy, and crunchy with croutons, and a sauerkraut risotto heaped with sautéed wild mushrooms. Entrées define "Dutch" as broadly as possible, including a commendable Indonesian rijsttafel that includes beef rendang, satays, sambal, and achar; and a deconstructed Surinamese roti that features a chicken breast stuffed with lobster. Truly weird! Turn as you leave to discover a digitized portrait of Queen Beatrix composed of blue and white ceramic tiles.

German

HALLO BERLIN ☆ ☆
402 West 51st Street, Manhattan, 212-541-6248; 626 10th Avenue, Manhattan, 212-977-1944 A paradise for sausage lovers, these German beer gardens claim to be "the wurst restaurants in New York." The menu runs the gamut from the lowly wiener to the imperial Berliner curry — a supremely delicious knockwurst dusted with raw curry powder. Bring your vegetarian friends, since the sides are so good, they can stand alone: crusty fried potatoes, sweet-and-sour red cabbage, German pickles, and homemade spätzl. There are several forms of pickled herring, but also a fresh herring filet doused with a choice of six different sauces, of which mellow mustard is the best. Skip the Königsberge klopse, stark white meatballs that do a good imitation of cream of wheat. Wash it all down with the sinister-sounding Köstritzer Black Lager.

KILLMEYER'S OLD BAVARIA INN ☆ $
4254 Arthur Kill Road, Staten Island, 718-984-1202 Here's the place to conclude your discovery tour of Staten Island, a rambling frame structure housing a kitsch-encrusted 19th-century German restaurant. The bar alone is worth a look, with its intricate carvings, and the list of nearly 100 beers will make any swiller happy. The food, alas, does not place Killmeyer's among the foremost German restaurants in town, so stick with sausages and pork roast (called "fresh ham") and skip the rubbery Wiener schnitzel. The setting alone — in a decaying industrial slough only a stone's throw from Perth Amboy, New Jersey — merits repeat visits.

NIEDERSTEIN'S ☆ $
69-16 Metropolitan Avenue, Queens, 718-326-0717 It's poised in the middle of Lutheran Cemetery, with gravestones and funerary sculptures climbing the hill out back like a well-framed shot from *Night of the Living Dead*. On Sunday the thronged rooms are dotted with funeral-goers. Germans have never been known as light eaters. Appetizers include chewy headcheese, ox tongue salad, a heap of intensely smoked ham called rauchfleisch, and sweet herring in oniony cream sauce. Soups change daily and run to ponderous goulash (heavy on the ghoul) and the dieter's choice, consommé with liver dumplings. Other Teutonic fare includes the oink-intensive Bavarian platter featuring knockwurst,

bratwurst, and pork loin on a generous bed of homemade kraut flecked with bacon. There's also a safety cushion of sculpted mashed potatoes in case a heavy forkful sends your hand plummeting to the plate. The sauerbraten is somewhat less satisfactory because the massive slabs of beef are short on vinegary tang.

SCHLITZ INN ☆

767 East 137th Street, Bronx, 718-585-8086 A low wood wall barely separates the bar from the dining room, which is painted with Germanic scenes featuring a hilltop castle and a sailboat floating full sail with no one aboard, and a big-busted fraulein hoisting two frothy steins. This ancient bar and café in the shadow of the Bruckner Expressway used to be open only in the afternoons. Under new Turkish owners, it recently extended its hours and expanded the menu to include the usual bar food, from hamburgers to jalapeño poppers to chicken parmigiana heroes. In the recesses of the menu the old Teutonic stuff still lingers — a pair of bratwurst sided with sauerkraut, say, or a choice of veal cutlets with or without sauce. Best of all is bauernwurst, a pair of beef links a very deep color of pink with a slight black pepper studding. Look up from your meal, and the dark wood paneling, bric-a-brac, and beer signs might cause you to expostulate: "Geeze! I must be in Milwaukee."

THE WURST IS YET TO COME

Germans cede ground to no one in their admiration of the lowly sausage. Called "wursten," these links come in so many forms — though nearly all are the same size — that it's difficult to keep them straight. King is the bratwurst, of course, a sausage mixing pork and veal with mild spices like nutmeg and ginger. This sausage has attained quite a following in America among states with a Teutonic population — Wisconsin in particular springs to mind, where the natives boil the raw sausage in beer and then grill it over charcoal all summer long. Bratwurst's closest competition comes from knockwurst, a pink beef or beef-and-pork sausage strongly flavored with garlic, a cousin of the slender frankfurter, Americanized as our beloved hot dog. Weisswurst is a pale veal sausage laced with cream; it's a specialty of Oktoberfest because it goes well with bitter beer, though you'd think bierwurst, a fatty combo of pork, beef, and veal. Blutwurst is, of course, blood sausage, while schinkenwurst is a lean sausage featuring beef and pork. Leberwurst is a funky combo of pork and pork liver something like braunschweiger, while the even funkier zungenwurst contains blood, liver, and heart.

The best place to find these diverse wursten is at any of the **Karl Ehmer** stores in the metropolitan area, or at the wonderful **Forest Pork Store** (66-39 Forest Avenue, Ridgewood, Queens, 718-497-2853) in Ridgewood, until recently, New York's premier German neighborhood. Savor the smoky aroma as you swing through the plate-glass doors, and be regaled by more types of wurst and bologna than you've ever imagined. Also don't miss the double-smoked bacon. After you make your selection, take your ticket to the silver-haired lady in her fortified corner booth, whom all the jocular butchers refer to as "my grandmother." She's the only German in the place — all the butchers are now Romanian.

SILVER SWAN ☆ $
41 East 20th Street, Manhattan, 212-254-3611 Like Hallo Berlin, one of the draws of this place is its modernity, with none of the appeal to nostalgia of the old joints. While the dining room in the rear emphasizes boar, the bar in front sports its own menu of cheaper stuff, including the usual schnitzels, wursts, sauerbraten, and goulash. Beers are an especial strong point, with seven wheat beers alone, served in half-liter flasks.

ZUM STAMMTISCH ☆ ☆ ☆
69-46 Myrtle Avenue, Queens, 718-386-3014 This German restaurant may indeed be 100 years old. It certainly looks like it with its dark wood decor and ranked beer steins. The name translates something like "the communal table" and anchors the dwindling German communities of Ridgewood, Middle Village, and Glendale. Begin with ox tongue salad — the pickled meat sliced thin and served with lettuce and onions. The standard schnitzels, wursts, and tangy-sweet sauerbraten are here evoked in superior renditions, and peripheral dishes of oxtail salad and homemade headcheese provide a certain culinary kinkiness. Best of all, though, is an amazing take on steak tartare, deep red and nearly fatless beef molded on bread points and garnished with capers and raw onions. And no egg! For dessert don't miss the hot raspberry sundae.

Swedish

GOOD WORLD ☆ ☆ 🐟

3 Orchard Street, Manhattan, 212-925-9975 Located in a former barber shop on the Chinatown frontier, Good World flaunts antique wood floors, tin ceilings, and a pleasant nighttime gloominess that makes you feel like you're in an obscure hideaway. Who cares if the service is spotty? Most of the food — Swedish, believe it or not! — is right on the money, including a cheap and massive preserved herring platter, a memorable multifish soup, and a juicy burger uniquely accompanied by pickled beets and capers. There are also lots of bar snacks, foremost of which is a lemongrass-smoked duck breast that looks like bacon. Wash everything down with a Finnish porter and admire the quirkiness of it all.

ULRIKA'S ☆ ☆ 🐟 $

115 East 60th Street, Manhattan, 212-355-7069 In contrast to the well-heeled gourmet crowd that worships Aquavit, Ulrika's attracts a loyal fraternity of doughty Swedes, who crave flavored aquavits and big plates of laxpudding, a potato and salmon casserole that outsiders may have difficulty appreciating. Much more spectacular are the appetizer of pickled herring — five varieties cured in diverse and delicious ways, and the entrée of mackerel tied like a Christmas package with a ribbon of its own skin. The interior is purely IKEA, and it may lull you into ordering the excellent Swedish meatballs. Not a bad choice.

For additional Swedish food, also see All Star Café Restaurant in the Albanian section of the Eastern European chapter.

Ghanaian and Nigerian

Just as the 1990s were the heyday of Senegalese immigrants, the first decade of the new century is the day of the Nigerians. This group has been prevalent in Chicago for over a decade already, where meals of fufu and soup sold from the backs of trucks has been the rule. As in New York, Nigerians first worked as cabdrivers intending to stay, contrasting with the Senegalese, who sell doodads on the street and then return home after six months. The Nigerians find friends in the Ghanaians, sharing a common language and an interest in all things mashed. The structure of their meals is also identical, with a mash and soup, and a piece of meat or fish served almost as a luxury afterthought, probably indicating how recently that hunk of meat or fish has become part of their meal.

LOOK FOR:

agbono *bush mango–seed sauce*

amala *Nigerian yam-flour mash*

asaro *imported Ghanaian yams*

atariko *seeds of the alligator pepper*

cocoyam *leaves used as a vegetable*

efo *any leafy green used in cooking*

egusi *Nigerian melon-seed soup*

ewedu *crain-crain leaf, used in sauces*

fufu *mash of yuca, plantain, or potatoes*

garden eggs *eggplant*

groundnut *peanut*

indi ungo *a "butter" made from dried fish and palm oil*

kenkey *Ghanaian fisherman's fermented cornmeal mash*

moi moi *fried patty of mashed black-eyed peas*

okazi *green leafy vegetable used in fish soup*

omotuo *mashed rice*

romo lamb "light soup"
spinach any leafy green used in cooking
suya Hausa tribe beef skewers dipped in crushed
       peanuts
waachi black-eyed peas and rice

Ghanaian

AFRICAN AMERICAN RESTAURANT ☆

1987 University Avenue, Bronx, 718-731-8595 This culinary combination has arisen, not as a result of a middle-class intellectual movement, but out of the necessity of working-class economics. This successor to African Restaurant is an alliance between a Ghanaian and an American cook, who present the food of two continents side by side on the same steam table. On the African side, you have a choice of two or three mashes every day, including kenkey and a fufu based on potatoes rather than yuca or plantain. There are also a couple of soups offered for the mashes, and a choice of stewed chicken, resilient and fatty oxtails, or a fried fish, usually porgy. On the American side of the menu are collards, macaroni and cheese, meat loaf, fried chicken, black-eyed peas, and Creole rice. The only thing I didn't like was the candy-coated barbecue chicken. Open 24 hours on the main drag in University Heights.

EBE YE YIE ☆ ☆ 🌶 🐟

2364 Jerome Avenue, Bronx, 718-563-6064 Run, don't walk to this Ghanaian eatery, situated among the rolling hills of University Heights. A neon sign in the window, modified from a previous occupant, says simply "A Restaurant." The homemade kenkey, made from fermented corn pone, is particularly tasty — dense and beige and served with a plastic knife so slices can be lopped off. Or go with a milder mash like omotuo, made from rice, or a potato-based fufu with the texture of rubber and silk. To accompany the mash choose soups like goat and beef, or simple fried fish garnished with an amazing dried-shrimp relish. For vegetarians, there's waachi, a combo of black-eyed peas and rice that's the forerunner of the soul food staple, hoppin' john.

IN GOD WE TRUST ☆ 🌶

441 East 153rd Street, Bronx, 718-401-3595 Among the many amazing features is a wall of Astroturf next to the tables, which makes for some comfy leaning after downing your fufu and soup. This Ghanaian café, just north of the commercial South

Bronx area known as the Hub, is a neighborhood oddity — its steam tables loaded with fragrant peanut and palm oil soups rather than the pork, beans, and rice of neighboring Latin joints. Begin by selecting a mash, a hefty starch cylinder that arrives wrapped in aluminum foil, each variety with a distinct texture, flavor, and aroma. Yam fufu is bland and soft as a pillow, springing back when you poke it. Omotuo, pounded from rice, has a clean taste and a pellucid whiteness that's almost disturbing. Made from fermented cornmeal, kenkey generates a flavor somewhere between caviar and old gym socks. Next pick a soup: peanut is my favorite here — tomato-tinged and minimally goobery. Palm nut comes a close second, tasting more of meat than palm oil. Into the soup is dropped your choice of whatever flesh presents itself on a given day — oxtail, goat, beef, chicken, or fried fish. Alternately, choose romo, a "light soup" containing lamb in a strong broth. To further vary the terrain, ask to have okra or spinach dabbed on the surface of your combo.

HOW TO EAT A MASH

Here's how it's done: pieces of mash — whether it be made from manioc, sweet potato, plantain, rice, or, more common nowadays, instant mashed potatoes — are nipped off with the fingers of the right hand from a bowl heaped with mash, then dunked in a gravy that comes on the side known as "soup." At your option, pieces of meat or fish are put into the soup. There's no protocol for consuming these morsels, another indication of the recent date of their inclusion in the meal. A tough piece of lamb, or bony piece of fish, or gummy gluey fragment of cow foot presents certain problems, and the Africans have no concept of what "tough" is, so they don't expect meat to be fork tender. Boldly pick these pieces of flesh or fish up with your hand and gnaw at them without embarrassment.

Soups available in Ghanaian eateries run to okra, peanut, palm nut, while, in Nigeria, egusi, a raunchy puree of melon seeds flecked with greens, somewhat resembling runny scrambled eggs, is preferred. The delightful musky flavor of egusi comes from dried shrimp. Egusi is an acquired taste that produces an intense craving after two or three exposures. Unless you drink the soup after you eat the mash, there's likely to be a lot left in the bowl.

MOTHERLAND CUISINE ☆

3926 White Plains Road, Bronx, 718-515-5400 This Williamsbridge café is the Ghanaian mother lode, serving up comfort food like mashed potato fufu and crushed-rice omotuo with the usual range of sauces (called "soups") — egusi is particularly good, made with crushed melon seeds and greens stewed into vegetable richness. A few surprising forays into American cuisine round out the menu: spaghetti and meatballs, Buffalo chicken wings, and bagels.

Nigerian

AZIZA ☆

3716 White Plains Road, Bronx, 718-882-5100 Even though Aziza is a Nigerian café, bottles of shito, hot pepper paste, are displayed on the counter for Ghanaian patrons, and the provender would be instantly familiar to immigrants from either country: big fluffy mounds of potato fufu, white rice, and joloff rice, any of which could serve as a launching pad for the soup and meat combos. Vegetable soup is delicious, but decidedly not vegetarian, flavored with little bits of dried fish and goat rib. The fish soup contains a steak of the fresh product, and some bonus chunks of goat stew meat if you request it. The staff is very congenial and will gladly help you along if you're unfamiliar with West African food.

DEMU CAFÉ ☆ 🐟

773 Fulton Street, Brooklyn, 718-875-8484 Yam porridge, a dappled mixture of white and orange yams, is lightly mashed and flecked with plenty of crushed red pepper. Also sampled: amala, a mash made from yam flour — moist, dark brown, and shaped like a small beret. We asked for vegetable soup, which turned out to be a tomato and palm oil blend that was thick with a chopped, spinachlike green. We also ordered fish and goat, to be flung in the soup. Our fish consisted of the front half of a bluefish and back half of a mackerel, like some gene splicing experiment gone bad. The dining room is spacious and comfortable. A serving window looks into the kitchen, where the Demu family is busy cooking. Each day the café has only a few of the dishes listed on the menu. Ask your Demu what's available. If you want to eat with your right hand the way most Africans do, the server will bring you a white plastic tub of water to wash with. This neighborhood hangout often hosts literary events in the evenings, and it's only steps away from BAM.

ICONS AFRO-WEST ☆ ☆ 🌶 🐟

197-13 Linden Boulevard, Queens, 718-978-2003 Hidden in the basement of this West African store — a jumble of chew sticks, wonderful small roasted peanuts in salvaged colonial booze bottles, stockfish pitched into cardboard boxes, and other toothsome treats — is a Nigerian restaurant, where a friendly hostess with cowry shells woven into her hair serves mashes like pounded yam

THE KOLA NUT

We sat down at the end of the long table, which looked like it could accommodate 20 or so. The gal with cowries in her hair waited on us. As usual, our plea for a modest amount of food remained unfulfilled, and we hunkered down to prepare for another big feed. First came four plastic-wrapped loaves of mash. Next, two huge bowls of soup, in this case goat, with plenty of strips of fat and gristle. Finally, for Adrian, who is a fishetarian, a bowl of okra and stockfish soup that must have been made with salt cod and not stockfish, since the flavor was relatively delicate. The beverage of choice was palm wine, which, though not alcoholic, had a pleasantly clean and slightly medicinal taste.

As we finished up, a man who'd been conferring with an earnest pair at the other end of the table drifted over. He pulled a kola nut out of his pocket and offered it to us with a flourish. As we accepted it, he launched into a speech: "Do you know what that is?"

"A kola nut," we hesitantly replied.

"Not just a kola nut, but all sorts of things. It represents love and family and community and food. And justice and culture and history. It means a whole lot of things to those in my tribe. I'm the chief."

"A village chief, or a bigger chief than that?"

"Oh, a bigger one. A chief of the Ebo tribe."

He told us he was going to Houston the next day to confer with more of his subjects. Then he pulled a plastic knife from his pocket like the kind you get at fast-food stores and deftly cut the fresh kola nut into several pieces, and handed one to each of us. Then he fetched a wooden board that had some carving around the edges, and a lidded receptacle in the center. When he flipped it open, it contained a smear of powerful looking hot sauce, so red it was almost black, dotted with dried seeds, and oozing palm oil at the edges. Chief showed us how to dip a bit of bitter seed and popped it in his mouth, and we followed suit.

and amala (sun-dried cassava) with goat in a pepper-laced sauce. This is one of the few places in town where you can wash your dinner down with palm wine, which, though it doesn't contain alcohol, is refreshing nonetheless.

LAMS KITCHEN & SPORTS BAR ☆ ☆ ☆ 🌶

268-A East 98th Street, Brooklyn, 718-342-8380 This friendly and comfortable refuge directly beneath the No. 4 tracks is evidence of Brownsville's burgeoning Nigerian community. Though the "sports bar" part is really just wishful thinking, the food is superb — satisfying combos of mash + soup + meat, best eaten with your fingers. On a recent Saturday, the fufus included white yam and the coarser, more flavorful cassava. Either goes well with egusi soup or okra soup. You can also toss in a piece of fish or meat. I'd recommend mutton, which comes in big challenging chunks. The jolly gals who cook are enough reason to go back again and again.

MIRAGE ☆ 🌶

2143 Cortelyou Road, Brooklyn, 718-941-0447 It's no mirage — just off Flatbush Avenue a new Nigerian has appeared, decorated with a backlit transparency of the World Trade Center and a colorful poster entitled "The Historic Visit of President Bill Clinton of U.S.A." A bowl of water on each table invites you to wash your hands before proceeding. We enjoyed a bowl of "mixed meat soup" containing many cow parts, including steak, impenetrable tripe, feet, skin, and heart matched with a tasty plantain mash called amala that's a rather alarming shade of brown. Easier to eat, and not as fiery hot, was a combo soup of melon seed and manioc leaf sided with pounded white-yam fufu.

NEW COMBINATION ☆ ☆

568 Utica Avenue, Brooklyn, 718-604-0964 I've got to admit the dish of snails was one of the stranger things I've enjoyed lately — three dark masses shaped like the lungs of a small petrified mammal, and with a chewy texture to match, deposited in a wonderful pepper sauce to be scooped up with a gobbet of yam fufu. Now farm-raised, the giant land snails known to taxonomists as *Achatina achatina* are unique to New Combo. The majority of the bill of fare is Nigerian, listing lots of soups like ogbolo, ewedu, and edikaikon that, were they regularly available, would make the menu the most comprehensive of its type in the city. The redsauced fish was eminently fresh and a lot more familiar, as was a side of spinach dotted with dried stockfish. Moi moi is a patty made of ground black-eyed pea meal and fried in palm oil — fluffy, brown, and altogether tasty. This unique establishment, recently moved from a much smaller space on Clarkson Street, combines Nigerian food with American and Jamaican, featuring French toast and grits, jerked goat, and a wide range of mashes and soups.

PALAVA HUT ★ 🍢 🐟

992 Atlantic Avenue, Brooklyn, 718-783-8806 Located in the warehouse-dominated no-man's-land between Clinton Hill and Prospect Heights, this eatery keeps a low profile, with the gate pulled halfway down most of the time. But persevere inside and be rewarded with a pair of beautiful fresh sea bass with wobbly black stripes swimming in pepper soup — red and only moderately spicy by African standards. We had two mashes: the usual pounded yam, and the harder-to-find amala, which is made out of sun-dried yuca that develops a lovely brown color, a grainy texture, and a strong flavor that tastes almost fermented.

SKIPPERS ★ ★ 🌶

977 Bay Street, Staten Island, 718-556-5600 This is the most user-friendly of the new spate of Nigerian restaurants, with a menu that takes the guesswork out of ordering by prematching soup, starch, and meat as numbered items. The dishes, however, are the unreconstructed originals, including a fine spicy goat stew laced with palm oil, a mash of broken rice with a clean and mild flavor, and boiled white African yam made with fresh specimens imported from Ghana and tasting nothing like the American variety. Decorated with bright orange posters advertising a Friday buffet, the facade shines like a beacon on Bay Street.

Greek

Even though much of the Greek population has departed Astoria — migrating east to Bayside, Queens, and further into Long Island — the vast majority of the city's Greek restaurants are still located there. The restaurateurs know that when New Yorkers want to eat Greek, they hop the N train. While most Astorian spots are not quite as inexpensive as you'd like them to be (full dinners often average $20 or more), they're still less than half the price of Greek spots in Manhattan like **Molyvos** and **Estiatorio Milos**. Don't forget that many coffee shops are still being run by Greek immigrants. These places usually offer a handful of Greek specials, which means that your cheapest taste of Greek will often be found right on the corner.

LOOK FOR:

avgolemono *lemon soup or sauce*

baklava *nut and honey phyllo pastry*

dolmades *rice-stuffed grape leaves*

fassolakia *green bean and tomato ragu*

galaktoboureko *custard-filled Cypriot pastry*

haloumi *Cypriot cheese*

horiatiki salata *classic Greek salad*

kataifi *shredded wheat pastry*

kefalograviera *Cretan sheep cheese*

kiousour *bulgur salad*

kokoretsi *bundled lamb-innard kebab*

kotopoulo sartsa *crock-baked chicken stew with cheese*

loukanika *Cypriot sausage*

melitzanosalata *pureed eggplant spread*

moussaka *eggplant and ground meat casserole*

orzo *rice-shaped pasta*

panakorizo *spinach-rice pilaf*

pastitsio *Greek lasagna, topped with bechamel*

phyllo *ultrathin dough sheets for sweet and savory pastries*

psaronefri ipirotiko *crock-baked pork stew from Epirus*

retsina *resin-flavored white wine*

saganaki *fried cheese*

skordalia *Macedonian garlicky mashed-potato dip*

smelts *fresh anchovies, usually fried*

stifado *rabbit-and-onion stew*

taramosalata *fish-roe spread*

tzatziki *yogurt, cucumbers, and garlic*

CHICKY'S ON 86 ☆

355 East 86th Street, Manhattan, 212-996-8277 Don't confuse this with the other grilled chicken places in town — Chicky's chicken is significantly tastier and moister, with skin burnished a deep brown, and an herby flavor that penetrates the entire bird. The massive Greek salad, too, is a thing of beauty, with railroad ties of good feta and plenty of olives in a good red-wine vinaigrette.

CHRISTOS HASAPO-TAVERNA ☆ ☆ $

41-08 23rd Avenue, Queens, 718-726-5195 If you're tired of the usual steakhouse, here's a welcome alternative. Located in an obscure corner of Astoria and comfortably furnished with antiques, this Greek taverna concentrates on beefsteaks, serving charbroiled T-bones, filets, shells, and chops, all displayed in their raw state by the front door. Starters are more recognizably Attic — old favorites like tzatziki, taramosalata, stuffed grape leaves, and grilled octopus, and harder-to-find items like steamed dandelion greens, home-cured sardines, and kokoretsi — bundled and skewered lamb innards heavily flavored with garlic and oregano.

JOE JR. ☆ ⚘

482 6th Avenue, Manhattan, 212-924-5220 This sometime celebrity hangout, the king of Greek coffee shops, offers a handful of Hellenic specialties each day. The moussaka is particularly fine, layered with eggplant, tender potatoes, and light bechamel, though you can skip the canned peas on the side of the plate. Also avoid the gyro platter, made with a rubber version of the good lamb you sometimes get. Best bet is an abundant Greek salad made with crisp ingredients and avalanched with sharp feta.

LATERNA ☆

47-20 Bell Boulevard, Queens, 718-423-1245 Reflecting Greek migration out of Astoria to far eastern Queens and Long Island, this nifty bi-level banquet space serves excellent lamb roast, Macedonian sausages, Greek salad, and skordalia – the potato dip with mouth-searing quantities of raw garlic. Don't miss the mezedes (appetizer) platter, which is a wonderful meal in itself: grilled sweetbreads, sausages, skordalia, and haloumi.

SKORDALIA

It's only cold mashed potatoes laced with olive oil, lemon juice, and raw garlic, but skordalia is one of humanity's greatest culinary inventions. Whether you scoop it with matchsticks of fried zucchini and eggplant, with gobbets of breaded cod, or with pita bread or some variation, this wonderful dip fills your mouth with 240 volts of pure raw garlic, lighting up your eyes and warming your tummy. It's especially good on a date, when there's kissing to be done. Skordalia originates in Macedonia, where bread smashed and whipped into oblivion is an added component, making the dip lighter and airier. Skordalia is the Greek answer to French aioli.

MYKONOS ☆

7616 3rd Avenue, Brooklyn, 718-491-0622 Already stuffed from eating several consecutive meals, I was determined to pass this place by, with just a notebook scribble to remind me to return. But one look in the window revealed a billowing steam table with a leg of lamb sticking out, appearing to have been just yanked from the oven. Our avuncular host turned out to be generous as well, piling a Styrofoam container high with garlic-strewn slices of tender freshly sliced meat, ringing them with lemon potatoes roasted in meat juices. Various other viands also presented themselves, including miniature barbecued lamb ribs and herb-slagged roast chicken, as a pair of pork shish kebabs sizzled seductively on the grill.

NICK'S PLACE ☆ ⏱

550 7th Avenue, Manhattan, 212-221-3294 This nominally Greek luncheonette is hidden in the bowels of a building with no sign of any sort – you have to know it's there. Neighborhood "garmentos" go for the entrée-sized salads, the best of which features slices of fresh turkey with beaucoup greens. Nick also does kebabs and burgers at a small grill at the end of the room (the feta burger is tops). On the whole, Greek standards like spinach pie are average, the best being moussaka.

PERIYALI ☆ ~< $
35 West 20th Street, Manhattan, 212-463-7890 While most upscale Greek restaurants in Manhattan pick the easy route to riches, concentrating on expensive but simply grilled whole fish, Periyali serves a Panhellenic menu, painting a fairer picture of Attic cuisine. At a recent lunch, we enjoyed stifado, a brick-red rabbit stew bombarded with baby onion bulbs, the meat copious and tender, and a chorus line of tender sautéed shrimp kicking in olive oil and lemon. The dining rooms in the rear are preferred, rustic within but offering a vertiginous cityscape through the skylights.

PYLOS ☆ ☆ ☆
128 East 7th Street, Manhattan, 212-473-0220 Inspired by the cookbooks of Diane Kochilas, Pylos voyages to some of the outer islands and hikes into the mountainous interior of the mainland to discover regional Greek cuisine unavailable in most other Hellenic restaurants in town. Kotopoulo sartsa is a case in point — a crock-baked chicken stew floating rafts of gooey cheese, from the region around Odysseus' home port of Ithaca. Named after the clay pots that hang precariously from the ceiling, Pylos does the more familiar Greek provender well, too, including grilled sardines and a particularly persuasive take on the macaroni pie pastitsio. The extensive Greek wine list is unique in the city.

S'AGAPO ☆ ☆ ~<
34-21 34th Avenue, Queens, 718-626-0303 In the shadow of the Kaufman Astoria Studios and a little off the beaten path, S'Agapo is my second favorite among the Astorian Greeks, recently confirmed by a meal that featured a special of Macedonian-style roast pork well marbled with fat and bathed in drippings alive with subtle flavor. Good too was a red snapper done "savori" — rubbed with fresh tomato and braised in a wine and citrus marinade. In spite of an excellent grilled octopus, the best starter is a zingy puree of roasted red peppers and garlic that goes great on the crusty bread.

SCOUNA TAVERNA ☆ ☆ ☆ ~<
23-01 31st Street, Queens, 718-545-4000 The decor of this grottolike and gracefully windowed space might be termed Nautical Lite: apart from an absurd little statue of a rotund salt who looks like the Gorton's fisherman (or maybe the murderer in *I Know What You Did Last Summer*), there are thankfully few kitschy

touches, and a close examination reveals that the fishing nets suspended from the ceiling are real. Apart from a small selection of meats, most of the main courses are whole fish, and an inspection of the iced selection will cue you to what's freshest. Grilled porgy is always a good choice; it comes carefully deboned and sprinkled with olive oil and dried oregano. If they're out of it, opt for the modest-sized red smelts, four to an order, though they come fried rather than grilled. Best of all, though, and closest to the hearts of the Greek patrons, are the smelts, a school of tiny fish that gleam silver among the chunks of ice. Deep-fried and served 100 to a plate, they arrive crunchy, chewy, barely bony, and fresh as the ocean's salt spray. For starters, anything featuring skordalia is a good bet. This being a Cretan joint, the saganaki is superb, and so is the octopus.

SNACK ☆ ☆ ☺

105 Thompson Street, Manhattan, 212-925-1040 Doubling as a grocery, this nifty café and carryout is festooned with symmetrical piles of Hellenic products facing a neat row of bright white tables decorated with tiny Greek flags. The fare is all room temperature, all vegetarian, and you can probably guess the menu: cheese and spinach pie, eggplant dip, Greek salad, stuffed vine leaves, and an especially delicious beet salad incorporating roots and stems sprinkled with olive oil, red-wine vinegar, and oregano, then topped with a dollop of skordalia. Just the thing for a Greek picnic in your apartment.

SNACK TAVERNA ☆ $

63 Bedford Street, Manhattan, 212-929-3499 Last year when Ithaka pulled up stakes and absconded to the Upper East Side, it left the West Village without a Greek restaurant. Rising to the challenge, Snack Taverna appeared, assuming the real estate from which quirky and beloved stalwart Shopsins had been cruelly evicted earlier in the year. The Taverna is more like a bistro, a branch of the tiny SoHo carryout and café called Snack, which has always been better than OK in my book. Unfortunately, Snack Taverna diddles with the bread dips so you might not recognize them. Some of the other modern, cooking-school stuff is good anyway, and the location may be just what you're looking for, among the warren of ancient Greenwich Village streets.

STAMATIS ☆ ☆ 🐟

31-14 Broadway, Queens, 718-204-8968; 29-12 23rd Avenue, Queens, 718-932-8596 Cynics contend there's no great Greek food left in Astoria. Today we encountered evidence to the contrary. After eyeballing the iced display of fish, we made our way into the spare skylit interior and noshed on a very garlicky skordalia and an abundant beet salad while waiting for our sea bass to cook. It arrived 20 minutes later, grilled over charcoal and singed on the edges, flooded with olive oil and herbs, every bite sweet, salty, and smoky. It was altogether the best grilled fish I've had in ages, visits to the ultrapricey Estiatorio Milos in midtown included.

THALASSA ☆ ☆ 🐟 $
179 Franklin Street, Manhattan, 212-941-7661 Restaurant-wise, it seemed that all TriBeCa lacked was one of those upscale Greek fish places that have been all the rage in midtown the last few years. Voila! Despite my cynicism, I found Thalassa far superior to Milos and Molyvos. The professional staff gleefully explains the merits of each species in the iced fish display, from which we picked sargos, a Mediterranean fish something like a porgy. The whole fish soon arrived crisp-skinned, deboned, and festooned with parsley and capers. Charred octopus flown in from Portugal, baby arugula salad, and baklava rife with toasted almonds were equally delicious.

UNCLE GEORGE'S ☆ 🐟
33-19 Broadway, Queens, 718-626-0593 Revisit the mother of all cheap Greek restaurants and be regaled by the flame-licked carcasses of lambs, chickens, suckling pigs, and sometimes even kids rotating horizontally in the window. A big portion sided with lemon-baked potatoes is still around $10, and the aluminum flagons of retsina are one of the city's great inexpensive hangovers. Saturday is the only day you can savor rabbit-and-onion stew.

UNCLE NICK'S GREEK CUISINE ☆ 🐟
747 9th Avenue, Manhattan, 212-245-7992 The photos of turn-of-the-century peasants set the stage for the thoroughly un-pretentious grub you'll find at Uncle Nick's Greek Cuisine. Cuisine? Not by a long shot. This joint's a monument to just plain food. A squeeze of lemon here, a splash of wine vinegar there, a sprinkle of dried oregano, and maybe some garlic, all applied with a re-strained hand — the art here is not in the seasoning, but in the grilling. In fact, as you enter the long dining room, the most promi-nent feature is the tandem charcoal grills behind a counter. The red snapper is the most celebrated fish, prepared for the grill by simply rubbing it with salt; but even better is the humble porgy, served two to a plate. Its sharper flavor — almost mackeralish — complements the dark flavor of the charcoal. Note that the propri-etors have opened a fancier Greek wine bar next door.

THE YOGHURT PLACE II ☆ 🕭
71 Sullivan Street, Manhattan, 212-219-3500 Other yogurts will turn to sawdust in your mouth once you've tried the home-made product at SoHo's The Yoghurt Place II. The full-fat product (called "Greek Strained Yogurt") is the tastiest, but so thick it's

110

best spread on bread or crackers. To eat plain or serve with fruit, thin it out with water. Also don't miss the garlic-laced tzatziki and the Greek desserts at this narrow carryout.

ZENON ☆ ☆ 🐟 🐂

34-10 31st Avenue, Queens, 718-956-0133 Zenon is from Cyprus, although the constituency is mainly Greek. Accordingly, don't miss Greek Night every Wednesday, when the place blows up (well, not literally). The menu features rotating specials, with heavy emphasis on seafood and lamb. Valiantly we ate our way through the menu: squid and shrimp salad, pickled beets, deep-fried zucchini, tzatziki, taramosalata, lamb chops, chicken, grilled octopus, fried calamari, and smelts so fresh they could have flung themselves out of the pan. All admirable, but the dishes you'll remember as you make your way home are skordalia, a garlic and potato puree served as a pita dip, and grilled haloumi, a Cypriot cheese that's been boiled in whey and mildly flavored with mint.

ZODIAC ☆

30-15 Newtown Avenue, Queens, 718-726-3995 Named after a famous mass murderer? This coffeehouse forgoes all the standard big feeds of Greek cooking, like moussaka and grilled fish and meats. Instead, the menu concentrates on hot and cold meze, plus pizza and burgers. The grilled octopus, engulfed in lemony broth, is especially tasty, while a dish of baked shrimp and feta is sometimes marred by rubberiness. You can't go wrong with the Greek salad, abundant in volume and dressed with olive oil and sharp red-wine vinegar. The breezy dining rooms are bordered by sidewalk tables, and Zodiac is recommended especially for enjoying a snack and a retsina.

Haitian

A walk down nearly any major thoroughfare in Flatbush will take you past a string of tiny Caribbean eateries, mainly Trinidadian, Jamaican, Guyanese, and Haitian. For a recent stroll I picked Nostrand Avenue, decamping the No. 2 train at Newkirk Avenue, one stop short of Brooklyn College. Topside I found a neighborhood of brick storefronts and three-story apartment buildings interspersed with modest Victorian homes. Standing on the corner is St. Jerome's, whose crenellated towers ringed with fierce griffins make it look more like a castle than a Roman Catholic church. Many of the local businesses are Haitian, including botaniques, bakeries, convenience stores, and a radio station so small that the DJ sits in a miniature booth a few feet from the sidewalk. Explore this area and the other not-too-distant Haitian district centered at Rutland Road and Rockaway Parkway in East Flatbush, and you'll find a good number of small, pleasant eateries where little English is spoken and the food is a tasty combination of African and French. Though little known to non-Haitians, it's one of the best cuisines of the Caribbean.

LOOK FOR:

accra *taro fritters*

achards *pickled vegetables*

bouyon or bouillon *beef and vegetable soup*

djon-djon *spindly native Haitian black mushrooms*

griot or grillot *marinated, boiled, and fried pork*

kabrit *baby goat*

lambi *conch ragu*

légumes *vegetable stew*

mayi moulin *cornmeal porridge*

poisson frite *simple fried fish, usually red snapper*

> **ragu** *red stew of cow feet and tripe*
> **riz noir** *rice cooked with djon-djon*
> **taso** *grilled goat*
> **ti-malice** *fiery cabbage relish*
> **touffée** *sautéed vegetables and meat served over rice or mayi moulin*

E & R ☆ ☆ ☆ 🐟

907 Church Avenue, Brooklyn, 718-941-0349 There's not much to be said about the decor at E & R. The boxy walls are smeared industrial green, interrupted by crazy red stencils of stars, flowers, and musical eighth notes. Next to a carryout window, there's a calendar touting a butcher shop on Coney Island Avenue with the uninspiring name of OK Meat Place. As a warning against overindulgence, a used Stairmaster is offered for sale in one corner. The female chef makes some of the liveliest French food in town, with a marvelous African twist. Pork griot is a confit of rich meat that's been soaked in a tart marinade, while bouyon is a thronged beef-and-vegetable soup, a hearty meal that would send any French peasant back, bowl in hand, to plead for more. Lambi can't be beat, torn into irregular pieces and drenched in a soothing and subtle red gravy. The rice is similarly delightful, bumpy with red beans and fragrant with fresh thyme and cloves.

EVE'S RESTAURANT ☆

1366 Flatbush Avenue, Brooklyn, 718-859-4874 It's a pleasant room, simple and spotless — eight tables with red-and-white tablecloths, ceramic seashells filled with paper napkins, and red artificial flowers. A woman in a white apron is seen cooking through a door at the rear of the room. Even though it was 12:30 p.m., lunch was not yet being served. So I had breakfast, a choice of cornmeal porridge or plantains served with fish, beef liver, or cow's feet. I picked the porridge and was served a very African-style plate of cornmeal mash dotted with pink beans flavored with fish stock. Accompanying the mash was a small bowl of stewed cow's feet, big squares of foot flesh with a rubbery texture, seasoned with thyme, garlic, carrots, and onion. I poured the stew over the porridge and dug in.

FRITTAILE LACAYE ☆

3974 Church Avenue, Brooklyn, 718-282-7900 Attractively decorated with Caribbean Primitive paintings and a dizzying wall of mirrors, this wonderful Haitian eatery specializes in fried things like griot — nuggets of pork marinated in citrus and shallots, boiled in

113

RIZ NOIR

Rice is a staple that Haitians make much of, whether it's well-oiled white rice cooked to perfection, rice dotted with red beans, rice cooked with petits pois, or rice salads rife with smoked herring and eggplant. But most beloved of Creoles is "riz noir," black rice colored with djon-djon mushrooms. Botanically known as *Psathyrella hymenocephala*, the mushroom is long and spindly, with a delicate fluted cap, and is most often used in dried form — nearly any Haitian market in Brooklyn sells them in tiny packets. Yet few Haitian restaurants serve black rice, perhaps because of the relative expense, or perhaps because it's considered a home-style dish. Nevertheless, you can often find it on the menu at **Krik Krak**. While the normal version of this dish involves mushrooms, lard, and shallots or onions, there are more elaborate preparations that make it into a festive full meal, including the introduction of shrimp and hot peppers and additional flavoring with cloves and garlic. Note that in most recipes the mushrooms are used to color and flavor the water that the rice is cooked in, but the mushrooms themselves are discarded — the stem, at least, is too tough to be edible.

the marinade, then fried in lard. The result is a very rich dish the French would call pork confit. Queen of the nonfried side of the menu is lambi, the national dish of conch swatches stewed in a thick tomato and pepper sauce. Between these two extremes are Haitian standards like goat tasso, poisson frite, and mais, a thick corn porridge.

KRIK KRAK ☆ ☆ 🐟 $

844 Amsterdam Avenue, Manhattan, 212-222-3100 This tiny Manhattan Valley Haitian lunch counter, brainily named after Edwige Danticat's first book, soared to excellence the minute it opened a few years ago. The lambi, a savory conch stew widely reckoned to be the national dish, was as tender as I've ever tasted it, the gravy laced with strips of sweet red pepper. So too was the griot exemplary — pork chunks marinated, boiled, and then fried to produce a concentrated porkiness. Deploy the blistering hot sauce, which masquerades as a tiny serving of cabbage slaw. Feeling flush? Get the fried snapper, strewn with onions and peppers and accompanied by a fine Creole sauce. On the weekends there's sometimes bouillon, a home-style stew that's the Haitian answer to Mexican pozole.

ROSE'S RESTAURANT ☆

1046 Rutland Road, Brooklyn, 718-774-1635 This East Flatbush café, perpetually festooned with Christmas lights, is the ideal spot to get some down-home Haitian cooking, and the ineffable Frenchness of it all will be readily apparent. Tender medallions of conch are fricasseed with plenty of lima beans and other vegetables in a rich red sauce. The dish called légumes — French for vegetables — is mainly goat, with only a smattering of vegetables to justify the name. Another Haitian favorite is griot (here spelled "grillot") — pork chunks boiled in a marinade of lemon, garlic, and spices, then fried in oil, for a crunchy exterior and mellow, chewy interior. Don't miss the Haitian bakery between the subway stop and the café, where they have an interesting collection of Haitian cookbooks in French and English.

LE SOLEIL ☆

877 10th Avenue, Manhattan, 212-581-6059 Favored by Haitian cabdrivers, and one of the last remaining vestiges of the Upper West Side Haitian community known as Bois Verna, this restaurant boasts a dining room decorated with brightly colored paintings of palm trees and island huts. The all-male clientele converses amiably and eats with evident gusto. There is a different menu for each day of the week comprising eight or so dishes. Last time I stopped by, three were available. I ordered the conch (lambi) and a fried red fish with sauce. The lambi was smothered in brown gravy tasting of garlic and onions. The fish — a red snapper strewn with onions and sweet red peppers in a spicy red sauce laced with vinegar — was large and done to perfection. All entrées were accompanied by plain rice cooked with beans or white rice with soupy red beans.

YOYO FRITAILLE ☆ ☆ ☆

1758 Nostrand Avenue, Brooklyn, 718-469-7460 A Haitian friend recommended this place with a rollicking name. Red neon signs sputter "YOYO" in the windows, and a yellow overhang offers Bega, Accra, Marinade, Lambi, Tassot, Griot, Banane, Patate. Most fall into the category of "fritaille," or fried things. Once inside, I found steam pouring from the receptacles. The counterman removed every lid to show what was underneath. The first held big chunks of griot, one of Haiti's greatest dishes, which looked so delicious I immediately ordered some. It's made from chunks of pork marinated in garlic, shallots, spices, and bitter orange, then boiled until the liquid evaporates. Next, the pieces are fried, which further anneals the ingredients to the surface, resulting in a chewy exterior and moist interior with the flavors intensely concentrated. Other fried items included slices of white sweet potato, plantain, sausages that tasted suspiciously Polish, and, most interesting of all, accra — amorphously delicate fritters of shredded taro root reminiscent of ones made in West Africa.

There's a whole lot of fusion going on, and it's not just in the fancy places where cooking-school chefs have been taught to toss wasabi into their French dressing. The places listed here resist our attempts to cram them into a single national category. They are interesting studies in cultural assimilation and fraternization, but are also perfect choices for contentious groups of diners who cannot agree among themselves exactly what they want to eat.

BIS MILALH ✕
1235 Fulton Street, Brooklyn, 718-783-2165 Following a trend that has taken this Bed-Stuy neighborhood — anchored by Brooklyn's foremost mosque — by storm, this place sports an imperially long steam table merchandised by the pound and loaded with African, Caribbean, and North American delicacies. The African stuff is nominally Senegalese, with a decent bluefish cheb, wonderfully slimy chicken-and-okra casserole, and sauté of diverse cubed organ meats. From the island roster comes a fiery jerk chicken, while African-American cooking is ably represented by stewed greens and mac and cheese. There are also usually three or four fried fish choices.

BLACK BETTY ✕
366 Metropolitan Avenue, Brooklyn, 718-599-0243 Taking a page from the Oznot's Dish book, this jazz bar has mounted a menu loaded with North African and Middle Eastern influences. The biggest thrill was the Moroccan paella, the standard Iberian product with couscous substituted for rice. It came saturated with an excellent shellfish-and-chicken broth that would have made cardboard taste good. The rest of the menu is a mixed bag: the Israeli avocado salad needed more dressing, the eggplant done three ways was delicious, while the turnovers called boreks had a crust like cast iron.

BOCA CHICA ✕
13 1st Avenue, Manhattan, 212-473-0108 The food at this lively pan-Latino is all over the map: Brazil, Mexico, Chile, Puerto Rico, Cuba, even Spain. Some of the dishes lack authenticity, but

117

who cares when they taste so good? Brazilian is best — check out the Bahian moqueca de peixe, which features shrimp and red snapper in a sauce made with coconut milk, bell pepper, garlic, and onion. Another triumph is conch ceviche with diced cucumber, tomato, and cilantro — a perfect summer salad.

BROOK LUNCHEONETTE ☆
504 East 138th Street, Bronx, 718-585-5880 Over the last 20 years, this old-time Mott Haven lunch counter has compiled pastrami sandwiches, served eggs with grits, and dished up Caribbean steak and onions, satisfying three constituencies simultaneously. Now Mexican has been added to the mix, and the well-stuffed barbacoa tacos — dressed with only onions and cilantro — are the best in the Bronx.

CAFÉ ASEAN ☆ ☆ 🐟
117 West 10th Street, Manhattan, 212-633-0348 The short menu at this thumb-sized Pacific Rim café offers the greatest hits of Vietnamese, Thai, and Malaysian cooking. Top honors among starters go to chicken satay, beef and vermicelli salad topped with crushed peanuts and ringed with basil, and crab and asparagus soup. Nor did the entrées disappoint: our faves were tofu and perfectly cooked vegetables in a lemongrass stir-fry, and an awesome curried squid. Refreshingly for this type of restaurant, the decor is strictly Martha Stewart, and the staff couldn't be nicer.

CALIDAD LATINA ☆
132 9th Avenue, Manhattan, 212-255-3446 Serving the unbeatable combo of Cuban, Dominican, and Puerto Rican cuisine, this villa of vinegar combines a budget weekly rotating menu with more expensive pork, beef, and seafood dishes. The made-to-order chicharron de pollo is especially fine, while Thursday's asopao de gallina is just about the best chicken stew you've ever tasted.

ELORA'S ☆
272 Prospect Park West, Brooklyn, 212-718-6190 A pair of cooks — one Mexican and one Dominican — make this Windsor Terrace eatery unique. Add the proclivity of both for Iberian chow, and you have a vast range of culinary territory. From a menu of biblical proportions choose paella, Cuban sandwich, tripe soup, pork burrito with mole verde, oxtail stew, or a simple plate of pernil or tacos. One of my faves is the home-style Mexican dish called chilaquiles: crisp strips of leftover tortillas mobbed with cheese, chiles, and tomatillo sauce. Delicious! French doors open onto the pleasant street, on the northern verge of Greenwood Cemetery.

EMERALD PLANET ★ ★ ☾

2 Great Jones Street, Manhattan, 212-353-WRAP Just when you were getting terminally bored of burritos, along comes the wrap — the burrito reborn with an international catalog of ingredients ensconced in wildly colorful flour tortillas. In pleasant digs, this place purveys downtown's best, with silly geographic identifications such as Kathmandu: grilled coconut shrimp in green curry with mango salsa, green beans, bamboo shoots, and rice. (Hey, where do you get shrimp in Nepal?) The other half of the menu is devoted to smoothies that feature fruit combinations with optional additions like spirulina, bee pollen, and lecithin. The decor is high tech, and you'll feel welcome to sit around, either inside or out, as long as you like.

GOBO ★ ★ ☾ $

401 6th Avenue, Manhattan, 212-255-3242 Almost-vegan Gobo — which possesses a familial connection to the Zen Palate chain — is one of the Manhattan's odder restaurants. The menu goes for the global, moving effortlessly from South America to China with many stops in between. I really dug the papaya ceviche and the Peruvian root-vegetable stew, especially since the agreeable

---

FOOD COURTS

The idea is not a bad one: divide a space into food stalls that will offer competing cuisines. Unfortunately, the overwhelming majority of the food courts now in service interpret "competing cuisines" to be competing fast-food chains. Demonstrating the excellence of the idea are places like the **Flushing Mall Food Court** (39th Avenue and Prince Street, Queens, 718-762-8787), which features 11 stalls. As the name leads you to expect, Cheg Du slings Sichuan fare, though tailored to Taiwanese tastes, including one of the city's best versions of dan dan noodles. There's also a sushi conveyor belt, and a big open area for shabu-shabu, with radiant cooking stations at each table and a small adjacent grocery that sells fixin's. While the counters called Tasty Congee and Taiwanese Food are self-explanatory, the cryptic Beggar Dish may leave you gawking: arrayed with compulsive precision are juliennes of various pig and duck parts, sold by weight, with no broth or noodles or rice of any sort. What you do with them is up to you.

orange broth also contained pozole. At less than $10, lunch specials are a great deal, and the green-tea-colored dining room, open kitchen, and multiculti staff make dining a pleasure.

GO-GO SOUVLAKI KING ☆

2218 Hylan Boulevard, Staten Island, 718-667-0080 This modest eatery boasts "Largest Menu on East Coast," including Italian, Greek, French (well, quiches), seafood, and good, cheap breakfasts all day, the latter with Hylan Boulevard's best home fries. Otherwise, go for the Greek: the gyro sandwich bulges with pungent mystery meat hacked from the rotating cylinder, dressed with tart yogurt sauce and plenty of roughage. Request grilled peppers.

HAVANA PIES ☆

219 East 23rd Street, Manhattan, 212-684-3330 Empanadas, invented in Galicia and perfected in South America, are turnovers filled with meat or cheese. Here the humble pie is redefined by international stuffing. The crawfish étouffée is fantastic, jammin' with pink tails in a lively sauce, as is the curried vegetables, creamy with coconut milk that provides a slightly sweet edge. But the greatest praise should be reserved for Cuban pernil asado — thick slices of garlicky pork roast. Pies may be ordered deep-fried or baked (the latter surprisingly good), and you'll have trouble choosing among the 20 varieties offered.

JOYA ☆ ☆ ♻

215 Court Street, Brooklyn, 718-222-3484 This Cobble Hill crowd pleaser, designed to look like a disco or maybe a bus garage, offers bounteous quantities of Thai and other Southeast Asian fare at remarkably low prices, given the real estate aspirations of the neighborhood. Expect a congenial and noisy throng, and food with bright but simplified flavors.

KOMODO ☆ ☆ $

186 Avenue A, Manhattan, 212-529-2658 Those who knew Avenue A when this was a crack block will be surprised at Komodo, a neighborhood joint that melds the cooking of Mexico and Southeast Asia. Also surprisingly, most of the dishes work. The chicken corn chowder blew us away, laced with coconut milk and properly spicy, as did the sirloin topped with fried kumamoto oysters — a nifty idea — and shivered fried leeks. And while the snapper filet cooked in a banana leaf was a bit mushy and bland, the mesclun salad dressed with pecan vinaigrette more than made up for it.

MARKET CAFÉ ☆ ☆ ♻

496 9th Avenue, Manhattan, 212-967-3892 Though nominally a French bistro, the long-running Market Café also proffers a menu of delicious individual pizzas (my favorite: clam and mozzarella) and formidable pasta choices, in addition to maverick Swedish specials come Christmastide. The Formica fixtures date from an earlier establishment, and the neighborhood hipsters and in-the-know tourists who frequent the place like it that way. Generally regarded as the best place to eat within walking distance of the Javits Center.

MEZZE ✩ ⌀

10 East 44th Street, Manhattan, 212-697-6644 This lunch-only pan-Mediterranean — created by celebrity chef Matthew Kenney — can't decide whether it wants to be a fancy salad bar or a real restaurant. Feathery baba ghanoush and hummus, ordered from the menu, were without peer; the curried shrimp risotto was spectacularly briny and cheesy. Also recommended are Moroccan spicy carrots, charcoal-grilled asparagus accented with preserved lemon, and, especially, a salad that paired potatoes and yams flavored with cilantro and astringent curry leaves (no relation to curry powder). Perch on the balcony to be waited on, and compare the bald spots of the men grazing at the salad bar far below.

MOONCAKE FOODS ✩ ✩ ✩

28 Watts Street, Manhattan, 212-219-8888 Mooncake demonstrates what the Greek diner would have been like if it had been invented in Asia. Hero sandwiches are replaced by Vietnamese banh mi (often with Western twists like dill mayo); chef's salads have become a series of Thai yums, sporting a choice of main ingredients; and Chinese peasant classics like Shanghai wonton soup and sticky rice with sausage are presented unaltered. Full dinners are available at less than $10, keeping this jewel of a spot — located on ultraobscure Watts Street — well within the price range of the traditional diner.

MOSAICO ✩ ⌀

175 Madison Avenue, Manhattan, 212-213-4700 What's almojabana? A Colombian cousin of the bouncy Brazilian cheese breads called pão de queijo. You can get it in two sizes at Mosaico, an upscale pan-Latin lunchroom that always has a few things I crave on its rotating menu (the meal-size tamales and pressed sandwiches are always tasty). The almojabana is a little more crumbly than its Brazilian counterpart, and a little cheesier. It comes in two sizes, and tastes even better if you ask them to pop it in the microwave.

LOS POLLITOS ✩ ✎

5911 4th Avenue, Brooklyn, 718-439-9382 Nearly a decade ago, Los Pollitos brought Peruvian-style rotisserie chicken and its dark mystery coating to Sunset Park, and it was damn good. But with a weird twist — the balance of the menu is Mexican food of a type that suggests bar food, but plenty edible nonetheless.

RADIO PERFECTO ✭

190 Avenue B, Manhattan, 212-477-3366 Niftily furnished with dozens of Bakelite radios from the 1930s and 1940s, and lighting sconces made from electric drills, this alphabet bistro offers a range of relatively inexpensive possibilities from solid comfort food like chicken pot pies, fried calamari, and pastas, to attempts at haute cuisine like a mousse of chicken livers and port wine garnished with onion marmalade — it's weird at first, but gradually grows on you. Pork roast with black beans and yellow rice — a tip of the hat to the neighborhood — is often less than perfecto, but the Belgian fries are some of the best in town.

REPUBLIC ✭ ✭ 🥢 🍎

37 Union Square West, Manhattan, 212-477-3366 Ambitiously taking the entire world of Asian noodles as its purview — fried, stewed, and souped — Republic gives you a chance to compare cooking styles from China to Thailand to Malaysia, while satisfying diners with divergent tastes. Service is quick, the space is attractive, and the price is right. I can never resist their deep-fried wontons.

RICE ✭ 🍎

227 Mott Street, Manhattan, 212-226-5775 What a concept! This café and carryout specializes in rice-based dishes, with a choice of basmati, Japanese short grain, sticky, brown, and, somewhat inconsistently, barley and couscous. Available in large and small sizes, the majority of the dishes are in an Asian vein, like Vietnamese grilled chicken, Thai beef salad, and Indian curry with yogurt and banana. There's also a selection of plain sauces priced at a dollar apiece which can be paired with any grain, including eggplant caviar, almond yogurt, and mango chutney.

TIKKI MASALA ✭

71-03 Grand Avenue, Queens, 718-429-0101 This combo Indian/Indonesian restaurant might be called the "Miracle of Maspeth" for its unusual menu, odd location, and semielegant dining room. Find plenty of South Asian dishes unavailable elsewhere, like chicken sabjee (boneless poultry in a mellow yellow sauce loaded with green vegetables), and Malai curry (lamb chunks bathed in rich coconut sauce). The Indonesian dishes are pallid by comparison, but desirable in the context of a broad-ranging meal with many diners — so bring your friends. Breads are a strong point, though the addition of sugar to several proved somewhat unnerving.

SOUPER DUPER

All the soup joints, including the ubiquitous and not-that-good **Daily Soup** chain, owe their inspiration to **Soup Kitchen International** (259A West 55th Street, Manhattan, 212-757-7730), a quirky joint that you know all about if you've studied the "Soup Nazi" episode of *Seinfeld*. Despite criticism leveled at the TV show, the rules of engagement are accurately represented — you do have to abide by a set of inflexible rules that will make you feel like you're in boot camp. Be prepared to line up in an orderly fashion, observe the posted rules, and be sure to have your money ready or you won't get any soup. The soup is from the dense and complicated school. The seafood bisque is the pièce de résistance — pieces of lobster, shrimp, real crab, and scallops in a thick pink puree. Other varieties include lentil, matzo ball, sweet red pepper, chicken vegetable, and creamless mushroom. Flavor secrets run to garlic in huge chunks, parsley, lots of dill, and mustard seed.

12 CHAIRS ☆ ☆ ☺
56 MacDougal Street, Manhattan, 212-254-8640 Not to be confused with the East Village joint 26 Seats, this SoHo café offers the pleasing combination of all-day breakfasts, bistro-style sandwiches, Middle Eastern salads, and — Surprise! — Soviet food. The so-called Russian ravioli are really Siberian pelmeni, a profuse serving of tiny dumplings loaded with oily meat, perfect brunch fare as far as I'm concerned. Also find a range of blintzes and potato pierogi, as well as one of downtown's best baba ghanoushes, and perfect breaded chicken cutlets sided with mashed potatoes. Open 8 a.m.

WILD LILY TEA ROOM ☆ ☺
511 West 22nd Street, Manhattan, 212-598-9097 Architecturally, Wild Lily is consistent with the Chelsea galleries that surround it, paradoxically achieving coziness with a brick-clad industrial space flaunting a burbling ornamental pool. In addition to dozens of annotated teas, food offerings run from gallery-hopping snacks to full meals. Trying to encompass all the tea traditions, the menu juxtaposes English scones and Chinese noodles. The cream of asparagus soup is delicately flavored; the salad of beets, goat cheese, and mushrooms on baby spinach vastly satisfying in its sweet citrus dressing; but proceed with caution when it comes to the subpar dumplings.

Italian

Heroes; Italian-American; Osteria, Trattoria, and Locandi; Pasticerria and Espresso Bars; Pizza; and Wine Bars

This chapter demonstrates the wide spectrum of Italian cooking styles currently available in the city, many at bargain prices. These range from Neapolitans and Sicilians — New York's earliest Italians — to such recent introductions as Milanese panini bars, Abruzzi pizza joints, Emilia-Romagnan piadina parlors, and Tuscan trattoria. Not all involve smotherings of red sauce, but if you really love tomatoes, as I do, you'll visit one of the more ancient places in Brooklyn, like **Bamonte's, Romano, Joe's of Avenue U**, or **Totonno's Pizzeria Napolitano**. You'll feel like you've been dropped into a movie set, and the greatness of the food will show you how far Chef Boyardee has gone to ruin it. In this edition, for the first time we organize the restaurants according to product rather than point of geographic origin. Note that the Italian-American category includes Neapolitan and other Italian food as it has been reworked here for a century and more; the Osteria, Trattoria, and Locandi designation catalogs more modern places that have been inspired by restaurants back in Italy, though they sometimes add Italian-American offerings (e.g., spaghetti with meatballs) to the menu because of their ready-made appeal for American diners.

An Italian restaurant renaissance has been percolating in the East Village for a decade. While pricey uptown Italians grabbed the spotlight, microcafés with simple names like **Max and Frank** flourished south of 14th Street, winning over nabies with simple, cheap, and often innovative food. The first of these was **Il Bagato**, a place that made the twin discoveries that you could run a restaurant with the tiniest of kitchens, and that customers were willing to come to a joint just off Avenue B if they thought it hip enough.

LOOK FOR:

arancine *Sicilian rice balls*

bagna caôda *Piedmontese garlic-anchovy dip for raw vegetables*

bistecca alla fiorentina *grilled Chianina steak slicked with olive oil*

bocconcini *little balls of fresh mozzarella*

bottarga *dried mullet or tuna roe*

braciola *Calabrian beef rolled around a filling and stewed*

bresaola *Lombardian beef cured like prosciutto*

calamari *squid*

cannoli *pastry shell stuffed with sweetened ricotta*

carpaccio *thin shaved raw meat or fish*

crespelle *crepes with a sweet or savory filling*

crostini *toast with topping*

crudo *Venetian sashimi*

eggplant rollatini *baked ricotta-stuffed eggplant*

focaccia *thick flatbread with many regional variations*

gelato *egg-enriched ice cream*

giardinera *tart Sicilian mixed-vegetable pickle*

gnocchi *small dumplings made with potato, bread crumbs, or flour and ricotta*

lardo *cured pork fat*

minestrone *"big soup" of macaroni and veggies*

mortadella *large-circumference pork sausage with chunks of lard*

mostarda *Cremonese chunky relish of sugar-cured fruits in mustard*

panelle special *small sandwich of chickpea raviolis from Palermo*

panzanella *Tuscan bread salad*

pasta e fagioli *pasta and bean soup*

ribollita *Tuscan bread soup*

scungilli *conch*

soppressata *air-cured pork salami*

straccetti *Roman eggdrop soup*

tartufo *truffle*

torta al testo *Umbrian flatbread*

tortelli   *elongated sacklike ravioli*

tortellini   *small filled pasta shaped like Venus'*
   navel

tramezzini   *crustless sandwich*

vastedda   *Sicilian spleen sandwich*

vitello tonato   *Piedmontese veal with tuna sauce*

Founded in most cases by Italian immigrants, these East Village novo-Italian cafés effortlessly blend modern fare from several regions with Neapolitan-American standards.

The restaurant success story of the new millennium is the Italian wine bar. By my count, we now have nearly 30 to choose from, mainly in downtown Manhattan and in various Brooklyn neighborhoods. As far as I know, none have yet failed. The earliest examples, like 'ino, were inspired by Milanese quick-food establishments, concentrating on pan-Italian snacks that went well with wine, mainly panini and platters of cold meats and cheeses. Eventually, menus became both more specialized and more ambitious. Illustrating the first principle, there are now two places — **D.O.C. Wine Bar** in Williamsburg and **Assenzio** in the East Village — that concentrate on Sardinian fare, scooped with the crisp flatbread eaten by shepherds called o pane carasau. In the latter category, the most ambitious so far is **Giorgione**, which has extended its menu to include raw oysters, imaginative antipasti, small pizzas, and a short list of pastas and main courses, with nary a panini in sight. Can it still be called a wine bar if it quacks like a restaurant?

Heroes

CATENE DELI ☆ 🐟
237 9th Street, Brooklyn, 718-788-0929 The arrival of your hero may be delayed by a lively discussion of an *Odd Couple* episode — quick, what were the names of Felix's kids? — and you can join in if you're old enough to remember. If not, it's still worth the wait. The signature sandwich of this ancient deli is the fried calamari hero, made of breaded squid cooked to order and generously heaped on a demi-baguette. Your choice of tomato sauce: sweet, medium, or hot. This is New World Italian food at its lushest and most creative. Other Sicilian holdovers include a very vinegar giardinera salad.

126

HOT ITALIAN ROAST BEEF HEROES

Sylvia Carter once told me that, decades ago, what beach-bound Brooklynites craved was not Coney Island franks or Brighton Beach knishes, but hot roast beef sandwiches. After spending years doggedly investigating this phenomenon, I can happily report that a series of antique establishments still thrive, strategically located on the borough's ocean approaches. Several are worth seeking out for their own sake any season of the year. Though gravy and mozzarella on a hot roast beef sandwich may sound weird, this treatment is standard in maritime Brooklyn.

CLEMENTE'S ✯ ✯

138 Avenue T, Brooklyn, 800-427-0556 Clemente's remains a neighborhood butcher shop, so that you have to pass Italian sausage, pork loin, and steaks pinwheeled around a filling of ricotta to reach the sandwich counter. The roast beef hero might be Brooklyn's best, and an astonishingly good deal. It's made with a chewy semolina loaf pummeled with thin-sliced roast beef veined with fat and still pink in the middle. The edges of the meat are slightly caramelized. The standard presentation involves no mustard, no mayo — but plenty of warm brown gravy that, canned or not, is pretty damn good. And no cheese. Wear a raincoat to eat this beauty.

DEFONTE'S SANDWICH SHOP ✯ ✯ 🖋

379 Columbia Street, Brooklyn, 718-855-6982 Founded by longshoreman Nick Defonte 80 years ago and now run by his grandson, Defonte's is one of Brooklyn's premier Italian hero shops, offering thirds and halves of sandwiches made from a crusty two-foot loaf. The roast beef is justifiably revered, but even better is the combo, advertised on a placard over the counter, that features wafer-thin fried eggplant and fresh mozzarella in addition to beef. The flavor of the eggplant blossoms in your mouth long after you've tasted the beef and cheese. Named after the patriarch, Nick's special is a heap of cold cuts, cheese, eggplant, hot peppers, lettuce, tomato, and pickled veggies so thick that you'll be hard pressed to wrap your mouth around it.

JACKIE'S DELICATESSEN ✯

3522 Avenue S, Brooklyn, 718-339-6556 Brooklyn roast beef heroes is a bona fide genre unto itself with enough variations to keep an ethnologist busy. Driving back from a softball game in Marine Park, I stumbled on Jackie's, where a line of eager guys poised on the balls of their feet await your order. The beef is homemade, and fantastic when matched with fresh mozzarella on a hot garlicky baguette in the "Roast Beef Grand Slam."

JOHN'S DELI ☆ ☆
2033 Stillwell Avenue, Brooklyn, 718-372-7481
Brooklyn's premier beach-going thoroughfare, Stillwell Avenue, is home to John's Deli. Favoring weekend beach-goers, the roast beef hero is offered Thursday, Friday, Saturday, and Sunday, assembled using a superior demi-baguette with an admirable crust. The beef is sliced from what looks like a Boar's Head roast, and then cooked to the mildest pink in a hot-water bath. Mozzarella several notches above the usual pizza cheese is welded to the sandwich as a first step, then dark gravy is flowed over it.

ROCKY'S ☆ ☆ ☆
2950 Avenue R, Brooklyn, 718-375-6137 When I did a piece on Brooklyn roast beef heroes, I didn't expect to find a place better than Clemente's. But then I hadn't been to Rocky's. It, too, is a meat market that makes heroes at the back of the store. I came upon Rocky himself on a Saturday afternoon carving up a fresh roast beef of smallish circumference, and I asked him to fix a hero in his usual manner. The beef — sliced thick, barely rimmed with fat, and tender as all get-out — was piled on a good Italian baguette, and slices of American cheese were layered thereon. Finally, salt and a mist of finely ground black pepper were blown over the sandwich. Spectacular!

ROLL N ROASTER ☆
Emmons Avenue and Nostrand Avenue, Brooklyn, 718-769-6000 While I don't exactly recommend the roast beef sandwich here — it's a little too much in the Arby's vein — this place, with its barnlike premises, represents one of the most unusual fast-food ideas ever spawned, and its continued presence in Sheepshead Bay is a monument to something, though I'm not sure what. This place probably doesn't merit its one star, but going there is enough of an adventure, and the prices are supercheap.

CROSBY CONNECTION ★ 🍅

172 Crosby Street, Manhattan, 212-677-8444 Founded by a Jersey ex-cop, this narrow encampment features sandwiches and little else, dispensed under garden umbrellas beside a snatch of suburban wooden fence, as the sandwich makers trade pleasantries with their lined-up clientele. No big surprises, other than a choice of excellent breads, fine cold cuts leaning toward the Italian, and mild innovations of the sort you might not even notice, like ricotta on a meatball hero, fresh basil leaves in unexpected places, and generous add-ons at no extra charge.

FAICCO'S ★ ★

260 Bleecker Street, Manhattan, 212-243-1974 Improvising within the hallowed canon of the Italian hero, Village pork store Faicco's takes advantage of their superior access to cold cuts to create the city's most formidable hero. With a flick of the knife, the crusty loaf is laid open, then successively piled with San Daniele prosciutto, hot cappicola, Genoa salami, house-made soppressata, fresh mozzarella, pickled red peppers, lettuce, and tomato. The $10 dreadnought easily feeds two.

JOEY'S COLD HEROES ★ ★ ★

554 Morris Avenue, Bronx, 718-993-1211 Italian heroes on excellent bread are Joey's forte, with a selection of cold cuts unrivaled in the commercial area known as The Hub, and perhaps in the entire Bronx. When you order the special ($3.75), you get good Virginia ham, Italian salami, and provolone that doesn't taste like rubber — an excellent combo, especially if you indulge in some of the extra add-ons displayed in the glass case, including thin floppy slices of eggplant, sautéed onions, or pickled hot peppers.

MONTE'S ★

156 Avenue O, Brooklyn, 718-259-1500 Isolated in a residential neighborhood, and nearly impossible to find, Brooklyn's most beloved sandwich parlor occupies a narrow nondescript storefront, and only an official city street sign outside — "Monte's Heroes Expressway" — lets you know that powerful forces champion the place. Choose either the Monte Deluxe — your choice of three meats (pick soppressata, mortadella, and hot cappicola) on a hero with fontinella cheese, lettuce, tomato, and pickled peppers or mushrooms — or that inscrutable Catskills favorite, roast pork on garlic bread with duck sauce.

WEST BRIGHTON ITALIAN GROCERY ★

1215 Castleton Avenue, Staten Island, 718-448-1168 This ancient salumeria, whose business card carries the cryptic inscription "Milk Farm," fabricates excellent hot and cold heroes on crusty bread, including one heaped with mortadella, cappicola, provolone, lettuce, and tomato, then inundated with wine vinegar and tasty olive oil. Watch carefully for the daily pasta specials, priced around $5. On a recent afternoon it was a perfect lasagna oozing equal proportions of mozzarella and ricotta, with a subtle Bolognese sauce, the finely ground meat taking a back seat to a tart, coarse tomato puree. The mild-tasting pasta fagioli soup wasn't bad, either.

Italian-American

BAMONTE'S RESTAURANT ☆ ⬻

32 Withers Street, Brooklyn, 718-384-8831 Founded in 1900, this restaurant was new when Italian immigrants from the town of Nola first carried the giglio through the streets of Williamsburg. When Robert Moses's BQE sundered the neighborhood five decades later, Bamonte's persisted beneath the superhighway as patrons retreated to the suburbs. Originating in Campania, the food is unabashedly Southern Italian: seafood-heavy and tomato-sauced, and yes, they probably have a tanker truck of the red stuff parked out back. Start your meal with an ancient concoction like clams casino or mussels marinara. In addition to seafood, the entrées favor veal, poultry, and pork. The homemade ravioli is absolutely superb: giant cheese-stuffed pillows bathed in sauce that remains light despite its ground-meat component.

BEATRICE INN ☆

285 West 12th Street, Manhattan, 212-929-6165 This ancient whitewashed restaurant recalls the day when everyone sought out their own Village Italian hideaway, and tried to keep it a secret. The food is straight out of the 1950s, from the iced shrimp cocktail, to the baked clams, both commendable, to a less-than-exciting fried calamari with a tomato sauce that will put you to sleep. For a second course, go with the homey pastas like a spaghetti with meat sauce and a doctrinaire lasagna oozing ground meat and cheese, and veer away from the heavier and more expensive meat courses.

CASA CALAMARI ☆ ⬻

1801 Bath Avenue, Brooklyn, 718-234-7060 The mascot of this Bath Beach Italian café is Squiddy the Squid, who appears high above the espresso bar in green neon like a deity. The lightly crusted specialty of the house — fried calamari — is a bit rubbery and the sauce is too bland — you've tasted better. Instead order the modest-sounding but magnificent escarole and beans, a green hummock rife with creamy white beans in a dense broth pungent with garlic. Many of the daily specials are also fantastic, including a Saturday dish of fried scallops on linguine with one of Brooklyn's best marinaras.

CHIANTI ✮ 🍽

8530 3rd Avenue, Brooklyn, 718-921-6300 Recommended by a beat cop as we desperately searched for a Norwegian restaurant that no longer existed, this Bay Ridge Italian's gimmick is "family style" — platters of pasta so big that you feel like a small child as they're delivered. The farfalle primavera was particularly good, hosed with cream and dotted with peas, carrots, and mushrooms. The chicken and veal platters were a profound anticlimax. Stick with the pastas!

EMILIO'S BALLATO ✮ 🍽 $

55 East Houston Street, Manhattan, 212-274-8881 This ancient Italian beanery has remade itself into a modern restaurant, with romantic flickering candles and a new green-and-buff sandpapered wall treatment. The food is much better than it needs to be, featuring generous appetizers of fried zucchini and red-sauced tripe. Pastas remain the center of the menu, and you need make no apology about treating them as your main course. Best are tagliatelle in a rich porcini sauce and spaghetti alla matriciani; in the Italian-American manner, there are four other choices featuring spaghetti. Our favorite secondi, hands down, are a stunning eight-chop rack of lamb and a humble platter of plump grilled sausages sided with broccoli rabe.

PASTA SAUCES

Alfredo *some combo of cream, butter, and cheese*

arrabiata *spicy tomato sauce (meaning angry, not Arab)*

boscaiola *woodsy tomato sauce with mushrooms*

carbonara *cream and bacon or porchetta*

con sarde *fennel and sardine sauce*

marinara *plain tomato sauce, used with seafood in the old country*

primavera *fresh vegetables*

puttanesca *sharp tomato sauce with olives, capers, and anchovies*

Siciliana *with eggplant and mozzarella, usually baked*

GIANDO ✮ ✮ 🐟 $

400 Kent Avenue, Brooklyn, 718-387-7000 If Tony Soprano were entertaining one of his paramours on the Brooklyn waterfront, you can be sure he'd go to Giando, a towering glass box sticking out among the decrepit warehouses and junkyards under the Williamsburg Bridge. You can't beat the East River panorama, nor the triple-thick veal chop wrapped in a thin strip of fat to preserve the moisture, as you watch the buses of Japanese tourists disgorge into the restaurant. The atmosphere and veal chop raise this place from one star to two stars.

JOE & JOE'S RESTAURANT ★ ⇒ 🍎
211 Church Avenue, Brooklyn, 718-854-3340 It's something of a shock to discover a Sicilian focacceria, even a vestigial one, in Kensington. Yet a steam table features silky broccoli rabe wreathed with caramelized onions, perfectly fried squid, penne with a nominal red sauce, even potato croquettes and rice balls. The balance of the establishment has evolved into a pizza parlor, and, more recently, a Northern Italian restaurant with an ambitious menu of chicken, veal, and fish. But further evidence of Joe's roots are found in the excellent square Sicilian slice, clumped with sauce and smothered in cheese.

L & B SPUMONI GARDENS ★ ★ 🍎
2725 86th Street, Brooklyn, 718-372-8400 OK, so this picturesque Bensonhurst old-timer (founded 1939) doesn't have the best Italian food in town, but the servings are voluminous and the price is right. My faves include eggplant Sicilian, a giant domed casserole of eggplant and ziti topped with browned mozzarella, and a garlicky vodka linguine dotted with peas and mushrooms. The perfect fried squid appetizer is enough to feed four, even though the "spicy" tomato sauce turns out to be bland. Though it seems out of character, the salad of oranges, walnuts, and baby lettuces is the second-best appetizer. Don't miss the spumoni ice cream, even if it's the dead of winter. Though often undercooked, the Sicilian pizza is notorious.

LENNY'S CLAM BAR ★ ⇒
161-03 Cross Bay Boulevard, Queens, 718-845-5100 Founded in 1974, this venerable Howard Beach seafood parlor looks like a radioactive jewel box on the horizon — just down the street from New York's most bizarre Starbucks — and features excellent stuffed clams, heaped with well-browned crumbs. The shrimp, mussels, calamari, and scungilli (conch) combinations are also worth contemplating, as are the pastas, especially Sicilian baked ziti, which should be sided with an order of the potent garlic bread. A hallway lined with celebrity photos leads to a painfully bright dining room, but if the weather's fine, sit on the deck that overlooks the Jamaica Bay canal known as Shellbank Basin.

LA LOCANDA ★
432 Graham Avenue, Brooklyn, 718-349-7800 That a nonhipster restaurant can still open in Williamsburg is a shock. This

132

ITALIAN MARKET

The **Arthur Avenue Retail Market**, at 2344 Arthur Avenue in the Belmont section of the Bronx, is one of the last operating covered markets in the city, built by Fiorello La Guardia in 1940 to get the pushcarts off the street. Stalls sell meat, cheese, fruits and vegetables, gardening supplies, dry pasta and pulses, coffee, and olives. Most products are unmistakably Italian; if you have any doubts, look up and see row upon row of small Italian flags under the lofty ceiling. Against the rear wall of the market is **Café al Mercato** (718-364-7681), with a seating area separated from the rest of the market by a low, faux-brick wall. Displayed in glass cases at this Sicilian spot are rice balls, crusty loaves of bread, roasted peppers, stuffed shells, and several rectangular pizzas, available by the slice, a recent collection including one with broccoli rabe against a backdrop of particularly good cheese. An olive slice had abundant green and black olives, chopped parsley, and a welcome dose of fresh garlic, while a tomato slice featured fresh tomatoes on a bed of cheese, with a sprinkle of dried oregano. If you're sliced-out, try the frittata, a crustless pie of eggs and vegetables cooked in the pizza oven.

nonconformist, decorated in Jersey Suburban, was founded by descendants of immigrants from the Italian town of Teggiano. Though the house tomato sauce is somewhat bland, there are many admirable nonna ("grandma-style") dishes, including an eggplant rollatini oozing good ricotta, deliciously plain escarole and beans, and spectacular linguine with broccoli rabe and garlic, a special some days. After dinner, hop across the street to enjoy the coffee and killer cannoli at Caffe Capri.

PATRICIA'S ★ ★ ⊘
1080 Morris Park Avenue, Bronx, 718-409-9069 Located in Morris Heights's alternative Little Italy, Patricia's is the quintessential outer-borough Italian restaurant, slinging excellent wood-oven pizzas and a roster of pastas that takes several minutes to contemplate, though the vast majority are tomato-sauced and cheesy, reprising most of the standards: carbonara, boscaiola, puttanesca, Siciliana, Alfredo, Sorrentina, primavera, and arrabiata (meaning angry, not Arab). If you can't make a choice, consider the daily specials, which often include more challenging fare. Tripe Gen-

ovese is a mass of tender cow stomach slicked with a tomato sauce and dotted with bacon, onions, and peas. Veal osso buco is similarly magnificent, served with polenta in a reduced barolo sauce.

LA PIAZZETTA ☆ ☆ 🐟 🐂

442 Graham Avenue, Brooklyn, 718-349-1627 The guazzetto alone would be enough to make me return to this Williamsburg Italian: mussels, clams, and scallops in a light tomato sauce laced with garlic, white wine, olive oil, and parsley. Croutons brushed with garlic and olive oil ring the bowl and gradually absorb the extra broth. We also enjoyed the featherweight potato gnocchi clumped with mozzarella. The soaring skylighted dining room, which appears to be a converted auto body shop, is oddly exhilarating.

RANDAZZO'S ☆ ☆ ☆ 🐟

2017 Emmons Avenue, Brooklyn, 718-615-0010 Sheepshead Bay's last remaining clam bar is, luckily, a paragon of its type: a fluorescently lit sea of Formica, where you can get them raw, fried, steamed, baked, chowdered, and sauced over pasta. The freshly shucked littlenecks are preferred over the cherrystones for their sweetness, and the New England chowder over the Manhattan for its briny depth of flavor. The fried clams are some of the best in town, accompanied by a powerful oregano-laced red sauce (pick hot or medium) that puts other dips to shame. Still, my favorite dish at this convivial working-class haven from the modern pretensions of the bay is pasta with lobster sauce.

ROMANO RESTAURANT ☆ ☆ ☆

7117-19 13th Avenue, Brooklyn, 718-232-5226 Built in an era when Rome was synonymous with Romance, the decor is right out of *Roman Holiday*: buckets of artificial flowers, acres of smoky marble, and masses of tiny white Christmas lights that hang from the ceiling like patriarchal beards in a Renaissance painting. A statue of Julius Caesar gestures approvingly at dating couples holding hands over bottles of Chianti. To further the illusion that you're dining in Rome, there's spediano. Not to be confused with the Sicilian shish kebabs of the same name, the Roman version is a lush double-decker mozzarella sandwich the size of a small dog, which is dipped in beaten egg and fried. I suppose fettuccine Alfredo is nominally Roman, too, created by restaurateur Alfredo Di Lelio in 1914 for a languishing postpartum spouse. The "homemade ravioli" ($10) is a particular delight, stuffed with crushed broccoli rabe. The baked ziti Siciliana with eggplant and melted cheese is another favorite. If you add a side of the intense garlic bread, the portions are enough for two or three.

"Focacceria" sounds like a trendy Tuscan bakery, but in parts of Brooklyn it denotes an old-fashioned Sicilian eatery specializing in snacks that can be eaten standing up, including short dishes of vegetables and seafood, and, especially, sandwiches made with seeded rolls called focaccia. Flooded with Sicilian immigrants in the 1950s, Bensonhurst boasts the biggest concentration. **Gino's Focacceria** (7118 18th Avenue, Brooklyn, 718-232-9073) exudes a glow that seems to come from the profusion of fresh vegetables heaped up inside: strips of breaded zucchini, stuffed artichokes, broccoli rabe sautéed in garlic, well-oiled fava beans, and a tart pickle called giardinera. The seafood selection is nearly as attractive, but the signature at Gino's is vastedda, a marvelous sandwich that piles boiled cow spleen on a split focaccia, avalanches it in snowy ricotta, then adds coarsely grated parmesan. Spleen? Pretend it's liver. **Caravello's** (2313 86th Street, Brooklyn, 718-946-5700) crouches in the shadow of the elevated D; the outside looks like a pizzeria, but penetrate deeper into the Formica interior and find a steam table offering a few dishes of real distinction. Powerful flavors of onion and garlic infuse a wan pork and potato stew, while the tomato-drenched lasagna is appealingly whomped with garlic. **Joe's of Avenue U** (287 Avenue U, Brooklyn, 718-449-9285) is like a 1960s diner, with booths large enough to accommodate extended families, who drift in Saturday afternoons to graze among old friends. The pasta con sarde (Friday and Saturday only) is spectacular: bucatini heaped with sardines roughly mashed with fennel, pignoli, and currants. Spoon in the toasted bread crumbs to form a thick sauce. At 96, **Ferdinando's** (151 Union Street, Brooklyn, 718-855-1545) is the oldest and most picturesque of the Brooklyn focaccerias, retaining its pot-bellied stove and ancient vastedda-making setup. More popular among its patrons is "panelle special," a sandwich of faintly smoky chickpea fritters, the perfect complement to the sharp grated cheese. Manhattan has a focacceria, too, appropriately named **La Focacceria** (128 1st Avenue, Manhattan, 212-254-4946). The present menu is vastly expanded over that of the original location, near the corner of 12th Street and 1st Avenue. It now provides one of the cheapest Italian meals in the East Village, though the food is of notoriously uneven quality. The contraption for making vasteddi — a shallow pan of oil for frying the cheese and spleen — is still the focal point of the restaurant, and the vasteddi are superb.

TONY'S & ELENA RISTORANTE ☆ ☆

7206 New Utrecht Avenue, Brooklyn, 718-331-7573 This daytime-only lunch counter is a blast from the 1950s, with its undulating beige counter and menu divided evenly between American diner food and Italian specialties. Though they make a good hamburger, spring instead for one of the heroes, like meatball Parmesan or, even better, pepper and eggs. Best pasta is cheese ravioli with the odd accompaniments of both meat sauce and meatballs, a protein orgy. Organ meat fans demand tripe in tomato sauce ladled over a big plate of linguine. Bonus: the hard-working espresso machine in the corner.

TRATTORIA MULINO ☆ ☉

133 5th Avenue, Brooklyn, 718-398-9001 A real contrast with the pretentious and expensive Tuscan-style restaurants of upscale Brooklyn, Trattoria Mulino highlights Neapolitan cooking of the sort that dominated the borough for a century, delivered in generous servings and atrociously misspelled on the menu. Manicotti is a pair of pasta cylinders bulging with spinach and fresh ricotta, topped with tomato sauce and melted mozzarella; grilled shrimp, refreshingly simple, lolls on a bed of arugula; while Sicilian calamari is a generous heap of well-braised squid served over linguine, reminding me of a similar dish at Babbo. The decor is deliciously unhip.

VALDIANO ☆ ☆ ✐

659 Manhattan Avenue, Brooklyn, 718-383-1707 The reclining statue of Saint Cono — who waves at diners from the top of the china cupboard — is your tip-off that the proprietors hail from the hilltop town of Teggiano, Campania. Amid a flock of predictable dishes, there are a few amazing ones. Penne all' arrabiata smothers the pasta in a hearty tomato sauce spiked with arugula and thick slices of the long green chile prized in the region. Stewed with sausage and white beans, a side of escarole makes a great shared appetizer. The restaurant is sometimes mobbed in the early evenings — so eat fashionably late.

136

VENICE RESTAURANT ☆ ☆ ☆ 🐟

772 East 149th Street, Bronx, 718-585-5164 Founded a half century ago by three guys from the Italian island of Ponza, 50 kilometers south of Rome, Venice reflects the island's culinary heritage with splendidly prepared seafood. Best of all is a conch (scungilli) salad, generously heaped over lettuce, tomatoes, and pickled vegetable giardinera. Also don't miss the succulent baked clams, stuffed with bland bread crumbs that don't interfere with the taste of the bivalves — which are scintillatingly fresh due to the proximity of the Hunt's Point Market. Pizzas are another strong point, Neapolitan style with a perfect mix of crispness, good cheese, and piquant tomato sauce.

VERONICA RISTORANTE ITALIANO ☆ 🍅

240 West 38th Street, Manhattan, 212-764-4770 Get there early if you want a seat at this venerable, lunch-only cafeteria in the garment center. The long counter presents a daunting array of choices, including nearly every Italian dish you've ever heard of. The linguine under the shrimp scampi is miraculously firm, with five jumbo shrimp well-coated with olive oil, garlic, and bread crumbs. Though many of the selections are swamped with red sauce, everything isn't red and dead — they do wonders with cream, veal stock, and pesto; if none of these appeal to you, there are plenty of salads and sandwiches, as well.

Osteria, Trattoria, and Locandi

BASSO EST ☆ ☆

198 Orchard Street, Manhattan, 212-358-9469 How did the East Village end up with so many great cheap Italian restaurants? In case you're keeping track, here's another one. Occupying a former taqueria, Basso Est nominally originates in the remote mountainous region of Abruzzo, and offers fettuccine with wild boar sauce to prove it. But check the pasta specials, too, since you might luck out and find them serving sacoletti, little pasta purses filled with roast peppers and smoked mozzarella — a ravioli I'm convinced the restaurant invented — deposited in a delicious butter sauce rife with fresh sage leaves.

BREAD TRIBECA ☆ ☆ 🐟 $

301 Church Street, Manhattan, 212-334-8282 BREAD 20 Spring Street, Manhattan, 212-334-1015 NoLita's cramped panini palace Bread has birthed a new place bigger and airier than its parent. The menu, too, is more ambitious. Reading like a greatest hits of trattoria dining, it deploys a wood-burning oven that perfumes the room and turns out products that range from cheese focaccia, to whole roast branzino stuffed with rosemary, to octopus that comes tossed with fingerling potatoes in a delicious salad. There's something for everyone, except when it comes to the wine list — which could use more choices, especially in the lower price ranges. On the positive side — the service is unusually friendly and solicitous.

CELESTE ☆ ☆ ⊘
502 Amsterdam Avenue, Manhattan, 212-874-4559 One came wrapped in juniper ash, another had been cured with saffron, while a third was dropped into a sterile pit and aged 100 days. "And I aged it for another month," noted the proprietor, who turned out to be a cheese fanatic. You're doing yourself a disservice if you don't try one of the amazing all-Italian cheese plates, which come sided with little smears of homemade compotes and flavored honeys. Wood-oven pizzas, pastas, nut-crusted chicken cutlets, fried fish, cured meats, and salads complete the menu at this Upper West Side trattoria, where you can eat very well for $25.

DA ANDREA ☆
557 Hudson Street, Manhattan, 212-367-1979 The warm octopus appetizer really stands out at this modern Village Italian, tossed with cubes of potato in a light pesto dressing, as does the vinegary salad of cucumber, tomato, and onion mantled with toasted bread crumbs. Dating couples have already discovered this dark and intimate retreat, pleasantly low on decor. Entrées of lamb shank sided with mushroom-dotted potatoes and zuppa di pesce with five types of seafood are also fab.

FELIDIA ☆ ☆ ☆ $
243 East 58th Street, Manhattan, 212-758-1479 The two-decade-old midtown Italian with an Istrian twist has remained popular based on its near-perfect pastas, and its connections with restaurateurs Joe Bastianich and Mario Batali. But on a recent visit, I was knocked out by a simple octopus salad, tender white swatches bedded on a row of creamy potatoes, punctuated by sweet grape tomatoes and black olives that were wrinkled like a thumb too long in the bathtub.

GALLO NERO ☆ ☆ $
192 Bleecker Street, Manhattan, 212-475-2355 While most downtown Tuscan trattoria make a half-hearted stab at authentic decor, this self-proclaimed osteria, by means of painted tiles and rustic wood furnishings, succeeds in convincing me I'm steps away from Florence's Duomo. The mixed cold cut affettati platter is a

138

good start to your meal, or a bowl of ribollita, the splendid bean-and-bread soup. Proceed to the perfect crespelles, semolina crepes wrapped around spinach and ricotta, done to a bubbly brown. While the lamb stew was a little boring, the salmi in coniglio, a quarter rabbit smeared with an herbal sweet-and-sour sauce called agrodolce, was as exciting as any I've tasted.

GRANO ☆

21 Greenwich Avenue, Manhattan, 212-645-2121 At this offspring of Borgo Antico, the rabbit is exemplary — swathed in a thick, dark sauce and heaped with polenta, sided by barely steamed baby carrots. A similar bunny ragout is also poured over papardelle, but king of the pastas is a spaghettilike tagliolini, blackened with squid ink and dotted with intensely flavorful baby clams.

LOCANDA VINI & OLII ☆ ☆ ⌖ $

129 Gates Avenue, Brooklyn, 718-622-9202 A "locanda" is a type of Italian country restaurant a little fancier than an osteria, and this obscure corner of Clinton Hill does indeed have a rural air. Occupying a former drugstore, and retaining many of the old fixtures, Locanda has a diverse menu, with entire sections devoted to house-cured olives, Italian cheeses, salads, individual appetizers, and ganged-up platters intended for sharing, littered with unfamiliar Italian terms in quotes. If the food weren't so good, the menu would seem like a snow job. Starters include a seafood charcuterie platter of octopus soppressata and tuna salami. Pastas are refreshingly light, and served in small enough portions so you can do the classic antipasti-pasta-secondi progression. My favorite is eggplant ravioli — irregularly shaped, stuffed with a mild vegetable puree, and served in an oily dice of fresh tomatoes. The best entrée is astonishingly good, a Piedmontese steak "tagliata" (which just means "sliced"), planks of pink charred meat standing like dominoes around a pile of arugula.

LUPA ☆ ☆ ☆ $

170 Thompson Street, Manhattan, 212-982-5089 In a city gone crazy for the rustic pleasures of Tuscan food, and still carrying a torch for Neapolitan, Lupa adjusts the geographic focus to Rome, delivering bold flavors like fennel, lemon peel, mint, anchovy, raisin, and, of course, garlic. Among the Roman offerings are an unforgettable potatoless gnocchi, and a fettuccine Alfredo profound in its buttery and cheesy simplicity. Patrician, too, is an oxtail alla vaccinara ("butcher's style") sloughing handsome quantities of meat and fat into a sweet-and-sour gravy, finalized with a spray of toasted pignoli. And when you order pollo alla diavolo, don't expect it to come Florentine-style, smeared with a paste of onions, garlic, and parsley. Instead, Lupa paves its crisp-skinned

version with crushed black peppercorns, a killer variation on southern fried chicken.

MALATESTA TRATTORIA ☆ ☆ ⌀

649 Washington Street, Manhattan, 212-741-1207 The
menu offers simple Northern Italian fare with a focus on Emilia-
Romagna. One evening a delectable special of risotto con funghi
was creamy with grana, a lighter, sweeter cousin of Parmesan, and
underscored with white wine and mushrooms. As befits a restaurant with its origins in the Italian breadbasket, baked goods excel.
Most remarkable is piadina, a regional flatbread that's like a flour
tortilla, only stiffer. It comes warm from the oven and folded over a
choice of four fillings. Predictably, the foremost pasta is tagliatelle
al ragù, airy ribbons in a hopelessly rich sauce of ground meat,
butter, and disintegrating vegetables. You will recognize it as Bolog-
nese sauce.

MAX ☆ ☆ ⌀

**51 Avenue B, Manhattan, 212-539-0111 MAX CAFÉ 1262
Amsterdam Avenue, 212-531-1210** The menu at these tersely
named Italians is largely based on the recipes of the proprietor's
mother, and the surprise favorite is a sleek, ocarina-shaped individual meat loaf that conceals a sliced egg and wad of mozzarella.
There's also a fine beet salad geometrically arrayed on the plate
with avocado and goat cheese, and a meatless, beanless, and
pasta-free minestrone that manages to do the job anyway. The majority of the menu, however, is devoted to bargain-priced pastas, like
a wonderful rigatoni Siciliana chunked with eggplant and cheese.

OTTO ☆ ☆ ☆ ⌀

1 5th Avenue, Manhattan, 212-995-9559 Ultra-thin-crust pizzas are the forte of this casual joint in the former Clementine's
space, now done up to look like an Italian railroad station — in the
front part, at least. The pies run the gamut from the conventional
(margherita made with buffalo mozzarella) to the unusual (house-
cured lard strips scented with nutmeg). The menu goes way beyond
pizzas, though, including cold pungent vegetable preparations,
cured meats and fish, salads, bruschetta, and a fritter of the day.
The wine list is exclusively Italian and fills three pages. Don't miss
the olive oil gelato for dessert, sprinkled with sea salt.

PEPE VERDE ☆ ⌀

**559 Hudson Street, Manhattan, 212-255-2221 PEPE ROSSO
149 Sullivan Street, Manhattan, 212-677-4555 PEPE GIALLO
253 10th Avenue, Manhattan, 212-242-6055** It's rare to find a
café where a new language is being invented, but that's the case
at the wonderful Pepes, where the Italian managers and Mexican
cooks have developed a patois halfway between Spanish and Ital-

ian. This synergy also extends to food, especially the amazing chicken, bacon, and guacamole hero, a personal favorite. It represents one of the most righteous uses for boring chicken breast. The pastas here are also excellent, made on the spot and bursting with garlic and fresh herbs. Enjoy soccer and motorcycle racing on the tube as you wait.

PEPOLINO ☆ ☆ $

281 West Broadway, Manhattan, 212-966-9983 Founded by a couple of refugees from the famous Florence restaurant Il Cibreo, which presents a revisionist approach to the cooking of Tuscany, with good results. So, too, does Pepolino offer a vegetable flan called sformato, and a wonderfully sludgy squid dish called inzimeno. Pastawise, go for the eggy tubes called garganelli, served in a peppery broth, or the featherweight gnocchi, that seem ready to float out of the bowl like little helium balloons. An altogether convivial space, whether you sit downstairs or up.

ROBERTO'S ☆ ☆ ☆

632 East 186th Street, Bronx, 718-733-9503 Obscurely berthed in the Bronx's Belmont section, Roberto's boasts a facade that looks like a ship's prow. Culinarily, this no-reservations place turns its back on its Arthur Avenue brethren. But that doesn't mean the chef ignores local markets, where ricotta and mozzarella are sold within minutes of manufacture, dozens of olive oils fill the shop windows, and fresh lamb, rabbit, and kid carcasses hang in butcher shops. Taking full advantage, the mozzarella in insalata di bocconcini has the ethereal fluffiness of just-made. The little balls play hide-and-seek among roast red peppers, slices of soppressata, cured olives, and sun-dried tomatoes in a salad so generous that four of us shared it as an appetizer. Regulars never open the regular menu, rather, they gaze in wonder at the specials chalkboard propped on the window sill. One day there were pieces of duck sausage cavorting with artichoke hearts and porcinis in a light tomato puree. Another time, there was an herby roast rabbit, surrounded by potatoes and basting juices.

TASTY PIZZA AND PASTA RISTORANTE ☆ ☆ ～

1709 86th Street, Brooklyn, 718-331-7100 You might not expect an innovative Italian restaurant to be yoked to a Bensonhurst pizza joint of no particular distinction, but there it is, part of a culinary empire that also includes an adjacent bagel shop, home of the big wheel bagel and the flagel. Delicious inventions at the restaurant include a perfect Greek-leaning grilled octopus salad heaped with garlic and a wonderful take on linguine with white clam sauce that features — in addition to a mother lode of chopped fresh clams — a touch of cream and a ring of plump shrimp around the periphery.

141

TRATTORIA PAOLINA ☆ ☆ ⓒ

175 Avenue B, Manhattan, 212-253-2221 Despite being the fourth in a series of Emilia-Romagnan restaurants south of 14th Street, Paolina manages to stake out new culinary territory. At this new and whimsically decorated restaurant (up near the ceiling lurks a miniature multicar pile-up that would do Godard's *Weekend* proud, as the blockheaded kickers of a Foosball machine have disported themselves around the room in unexpected places), you can get the usual piadinas and tagliatelle al ragù, but there's also fagotti — blistered fried pies loaded with ham, cheese, mushrooms; and maialino al latte — a substantial pork filet browned in oil, then braised in milk. Best of all is the breaded chicken cutlet named after Italy's favorite superhighway: cotolette autostrada. Sit outside on the comfy deck chairs and watch the world go by.

VIA EMILIA ☆ ☆ ☆

240 Park Avenue South, Manhattan, 212-505-3072 Grounded in the rustic cooking of Emilia-Romagna and named after the road that connects its greatest food destinations, this restaurant excels at appetizers like tortellini in brodo, little stuffed pasta curls said to resemble a woman's belly button, deposited in a rich chicken stock; and gnocco fritto, a plate of good cold cuts sided, in the quirky manner of the region, with puffy trapezoidal fritters hot from the fat. Tortellini in several variations leads the pasta list, and among secondi, there's a fine thick pork chop, braciolona di maiale. Bravely, the wine list favors Lambruscos, the fizzy reds of the north.

LE ZOCCOLE ☆ ☆

95 Avenue A, Manhattan, 212-260-6660 A project of the gang that brought us Chelsea's Venetian trattoria Le Zie, the present premises are nominally dedicated to the propagation of cicchetti, the Northern Italian answer to Spanish tapas: short dishes of octopus, artichokes, beans, pickled fresh sardines, etc., pleasantly reeking of garlic and olive oil. The combination of 10 or more dishes is an excellent deal at $15.95, perfect snack food to go with the well-chosen and relatively inexpensive wine list. The full trattoria menu includes lots of pastas and secondi.

Pasticceria and Espresso Bars

CAFFE CAPRI ☆ ☆ ☆ ⓐ

427 Graham Avenue, Brooklyn, no phone There's no place I'd rather nurse an espresso than Caffe Capri, a charming Italian coffee shop that transplanted a little bit of glamorous Capri to Williamsburg in 1974, and never changed one bit thereafter. The shells are trucked in, but the ricotta filling is concocted on the spot, white as driven snow. The cannoli are filled when you order them, guaranteeing a supremely crunchy shell.

ESTRABAR ☆ ⓐ

186 Cypress Avenue, Brooklyn, 718-821-6080 Of course, to even qualify for the prestigious designation of best cannoli of the year, the shell must be filled right before your eyes just before the pastry is handed over the counter. The ricotta has to be fluffy, taste just-made, and be dotted with only a modest number of useless distractions like candied fruits and chocolate chips — the shell is responsible for providing the crunch, not the extraneous matter. This year the bronze cannoli goes to Estrabar, an excellent Italian espresso bar teetering on the Brooklyn-Queens border in a postage-stamp-size Sicilian neighborhood.

MADONIA BROTHERS BAKERY ☆ ☆ ⓐ

2348 Arthur Avenue, Bronx, 718-295-5573 Grab a cannoli — the rich ricotta filling is squirted into the shell when you order, so the pastry stays crunchy. Cookies are another forte in this busy, venerable bakery.

MONA LISA ☆ ⓐ

1476 86th Street, Brooklyn, 718-837-9053 The imposing stucco and orange tile facade is surmounted by a vignette portrait of — you guessed it — the Mona Lisa, but it can't hold a candle art-wise to the ceiling of the gelato parlor, painted with the most twisted Sistine Chapel rip-off imaginable, with Adam's torso twisted as if he'd been in an auto wreck. Much better than Louie G.'s, the gelato is Brooklyn's best, rich and fresh tasting. Favorites include sanguinella (blood orange) and a very intense coffee that would make a splendid breakfast. Avoid the pastry side of the establishment, however; there are better pastries to be found on nearly any block in Bensonhurst.

VENIERO'S PASTICCERIA ☆ ☆ ☆ ⓐ

342 East 11th Street, Manhattan, 212-674-4415 There's not a pastry shop in Little Italy, or Arthur Avenue for that matter, that can hold a candle to Veniero's Pasticceria, the East Village old-timer where, up until a few years ago, you could run in and buy a pastry just about anytime unimpeded. Nowadays, due to tourist inundation you have to plan your assault more carefully. The custard éclair is good as ever, crammed with thick egg custard and striped with a rich chocolate frosting that's more like fudge. The best way to get your feet wet here is with a box of eight or 10 miniature pastries, still miraculously cheap. The biscotti also rock, as does the wedding cake called zuppa inglese, a concoction of white cake, whipped cream, and rum, available by the slice.

Pizza

A SHORT HISTORY OF NEW YORK PIZZA

Pizza as we know it was invented in 1905 down on Spring Street, when Neapolitan immigrant Gennaro Lombardi fired up his coal oven to nearly 900 degrees and popped in the first pie. Though Gennaro's pizza had distant cousins in Naples — a pie created for Princess Margherita in 1889 was the first to use tomatoes and mozzarella — his new creation was far more cheesy and tomatoey, a substantial meal in itself that eventually came to be strewn with all sorts of toppings. One hundred years down the road you can still eat superb pizza at **Lombardi's,** still made in the same sainted oven. The clam pie is especially recommended — some say it has aphrodisiacal powers.

The charismatic Lombardi inspired his bakers to spin off their own pizza parlors. **John's** in Greenwich Village, **Patsy's** in East Harlem, and **Totonno Pizzeria Napolitano** in Coney Island were all founded in the 1920s and '30s by Lombardi alumni. All generate superb thin-crust pizzas with good mozzarella, but none of these places (with the exception of Patsy's northernmost storefront) sell slices, so bring friends or be prepared to eat a whole pie by yourself.

Though there have been imitations of this original style, most notably at **Joe and Pat's** in Staten Island, most New York pizza has evolved considerably from this model, with a conventional gas oven in the 500-degree range being substituted for the hotter coal oven. Twenty years ago there were virtually no

McDonald's and Burger Kings in the city, and citizens depended on the corner pizza parlor for fast food: two slices and a soda constituted the standard proletarian lunch. The gas ovens cooked the pies more slowly, so pizzas prepared therein could flaunt thick crusts and profuse toppings. According to journalist Jonathan Kwitny in *Vicious Circles*, the mob came to control the manufacture of pizza cheese (supplied by Al Capone in Fond du Lac, Wisconsin), and forced the neighborhood parlors to use the mediocre Wisconsin mozzarella. The ancient places like John's and Lombardi's were grandfathered out, however, and could still use locally made fresh mozzarella, as long as they never sold individual slices. Hence, according to Kwitny, John's still carries the warning "No Slices" on its awning to prevent fire bombing or other signs of Mafia displeasure.

Independent neighborhood parlors are thankfully still an important feature of the New York landscape, even though terrible national outfits like Domino's and Little Caesar's have tried to horn in. One of my favorite local parlors is the sweet-sauced **Stromboli's** in the East Village; further uptown in the Flatiron district, **Bella Napoli** (favoring an herby sauce) and **Pizza Supreme** near Penn Station (favoring a garlicky one). Way north in Riverdale **Denise Pizza** mounts a very refined slice with good cheese. In neighborhoods with a substantial Sicilian presence, often dating from the early 1950s, thicker-crust pies have come to be preferred. Known as Sicilian pizza, the slice is square rather than wedge-shaped. **L & B Spumoni Gardens** in Brooklyn's Gravesend is a notorious purveyor of these pies in a setting that feels like an outtake from *Grease*. The spumoni rocks, too. Better yet is the Sicilian slice at **Rose & Joe's** in Astoria, which is not a pizzeria at all, but an Italian bakery. Their luscious square only finds its equal at **Krispy Pizzeria** in Dyker Heights, Brooklyn, where the nonna ("grandmother") pie comes festooned with some of the best fresh mozzarella in town.

Long isolated from the other boroughs, Staten Island has developed its own distinctive style of pizza, halfway between thin crust and thick. Meriting the encomium "low dive," **Denino's** has been slinging

Staten Island pizza and incredible scungilli salad for over 50 years, and is also a great place to sit and drink beer. Another sterling producer of this style is **Nunzio's,** located a stone's throw from the beach.

Recently, upscale pizza parlors have begun looking back to Italy for their model of what a pizza should be. It never occurs to them that contemporary pizza in Italy has been partly inspired by the worldwide popularity of American pizza. **La Pizza Fresca** turns out thin-crust pies in a wood-burning oven, and is actually certified by some crank organization (editor's note: the Associazione della Vera Pizza Napoletana) as the producer of a true Italian product. This certification shouldn't dissuade you from enjoying their pizza, though the high price tag might. Also harkening back to Italia is **La Villa**, which offers a fresh-mozzarella nonna focaccia gobbed with fresh garlic. Another oddity served there originates in Abruzzo, though it's named after Rome: the Romano, a double crust rustically stuffed with potatoes, pepperoni, and Italian sausage. Gutbomb time!

New York being New York, there are all sorts of oddball pizzas invented by crackpots who don't realize there's a fine line between genius and insanity. **O'Neill's** serves up a pizza with stunningly high-quality ingredients in the middle of an OTB parlor: down your pie while watching the ponies run on dozens of TV screens. Devotees of chowhound.com are obsessed with the pizza at **DiFara's**, painstakingly created in a conventional oven by aging master Domenico DeMarco, who will fiddle with your pie endlessly before he turns it over to you. The artichoke slice is legendary. **Otto** caused a sensation this year when it introduced pizzas with a thin crust something like a big cracker, though this type is standard in parts of central Italy, which once again proves there's no such thing as "real Italian pizza." Toppings run from the fairly normal (buffalo mozzarella) to the bizarre (lardo — strips of cured pork fat). Also on the very frontier of experimentation is **Famous Pizza** of Jackson Heights, where there's never been anyone named Ray. Their Indo-Pak pizza begins with the usual cheese and tomato sauce, but not content to stop there, the baker rains on onions, fragrant masala powder, and fresh green chiles, making the pie scaldingly hot as well as delicious. Hell, I like it so much that I'm willing to take one back to Italy and certify that it's the only true New York pizza.

BELLA NAPOLI ★ ⏺

130 Madison Avenue, Manhattan, 212-683-4510 One of the best neighborhood pizza parlors in town, using an herby tomato sauce on the pies.

BRICK OVEN GALLERY ★ ⏺

33 Havemeyer Street, Brooklyn, 719-963-0200 Topped with the legendary mozzarella made by a little old lady in her garage on Metropolitan Avenue, the splendid pizza puttanesca more than lives up to its name, with a peppery, lip-curling brininess that would make a sailor curse with pleasure. "Peter's Favorite" is another good showcase for the crust, heaped with arugula, prosciutto, and shavings of Parmesan, but skip the Eddie's 1960 Brooklyn, a soggy and cheeseless pie smothered with a too-sweet tomato sauce. The outdoor tables and list of cheap decent wines make this a very pleasant summer-evening venue.

CORONA PIZZA ★ ⏺

51-23 108th Street, Queens, 718-271-3736 Some claim this joint serves the best pizza in Queens. I go for the splendid meatball Parmesan hero, planted on a profusely seeded bun, with plenty of melted mozzarella, a tart tomato sauce a little thicker than usual, and – their innovation – the meatballs sliced thin and evenly distributed along the length of the sandwich. The pizza is OK, too, and those made in the brick oven ("il forno") deploy the same wonderful cheese. For your convenience in completing the meal, the Lemon Ice King is right across the street. Now tell me: Why is it called meatball Parmesan, when the cheese is obviously mozzarella? Answer: In this case "Parmesan" refers to the city of Parma, not the cheese.

DENINO'S ★ ★ ★ ⏺

524 Richmond Avenue, Staten Island, 718-442-9401 Small surprise that Staten Island, where 40 percent of the population traces Italian roots, has some of best pizza in town, developed in isolation from its Manhattan and Brooklyn counterparts. Denino's turns out the superior pie on the island – topped with lush tomato sauce and creamy mozzarella. The crust is a bit thicker than usual, carefully browned but never charred, remaining light in texture. Also don't miss the cold scungilli (conch) salad.

DIFARA PIZZERIA ★ ★ ★ 🍎

1424 Avenue J, Brooklyn, 718-258-1367 The artichoke slice is every bit as good as its obsessed advocates claim. The freshly cooked vegetable is carefully laid on a perfect thin crust with two types of cheese by a dude who's become a Brooklyn legend, and the seedy premises only makes the slice tastier.

DRIGGS PIZZERIA ★ 🍎

558 Driggs Avenue, Brooklyn, 718-782-4826 The front is a pizzeria with all the usual stuff; in back is a dining room with plastic-covered tables and pictures of sports figures. The eats selected from a chalkboard over the kitchen are much better than you'd expect: ricotta-stuffed eggplant Parmesan and penne a la vodka, which comes in a light tomato sauce fortified with cream, blessedly light on the booze. But it would be a mistake to neglect the grub in the front part of the joint, especially the pizza tri-colore and the wonderful, retrograde meatball Parmesan hero.

FAMOUS PIZZA ★ ★ 🍎

75-12 37th Avenue, Queens, 718-205-5000 Not to be confused with the execrable Famous Ray's and their cheesy ilk, this Famous is champion of the individual, made-to-order pie. Most delectable is the Indo-Pak, topped with jalapeños, onions, and a complex and aromatic masala, and really quite amazing.

FORTUNATA'S ★ 🍎

65-26 Metropolitan Avenue, Queens, 718-456-4786 Bulging with good mozzarella and creamy ricotta, and flecked with bright green parsley, Fortunata's calzone is an oasis of culinary pleasure in Queens's cemetery zone (Goths take note). Four kinds of Sicilian slices (choose the one called "grandpa") clue you to the orientation of this miniature restaurant; there's a more ambitious menu and waiter service in a rear dining room.

LIL' FRANKIE'S ★ ★ 🍎

19 1st Avenue, Manhattan, 212-420-4900 This diminutive offspring of Frank's on 2nd Avenue is driven by a wood-burning oven that supposedly includes stone from Mount Vesuvius (who cares?) and reaches temperatures of nearly 900 degrees. The pizzas — 11 combos with a few specials — are thin-crusted, of irregular shape, and boast top-quality ingredients. The polpettine pie, littered with tiny meatballs and flavored with sage, is a particular favorite. Alternatives include a modest selection of roasted poultry, fish, and vegetables. Skip the pastas, which get mushy in the oven.

GIOVANNI'S ✕ ⚅

2343 Arthur Avenue, Bronx, 718-933-4141 This pizzeria specializes in brick-oven pies with an unusually thick crust, chunky tomato sauce, and great latitude in topping options. The same pies are cheaper if you get them made in the regular oven, but who would be so crazy?

JOE AND PAT'S ✕ ✕ ⚅ 🐟

1758 Victory Boulevard, Staten Island, 212-981-0887 Resurrected after a severe fire over the pizza oven, J & P's gives Denino's a run for its money as the isolated island's finest pizza parlor. The pie is thinner crusted, dotted with fresh mozzarella, and every bit as good as its prototypes at Lombardi's and Patsy's. Choose from dozens of toppings. My favorite is scungilli (conch) slagged with extra garlic. Soups like lentil and pasta fagioli are fab, and there's also a lengthy list of heroes — including one confusingly designated "submarine" — and a menu of pasta and seafood.

KRISPY PIZZERIA ✕ ✕ ⚅

7112 13th Avenue, Brooklyn, 718-748-5797 Among the Sicilian-leaning pizza parlors of Brooklyn neighborhoods like Bensonhurst, Bath Beach, and Dyker Heights, a current fad is the nonna ("grandmother") slice, which turns back the calendar by offering fresh mozzarella and crushed tomatoes, sometimes fresh, on a thick crust. The nonna at Krispy is superb, and I swear the cheese is only a few hours old when it's thrown on the pie.

LUCA LOUNGE ✕ ⚅

220 Avenue B, Manhattan, 212-674-9400 Pushing the northern verge of Avenue B's restaurant row almost to Stuy Town, this glorified pizza joint has one of the nicest backyard gardens in the East Village. Beyond the handful of excellent, thin-crust pizzas, the pickings are slim: a couple of salads, a slender cheese-and-fruit plate, tomato bruschetta. So stick with the wine and pizzas, the best of which is carciofi, topped with plenty of artichokes on a crust imbued with a smoky taste from the wood-fired oven.

O'NEILL'S ✕ ✕ ⚅

64-21 53rd Drive, Queens, 718-672-9696 Irish pizza may sound oxymoronic, or just plain moronic, but this Irish steak pub with an implanted OTB inside turns out some of the city's best pizza. We're not talking 900-degree, coal-fired pies like Lombardi's, but pizza turned out in a conventional oven with a roster of exemplary ingredients by an artisanal pizza impresario who knows how to coax maximum performance out of his equipment. You can watch the nags run and even blow a Hamilton or two as you down perfect slices. Finding this Maspeth institution — which I sought after seeing Mario Batali eating there in an OTB commercial — is half the fun.

PIE ★ ★ ⏱

124 4th Avenue, Manhattan, 212-475-4977 Each day a dozen oblong thin-crust pizzas are laid out on the counter like Turkish carpets. Make your choices and — snip, snip, snip — the portions are scissored, weighed by the pound, and arranged on a tray. On a recent afternoon, I tried the six best-looking pies: minced broccoli and cheese; salad with feta and green olives on tomato-sauced crust; potatoes, ricotta, walnuts, and rosemary; prosciutto and arugula; four cheeses; and finally, an oddball pie with potato, green chiles, prosciutto, and ricotta, inset with multiple sunny-side-up eggs.

LA PIZZA FRESCA ★ ★ ★ ⏱ $

31 East 20th Street, Manhattan, 212-598-0141 Lofty-ceilinged and skylighted, this handsome café highlights pizzas flash-cooked at high temperatures in a wood-burning brick oven, featuring toppings of scintillating freshness. Unfortunately, the prices will make you gasp. Pastas, salads, and desserts are also offered, but highest honors go to a pie: quattro stagione, topped with prosciutto, mushrooms, mozzarella, and artichoke hearts that never saw the inside of a can.

PIZZA SUPREME ★ ⏱

413 8th Avenue, Manhattan, 212-594-8939 Another great neighborhood pizza parlor, using a particularly garlicky tomato sauce. The best slice, however, is the cheeseless Sicilian Square.

ROSE & JOE'S ITALIAN BAKERY ★ ★ ⏱

22-40 31st Street, Queens, 718-721-9422 The square Sicilian slice is absolutely scrumptious — artfully smeared with a semi-chunky red sauce that's on the sweet side, clumped with good mozzarella, scattered with oregano. But good as the toppings are, the dough's the thing, cooking up light and airy, crisp on bottom and sides, with virtually no wasted "bone" (the humpy part). The slice brought back fond memories of Boston's North End, where pizza is sold out of bakeries, and folks line up to wait for the next pie.

SERAFINA FABULOUS PIZZA ★ ★ ⏱ $

1022 Madison Avenue, Manhattan, 212-734-3165 Eschewing coal, this place fires its brick oven with wood, which snuggles up to the pizza and gives it a magnificent smoky flavor. Like La Pizza Fresca, Serafina looks to Italy for its model, seeking to undo over a century of American pizza history. The crust is cracker thin, pleasantly charred in places, and sometimes lacking tomato sauce; uncooked ingredients like arugula and big shavings of Parmesan are often thrown on after the pizza emerges from the oven. Serafina has a breezy upper floor that furnishes sweeping views of the neighborhood.

STROMBOLI'S ☆ ⏻

83 St. Marks Place, Manhattan, 212-673-3691 For over a decade Stromboli was my late-night refuge. This East Village landmark usually has a fresh pie working on the counter, so you rarely get a reheated slice. The cheese is good, the sauce on the sweet side, and the crust so perfect I always eat the rind (also known as the "bone"), which would otherwise be discarded.

SULLIVAN STREET BAKERY ☆ ☆ ☆ ⏻

73 Sullivan Street, Manhattan, 212-334-9435 When I want pizza like I get in Tuscany and Umbria, I go to Sullivan Street, where simple flatbreads with single toppings like mushrooms, zucchini, and potatoes are cut into big rectangles and sold by weight. Nowhere in town is the relationship of dough to pie more apparent, with the possible exception of Rose & Joe's.

TOTONNO PIZZERIA NAPOLITANO ☆ ☆ ☆ ⏻

1524 Neptune Avenue, Brooklyn, 718-372-8606 Another old-timer prey to rumors of sliding downhill is Coney Island's Totonno Pizzeria Napolitano, located a couple of blocks inland from the beach in a neighborhood of auto body shops and rickety wooden houses. I'm happy to report that on a recent visit the pizza was still wonderful in all its sloppy glory, with a thin, charred crust, high-quality mozzarella in slices, and especially rich pepperoni. The pie is awash with a sauce that some may regard as too damp, but so what? Eat it with a fork. *Zagat* calls the staff rude, but to me, they're the soul of hospitality. Note: Pies only, open Wednesday through Saturday, dough runs out early in the evening.

LA VILLA ☆ ☆ ☆ ⏻

261 5th Avenue, Brooklyn, 718-499-9888; original locations, no wood oven: 6610 Avenue U, Brooklyn, 718-251-8030; 82-07 153rd Avenue, Queens, 718-641-8259 Pizza's the thing at this new branch of a Howard Beach place, whether you pick the focaccia di nonna (a "grandma's pizza" topped with house-made mozzarella and fresh garlic) or the Romano, a double-crust extravaganza stuffed with meats, cheese, and potatoes already roasted once in the wood-burning oven. The shareable antipasto platter ($8.50) is a particularly good deal, a vast assortment of grilled, pickled, and sun-dried vegetables, plus mozzarella, provolone, and olives. Among pastas, opt for anything done in that high-temp wood oven. The decor might have been borrowed from a Dallas strip mall.

VIVA HERBAL PIZZERIA ☆ ⌀

179 2nd Avenue, Manhattan, 212-42-8801 If "healthy" and "good" seem like contradictory pizza concepts, check out Viva Herbal Pizzeria. All offerings are vegetarian, and a third go all the way to vegan, discretely deploying faux cheese and soy sausage (not bad) as necessary. Most slices, which come on crusts of whole wheat, cornmeal, or spelt, are verdantly mounded with veggies. My favorite is the mozzarella-laced Mexicali, with onions, tomatoes, cilantro, and enough jalapeño peppers to fry your tongue. The strangest is ganja, incorporating garlic marinated in hemp oil, roasted hemp seeds, hemp-seed "nuts," and hemp/basil pesto. Deprived of THC, of course. Damn!

Wine Bars

AQUILONI ☆ ⌀

172 Avenue A, Manhattan, 212-777-9342 It was inevitable that 'ino would spawn a slew of hip Italian sandwich-and-wine shops downtown, though none has yet learned to make sandwiches as pristine and symmetrical. But Aquiloni beats its predecessor for sheer elbow-wagging comfort — with a corner premises offering a wonderful view of the street — and a couple of novelties you won't find elsewhere. One is a tramezzini of sliced egg, onion, and radish with a yummy herb mayonnaise, while another is a bruschetta of funky gorgonzola, green apples, nuts, and honey that probably ought to be a dessert.

ASSENZIO ☆ ☆

205 East 4th Street, Manhattan, 212-677-9466 Beginning with the crackling flatbread called pane carasau, the city's second Sardinian wine bar cordially promotes the foods beloved of the hulking isolated island: cold sliced porchetta, wild boar ragu, herbed suckling pig, goat cheese served with pears, and a salad featuring fennel, oranges, and pungent oil-cured olives. But the pleasant and relatively inexpensive Italian wine list neglects the island somewhat, though there's a Monica di Sardegna called Perdera that's among the best reds I've tasted this year. In summer, the entire front of the restaurant opens up to catch the East River breezes.

BAR VELOCE ☆ ⌀

175 2nd Avenue, Manhattan, 212-260-3200; 17 Cleveland Place, 212-966-7334 The East Village branch of this wine bar and panini shop endured a shooting and hostage drama in 2002 and survived. Bar Veloce's shopcoated wine geek and sandwich fabricator still pour good Italian vintages and serve up exceptional accompanying grub in an oddly lit and relaxing setting. Go for the eggplant panini and, if pocketbook permits, a glass of Gutturnio.

D.O.C. WINE BAR ☆ ☆
87 North 7th Street, Brooklyn, 718-963-1925 Among the avalanche of new wine bars that have smothered the city, this is one of the simplest and best. The setting is virtually indistinguishable from an Italian farmhouse, especially late in the evening with the lights turned low. The proprietors are from Sardinia, and their homey pride is evident in the all-Italian wine list, and in the bread provided with platters of cheese and cured meats — carta da musica (sheets of music), crisp broad irregular crackers fragrant with rosemary. The usual pressed Italian sandwiches are also served from the tiny open kitchen, but plain cold cuts go better with the boldly flavored reds.

ENOTECA I TRULLI ☆ $
124 East 27th Street, Manhattan, 212-481-7372 A visit to this pleasantly austere wine bar is an education in Italian wines, allowing you to sample Barolos, Brunellos, Barbarescos, Chiantis, Proseccos, and vini dolci by the glass or, even better, in flights of three two-ounce tastings. But the snacks alone are worth the visit, including cheeses, cured meats, and olives, all from Italy. From Lazio comes porchetta d'ariccia, a silky pork roll stuffed with fennel, while Veneto provides sottocenere, a delicious cow's milk cheese shot with truffles.

GIORGIONE ☆ ☆ ☆ 🕐 🐟
307 Spring Street, Manhattan, 212-352-2269 The most ambitious wine bar so far, Giorgione has extended its menu to include raw oysters, imaginative antipasti, small pizzas, and a short list of pastas and main courses, with nary a panini in sight. Can it still be called a wine bar if it quacks like a restaurant? Let's just say Giorgione is a restaurant organized according to wine bar principles, which encourage sipping and snacking with no obligation to pursue a multicourse meal. The food is so good, however, that you might want to. The octopus appetizer is justifiably notorious.

'INO ☆ ☆ ☆ 🕐
21 Bedford Street, Manhattan, 212-989-5769 This was the first of the postage-stamp-size Milanese sandwich shops, offering glasses of wine and small mugs of real cappuccino with panini, tramezzini, and bruschetta. And it's still one of the best. Thrill to the Italian BLT, made with crisp cubes of pancetta mired in lemon mayo, or the special of four minipanini that lets you sample the entire range of cured meats and aged cheeses, or the bruschetta tumbled with a dozen oil-slicked cloves of caramelized garlic.

153

'INOTECA ★ ★ ☺

98 Rivington Street, Manhattan, 212-614-0473 Following in the footsteps of 'ino, which invented the genre here in New York, this is one of the best wine bars so far, with an Italian wine list filled with unexpected finds, a fine list of cheeses and cured meats, fritters, and the trademark panini and tramezzini that made its forebear justly famous. The trendy Lower East Side premises are markedly more spacious, but the sense of intimacy is lost. It gets two stars rather than three because it's derivative of the original place.

Jamaican, Bajan, Grenadian, and Vincentian

Of all the Caribbean islands, Jamaica has the most interesting and varied cuisine. It makes abundant use of fresh seafood, chicken, and pork and deploys a broad range of flavors from a variety of sources. Chinese indentured workers introduced soy sauce. African slaves provided green onions, cilantro, many of the cooking techniques, and the love of garlic and hot peppers. The Spanish, both directly and via Spanish-speaking Caribbean islands, introduced the use of salt cod and cooking techniques involving yellow onions, green peppers, and vinegar. Curries came directly from India and via England and Trinidad and Guyana. Jamaicans also cook with unusual botanicals: ackee, breadfruit, and allspice, the latter an indispensable indigenous spice that Jamaican cooking (especially the technique known as jerking) makes spectacular use of.

Jamaica's only competition for complexity and excellence of cuisine is from Trinidad, which owes more culinarily to the Indian subcontinent than Jamaica does. Only recently the city has been blessed with many of the more minor cuisines of the Caribbean; each is estimable in its own way and shows a welter of historical influences. Bajan eateries, for example, owe much to England pastrywise, while the main courses show a profound African influence. By contrast, the city's restaurants hailing from Saint Vincent and Grenada do less to distinguish their cuisines from Jamaica's at this point in culinary history. Grenadian, however, provides an estimable contribution to world cuisine: the poetically named "oil down." A walk up Nostrand Avenue in Crown

155

Heights and Bed-Stuy is the perfect way to acquaint yourself with the breadth of anglophone Caribbean cooking.

LOOK FOR:

callaloo *stewed taro leaf*

coco bread *starchy accompaniment to patties*

coo coo *Bajan cornmeal porridge*

corned oxtail *Grenadian brine-cured meat*

cow cod soup *Jamaican bovine penis potage*

cowfoot souse *Grenadian pickled delight*

curried lambi *spicy conch*

cutters *Bajan sandwiches*

escabeche (or escovitched) porgy *fried and pickled fish, a Spanish contribution*

festival *Jamaican sweet fried dough*

flying fish *Barbados's favorite catch, always served with coo coo*

Irish moss *sweet seaweed beverage*

jerked *barbecued with spice paste containing allspice*

lead pipe *Bajan cylindrical pastry*

oil down *Grenadian multistarch oxtail stew*

patties *beef or vegetable turnovers*

pepper shrimp *crawfish in Tabasco, a specialty of western Jamaica*

puddin' and souse *Bajan sweet-potato sausage and pickled pig face*

rice and peas *coconut-drenched red beans and rice*

sweet bread *Bajan sweet pastry stuffed with coconut*

Bajan

BAJE'S P & T EATERY ☆
3513 Church Avenue, Brooklyn, 718-826-8375 How does this place manage to look so much like a rural Caribbean grocery? The dusty ranked bottles of spices and cleaning products are made to play second fiddle to the steam table set into the counter, from which a head-scarfed and skinny old lady ladles goat curry and

various other stews that vary by day. There's a Bajan touch to the pan-island menu: anything can be ordered with coo coo, the okra-dotted cornmeal porridge of Barbados.

COCK'S ✯ ✯ ✯
806 Nostrand Avenue, Brooklyn, 718-771-8933 One of the city's rare Barbados cafés, Cock's offers the full range of culinary delicacies, from the signature flying fish with coo coo (a sculpted mass of cornmeal porridge with fried fish in a zippy gravy) to pud-din' and souse (the former a cross between haggis and blood sau-sage stuffed with sweet potatoes, the latter a pickle of pig face parts). As if these weren't enough, there is also a line of humor-ously named baked goods, like lead pipe and conkies. Don't miss sweet coconut rolls and other more perishable pastries available mainly on the weekends.

CULPEPPER'S ✯ ✯ 🐟
1082 Nostrand Avenue, Brooklyn, 718-940-4122 Bajan food is a gentle mixture of English and African, and Culpepper's is one of the friendliest restaurants around. The menu offers Brit-leaning baked goods like tennis rolls, and familiar Caribbean standards like curry chicken and brown-sauced goat, but go for the national dish of coo coo, a cornmeal porridge in a light red sauce that's strikingly different from the "brown stew" gravy of other Caribbean joints. Though kingfish is a popular choice, go for steamed flying fish instead, the island's favorite catch and a real Bajan passion. Dewinged, deboned, and cut crosswise into thin pieces with the hatched skin adhering, flying fish has firm white flesh and a mild, almost meaty flavor that goes well with the delicate sauce.

Also see Halal Roti and Roti Shack in the Trinidadian section of the Trinidadian, Guyanese, and Surinamese chapter.

Grenadian

PYSNE'S ✯ 🐟
249 Empire Boulevard, Brooklyn, 718-282-2000 If you've ever wondered what Grenada looks like, Pysne's is your place. This handsome restaurant is lined with color photos of the tiny nation, and regulars use them as a point of reference while trading stories of island life. The menu includes brown stew chicken, goat curry, a couple of fried fish, oxtails in a deep brown sauce, and BBQ chicken. Sometimes there are also uniquely Grenadian specialties like oil down, cow heel souse, tanya log, and an especially deli-cious and African-leaning callaloo — fresh taro leaves stewed with hot pepper sauce. The macaroni pie (mac and cheese) is also commendable.

TCB'S ✶

769 Nostrand Avenue, Brooklyn, 718-363-8100 TCB's, a narrow Crown Heights carryout with a multinational menu, lists lambi, rotis, jerks, cowfoot souse, and other island specialties that may be unfamiliar to those born on larger landmasses. I was curious about oil down, which prompted the counter guys to divulge they were from Grenada, not Jamaica — I'd stumbled on their national dish. This Fridays-only tour de force is a farrago of green plantain, cocoyam, corned oxtail, and dense flour dumplings shaped like swollen fingers, simmered for hours in coconut milk. A few pieces of curry chicken are thrown in at the last minute. With only a trickle of concentrated sauce, this ridiculously rich dish needs to be chased with an island drink: white foamy Irish moss, made from seaweed; mauby, concocted of bitter carob bark; or sorrel, a blindingly red hibiscus-flower tea mimicking Kool-Aid. Antilleans do know how to live large.

Jamaican

BLUE MOUNTAIN CAFÉ ✶ ✶ ✶ 🌶

1377 East New York Avenue, Brooklyn, 718-342-5850 This establishment is an eats beacon in downtown Brownsville, and one of the rare local places to produce jerk pork. The handsome nuggets are grilled over charcoal and doused with a distinctive homemade sauce. Though the regulars seem to prefer the oxtails, we scarfed an excellent goat curry, damper and hotter than most, served over rice and peas. Chef Shorty qualifies as one of the most painstaking cooks in town.

BOSTON JERK PALACE ✶ ✶ 🌶

224-15 Linden Boulevard, Queens, 718-525-7928 Invoking the name of the world's most famous jerk destination (Boston Beach, near Port Antonio, Jamaica), BJP specializes in flame-cooked chicken and pork well slathered with jerk spices and tendered with three sauces — sweet, pepper, and jerk. A combination of the latter two is preferred, but the well-charred chicken tastes fine without them. Depending on the cook's whim, there may be oxtails and stewed chicken, and traditional breakfasts like saltfish and ackee. On the day we visited there was also an excellent vegetarian red bean soup rife with manioc and finger-shaped dumplings.

BRAWTA ✶

347 Atlantic Avenue, Brooklyn, 718-855-5515 This slightly upscale Jamaican has proved its durability over the years, even though the versions of jerk chicken (baked, not barbecued) and escabeche fish are tame by Flatbush standards. The dining room is fancy enough to invite your parents to eat there.

CARIBBEAN TASTE INC. ★ 🐟

3925 Baychester Avenue, Bronx, 718-994-9820 The area north of Gun Hill Road is swarming with Jamaican restaurants, and The Bronx clearly aims to give Brooklyn a run for its money as far as jerk chicken goes. Surrounded by gas stations, Caribbean Taste

JERK EVOLUTION

The quintessential dish of Jamaican cuisine, and one served by nearly every self-respecting Jamaican restaurant, is jerk chicken. It was invented by the long-exterminated Arawak Indians, who would dig a pit, line it with wood from the allspice tree, and smoke wild boar therein. The technique evolved in Jamaica, where pork or chicken are soaked in a thick marinade of ground allspice berries (native to the island and imparting a flavor something like cloves), garlic, and green onions, then barbecued on a grill made from an oil drum. Some say the best jerk chefs use blood from the animal in the marinade. The marinade recipe has been picking up ingredients over the years, so that it's often complex in formulation, varying according to the taste of the chef. Soy sauce is now a common ingredient, the contribution of Chinese immigrants who came to the Caribbean around 1900 as indentured sugarcane workers.

While the marinade for the raw meat is often a thick paste, there is another solution that has been traditionally used to moisten the bird just prior to serving. This "jerk sauce" is mainly a vinegar solution laced with incendiary Scotch bonnet peppers, and should be used sparingly. This sauce, too, has evolved, and most modern jerk sauces that you find in the city are combinations of traditional jerk sauce and bottled barbecue sauce. Sadly, within the last few years some of the jerk joints in Brooklyn and the Bronx have started serving bottled commercial barbecue sauce on the side, though they may hide a grease-smeared bottle of the fiery original concoction behind the counter. Thus, it's necessary to inquire about the nature of the jerk sauce before directing the counter guy to dump it all over your chicken. Typically, jerk chicken is already a bit spicy without it.

offers a version smoked over charcoal and doused with a jerk sauce a little on the sweet side and less fiery than most. The escabeche fish is another spectacular entrée, a whole fried mackerel bedded in a julienne of pickled vegetables in a clear vinegar sauce with plenty of heat. Best liquid accompaniment: the lovable grapefruit soda called Ting.

DANNY AND PEPPER ☆ ☆ ☆ 🐟 🐟

771 Flatbush Avenue, Brooklyn, 718-284-9187 Widely believed to produce the city's best jerk chicken, this counter shares a store with a Korean fish market, and the fishmongers and jerk sellers size up every customer and seem visibly disappointed if you move to the opposite side of the store. A serve-yourself refrigerator holds tonics with names like Agony Drink and Front-end Lifter, as well as D&G ginger beer. The chicken is moist and pink inside, with the pinkness resulting from marination rather than undercooking. The skin is nicely charred and crusted with jerk seasonings, which in this case run more to green onions, oregano, and thyme. Refuse the offer of free bread; instead, ask for festival, a sweet torpedo-shaped fritter.

DEE'S WEST INDIAN BAKERY ☆ 🔥

97-17 57th Avenue, Queens, 718-699-1398 Situated on the ragged northern frontier of Lefrak City, this minuscule Jamaican café has two hot selections per day, plus the usual array of patties, cakes, and tonics like Tan-Pon-It Long and Zion. Oxtails stewed with butter beans are particularly savory; alongside you get stewed cabbage, and rice and beans cooked in coconut milk. Other typical choices include brown-stew chicken, curried goat, and, only at breakfast, saltfish and ackee. For something sweet, try tamarind balls or rainbow cake.

FINGER LICKIN'S "R" US ☆ 🔥

14 Duryea Place, Brooklyn, 718-693-7927 Who could help diving into the doorway of a place with a name like that? Decorated with a de rigueur picture of Haile Selassie, this Rasta joint has good food at spectacularly low prices. Breakfast is available all day, in this case leafy green callaloo stewed with salt cod, spread over ripe tomato, topped with rounds of white yam.

FI WIH KITCHEN ☆ ☆

1451 Bedford Avenue, Brooklyn, 718-230-5651 We were lured inside this handsome corner store — where the slogan is "For a taste of the yard, abroad" — by the smell of jerk chicken cooking on the drum outside. The bird turned out to be superb — with a homemade jerk coating thinner and more herby than most that nevertheless featured an authoritative bonnet-pepper kick. Another great offering is brown stew beef, a thick and odiferous dish that owes a debt to Worcestershire, served with rice and peas and salad. For a starch overload, dig the orb-shaped fried dumpling. Fi Wih means "For what?" in Jamaican dialect.

FOOD HUT ☆ ☆
1709 Amsterdam Avenue, Manhattan, 212-491-4492 Formerly known as Toyamadel, this spacious storefront boasts the same gleaming kitchen and list of dishes that goes way beyond the standard handful of daily offerings. Omnibus platters come in three sizes to suit any appetite. The chicken curry and jerk chicken are among Harlem's best, and there are also roots tonics to cure a hangover or prime you for a wild Saturday night. My advice: Ask for dumplings with everything.

H.I.M. ☆ ⵁ
2130 White Plains Road, Bronx, 718-239-7146 The initials stand for His Imperial Majesty Haile Selassie, and this vegan lunch counter is decorated with multiple likenesses. Pay $6.50 and get generous servings of five dishes. My choices on a weekday afternoon: a boil-up of lavender taro root and purple onions tasting of bay leaf; a stir-fry of sweet plantain and orange bell peppers; a swirl of tofu, celery, and onions that looked just like scrambled eggs; African-tasting chopped kale; and, welcome mainly for its colorfulness, sliced boiled beets.

HOUSE OF JERK ☆ ☆ ✒
1060 Classon Avenue, Brooklyn, 718-623-5499 Though the name makes it sound like a National Lampoon movie, H of J is one of the most formidable Jamaican carryouts in Brooklyn, with a more complete menu of roots cuisine, including thick sweet cornmeal pudding, meat and fish cook-ups, and ackee and salt cod. The fish soup is especially fantastic, with a roster of ingredients that runs to christophene, taro, potato, and carrot in a fish fumet worthy of a bouillabaisse. Beckoning you in the right direction is a plume of barbecue smoke which drifts up Classon, crosses over Fulton, and heads toward Clinton Hill.

JERK CENTER ☆ ☆ ☆ ✒
1296 East Gun Hill Road, Bronx, 718-798-4966 Nearing its seventh anniversary, this converted gas station still makes slammin' jerk chicken, even though a cell phone business seems to have moved in, offsetting half the tables. Still, the goat curry remains top-notch, and there's plenty of other Jamaicaniana, too, including pepper shrimp, cod fritters, and festival (pronounced "fes-tee-val"), a sweet fry bread. Warning: The jerk chicken will blow the top of your head off if you request the vinegary sauce that goes with it.

PATTIES

While jerk may be the favorite meal of islanders, the most popular snack is clearly the patty. This name designates a hand-held pastry that was certainly inspired by the empanada, though whether the idea was transmitted via the Cornish pastie, or directly from Spanish Caribbeans, is a matter of contention. While patties made by Tower Island and similar concerns are widely available around the city, even in pizza parlors, or from the **Golden Krust** chain that's been expanding all over town, you'll find a better product if you seek out ma-and-pa places that specialize in these turnovers. While the traditional type is fried and utilizes a dough laced with annatto, which turns the crust bright orange (and provides further evidence that the pie may have come from the Spanish), the modern patty shop fabricates varieties made by other methods, including a healthier baked version that usually lacks annatto. Moreover, fillings have gone far afield from the original mince (hell, it's almost a puree) of beef laced with hot peppers. One New York invention unites two Jamaican culinary passions in the jerk chicken patty, while other choices also include fish, callaloo, and various soy-based substances popular among the Ital places run by Rastas. While patties mainly function as snacks, they also do service as full meals, usually via the use of coco bread. This baseball mitt of a doughy bun usually costs a dollar and is folded around a patty to make it a full meal.

MARCUS ISLAND DELI ☆
2709 Avenue D, Brooklyn, no phone Operated by a father and son team who immigrated from Brixton, England, the deli is no longer a deli, but an excellent jerk chicken joint, as evidenced by the tandem drum smokers prodigiously smoking out front. Inside, the motif is still drums, but in this case African drums ranged along the top of the soda case.

MAROONS ☆ 🐟 🍽 $
244 West 16th Street, Manhattan, 212-206-6640 Nothing better than a plate of green tomatoes, crumbed and carefully fried.

They join a list of other distinguished appetizers at this upscale Jamaican and soul food café, cunningly fitted into a pair of tenement apartments. Barbecue ribs are dense and sweet, cooked to the point where the meat and sauce fuse. The cod fritters are equally accomplished, dotted with scallions and miraculously devoid of denseness. For sides, pick the callaloo over the mac and cheese.

MO-BAY ☆ 🐟
112 DeKalb Avenue, Brooklyn, 718-246-2800 The name is slang for Montego Bay, Jamaica's biggest tourist trap, but the food is much better than the name would suggest. Right across from Fort Greene Park, this cheery spot serves a meaty goat curry with plenty of zing, jerk chicken with an aromatic sauce, and deep-fried cassava cakes called bammie that one sees too infrequently. There are also soul food selections like fried whiting, mac and cheese, and collards, but the best dish is escovitched fish — a whole snapper bathed in a sauce of pickled vegetables and righteously hot.

NEGRIL ☆☆ $
362 West 23rd Street, Manhattan, 212-807-6411; 70 West 3rd Street, Manhattan, 212-477-2804 This is a good place for an island splurge, if you don't mind paying around $15 for entrées, and want something with that vacationland ambiance and plenty of fruity cocktails. The skillfully spiced fare runs to curry goat (dig it), jerk pork (dig it), and jerk chicken salad (skip it). There's a slightly less desirable version of this place in Hell's Kitchen called Island Spice (402 West 44th Street, 212-765-1737).

NORMAN'S JERK CHICKEN RESTAURANT ☆
167-20 Hillside Avenue, Queens, 718-297-2803 The chicken has a lot more soy sauce in the jerk covering than is usual, and I figure it's the influence of the Guyanese and Trinidadian restaurants in the neighborhood. Norman's occupies a corner store and looks like an old lunch counter, with a couple of booths and a row of stools. A sign over the counter offers breakfasts of mackerel and banana, ackee and codfish, and porridge and liver.

ONE STOP PATTY SHOP ☆
1708 Amsterdam Avenue, Manhattan, 212-491-7485 Reggae booms out the door as you cross the threshold and behold the glass cases filled with hot patties, a list of the varieties contained therein scrawled underneath. The hot beef is always admirable, with a fine mince zapped with Scotch bonnet sauce. Have it with coco bread, a white roll something like a baseball mitt to catch the patty in. Low-fat patties like jerk chicken are also available, but I'll go for the greasy annatto-yellow pastry every time.

PEARLY'S ☆

346 Rogers Street, Brooklyn, 718-703-1770 OK, so it's not done on a barbecue made from an oil drum, and charcoal isn't involved. Still, contrary to expectation, Pearly's jerk pork is one of the best in Brooklyn. The pieces are large and succulent, rimmed with fat, and slightly gritty with generous quantities of jerk spices. And this tiny café is like a Jamaican clubhouse, with friendly guys sitting around slurping Red Stripes, each willing to give his own testimony to the excellence of Pearly's cooking.

RICKY'S EAT-WELL ☆

841 Utica Avenue, Brooklyn, 718-342-2490 That's Ricky up on the awning, wearing chef's whites and turning chicken on the oil-drum barbecue with a long fork. Good jerk chicken is the raison d'être for this carryout, with a good smoky flavor and crisp skin. Don't ask for the jerk sauce, though, because it's a little too much like bad barbecue sauce. Even better than the chicken is goat curry, a mass of well-seasoned meat in a zingy gravy, served with cole slaw and rice-and-peas. Don't miss the Plexiglas case flaunting risqué island comic books.

ROYAL BAKE SHOP ☆

215A East 170th Street, Bronx, 718-681-9160 What a contrast between the beef patties they sell at pizza parlors and the ones served here! The annatto-tinged pastry is fresh and light. The filling is very spicy, with the meat ground so fine it's almost pureed. Eat them as the Jamaicans do, in a coco bread. The combination of coco bread and patty is sublime — the spicy filling of the patty shining through two carbo layers, one puffy, one oily. Royal Bake Shop doesn't sell much else, but these are good enough to warrant a special visit.

ST. JOHN'S CAFÉ AND RESTAURANT ☆ ☆

1173 St. Johns Place, Brooklyn, 718-773-0701 Despite the grandiose name, this place is a hole in the wall. The very pleasant staff offers a choice between excellent renditions of both fried chicken and jerk chicken, reflecting the Carolina-meets-Jamaica roots of the community. And St. Johns Place is one of the most pleasant for strolling in Crown Heights.

STRICTLY ROOTS ☆ ⊘

2058 Adam Clayton Powell Jr. Boulevard, Manhattan, 212-864-8699 This vegetarian eatery — their slogan: "We serve nothing that crawls, walks, swims, or flies" — with its comfortable tables and velvet painting of Haile Selassie in a suit, goes way beyond Ital fare to create a cuisine that rivals any in depth and interest. Sure, there are predictable Jamaican standards like vegetable-stuffed patties, banana bread, and sorrel punch, but take a gander at the steam table: a delicious succotash of green beans and limas, crisply fried tofu balls, an herby potato mash sweetened with orange yam, and a lasagna that substitutes TVP (textured vegetable protein) to create a dead-ringer for its Italian prototype.

SUN SHINE KITCHEN ☆ ☆

695 St. Nicholas Avenue, Manhattan, 212-368-4972 Jamaicans don't cotton to the Trinidadian roti, preferring to eat the curried meat or poultry filling plain, or jazzed up with spicy shredded cabbage and other vegetables. This establishment is just a Plexiglas kitchen with no dining room, so you have to sit on the nearby A train stairs in order to dine. Nevertheless, the goat roti is one of the best in Harlem. You don't have to wrestle with the bones, 'cause they've all been carefully extracted, leaving tiny savory cubes of curried meat.

SYLVIA'S RESTAURANT ☆

674 Nostrand Avenue, Brooklyn, no phone The restaurant's name and the mural — a straw-hatted boy fishing while, over his shoulder, a family picnics in a lush meadow — might make you think this is a soul food joint. Think again: this eatery, which features a savory liver-and-dumpling breakfast, is Jamaican. Heartier meals are based on fried fish, curry beef, and brown stew chicken, and come with a salad, slices of fried plantain, a hunk of cassava, and white rice soaked with a generous quantity of brown lentils. Tell them not to stint on the habanero hot sauce, and expect the regulars lined up along the counter to be impressed.

TUMMY PARADISE ☆

932 Utica Avenue, Brooklyn, 718-282-5100 Ever seen tripe in a Jamaican joint before? I hadn't, until I stumbled over the sidewalk chalkboard menu. The pillows of well-tenderized cow stomach recline in a tasty stew flavored with allspice, the brown terrain varied by humongous white beans. Though bony, Tummy's goat curry is similarly lip-smacking and abundant. Other entrées included curry chicken, brown stew chicken, and escabeche fish, with fish cakes, fried dumplings, and the long doughnut dubbed "festival" offered as snacks.

VERNON'S NEW JERK HOUSE ☆ ✍

987 233rd Street, Bronx, 718-655-8348 Allan Vernon is one of the city's foremost jerk theorists, and his jerk sauce is readily available in specialty stores. While jerk sauce is traditionally a thin bonnet-pepper vinaigrette, his is loaded up with all sorts of ingredients to give it the consistency of ketchup, and a flavor that owes

165

too much to Worcestershire. That said, his jerk pork is fabulous, meaty and tender. The chicken is more succulent than most, leaving a faint burn in your mouth. Look for daily specials like brown stew chicken and tripe and beans.

Vincentian

LOUISE'S ☆ 🐟 🐠
54 Rockaway Avenue, Brooklyn, 718-574-7514 Heralded by a wall-size mural of palms flanking a cool lagoon and an outsize papier-mâché hamburger, this cavernous East New Yorker specializes in the food of the Caribbean island of Saint Vincent. Antillean specialties run to savory oxtails, deep-fried fish filets, and an awesome curried chicken with just the right amount of heat (lots). The island women who run the joint couldn't be nicer; and when they ask how you liked your meal, you'd better say "Very much, thank you." The menu is rounded out with burgers and further mainland fare.

Japanese

Noodle Shops, Other Specialties, Restaurants, and Sushi Bars.

Japanese businessmen swarmed the city in the 1980s, and generated a campus of upscale sushi parlors and other quasi-luxury establishments radiating north from the corner of 5th Avenue and 42nd Street. Though somewhat faded, many of these institutions — nearly 30 in number — still exist. Meanwhile, the East Village became the hippest imaginable destination for young Japanese expatriates and tourists, many of whom settled down to become artists and restaurant employees. Over the years, Japanese sushi bars became the downtown equivalent of Greek diners, the place to get a quick and familiar katsudon, bowl of noodles, or set meal of sushi. Astonishingly, this type of place never existed in Japan, where eateries tended to pursue the perfection of a specialty or two, and few attempted to present the entire range — at least the downscale part — of Japanese cuisine.

Whether you crave soba or udon, hot or cold, in soups or dry, Manhattan provides a plethora of great Japanese noodle houses. All can be counted on for a satisfying bargain meal, where it is considered good form to be as noisy as possible as you slurp your noodles. In Japan, a majority of the restaurants would fall into the Other Specialty category — small places that do one thing only, and do it very well. Luckily, several of these places have materialized here, including a tonkatsu-ya that specializes in frying breaded pork cutlets, and another place, a carryout window on East 9th Street, that concentrates on the catch-all pancake called otafuku. Finally, the Americans are largely responsible for the democratization of sushi, pricing it low enough in many restaurants that the general population can enjoy decent-quality fish without mortgaging their SUVs.

Noodle Shops

HONMURA AN ☆ ☆ ☆ 🐟 $

170 Mercer Street, Manhattan, 212-334-5253 Decade-old Honmura has stayed the course, turning out perfect soba every day starting with imported Japanese buckwheat. While it seemed expensive when the place first opened, now the $21.95 bowl of soba and broth topped with two tempura shrimp so large they must have frightened swimmers seems like a deal.

MENCHANKO-TEI ☆ ☆

39 West 55th Street, Manhattan, 212-247-1585; 131 East 45th Street, Manhattan, 212-986-6805 Don't look for teriyaki, sushi, or tempura at this king of the authentic Japanese noodle joints: the menu is centered on soups crammed with noodles or rice and served in big metal bowls. Try the eponymous menchanko, weighed down with udon, chicken, Chinese cabbage, fish balls, Japanese sweet potato, tofu, and gooey rice cake. Another specialty is oden, a Japanese comfort food that lets you mix and match from among a list of nine strange-sounding elements, including "fish cake bar fly" and devil's tongue jelly.

ONY ☆ ⊘

357 6th Avenue, Manhattan, 212-414-8429 Brought to you by the folks responsible for Menchanko-Tei and Katsuhama, Ony modestly bills itself as a noodle bar, specializing in pristine soba, udon, and ramen. As an added bonus, sushi is also offered, focusing mainly on nori rolls and reaching a level above the East Village average.

RAI RAI KEN ☆ ☆ ☆

214 East 10th Street, Manhattan, 212-477-7030 You've never tasted ramen this good before — and the reason is right on the other side of the narrow lunch counter: giant bubbling stockpots. In one you can see scallions, carrots, apples, and an entire chicken, whose combed head sticks out of the broth like a periscope. This astonishingly good broth is used as the basis for the simple and elegant noodle soups. You'll feel like you've been whisked away to Tokyo for the 15 minutes or so it takes to eat a bowl.

RESTAURANT NIPPON ☆ ☆ $

155 East 52nd Street, Manhattan, 212-758-0226 If you thrilled to *Tampopo*, you can recreate the experience of eating freshly made soba noodles, made from scratch using buckwheat grown at the restaurant's Canadian farm. Dig the warm-weather lunch special, starting with a couple of pieces of inari-zushi, followed by a green salad, and climaxing in a heap of cool morisoba — buckwheat noodles displayed on a bamboo screen.

SOBY-YA ☆

229 East 9th Street, Manhattan, 212-533-6966 Who would guess that the elegant premises is a humble Japanese noodle shop, offering mainly hot and cold assemblages of udon and soba. You can eat for around $10, but who could resist appetizers like homemade shumai, tempura by the piece, and, lost in the extensive sake menu, a bar snack of raw baby squid marinated in a fragrant dark liquid?

TOKYO LA MEN ☆ ⊘

90 University Place, Manhattan, 212-229-1489 This place is all about puns. Thrill to hokey names like Viking La Men and Stamina La Men, then order ten sin, brought in a huge white bowl that

169

holds a quart of brown broth laced with mushrooms and beef. A broad omelet strewn with shredded red ginger and ribbons of spinach floats on top.

Other Specialties

CHIKUBU ☆ ☆ 🐟 $

12 East 44th Street, Manhattan, 212-818-0715 Probably the only spot in town that serves fugu caught in the wild is midtown's Chikubu. The fugu chef's certificate of qualification is displayed in the cloakroom. The fugu sashimi is sublime, pinwheeled on the plate in thin translucent slices crazed with fine filaments and topped with a little wad of dyed radish. The condiment of choice? Tabasco sauce — in Japan an exotic ingredient. The other sushi and sashimi also rock, and wash it all down with a tipple of sake flavored with toasted fugu fin. Also watch for seasonal specialties like "sweet young honey bee with soy sauce."

KATSUHAMA ☆ ☆ ☆

11 East 47th Street, Manhattan, 212-758-5909 This authentic Japanese tonkatsu-ya does only one thing, but they do it spectacularly: thin pork cutlets breaded and deep-fried. They're merged with egg, shredded cabbage, and scallions to make the luncheon favorite katsudon (available all day), or presented without further diddling in all their sprawling magnificence, sided with an elemental cole slaw. You can substitute chicken or shrimp for pork, but don't expect it to be nearly as good.

OTAFUKU ☆

236 East 9th Street, Manhattan, 212-353-8503 Think it might be a new nightclub owned by Joey Buttafuoco? Nope — it's a Tokyo-style street-food stand where the specialty is a gooey pancake called okonomiyaki, which means "cook what you like." While the range of offerings doesn't match a similar establishment at the Japanese mall in Edgewater, New Jersey, Otafuku provides a fine intro to the genre, featuring ingredients such as shrimp, unsmoked bacon, and squid. Also offered: fried octopus balls (gee, I didn't know they had balls).

WIN49 ☆ ⏛

205 Allen Street, Manhattan, 212-353-9494 Just when you thought Manhattan already harbored every kind of Japanese specialty restaurant that you could find in Tokyo, another unique one pops up. Win49 specializes in kushikatsu — anything breaded, fried, and skewered. Fish, pork, shrimp, potatoes, and even asparagus are all fair game, and you can combine these brochettes with side dishes to form bento-box lunches. Also on the menu are an appealing array of sushi rolls, the best of which is made with salmon skin gobbed with sweet sauce.

YAKINIKU WEST ☆ ☆ ☆ $
218 East 9th Street, Manhattan, 212-979-9238 Billing itself as a Japanese rural steakhouse, Yakiniku features acres of polished woods, broad low tables with recessed legroom, and a trickling fountain at the end of the dining room framed by a bamboo grove. In the center of each table is a ventilated barbecue grill, and you will be held responsible for cooking most of your meal on it. Choices range from steak to seafood to chicken, and a nifty set meal includes salad, soup, rice, kimchee, grillables, tea, and dessert. More exotic meats, like tongue, tripe, and intestines, are available à la carte.

YOSHINOYA ☆
255 West 42nd Street, Manhattan, 212-703-9940 Following in the footsteps of Teriyaki Boy, this Japanese franchise is preparing an all-out assault on Manhattan. The specialty is East-West fusion, par excellence: the splendid beef bowl, meat like you'd expect to find in a Philly cheese steak sautéed with onions and heaped over rice like sloughed tire treads over a snow-capped mountain, exuding a light soy aroma. There's also a chicken teriyaki bowl, a vegetarian bowl, a couple of soups, and not much more. If you want to really go Japanese, request a brown egg and crack it over your bowl.

Restaurants

HANAMAI ☆
525 6th Avenue, Manhattan, 212-255-9981 A little piece of the East Village in the West, Hanami offers the usual downtown Japanese mix of sushi, noodles, tempura, teriyaki, donburi (over-rice dishes), and appetizers, where much of the culinary excitement is. Briefly seared tuna tataki, lightly fried age tofu, and the badly misnamed "squid legs" are recommended. But the real utility of this place lies in its unexpected location, and in the fabulous $12.95 bento box at dinner.

MICKEY'S PLACE ☆
101-16 Queens Boulevard, Queens, 718-897-9898 Most patrons are greeted by name like old friends when they wander into this neighborhood Japanese, but one glance at the sushi counter demonstrates that the three busy chefs take their fish very seriously. We turned them loose on an omakase (chef's choice) one recent evening, and they worked magic, producing six courses of yellowtail, fluke, eel, snapper, and a showy carved apple of avocado stuffed with spicy tuna.

NIKONIKO ☆

80 Wall Street, Manhattan, 212-232-0152 This handsomely decorated Japanese fast-food outlet describes itself as "sushi & bowl." The sushi part features the most obvious combinations, which are as good as prefab sushi can get. While soups like beef with noodle suffer from a boring stock, the over-rice dishes are much tastier. Six bucks gets you katsudon, a fried pork cutlet mired in a scallion-laced omelet; bibimbop don, an adaptation of a mix-it-yourself Korean favorite; or, best deal of all, una don, a giant sauce-smeared eel fillet

SAJI'S ☆

2810-18 Broadway, Manhattan, 212-749-1834 Entered via a side street, Saji's is a microscopic noodle shop/sushi bar/donburi parlor with a couple of narrow counters for eating on the premises. Long a secret of Columbia students, the prices are phenomenally cheap and the food much better than it needs to be. If you carry out the shrimp tempura udon, the staff will thoughtfully wrap the shrimp separately, so they won't get soggy until you're ready to eat them.

SAPPORO ☆ ☆

152 West 49th Street, Manhattan, 212-869-8972 Long the choice of students and slumming Nipponese businessmen, it's one of Times Square's last good, cheap ethnic eateries. With nary a piece of sushi in sight, the menu is no-nonsense comfort food. Don't miss the gyoza, stuffed with savory meat and greens and pan-fried to a crisp brown. Come during the summer, and get the pièce de résistance: hiyashi chuka, a bowl of cold noodles in a slightly sweet broth, topped with ham, chicken, egg, fish cake, green onion, shredded ginger, cucumber, and corn.

SAPPORO EAST ☆

245 East 10th Street, Manhattan, 212-260-1330 This budget old-timer (no relation to Sapporo at Times Square) is pushing 20, the place that was almost single-handedly responsible for popularizing Japanese food in the East Village. In the process, it filled the shoes of the Greek coffee shop in other parts of town: a place where good cheap meals can be regularly taken, and old friends met without premeditation.

TOMO ☆ ☆

4561 Amboy Road, Staten Island, 718-227-5100 Yoked to a beauty parlor and located most obscurely at the end of a narrow parking lot in downtown Eltingville, Tomo carves a diverse range of near-perfect sushi, and rounds out the menu with budget noodle soups and pricier Japanese entrées. The well-conceived rock garden at the front entrance is a charming emblem of the restaurant's excellence. Lunch specials an astonishingly good deal.

Sushi Bars

AKIDA ☆ 🐟

42-32 Bell Boulevard, Queens, 718-224-8196 Of the Japanese restaurants on Bayside's burgeoning sushi strip, this one looked the best. We knocked back yellowtail, mackerel, and broiled eel nigiri-zushi in short order, then switched to the more exotic assemblages from the Chef's Special Roll section of the menu. Best was the spider roll, spiny with fried soft-shell crab and cooled with cucumber. Also memorable was the tiger roll of eel and shrimp moistened with ginger dressing.

GENKI SUSHI ☆ 🐟

9 East 46th Street, Manhattan, 212-983-5018 Why is the face on the logo frowning? This sushi bar serves some of midtown's best in a sunny, street-level room that's the atmospheric antithesis of the usual nigiri-sushi purveyors. The plates rotate around an amoeba-shaped prep area on a cunning metal conveyor belt, color-coded according to price, as Brazilian music floods the premises. Most mind-boggling was the eel, broiled to order and flopping extravagantly over the rice lozenges, but nearly its equal was the belly tuna (toro) imported from Chile, intensely pink and creamy.

HARU ☆ 🐟

433 Amsterdam Avenue, Manhattan, 212-579-5655; 1501 Broadway, Manhattan, 212-398-9810; 1329 3rd Avenue, Manhattan, 212-452-2230; 280 Park Avenue, Manhattan, 212-490-9680 Finally, the Upper West Side has broken the sushi barrier, and it's no longer necessary to go south to get a decent piece of fish. Haru's menu concentrates on incredibly fresh sushi and sashimi, often sprinkled with electric-red flying fish roe and served Korean-style in filets so huge that they droop over the ends of the rice and trail along the plate.

HASAKI ☆ ☆ ☆ 🐟 $

210 East 9th Street, Manhattan, 212-473-3327 Kudos to the architect who designed this timber-intensive subterranean space, preceded by a sunken patio and pair of anterooms decorated with dramatic stone treatments and a stand of live bamboo. In spite of credible versions of sukiyaki, teriyaki, and soba, the raw fish still rules at Hasaki, where four crackerjack chefs wield knives

173

HISTORY LESSON

When sushi first hit town almost 25 years ago, it came on a conveyor belt and your choices were limited to a couple of rolls and a few nigiri-sushi. Simultaneously, **Mie**, an East Village place, offered a slightly broader range of fish in a restaurant setting, even though the restaurant was subterranean and somewhat mysterious-seeming. Sushi has evolved in all directions since then. Haute purveyors like **Hatsuhana** spawned a generation of fancy sushi parlors that flew their specialties in from Japan on a daily basis, like **Kuruma Sushi, Sushisay**, and **Sushi Yasuda**. At about the same time, "new style" sushi was invented at **Nobu**. It really wasn't all that different from conventional sushi, only the oily fish were sometimes seared on one side, and the slices of fish sometimes painted with an unusual sweet sauce, or paired with something unexpected, like jalapeño peppers. Sushi also became democratized, and local parlors started selling it to hoi polloi as suitable lunch fare. As an extension of this downscale sushi were fast-food places that offered it prefab, and other establishments that inaugurated all-you-can-eat sushi, an idea that would have been an abomination in Japan, before they started doing it, too. Meanwhile, American sushi chefs were innovating, inventing things that seemed as wild as the California roll when it was first invented: sushi featuring shrimp tempura and soft-shell crab, deposited in the maki roll or hand roll while still hot. Other nationalities got into the act, with South Americans merging ceviche and sushi cultures, Korean restaurateurs professing their own love of sushi, and even Italians, at places like **Esca**, promoting an Italian form of sashimi known as crudo. Now you must begin any sushi binge with the question: What kind of sushi do I want to eat?

simultaneously. The regular combos are fantastic, but pay closer attention to the specials like negi toro, a huge wad of belly tuna ground up like steak tartare, tweaked by chopped scallions, topped with three kinds of damp seaweed and one kind of dry, and looking like a fatal undersea accident. The regular menu also offers sushi surprises, like kinuta eel, a maki roll sans rice with a superthin curl of cucumber standing in for the usual seaweed wrapper.

HATSUHANA ☆ ☆ 🐟 $

17 East 48th Street, Manhattan, 212-355-3345; 237 Park Avenue, Manhattan, 212-661-3400 The 48th Street location was the earliest purveyor of high-quality sushi in town, and many of its best itamae have gone on to bigger and better things. Meanwhile, the quality has been diluted somewhat by careless franchising around the country, yet Hatsuhana remains a sentimental favorite.

JEOLADDO ☆ 🐟

116 East 4th Street, Manhattan, 212-260-7696 Here's the gimmick: a Japanese restaurant with Korean touches combined with a screening room for independent films. The menu emphasizes sushi, which is painstakingly fresh and, for now at least, cheap by local standards. Typical maki rolls are sometimes priced two-for-one, but look to the "House Roll" section to find more colorful creations.

JEWEL BAKO ☆ ☆ 🐟 $

239 East 5th Street, Manhattan, 212-979-1012 The interior really does look like a jeweled coffin, where you can experience innovative appetizers like a yellowtail sushi plate that lets you compare four varieties of that fish. This natural successor to Nobu and Bond Street specializes in "new style" sushi and sashimi.

KOKO ☆ 🐟

168 Lexington Avenue, Manhattan, 212-481-8088 If you're one of those raw-fish enthusiasts who like to know a good sushi bar in every corner of town, add Koko to your list. This new restaurants specializes in sushi, while also offering a modest list of perennial Japanese favorites like katsudon, teriyaki, and a particularly good tempura. Though toro is often unavailable, the regular tuna sashimi is sleek and fresh. "Water eel," funky mackerel, and the yellowtail and scallion roll are all exemplary. Koko joins two other sushi parlors on the same block. If one more arrives, we'll call it Sushi Row.

KURUMA SUSHI ☆ ☆ ☆ 🐟 $

7 East 47th Street, Manhattan, 212-317-2802 I've seen sushi heaven and its name is Kuruma Sushi. Begin your voyage with toro sashimi, and the kindly sushi chef, who obviously knows his stuff, will inquire politely, "How fatty do you want it?" Your reply, of course, is "As fatty as you can make it." What floats over the partition and eases onto your plate are two wobbly diamonds of perfect flesh, bright pink and crazed with little veins of fat like Kobe beef, and so unutterably tasty that you could walk out the door right then and still feel satisfied. But you won't. Eating sushi there is like riding a very expensive taxi — plan on spending about $25 per person for every three minutes on the meter.

MATSURI ☆ 🐟 $
396 West 16th Street, Manhattan, 212-243-6400 Chef Tadashi Ono made his reputation imparting a Japanese twist to French food at La Caravelle and Sono. Now he finds himself in a sprawling subterranean space that recalls the dark ribbed interior of Jonah's whale. The conservative menu, described as "home-style Japanese cooking," owes more than a little to Nobu. The five-piece Matsuri sushi is a thrilling venture into "new style" sushi, with its searings and dabs of tart sauce, while other dishes one-up your neighborhood Japanese — like the 12-inch tempura eel — but with generally meager portions, you may wonder if you're trapped, not inside a whale, but inside a cash cow.

MIE ☆ ☆ 🐟
196 2nd Avenue, Manhattan, 212-674-7060 The proprietors must have been prescient when they opened this Japanese old-timer in 1965 — over the next three decades it was joined by dozens of comparable East Village restaurants. This was also one of the first places in town to serve sushi, and the output remains above average, with an intriguing list that sometimes includes butterfish, cockle, and smelt egg. Even more important — the comfortable subterranean rooms have empty seats when inferior joints in this sushi-wise neighborhood are mobbed. Favorite dish: a vinegary octopus salad found on the special menu card.

SUSHISAY ☆ ☆ 🐟 $
38 East 51st Street, Manhattan, 212-755-1780 Tracing its lineage to a Tokyo establishment founded in 1888, Sushisay is Manhattan's third best sushi bar, runner-up to Kuruma Sushi and Sushi Yasuda. It's also the most cheerful and spacious, with an L-shaped sushi bar 50 feet in length manned by six chefs. As at all the higher-quality establishments, begin with tuna sashimi offered in several degrees of fattiness, progress through various nigiri-sushi, then on to the hand rolls or maki rolls. All the fish in the cold case glistens, but we were particularly knocked out by the sardines, topped with little hillocks of chopped scallion, and the fresh-tasting river eel.

SUSHI YASUDA ☆ ☆ ☆ 🐟 $
204 East 43rd Street, Manhattan, 212-972-1001 Sushi Yasuda is all blond woods, accented by a single twig of pink orchids and the green banana leaves on which the glistening sushi and

sashimi are deposited. Contrary to form, the sushi's also great at the tables, and the matsua special allows you to pick from regular selections and specials alike — the fattiest toro, unrubbery Japanese octopus, four kinds of yellowtail, and two eels that have never seen the inside of a plastic bubble pack.

YUJIN ☆ ☆ ⇐🐟 $
24 East 12th Street, Manhattan, 212-924-4283 Evidence that the influence of Nobu is creeping northward, Yujin combines an aggressive and expensive sushi selection with a menu of substantial — one might even say humongous — entrées that vary little from the catalog established by places like Bond Street and Next Door Nobu. The sushi is as perfect as any downtown, supervised and sometimes even sliced by the former chef of Sushi Samba.

Jewish-American

Dairy and Meat

This section features Jewish-American eateries — some kosher, some not. Expect the food to be mainly in a German or Eastern European vein. Due to the Jewish dietary laws, these eateries naturally assort themselves into two camps. The delis are more profuse in this day and age, but as recently as a decade ago the dairy restaurants were just as important to the dining landscape of the city, including **Hammer's** on 14th Street (where *The Front* was partly filmed), **Dubrow's** in the garment center, and **Ratner's** on Delancey Street — now all sadly gone. Go to **Diamond Dairy Restaurant**, where you can be entertained by jewelry transactions on the trading floor below, for a little of the old atmosphere. When I first arrived in New York, I ate at Dubrow's, where I was amazed to see old men eating bowls of sour cream for lunch.

For Jewish Sephardic styles, consult the Middle Eastern, Central Asian and Caucasian, and South Asian chapters.

LOOK FOR:

blintz *Eastern European crepe*

borscht *beet soup hot or cold*

Cel-ray *celery soda pop*

challah *twisted egg bread*

cholent *bean stew*

corned beef *brisket cured with salt and spices*

halvah *dessert of compressed sesame seeds and honey*

kasha *buckwheat groats*

kasha varnishkes *Russian-Jewish bow-tie pasta and kasha*

kugel *sweet noodle pudding*

lox *brine-cured cold-smoked salmon*
mandelbrot *Jewish biscotti*
matzo *unleavened flatbread*
matzo ball *dumpling made from matzo crumbs*
matzo brei *eggs scrambled with matzo fragments*
Nova *translucent cold-smoked salmon from Nova Scotia*
pastrami *smoked beef brisket rubbed with spices*
stuffed derma *oniony cereal sausage*

Dairy

B & H DAIRY RESTAURANT ☆ ☆ ☆ ⏀
127 2nd Avenue, Manhattan, 212-505-8065 This lingering vestige of the theater district once known as the Jewish Broadway is also one of the few kosher dairy restaurants remaining in town. I dream about their soups — mushroom barley, borscht, cabbage, and vegetable, in descending order of preference — sided with two thick slices of buttered made-on-the-premises challah (here called "holly bread"), of which I always get a double order. The blintzes and overstuffed pierogi are homemade, too, and the East Village's best.

BARNEY GREENGRASS ☆ ☆ ◄●
541 Amsterdam Avenue, Manhattan, 212-724-4707 Barney Greengrass, which styles itself as "The Sturgeon King," couldn't be more serious about cured fish. This Upper West Side landmark dispenses chub, lox, Nova, kippers, sable, whitefish, pickled herring, sardines, and sturgeon. The faintly smoky and boneless white flesh of the last is likely to be preferred by youngsters. Examine the showcase and proceed into a dining room, curiously wallpapered with scenes of New Orleans. Here you can order thin slices of any fish served with lettuce, olives, tomatoes, onions, pickles, accompanied by a toasted bagel. Of several fish-and-eggs combos, my favorite is scrambled eggs with caramelized onions and Nova.

DIAMOND DAIRY RESTAURANT ☆ ◄● ⏀
4 West 47th Street, Manhattan, 212-719-2694 Dramatically poised on a balcony above the National Jewelers Exchange, this old-fashioned Jewish dairy restaurant features the usual dishes, including blintzes, puddings, and slow-moving glaciers of sour cream. Baked fish is a particular specialty, but even better is cholent, a garlicky bean stew. Enjoy watching the jewelry transactions down below as you dine.

HALL STREET KOSHER CAFÉ ⭐ 🐄
9 Hall Street, Brooklyn, 718-802-9638 Located in a rather trashy trailer a stone's throw from the Brooklyn Navy Yard, this is one of the few places to eat, period, in this hardscrabble nabe. Although the kugel, blintzes, and soups have probably been over-hyped by commentators like Leff and Schwartz, it's still an estimable place, as proved by a recent lunch of egg salad and pastries that enfolded weenies made of fish (the gefilte dog?). "It's for the kids," the jovial counter guy observed.

Meat

DELI CORNER ⭐
2001 Avenue U, Brooklyn, 718-891-1555 This faded lunch counter was here when John Travolta discoed out of Brooklyn into *Saturday Night Fever*, dispensing the same kosher franks and hot meat sandwiches, the latter well-smeared with grainy mustard and wrapped with a single brine pickle. Though cut on a machine rather than by hand, the pastrami, corned beef, and brisket are particularly flavorful and generously heaped on the sandwich (pick rye rather than the anemic club roll). Stand in the doorway to eat, and watch Russian and Chinese immigrants — Homecrest's newest residents — pass by.

DELI MASTERS ⭐ ⭐
184-02 Horace Harding Expressway, Queens, 718-353-3030 Sorry to disappoint all the fans of Second Avenue Deli, Katz's, and Carnegie Deli, but I had my best pastrami sandwich of the year late one evening at Deli Masters, an obscure kosher institution that hangs above the LIE like a goiter. Served on rye, the sandwich is full but not overstuffed, and the meat is greasy and flavorful.

GOTTLIEB'S RESTAURANT ⭐
352 Roebling Street, Brooklyn, 718-384-6612 The brisket sandwich with gravy really rocks at this old-time Williamsburg kosher deli, which remains picturesquely unrenovated since the 1960s. Go for the large size, and side it with the usually excellent (unless they've been reheated a couple of times) fries. The chicken cutlets that beckon from the window are also fab, and I can't remember tasting better Hungarian goulash, the potatoes and tender hunks of beef bathed in a mild, paprika-tinged sauce. Thursday the action really heats up with specials like chopped chicken liver and gefilte fish.

180

JAY & LLOYD'S ☆ ☆ ☆

2718 Avenue U, Brooklyn, 718-891-5298 Critics go crazy for Adelman's, a kosher deli on Kings Highway in Brooklyn. But I find their corned beef too fine-grained, their matzo ball soup too Campbell's-tasting, and their pastrami only adequate. And the twerpy decor is for the birds. Much better on all counts, and only a few blocks seaward, is Jay & Lloyd's. The pastrami's great, thickly rimmed with spices, moist, and generously wadded in the sandwich. Cut by hand, the slices are not too thin and not too thick, and delivered with no pretensions whatever. They also offer a kosher version of the Catskill sandwich fave RPG, usually made with anisey Chinese roast pork on garlic bread topped with duck sauce. Here, veal is substituted for pork.

YIDDISH BROADWAY

The period from 1880 to 1924 was the era of greatest Jewish immigration from Germany and Eastern Europe to New York, a time during which a quarter million Jews settled on the Lower East Side. Mainly speakers of Yiddish, this population entertained itself at a theater district that extended along 2nd Avenue from Houston Street to East 14th Street, an area that became known as the Yiddish Broadway. At one time there were as many as 15 theaters in this district, of which vestiges remain. The Fillmore East was once a Yiddish-language theater, as was the ornate theater located at the corner of 12th Street and 2nd Avenue, now used as a movie theater. This East Village thoroughfare also hosted a string of restaurants and coffeehouses that formed the literary center of the Jewish community, associated with writers like Isaac Bashevis Singer. **B & H Dairy** and the **Second Avenue Deli** both date from the Yiddish Broadway era, and the latter features photos of actors associated with those theaters in the Molly Picon Room, named after a prominent Yiddish-language actress. The most important remaining vestige of Yiddish Broadway, however, is the Hollywood movie industry, founded in the 1920s by such Lower East Side theatrical luminaries as Harry Cohn, the Warner brothers, Adolph Zukor, and Samuel Goldwyn, whose real name was Samuel Gelbfisz.

KATZ'S ★ ★ ★

205 East Houston Street, Manhattan, 212-254-2246 Visit this century-old Jewish deli (their slogan: "Send a salami to your boy in the army") and Wurst Fabrik (Yiddish for sausage maker) before someone decides to raze it and build a high-rise condo or install another Starbucks. Tip the carvers $1 before you order and get a sandwich big enough for two — my usual choice is a combo of pastrami and corned beef on a club roll. The preferred beverage is Dr. Brown's Cel-ray, a celery tonic that's a Lower East Side favorite, but skip the limp and mealy fries. Note: Not kosher, but "kosher style."

PASTRAMI QUEEN ★ ★

1269 Lexington Avenue, Manhattan, 212-828-0007 Even after a transplantation from Queens and a gender change (formerly Pastrami King), this deli serves up a pastrami sandwich more like Montreal's "smoked meat" than New York pastrami. It's smokier, more finely grained, freer of fat. Though the sandwich isn't overstuffed, one is enough to fill you up.

SARGE'S ★

548 3rd Avenue, Manhattan, 212-679-0042 Founded by a retired policeman in 1964 and now run by his grandchildren, Sarge's is one of the city's great Jewish delis. The pastrami is monumentally smoky, delicious even though it's usually cut way too thin (request thick slices). But the corned beef can't measure up. It finds the meaning of its life not in a sandwich, but in the corned beef hash — slivers of salty meat fried crisp that overpower the smidgens of potato. It's wonderful when topped with the optional trio of poached eggs. Servers are so gruff, they could be actors playing waiters in a deli.

SECOND AVENUE DELI ★ ★ ★

156 2nd Avenue, Manhattan, 212-677-0606 While the corned beef is superior at Katz's, pastrami is the thing to get at the Second Avenue Deli — leaner than usual, firm, smoky, and deep ruby in color. For those seeking a less rough-and-tumble venue, this kosher haven takes its theme from the Jewish theater district that used to flourish along this thoroughfare. The deli is also a good place to experience the arcana of Ashkenazy cooking, from stuffed derma, to kasha varnishkes, to creamy noodle pudding, achieved without cream, of course.

SIEGEL'S KOSHER DELICATESSEN ★

1646 2nd Avenue, Manhattan, 212-288-3632 It's deli as theater at Siegel's, where even the Trinidadian waitress speaks with a Brooklyn Jewish accent and the deli guys behind the counter trade lines like: "I'm not an idiot like you," and "You're a bigger idiot than me . . ." The garnet-colored corned beef is particularly good, with spider-veins of fat, while the pastrami and the brisket are sometimes too lean. Check the window for potato pancakes, served warm with apple sauce, two to an order, and don't miss the stupendous chicken soup, whose imperfect clarity signals superior flavor and density — order it with vegetables and find the flavor accelerated with, among other things, turnips.

Korean

Long gone are the days when every Korean restaurant in town had an identical menu, divided inexorably into barbecues, seafood stews, sushi, and noodle dishes — usually with no English translation. Fifteen years ago the patrons were almost exclusively Korean, and there was a particular thrill venturing into them. Though the welcome was never less than warm, it was disappointing to be served only the most unchallenging pan chan that could be dredged up, causing you to look tearfully down into your bowl of bland white-cabbage kimchee, while diners at the next table were enjoying wilder pan chan featuring raw meat, pickled skate, and kimchees of the deepest red — tinted with tons of hot pepper, of course.

Nowadays, many of these restaurants expect non-Koreans, and no longer give themselves the air of a private club closed to the general public. Restaurants with peculiar specialties — like dumplings, barbecued Kobe-style beef, or male-enhancing fodder like eel and animal penis — have appeared in profusion. Walk along West 32nd Street in Manhattan or Northern Boulevard in Murray Hill, Queens, and marvel at the sheer number of Korean establishments, and the welcoming nature of their facades.

Because they live in a country with hard winters, Koreans prefer food that is both spicy hot and thermally hot. Many stews are served from metal chafing dishes bubbling over Sterno flames, making it possible to eat a dish while it's actually boiling, not that you'd want to. I always extinguish the flames immediately, since steaming hot is hot enough for me. An assortment of small dishes, called pan chan, is served cold when you first arrive. These can be downed as appetizers, during dinner, or afterwards. You're encouraged to ask for more of any dish that you particularly enjoy. Many of the best of these dishes feature raw fish or meat.

LOOK FOR:

beebimbop *multi-ingredient warm rice salad*
bulgogi *beef barbecue*
chongol *hot pot*
chuk *rice gruel*
jaeook gooey *pork tenderloin barbecue*
kalbi *beef short ribs*
kerbing *black-bean buns*
kimbad *rice rolled in seaweed with a variety of fillings*
kimchee *spicy cabbage pickle*
kungjung chongol *meat-and-fish hot pot*
mandoo *meat-stuffed dumplings*
naengmyum *North Korean noodles*
nakji kpchang jungol *pork tripe stew*
pajun *giant gooey pancake*
pan chan *small appetizing dishes*
pokkum *stir-fry dish*
soju *sweet-potato liquor*
soondubu *soft homemade bean curd*
sujeonkwa *cinnamon dessert beverage*
tang *soup*
tchigae *stew*
toenjang tchigae *bean paste stew*

DO HWA ☆ ☆ 🐟 🐟 $

55 Carmine Street, Manhattan, 212-414-1224 This offspring of the East Village's Dok Suni, partly owned by Quentin Tarantino, pulls fewer culinary punches in its presentation of Korean fare in a hipster setting. Go for the wonderful deji kalbi, spare ribs annealed with a thick sweet sauce, or any of the several pajun, savory pancakes loaded with chiles, scallions, and your choice of seafood or vegetables. While a pricey pair of sea bass fillets left us cold, the beebimbop — a rice, beef, and vegetable assortment topped with a runny egg and delivered in a sizzling crock — was wonderful. Depending on where you live, going to Do Hwa might just beat going to 32nd Street.

DOSIRAK ☆ ☆ 🐟

30 East 13th Street, Manhattan, 212-366-9299 Forgoing the flotilla of free small dishes called pan chan, which you might not have been too fond of anyway, DoSirak offers what it calls "simple good Korean food," and I can't argue with that assessment. The soups are a particularly good deal (under $10), running from the unspicy but rib-sticking beef short rib to the searingly spicy pork and kimchee. The crock-seared rice salads known by the musical name beebimbop are often thrust into the wood-burning oven at the rear of the restaurant, a vestige of pizza parlors past.

EMO'S ☆ 🌶

1564 2nd Avenue, Manhattan, 212-628-8699 No, it's not named after the postpunk school of emotive rock, though the excellent eats may leave you tearful. Emo's is a Korean restaurant that doesn't stint on hot, vinegary, and fishy flavors, and the prices are lower than you'd expect to pay in these upscale surroundings, especially if you go for filling one-dish meals like beebimbop, a crock of warm rice topped with meat, diverse Asian vegetables, and a raw egg. Mix vigorously.

LEE PARK SA ☆ 🌶

158-15 Northern Boulevard, Queens, 718-321-9730 The specialty of this small rustic Korean barbecue is Kobe-style beef, cubed and grilled over a gas flame in the middle of the table. You won't miss the charcoal: the tidbits come out smoky and beefy tasting, and are best eaten without the rigamarole of wrapping them in lettuce. While the short rib seemed a little below par, the piping-hot and spicy-hot stew of mushrooms, baby octopus tentacles, and two kinds of pork tripe known as nakji kpchang jungol is transcendently good.

MANDOO ☆ 🌀

2 West 32nd Street, Manhattan, 212-279-3075 This nifty Koreatown stalwart specializes in dumplings, made right in the window. The modernistic dining room is all angles and blond woods, and selections include baby mandoo, nearly a score of tiny dumplings with a pork-and-scallion filling; kimchee mandoo, stuffed with the sweltering cabbage condiment; and the euphonious haemool mool mandoo, filled with a combination of shrimp and sea cucumber, colored fluorescent orange due to the addition of carrot to the dough. Noodles, rice dishes, and desserts round out the menu, and the perfect conclusion to a meal is sujeonkwa, a cold sweet broth flavored with cinnamon.

MANNA ☆ 🌀

289 Mercer Street, Manhattan, 212-473-6162 While the food hardly matches its biblical counterpart, it's pretty darn good anyway, and cheap for Korean fare. Priced around $10, the bento boxes contain 10 or more dishes, including pickles, kimchees, sautéed mushrooms, black-sesame rice, bean-thread vermicelli dressed with sesame oil, miso soup, and a generous heap of

KOREAN SUSHI
AND GENERAL TSO'S CHICKEN

Despite some differences of opinion over the years between Korea and her neighbors Japan and China, Koreans love to eat Japanese and Chinese food. Most big-ticket Korean restaurants feature a sushi bar, for example, and the Koreans were in on the ground floor of sushi evolution, by creating the "mega" style of preparation that has increased the average size of sushi around town, for better or worse. Immigrants from northern China brought their noodles with them; now they are very popular in both Koreas, and one of the few dishes acknowledged to be a foreign export by a sometimes xenophobic population. Following are some restaurants that groom Chinese and Japanese food for a Korean audience. Expect to find Korean flourishes like kimchee and other pan chan in all these places, with a higher level of chile heat available in some dishes.

SAM WON GAHK ☆ 🌶

82-53 Broadway, Queens, 718-458-4020 This modest noodle shop in a former diner features Chinese dishes with surprising twists that begin with the arrival of serious cabbage kimchee and sweet yellow daikon pickle — betraying the Korean bent of what's to follow. We especially enjoyed "rice with vegetable and pork with starch noodles," which, in case you had any doubt, is a carbohydrate barrage of rice tangled with mung-bean thread, and "noodles with hot chop suey soup," which was served in a bowl like a basketball cut in half, featuring squid and shrimp with Italian spaghetti in an incendiary red broth.

HAEJO ☆ ☆ 🌶

46-25 Kissena Boulevard, Queens, 718-461-4782 Immigrants from Shandong, China, brought wheat noodles to Korea in the 1950s, and induced a national preoccupation. Dig the freshly made product at Haejo, Flushing's answer to Honmura An. A surveillance camera pointed at the kitchen ensures that your noodles are freshly made, and the toppings run the gamut from "brown sauce" to "brown sauce Peking style" to "special brown sauce Peking style." You can also order noodles in a series of soup preparations, most of them fiery hot. Note the address carefully — there is a seafood joint with same name nearby.

ISHIHAMA ☆ 🐟

319 5th Avenue, Manhattan, 212-696-9386 Providing a dish of kimchee alongside, this restaurant concentrates on sushi with a Korean perspective, although other Japanese standards like teriyaki and tempura are also available. The sushi is well-formed and fresh, and recommended items include hwe-dup bop, a salad of rice, raw fish, and greenery in a sweet chile sauce; and natto hand roll, an if-you-dare combo of scallions and mucoidal fermented soy beans. Best of all — a free side dish of raw sea squirt in hot sauce that landed on our table one evening. Wash it down with O.B. beer (the favorite of gynecologists everywhere) or a bottle of soju, a sweet-potato liquor (now usually made from grain) that's like a weak vodka.

NOLBU SUSHI ☆ 🍊

162-20 Northern Boulevard, Queens, 718-939-7374 The Koreans have adopted the nori roll, and transformed it in much the same way the burrito turned into the wrap in the early 1990s. Taking Japanese futomaki as a license to innovate, this minichain has generated a series of thick rolls stuffed with sushi rice and a bewildering array of ingredients, including American cheese, kimchee, and smoked pig trotter. Several of the combos are quite good — I leave you to figure out which.

meat. The pork, which is a lot like bacon, is particularly good. Other favorites include a special of soft bean curd, sprouts, and rice in a sputtering stone crock. Stir in the raw egg to thicken the stew.

THE MILL ☆ 🐟

2895 Broadway, Manhattan, 212-666-7653 This Columbia favorite was a regular diner with a few restrained Korean dishes until a few years ago, when it morphed into a full-scale Korean restaurant. The prices remained eminently reasonable, and now it's one of the better bargains in town. My faves are the stone crock dishes, all priced under $10, one of which features spicy pork strips, watercress and lettuce, and various other vegetables heaped over rice that sizzles to the bottom of the vessel. Scrape off and crunch.

NATURAL BEAN CURD ☆ ☆ 🐟 🍊

40-06 Queens Boulevard, Queens, 718-706-0899 Soft bean curd, known as soondubu, has become all the rage in Queens, and this Sunnyside café offers it in five variations, partnered with things like kimchee, beef intestine, and mixed vegetables. With a limited menu, this fast-food chain hawks Korean standards at half the cost and in half the time of traditional restaurants. Though you don't get to barbecue the bulgogi yourself (actually, it isn't barbecued at all, but skillet-fried), the sweet and oniony pile is enough for two, especially considering the generous assortment of pan chan that accompanies each entrée.

NEW YORK KOM TANG SOOT BUL HOUSE ☆ ☆ ☆
🐟 $

32 West 32nd Street, Manhattan, 212-947-8482 This is the most reliable barbecue in Koreatown, and the "soot bul" in the name is your guarantee that it's also one of the few places left that use real charcoal in their grills. I've never explored all the nooks and crannies of the three floors, but bring a crowd and you can have the second-floor room with a picture window looking onto 32nd Street. Your first course might be the rubbery pancake filled with seafood called hae mool pajun, or hoe mu chim, a novel salad of raw fish tossed with vegetables. Besides the usual short rib and beefsteak, barbecuables include organ meats like stomach and tongue. Founded in 1979, it claims to be the oldest Korean restaurant in New York, though I have my doubts.

OLYMPIC GARDEN ☆ ☆ 🌶 🐟

79-06 Broadway, Queens, 718-335-4646 Occupying a commanding position opposite Elmhurst Hospital, Olympic Garden is a stone and glass box with a Vegas flair. It is priced on par with other Korean restaurants in the city, but the servings are significantly larger. Bulgogi was enough to share among four, although instead of arriving neatly pinwheeled on a platter, it came in a big wad. The beef is too lean, anyway, so order the jaeook gooey, ribbons of pork tenderloin that really are gooey with a dark marinade. And who could avoid ordering something called angler sea toad casserole? Not me. It's one of those red stews brought to the table boiling, rife with bean curd, cayenne, and green onions.

SEOUL KING DUMPLINGS ☆ ☆

Northern Boulevard at 150th Street, Queens, no phone The heart of Murray Hill's Koreatown is this humble green-roofed shack, serving but four specialties ($1 each): mandoo dumplings, pancakes filled with sweet syrup, cakes stuffed with red-bean paste, and black-bean-stuffed rolls that — according to the jolly chef — are called kerbing.

SHIN JUNG ☆ 🐟

136-33 37th Avenue, Queens, 718-460-5026 If you're a fan of chandeliers, here's your place — the double dining room has dozens. The food is straightforward Korean, entirely lacking Japanese flourishes, and deploying superior raw materials. The meat in the unmarinated beef rib — our favorite barbecue — was spectacularly well-marbled, ceremoniously snipped from the bone by our waitress as we watched. Also recommended are the mung bean pancakes, three to an order and crammed with vegetables and beef, and the whole grilled mackerel. The beverage of choice is soju, quaffed from tiny glasses between bites.

SOL BAWOO ☆ ☆ ☆

41-10 149th Place, Queens, 718-445-2542 Korean barbecue is never cheap, but this rustic spot excels at big portions, plenty of pan chan, and, sometimes, freebie platters of acorn jelly and noodles. The fresh eel totally rocks, two to an order and grilled over charcoal. The menu also boasts goat hot pots made from several intriguing animal parts. Beef and birds are grilled over irregular hardwood charcoal of the type obsessive barbecuers use, though pork and seafood will be fried. The menu also offers noodle dishes and stews, and to get you in the mood, the room is festooned with vines and lined with bark like a mountain cabin.

Malaysian, Indonesian, Philippine, and Singaporean

Though the Buddhist Chinese constitute 35 percent of the population in many parts of Malaysia, the Islamic majority is trying to make them scram — which probably explains the marked increase of Malaysian restaurants in town six or seven years ago. Now the number seems to be dwindling, as other immigrant groups appear. Nevertheless, Malaysian remains a fad among Chinese diners, for whom it represents only one in a mix of Asian restaurants found in modern Chinatowns. Malaysian food is a grab bag of Chinese, Indian, Portuguese, aboriginal Malay, Thai, and other Southeast Asian influences, all of which come together in the cooking of the Straits Chinese, a subgroup of expats resident in the Malay Peninsula for two centuries and more.

Though New York boasts myriad Malaysian restaurants, Indonesian boites can be counted on the fingers of one hand. Nearly 20 years ago Atlantic Avenue's adorable **Bali Rice Shop** introduced the satay to Brooklyn, then promptly croaked. That loss was finally redressed in 1993 when **Java Rijsttafel** surfaced in Park Slope, although, as the name implies, this pint-sized café specializes in the scarf of Java rather than Bali. Neither had much effect on the city's Indonesian deficiency, since these islands are only two in an archipelago of 8,000, many with unique cuisines.

As for Filipino — there are now fewer than there were 15 years ago, when nurses and doctors were imported en masse from the Philippines to work at area hospitals, especially Beth Israel, which gave rise to the concentration of eateries and groceries still found around the corner of 1st

Avenue and 14th Street. I can remember when a Filipino lady from a nearby restaurant near the corner of East 12th Street used to set up a stand in the summer on 1st Avenue and sell wedges of fresh pineapple on a stick. Sadly, the turo-turo joints that once graced 9th Avenue behind the Port Authority are now vanished, but there is still a substantial Little Manila in Woodside, Queens, along Roosevelt Avenue in the 60s.

LOOK FOR:

ABC *Singaporean ice dessert with wiggly jellies*
achar *sweet pickled vegetable salad*
ayam balado *chicken in hot chile sauce*
ayam opor *chicken in coconut sauce*
bakwan *Javanese corn fritters dotted with small shrimp*
balut *Philippine gestated hen or duck egg*
batchoy *Philippine pork organs in gingery broth*
beef rendang *dark coconut-milk stew*
dinuguan *Philippine pork in blood gravy*
embek-embek *Sumatran soup with dumplings*
gado-gado *Javanese boiled salad with peanut sauce*
ginataang sitaw *Philippine pumpkin stew*
golden chicken *Singaporean chicken wings stuffed with shrimp and fried in rice paper*
ketjap *vinegary Indonesian palm-molasses forerunner of ketchup*
laing *Philippine pork and taro-leaf stew*
laksa *Malaysian rice noodles*
matarbak *pastry filled with curried meat and eggs*
nasi rames *Indonesian set meal*
otak-otak *Sumatran fish mousse in banana leaf*
papaitan *Philippine tripe and heart soup*
pasembur *Indonesian sprout, jicama, and shrimp-fritter salad*
pastel *Indonesian-Dutch turnover*
pata *fried Philippine pork shank*
popiah *thin-skinned vegetable burritos*
prawn mee *pork and shrimp over egg noodles with broth*
rambutan *small round fruit with red hairy skin*

rijsttafel	*Indonesian-Dutch serial multidish meal*
roti canai	*Malay-Indian chicken curry with floppy pancake*
sambals	*Indonesian and Malaysian condiments often flavored with dried fish*
sate ayam	*Indonesian chicken brochettes with peanut sauce*
tosino	*sweet pickled Philippine pork*
trasi	*fish paste*

Indonesian

BALI NUSA INDAH ☆ 🐟

651 9th Avenue, Manhattan, 212-265-2200 The set meal called nasi rames is a parade of piquant Indonesian dishes: gado-gado, shrimp chips, achar pickles, tender beef satays dabbed with peanut sauce, chicken curry, beef rendang, a garlicky toss of shrimp and green beans, salty anchovy-and-peanut sambal, and a mound of snow-white rice. Indonesia is the botanical home of clove, nutmeg, mace, black pepper, and cassia — spices over which Arab and European traders contended for centuries. Luxuriant combinations of these intensify the meat and poultry offerings at Bali Nusa Indah. Ayam opor is my favorite: chicken chunks, crisp skin adhering, dunked in a sienna-tinted sauce redolent of coconut and sweet spices. But, hey, where's the Balinese food implied by the restaurant's name?

BOROBUDUR ☆ ☆ ☆ 🐟

128 East 4th Street, Manhattan, 212-614-9079 Named after a ninth-century pyramid encircled by seven stone terraces featuring bas-reliefs of Buddha's life, Borobudur is situated on the ground floor of an East Village tenement. Despite the Buddhist name, the food is Muslim halal, mainly from Java. This rare Indonesian café serves top-notch meals in a number of pleasing formats, from the fiery beef rendang over rice, to the generous (eight-stick) satay platter, to the omnibus meal of nasi goreng — a miniature rijsttafel of fried rice, chicken satays, and the clean-tasting pickle, achar. Don't be misled by the new dining room — the food remains as zesty and rough-hewn as it was at the outset. Find scads of things you'll get nowhere else: matarbak — a flaky pastry stuffed with ground meat and curried scrambled eggs, and sambal udang — shrimp, potatoes, and "stink beans" in a spicy orange sauce. They smelled fine to me.

JAVA INDONESIAN RIJSTTAFEL ☆ ☆
455 7th Avenue, Brooklyn, 718-832-4583 Native to Java is a sweet-and-sour marinade of palm molasses, soy sauce, and vinegar or tamarind called ketjap, the forerunner of the red stuff that comes in disposable packets. Java Rijsttafel's ayam panggang wraps this inky cloak, fragrant with garlic and ginger, around a chicken breast, then paints it with lemongrass oil for a patent-leather shine. A couple of other Javanese specialties are bakwan — splendid corn fritters dotted with shrimp, and pastel, turnovers stuffed with fine rice noodles whose pastry reflects four centuries of Dutch colonialism. Warning: The food might be blander than you hoped for, as a result of the restaurant pandering to tender-tongued neighborhood regulars.

WARTEG FORTUNA ☆ ☆ 🍎
51-24 Roosevelt Avenue, Queens, 718-898-2554 Smaller than a breadbox, the dining room at this working-class Indonesian is two narrow shelves along opposing walls and four barstools. Don't expect gringo-friendly satays; instead find a small selection of set meals and a few snacks, and expect a pleasant conversation with the regulars. Embek-embek are elongated taro dumplings stuffed with egg yellow in a thin, hot, sweet brown broth. There is also an alarmingly green angel food cake, a milky pink beverage that might have been Pepto Bismol, and a fried potato concoction that the Indonesians dining around us struggled to find an English word for. A friend swears by the avocado milkshakes.

Malaysian

MALAYSIAN RASA SAYANG ☆ 🍎
75-19 Broadway, Queens, 718-424-9054 Only steps away from the Jackson Heights stop, this Elmhurst Malaysian excels at popiah, refreshing summer rolls stuffed with tempeh, crisp fried onions, and greenery, then topped with a pair of sauces; and rendang, cubes of beef shank slow-cooked in a coconut gravy laden with sweet spices and garlic. Our loudest cheers, though, were reserved for tilefish braised in a gingery broth — a dish elicited by asking the waitress what kind of fish was on hand, and then letting the cook decide how to prepare it.

NYONYA ☆ ☆ 🐟
194 Grand Street, Manhattan, 212-334-3669; 5323 8th Avenue, Brooklyn, 718-633-0808 Ignore the pricey suggestions of the waitstaff and go for some of New York's best home-style Malaysian cooking at bargain prices. Start with the wonderful pasembur, a shareable salad of sprouts, jicama, cucumber, and

tofu surmounted by herb-flecked fritters smothered in chile sauce, then proceed to "squids wrapped in silver foil" — rings of steamed cephalopod made triply tart with lemon, lemongrass, and lime leaves. Other faves include achar, a plate of sweet pickled vegetables dotted with sesame seeds, and yam rice, featuring yam, pork, and assorted vegetables in a side dish that could almost be a main course.

PROTON SAGA ☆ 🐟 🐠

11 Allen Street, Manhattan, 212-625-1163 This attractive eatery — pridefully named after the first car to be manufactured in Malaysia and not some grade B science fiction movie — presents an Islamic perspective on Southeast Asian food. The achar is sublime, a tart and sweet salad of shredded vegetables topped with sesame seeds and crunchy peanuts. The no-pork menu focuses on seafood, of which stingray is something of a house specialty. Have it Malaysian style, smothered in chile sauce, the tender flesh pulling easily away from the radiating spines. Also don't miss peanut cake, an Indian-style paratha filled with crushed goobers.

SATAY HUT ☆ 🐟

135-25A 40th Road, Queens, 718-321-0842 Provocatively located just down the street from a public housing project called the Bland Houses, the food at Flushing's Satay Hut is anything but insipid. The roti canai, a gossamer pancake bunched and presented with a small bowl of chicken curry, is assertively hot, and so is the even-better coconut variation sometimes available. Out-hotting these is beef rendang rice — fiery gobs of meat with the spicing twisted in a decidedly Indian direction. Paradoxically, the "chili chicken (Indian style)" didn't taste very Indian at all, although these breaded and mildly spiced morsels beat the pants off Chicken McNuggets.

TASTE GOOD ☆ ☆ ☆ 🐟 🐠

82-18 45th Avenue, Queens, 718-898-8001; 53 Bayard Street, Manhattan, 212-513-0818 The name is an understatement at this homely Malaysian diner that, in its original location, hides behind a sign that reads "Chinese Noodles." The new branch in Manhattan's Chinatown is equally as good, but not quite as comfy. The good mood of the staff at both places is contagious, much of the food is prepared as you watch, and the excellent dishes run from humble roti canai and stuffed tofu (a slippery showcase of diverse curd), to grander creations. Dried curry asam prawn dumps nine behemoths into a sweet chile sauce. The waitress will offer to remove the heads and shells; don't let her, since the orange fat (and most of the flavor) is deposited in the head, and the crunch of the exoskeleton nicely offsets the fleshiness of these beauties. "Dried curry fish meat" is another estimable variation on the very wet "dried curry" formula, this one featuring slices of tilapia in a tureen of thick sauce enlivened, Thai-style, with chile peppers.

Philippine

ELVIE'S TURO-TURO ☆ ☆
214 1st Avenue, Manhattan, 212-473-7785 Founded a decade ago to serve the lunch needs of Filipino Beth Israel nurses, this Philippine lunch counter (whose name means "point-point" in Tagalog) offers a beguiling display of dishes that specialize in the abrupt juxtaposition of powerful competing flavors applied to ingredients that run from Chinese to aboriginal Malay to Mexican to European. Sample the daily specials or snack on satays, miniature whole fish, empanadas with braided pastry, a whole-black-peppercorn rendition of sweet-and-sour pork, oxtails in peanut sauce, or, Elvie's signature, anise chicken.

BALUT

Every region has food oddities idolized by residents and treated contemptuously by everyone else. My most recent encounter with a dish of this caliber is balut, boiled eggs sold in every Philippine grocery in town. At the **New Manila Food Mart** (351 East 14th Street, Manhattan, 212-420-8182), the duck version sits in a lidded wicker basket with a gingham liner that Rebecca of Sunnybrook farm might have carried down the garden path. The more pedestrian chicken version is colored violet and resides in the refrigerator case. Peel the egg and take a bite, and you're in for a big surprise. The white is tinged yellow, and has an almost cheesy quality, with a slight tang of fermentation. The flesh is crazed with red blood vessels.

Balut is the Tagalog term for a fertilized egg permitted to gestate for 15 days before being boiled. According to the counterman, the eggs should be reheated before serving. Duck eggs are most prized because of their size. A poll of Filipino friends revealed a diversity of opinion as to how the eggs should be eaten. One said they were good only immediately after boiling, still slightly runny. She also said that you throw the fetus away. Another claimed that, according to her mother, the crunchy fetus is the best part.

IHAWAN ★ ★ ★

40-06 70th Street, Queens, 718-205-1480 Since the demise of Manila Garden last year, Ihawan takes its place as the city's foremost Filipino, not just featuring barbecue (pick the pork), but regaling us with off-the-wall culinary combinations that mix Spanish, Chinese, and Malay influences. Several visits convinced us that Filipinos shame even the French and Taiwanese in their admiration for organ meats, as a succession of powerfully flavored offerings demonstrate: bopis (pork lungs and liver), bulalo (marrow bone soup), batchoy ("pork internal parts in ginger soup"), papaitan (tripe and heart soup), dinuguan (pork in blood gravy), and menudo, made with beef cubes and liver, rather than the tripe used in most Spanish-speaking countries. Another killer selection is laing, a loose and creamy dish of fresh taro leaves simmered in coconut milk, with a big shrimp cavorting on top. The dish has a mild oxalic tang and an appealing brininess. But most popular with Filipino families was pata, a massive pork shank fried till the skin is crisp and blistered.

Singaporean

SINGAPORE CAFÉ ★ ★

69 Mott Street, Manhattan, 212-964-0003 This gleaming facility in the heart of Old Chinatown flaunts a decor and extended menu that bespeak Singaporean sophistication. The menu offers the largest collection of hawker food to be found in the city, adding cart-style Chinese, Japanese, and Thai dishes to Malaysian. Highlights include crab with aromatic flavor, and golden chicken — stuffed with shrimp paste hemmed in with poh piah skin and fried to delirious perfection. But turn from this mire of strong seasonings for a moment and consider the lowly chicken satay. Though invented in Persia, this favorite is rendered in most Southeast Asian restaurants as a boring ellipsoid of breast meat pierced by a dowel and indifferently grilled. Singapore Café's features tiny morsels of poultry, both light and dark, swaddled in skin and adhering little bits of fat. Prawn mee is a Malay-leaning dish that modestly offers only two shrimp and a couple of pork slices to embellish its bounty of soft egg noodles. The center of attention, though, is a brick-red broth so irresistible you'll lick the last drops from the bowl.

CRAVING HAWKER FOOD

For such a tightly wound place — gum chewing carries stiff penalties — Singapore is freakishly casual about eating. Central to the food culture are thousands of street carts, each serving one or two specialties from a roster of hundreds flaunting Indian, Malaysian, Indonesian, and Hokkien Chinese pedigrees. This folkway arose in the days when the city had an overwhelmingly male population, uprooted from their homelands and too busy to cook for themselves. Though most of these carts have been moved indoors, first to open-air hawker centers, then to air-conditioned food courts, the intoxicating habit of wolfing down cart meals persists. This cuisine is collectively known as kiasu makan in Spinglish, the polyglot patois of the metropolis — "meals to be craved." Noodles form the basis of many hawker offerings — steamed, stirred into soups, and fried. Even the simplest-seeming dishes have complex sour and fishy flavors.

Mexican

A round 1990, the first trickle of Pueblans began arriving in New York, some say after a huge Volkswagen plant closed, throwing many out of work. The food they brought with them was a revelation — dense and thick moles (pronounced "moe-lays"), double-tortilla tacos containing organ meats dressed only with cilantro and raw onions, and grilled fresh cactus paddles, representing a complete contrast to the reworked Tex-Mex that was offered in the city's margarita mills, and the Cal-Mex burritos that were just becoming a fad around town.

Inevitably, as Puebla emptied out, immigration from adjoining states began, and now if we choose carefully, we can find ourselves eating food from the states of Guerrero, Michoacán, and Oaxaca. There's plenty of overlap, of course, but it's the unique dishes like huashimole and fiery caldo camarones that most fascinate us. Meanwhile, more Mexican neighborhoods have arisen with the full complement of taquerias, panaderias, and grocery stores well-stocked with imported merchandise we didn't have a prayer of finding before. Not sure what I'm going to do with sundried cow stomach I found in Bushwick, but it's nice to know it's there if I want it. Major Mexican neighborhoods are now to be found in East Harlem, Jackson Heights, Corona, East Williamsburg, Sunset Park, and, especially, Bushwick. Nowadays, you're never far from a Mexican meal, and don't forget those churros they sell down in the subway, or the line of taco trucks on Roosevelt Avenue, mainly in the 70s and 80s.

Also see Tex-Mex and Burritos in the Regional and Vernacular American chapter.

LOOK FOR:

adobo *meat or chicken in vinegary chile marinade*

aguacate relleno *half avocado stuffed with shrimp or chicken salad*

antojitos *corn-based snacks like enchiladas and tacos*

cemitas *round Pueblan sandwiches*

champurrado *lard-laced cocoa and cornmeal beverage*

chilaquiles *taco chips tossed with green or red mole*

chilate *red, chile-laced weekend chicken soup*

chile relleno *fresh chile stuffed with cheese*

chipotle *smoked jalapeño*

churros *linear donuts*

clayuda *Oaxacan pizza*

cochinita pibil *Yucatan pork marinated in bitter orange*

ensalada de nopalitos *cactus salad*

escabeche *Spanish-Mexican pickled fish*

flautas *stuffed and fried tortilla flutes*

guacamole *cold smashed avocado dip*

horchata *sweet rice beverage*

huachinango Veracruzana *red snapper in tart vegetable julienne*

huevos rancheros *ranch eggs served on tortillas with salsa*

masa *corn dough used to make tortillas*

menudo *tripe soup*

milanesa *pounded and breaded beefsteak*

mixiotes *meat or chicken wrapped in parchment and steamed*

mole negra *Oaxacan chocolate mole*

mole pipián *south Mexican pumpkin seed sauce*

mole poblano *Pueblan chile-chocolate gravy*

mole ranchero *south Mexican sauce made with dried chiles*

pan de pulque *egg bread leavened with beer*

panza *tripe stew*

pozole *weekend-only hominy stew*

> **quesadilla** *toasted cheese sandwich made with tortillas*
>
> **queson fundido** *Mexican cheese fondue*
>
> **tamale** *stuffed cylinder of corn dough*
>
> **tinga** *south Mexican fiery chicken stew*
>
> **tomatillo** *green husk tomato used in mole verde*
>
> **tostada** *corn tortilla fried flat and loaded like a taco*
>
> **verdolaga** *purslane*

ATLIXCO DELI ☆

37-18 31st Avenue, Queens, 718-777-2775 Named after a fertile valley in Mexico's geographic center, this modest grocery is festooned with plastic foliage and excels at tacos lushly topped with onions, cilantro, guacamole, and spicy pickled red peppers; the tortas are also spectacular. Wash them down with champurrado, hot cocoa laced with pork fat — an idea whose time has come?

LA CASA DE LOS TACOS ☆ ☆ 🌶

2277 1st Avenue, Manhattan, 212-860-7389 This airy and comfortable truck stop wrested the palm from La Hacienda as the foremost Mexican restaurant in El Barrio. The fiery red pozole is the best of its type, heaped with "flowered" hominy and small cubes of pork, served with a fulsome condiments bar brought right to your table, with three fried tortillas for crumbling into the soup. The usual range of antojitos is also available, but check the steam table for nonmenu moles and other southern Mexican fare.

CASTRO'S ☆ 🌶 🕐

511 Myrtle Avenue, Brooklyn, 718-398-1459 Food beacon in a neighborhood with few good places to eat, Castro's is probably the oldest real Mexican restaurant in Brooklyn, and I'm not including the tequila bars of Bensonhurst and Bay Ridge. The menu combines Tex-Mex and Pueblan specialties, and it's one of the few places in town you can get the fiery stew known as tinga.

EL CHILE VERDE ☆

222 Bushwick Avenue, Brooklyn, 718-381-0346 I watched with fascination as this grocery transformed itself into a full-service restaurant, the dried chiles and canned beans pushed into the corner while a new kitchen turned out deep-fried masa quesadillas (pick huitlacoche, Mexico's favorite fungus), cemitas on homemade rolls, and chicken enchiladas drenched in a near-perfect mole poblano. Breakfast served all day, including omelets, huevos rancheros, and chilaquiles — a loose toss of taco chips in — what else? — chile verde.

LOS COMPADRES ☆ ☆
5807 5th Avenue, Brooklyn, 718-492-3459 This humble panadería received an astonishingly high ranking (#13) in my "100 Best Latin Restaurants" feature via its astonishing cemitas — outsize Pueblan sandwiches on round seeded rolls as rich as challah, heaped with avocado, scarlet sun-dried chiles, onions, greenery, and your choice of meat. The bakery's milanesa (thin sirloin) is notorious in Sunset Park, whether served on a sandwich or with rice and beans.

LA ESPIGA ☆ ☆ ☆ 🖎
42-31 102nd Street, Queens, 718-779-7898 Its Astorian cousin La Espiga II first turned us on to great cheap Mexican food. The quality there has declined, while its Corona progenitor — a tortilleria that threw down some tables and began serving amazing and idiosyncratic antojitos — has only become better. Fix your famished gaze on the roast pig floundering in meat juices in the front window, best deployed in tacos dressed with guacamole, onions, cilantro, and jalapeños.

LA ESPIGA II ☆
32-44 31st Street, Queens, 718-777-1993 Useful for a pit stop in the neighborhood, but not worth trekking to from, say, more than six blocks away, La Espiga II has turned into something of a low dive. Still on offer are an extensive range of snacks: tacos, tamales, and tortas, Mexican-style sandwiches made with a crusty roll called a bolillo. The weekend special, barbacoa — goat steamed in a banana leaf with chiles and salt — is still stringy and delicious.

FLOR DE LUNA ☆
33-09 36th Avenue, Queens, 718-392-9349 Located on a strip hopping with an international restaurant roster, this very modest Dutch Kills Mexican café also boasts of its status as a carnicería, or butcher shop, and therein lies the clue to its most outstanding offering: a steak quesadilla jamming with tasty meat, cheese, and sautéed onions.

GABRIELA'S ☆ ⏾
685 Amsterdam Avenue, Manhattan, 212-961-0574; 311 Amsterdam Avenue, Manhattan, 212-875-8532 The food at this upscale Mexican diner is plain and honest, and better than you'd expect considering the appearance. Quesadillas are served three to an order, and what makes them amazing is the tortillas,

made right on the premises with a masa more finely textured than most. The specialty of the house is chile-rubbed rotisserie chicken. Three regional sauces can be ordered to go with the bird. My advice: order all three — mancha manteles from Sinaloa, pureed bananas and chiles with a surreal orange color; Oaxacan mole negro, a smooth dark sauce with a delayed incendiary kick; and a mole pipián from Jalisco. Dig the cured beef tongue Veracruz simmered with peppers, potatoes, olives, carrots, and tomatoes.

EL GRANO DE ORO 2000 ☆ ☆ ✒

96-15 Roosevelt Avenue, Queens, 718-205-8177 A friend from L.A. reports that this narrow, tile-clad taqueria is where he goes when he's homesick. Three to an order, picaditas are lipped rounds of masa heaped with lettuce, onions, cheese, and your choice of meat — on a recent revisit I selected cabeza (head meat), but you might want to stick with the steak. Considered one of the best taquerias in Queens.

LA HACIENDA ☆

219 East 116th Street, Manhattan, 212-987-1617 This is the most ambitious Mexican restaurant in East Harlem, though certainly not the best, with a menu that runs to 100 selections, helpfully including English translations like "spicy meat of the mole" and the appetizing-sounding "fat of chunk." I went right to the antojitos section of the menu, where there were two choices of "guaraches." Named after the sandal made with a rubber-tire sole, and of recent culinary origin, these are made with a footprint-shaped flatcake of masa with a rubbery texture and taste something like a Colombian arepa. The stripped-down version is spread with green tomatillo sauce and then mounded with shredded lettuce, onions, crumbly cheese, and crema, a runny Mexican sour cream. For an extra dollar, strips of griddle-fried beef are heaped on top, making a filling meal, and a flavorful one.

EL MAGUEY Y LA TUNA ☆ ⏱

321 East Houston Street, Manhattan, 212-473-3744 Miraculously, this decade-old Pueblan restaurant has closed its decrepit premises on Grand Street in Williamsburg, and moved to the Lower East Side. The moles remain a strength of the restaurant, especially the Michoacán standard mole ranchero. It employs two flavorful dried chiles — the guajillo and the costeno — trading licks in the sauce like heavy-metal guitar gods. The mole poblano is good, in a smooth rendition, while the tongue tacos are still a favorite. Unfortunately, the fiery chicken soup called chilate has vacated the menu, and a bunch of meaty Tex-Mex stuff has been added. Still, a decent Mexican choice in the East Village.

LOS MARIACHIS ☆

805 Coney Island Avenue, Brooklyn, 718-826-3388 Premiering a decade ago on a bleak stretch of Coney Island Avenue dominated by auto repair shops, Los Mariachis has blimped from a single storefront to an entertainment complex featuring a wedding hall and Tijuana-style curio shop. The signature dish, chicken mole poblano, is a good introduction to the earthy, sauce-driven cuisine of Puebla. Guisado de calabasas features chunks of pork and slices of zucchini slowly stewed in pureed calabash squash. Friday evenings there's a strolling mariachi band.

GROW YOUR OWN

There's no doubt that the most comfortable and thriving Mexican neighborhood in town surrounds Maria Hernandez Park in Bushwick, Brooklyn. Find bakeries, taquerias, and groceries, and there's even a Chinese restaurant that caters to Mexican tastes, partly via the inclusion of loads of jalapeños in the generally Cantonese offerings. The best grocery is **La Guadalupana** (1486 DeKalb Avenue). Aside from selling the usual dried and fresh peppers, cecina, cones of lump brown sugar called piloncillo, several types of dried hoja santa — a minty herb that, according to cookbook author Rick Bayless, exists in 27 distinct varieties — and plastic-wrapped kilos of products from competing Flushing Avenue tortillerias (corn only) in various shades of white and purple, it purveys many fresh botanicals unavailable from the local Korean greengrocers. Guahay are boomerang green pods, each containing a single row of small seeds, to be cooked into moles and sprinkled fresh on tacos. There are also bitter-smelling green leaves on long stalks named "papalo," and you can also buy papalo seeds — wispy like flax — to grow your own. When I bought a bag of seeds, the clerk wonderingly asked me if I had a big enough place to have a garden. Most amazing of all at Guadalupana were fibrous and flattened brown rounds, roughly the size of a deflated basketball. In answer to my perplexed gaze, one of the store employees identified them as dehydrated cow stomachs.

MATAMOROS PUEBLA GROCERY ☆ ☆ 🌶 🍎

193 Bedford Avenue, Brooklyn, 718-782-5044 Like a jungle explorer, push your way past hanging chiles, stacks of fresh tortillas, and mazelike shelves to find a tiny taqueria, where a laboring throng of Mexican women is evidence of the effort that goes into producing this seemingly simple fare. For five years Matamoros has furnished tacos, enchiladas, and particularly good sopes to the North Side community.

MEXICO DOS ☆ ☆ ☆ 🌶

1726 Amsterdam Avenue, Manhattan, 212-234-3334 Hamilton Heights, where Alexander Hamilton once strolled around his ranch, is a new hot spot for southern Mexican cooking, and Mexico Dos is home to some of the best-prepared moles in town. The green is compounded of fresh tomatillos, green chiles, and cilantro, spiced with epazote and hoja santa — unforgettable whether poured over pork ribs or mixed with tortilla chips in a splendid chilaquiles. Red mole, too, has its advocates, who love the complexity of flavor that arises from a combo of sesame seeds, raisins, almonds, and several kinds of chiles. Decent Tex-Mex is also available at this highly recommended spot. Tragically, the most obscure mole on the menu is usually unavailable: huashimole, originating in Guerrero and intriguingly described as "Traditional among Mexicans. Made with wild seed, salted huaje & dry pepper & sauce."

MI COCINA ☆ 🍎 $

57 Jane Street, Manhattan, 212-627-8273 This comfortable upscale dining room is a West Village favorite, though the food has been up and down over the last few years. The skirt steak in the style of the ancient city of Querétaro is sublime — charcoal grilled, cilantro strewn, and profusely sided. For vegetarians, there's a fine cazuela of zucchini, corn, onions, poblanos, tomatoes, and crema that's positively pre-Colombian.

MI MEXICO LINDO PANADERIA ☆ ☆

2267 2nd Avenue, Manhattan, 212-996-5223 Where's the best place to get a torta? At a Mexican bakery, of course, where the round telera roll is fresh out of the oven. The milanesa torta bombs a razor-thick breaded steak with mayo, jalapeños, onions, avocado, and lettuce. More wildly, you can get your torta topped with two tamales.

MISTER TACO ☆

2255 White Plains Road, Bronx, 718-882-3821 One end to the other, the miraculous White Plains Road is paved with cheap eateries. Located on the rump end of the Bronx Botanical Garden,

POZOLE

I have seen God in a bowl of pozole. This hearty soup, a weekend special at nearly every taqueria in town, never fails to please. The rich broth is heavy with chunks of pork, fragrant oregano, and hominy slow-cooked until it "flowers" (also known as pozole). On the side you get a bowl of vegetables to be mixed in, usually including shredded lettuce, onions, red radishes carved like crudités at a cocktail party, and sometimes chopped jalapeños. Most places also add a refried-bean tostada, which turns the soup into a full meal.

Eventually I became aware that this so-called white pozole, which I'd been enjoying up and down Sunset Park's 5th Avenue for years, was not the only one treasured in Mexico. In fact, there are dozens. White pozole probably originated in Guadalajara, where, cooked without oregano, it's eaten for breakfast and tends to be even blander. In Guerrero a green version — thickened with pumpkin seeds and tomatillos — is downed every Thursday for lunch. Another rendition incorporating dried and fresh shrimp is found all along the Pacific coast from Nayarit southward. In inland areas of Michoacán, a fiery red version finds its way onto tables.

Mister Taco is a dependable and delicious source of tortas; antojitos like enchiladas, tamales, and tostadas; and, of course, double-tortilla tacos bulging with meat, chopped onion, and cilantro. Just don't call him Señor.

LOS PAISAS ✫
898 Amsterdam Avenue, Manhattan, 212-961-1263 This cluttered grocery/café in an area sometimes known as the Valley serves a burgeoning Mexican community. Dig the flimsy-looking wooden loft that doubles the area of the café to accommodate four tables total. A steam table next to the cash register has the usual sauces: pipián, poblano, verde, rojo. The chicken, goat, or whatever, is brought up from the kitchen in the rear and sauced on the spot. A chorizo torta was an amazing bargain, the roll packed with sausage and scrambled eggs, onion, tomato, lettuce, and sliced avocado. Los Paisas is also a good place to stock up on Mexican groceries: spices, Brooklyn-made tortillas, candy, soda, beer.

PUEBLA MEXICAN FOOD ☆ 🍑

47 1st Avenue, Manhattan, 212-473-6643 Morphing first from an Italian bakery to a Mexican one, then into a Mexican greasy spoon, this beloved institution (formerly Downtown Bakery) has lately remade itself again, adding Tex-Mex to the menu. The breakfast burritos are especially wonderful, crammed with potatoes, bacon, and chorizo. Imagine my surprise — oh blessed fusion! — when the chorizo turned out to be Italian sausage.

RICOS TACOS ☆ ☆ 🌶

505 51st Street, Brooklyn, 718-633-4816 Reaching for novelty and big city sophistication, Ricos purveys tacos arabes and taquitos, in addition to the usual roster of tacos, tortas, tostadas, and soups. The former rolls a quantity of spicy chopped beefsteak into a flour tortilla, making an unfried flauta, an open-ended miniburrito, or a Middle Eastern pita sandwich, depending on your interpretation of this wonderful invention. The latter is a fetish of Mexico City: a taco made with a pair of comical miniature tortillas offered with the usual ingredients presented open-faced. Garnish it at the magnificent salsa table. Weekends feast on an incendiary caldo de camarones.

WHAT'S IN YOUR TACO?

al pastor *marinated rotisserie pork*

barbacoa *braised goat or lamb*

cabeza *anything from the head, including brains, cheeks, ears, etc.*

carne asada *grilled beef*

carnitas *deep-fried pork tidbits*

cecina *salt-cured or air-dried beef*

chorizo *skinless sausage*

lengua *tongue*

pollo *chicken*

rajas *chile strips*

RICO'S TAMALES OAXAQUEÑOS ☆

southeast corner, 5th Avenue and 46th Street, Brooklyn, no phone This rickety red shed — owned by the same Dominican dude who owns Ricos Tacos, and part of a burgeoning empire — dispenses some of the city's best tamales, the chicken version laced with chocolaty mole poblano, the pork with spicier mole verde, while chicken tamales with rajas — roasted green-chile strips — is another triumph. Wash them down with arroz con leche, a sort of liquid rice pudding, or champurrado, a chocolate-flavored corn beverage. The competing yellow lean-to across the street offers wonderful goat soup.

SALON MEXICO ★ ★ 🌶 🍐 🍴

507 9th Avenue, Manhattan, 212-868-7780 This place that partly caters to garment center workers — and the first Pueblan café to open in midtown — did fine under the name Los Dos Rancheros Mexicanos for nearly a decade, then something sent them searching for a slicker name. Maybe it was the addition of a few Italian dishes to the menu, with meatballs that do double duty in albodingas con chipotle and spaghetti and meatballs. Anyway, the food remains good, especially the tart homemade mole pipián that surrounds the quarter chicken like an algae-filled lake, the taste made tart with tomatillos. The fresh and spicy guacamole is similarly excellent. Only the fiery chicken soup called chilate bummed us out — fortified with too many vegetables, making it healthy but not particularly good.

TACO AZTECA ★ ★ 🌶

75 Victory Boulevard, Staten Island, 718-273-6404 This busy Tomkinsville corner is where day laborers shape up to be hired, and what better place to find the best tacos in Staten Island? Sit at the counter of this former pizza parlor and enjoy cemitas, Pueblan sandwiches served on huge rolls dotted with sesame seeds and heaped with chicken, pork, or, best of all, milanesa — beefsteak topped with melted cheese, avocado, and sun-dried chiles.

TACOCINA ★ 🍴

714 9th Avenue, Manhattan, 212-541-6969 Tacocina has a slick, fast-food presentation, and too many portraits of Frida Kahlo. The college-age staff are mainly from Mexico City, and somewhat bewildered. The tongue taco, though not fully stuffed, is first-rate. Other no-nonsense tacos from a list of 15 include hongos con elote (mushrooms and sweet corn), chuleta (pork chop), and the untranslated "suadero." The best thing on the menu is the tortilla soup ($2.75), which comes with extra tortilla chips for immersion in the red, red broth.

TACOS LA HACIENDA ★

96 Wyckoff Avenue, Brooklyn, 718-821-8816 Dominating the busiest corner in Bushwick's Wyckoff Heights neighborhood, House Tacos occupies a streamlined diner that hovers over the L train station. Blue plate specials like chicken mole poblano and bistek a la Mexicana are superb, served with perfect orange rice and savory black beans, and there's a juicy cheeseburger made from fresh meat that's a couple of notches above the diner standard. Antojitos like tacos, huaraches, and, especially, quesadillas, are also recommended, the latter stuffed with chicken and decorated with mole verde and queso fresco and bearing no resemblance to bar food.

WHAT? OAXACAN!

A pal from Los Angeles disdains Pueblan food, calling it some of Mexico's worst. Where the action is, according to him, is Oaxacan. Naturally, L.A. has a slew of eateries where you can get the region's legendary seven moles — and I've got to admit, they're pretty damn good, with lots of crazy flavors. Until recently, we had no choice but to cry into our mole poblano, but now there's another way, and I don't mean driving to Los Angeles. New Jersey harbors **Restaurant Oaxaqueño #2** (260 Drift Street, New Brunswick, 732-545-6869), and even if there is some question as to whether the current proprietors are really from Oaxaca, there are some serviceable Oaxacan specialties on the three confusing menus. Chuletas en huajillo turned out to be a trio of gnarled and tasty pork chops that won't lie flat in a brilliant red sauce. The black mole one-ups mole poblano — smoother, darker, subtler, with a bitter edge that comes from multiple overroasted chiles. Get it on lamb barbacoa or chicken. We also ordered carnitas in yellow mole, but instead of pork tidbits we got big floppy pieces of skin in a bright orange liquid. Dotted with pieces of cactus, the sauce was incredibly subtle, with an undertaste of cumin. As a side we ordered the nopales, but instead of the canned variety, we got three big fresh cactus paddles, spines burned off and both sides nicely charred, served with a few green onions with bulbs attached. When we carefully examined the menus at home, we discovered a dish that we had neglected — guisado de cabeza de chivo en amarillo, goat head soup. Damn! Not to mention tacos de chapulin — crunchy grasshopper tacos. The next time we went, they were gone, but we selected tlayuda, an outsize homemade corn tortilla baked to brittleness and topped with black beans, jagged pieces of cecina, greenery, and a roasted jalapeño — Oaxacan pizza.

TACOS NUEVO MEXICO ☆

491 5th Avenue, Brooklyn, 718-832-0050 The proximity of the Slope to this taqueria guarantees the patronage of gringos as well as campesinos — resulting in a crowd-pleasing menu of antojitos, egg dishes, and pan-Mexican entrées, but look to the chalkboard for funky regional specials like spongy shrimp cakes called torta de camarones, and a wonderful green mole laced with verdolaga (purslane).

TAQUERIA COATZINGO ☆

76-05 Roosevelt Avenue, Queens, 718-424-1977 Named after a Pueblan town, this brightly lit Jackson Heights taqueria excels at food of the region, including fine chicken enchiladas with chocolate mole, and the chile-laced beef soup called birria, garnished with fresh jalapeños, as if the dried chiles in the broth weren't hot enough.

TAQUERIA LA ASUNCION ☆

206 Knickerbocker Avenue, Brooklyn, 718-881-2732 Once the commissary kitchen that produced the city's greatest mole poblano from scratch, this Bushwick oasis has become a full-service taqueria, open all week instead of just on the weekends. The chicken enchiladas smothered with the rich and spicy mole poblano is still the thing to get, though observers believe the quality of the signature mole poblano has slipped.

TULCINGO #4 ☆ ☆ 🥄

25-26 Broadway, Queens, 718-726-1525 This unprepossessing Long Island City storefront is so much more: pharmacy, grocery, and social center, with the usual menu of Mexican tacos, tortas, and tostados. But glimpses of the gyrating kitchen staff and an examination of the signs hand-scrawled in Spanish reveal a more ambitious menu of central Mexican regional fare. Foremost on a recent visit was adobo de puerco con nopales, a searingly red stew of short ribs and cactus, and barbacoa, a regular weekend special of goat steamed with chiles and other seasonings, both served with orange rice, refried beans, and a half dozen warm tortillas.

EL VAQUERO ☆

2210 3rd Avenue, Manhattan, 212-426-0518 "The Cowboy" subtly announces its presence with a cactus-and-10-gallon-hat logo on the awning. A scatter of men with droopy mustaches swill Corona and Modela midafternoon. The menu has an assortment of platos, but the joint exists for its antojitos. The chivo taco features two fresh corn tortillas folded over shredded goat, onions, and cilantro, and while it's not overstuffed, the meat is tender, moist, and pleasantly gamy. A single sauce is offered, a fiery homemade puree of tomatoes and chiles.

ZARAGOZA GROCERY ☆

215 Avenue A, Manhattan, 212-780-9204 Until the day the East Village develops its own real sit-down taqueria, this place will suffice, serving double-tortilla tacos with a choice of three stuffings, rice and beans, tamales, and, sometimes, potato-stuffed flautas that are the glory of this well-stocked Mexican grocery.

Middle Eastern

Egyptian; Israeli; Jordanian; Lebanese, Syrian, and Palestinian; and Yemeni

The Ottoman legacy can be seen in the common dining heritage of these countries, most obviously in the small dishes known as maza or meze, often served at lunch or as appetizers: hummus, falafel, tabbouleh, and baba ghanoush (the spelling varies wildly). These can be found in almost all Middle Eastern restaurants; they are tasty and good for you. But if you've become familiar enough with them to be on the verge of boredom, search out those dishes that differentiate the cuisines of the Middle East rather than unite them, like the kibbeh pie found in Lebanese places, or the salta of the Yemenis.

In this region of political and religious tumult, I had to make some tough calls. Do the Jewish Yemenites, for example, have more in common with the Muslim Yemenis with whom they lived for millennia, or with the Israelis who have been their hosts for a mere half century? Whether to clump the Lebanese, Syrians, and Palestinians together as is the usual custom in matters culinary, or award them separate categories emphasizing distinctions? Following are my rather unsatisfactory groupings.

LOOK FOR:

assid *Yemeni giant dumpling with gravy*
baba ghanoush *pureed eggplant dip*
bourma *Egyptian vegetable stew*
foul *stewed fava beans*
glaba *minced lamb*
hilbeh *Yemeni fenugreek emulsion*
hummus *pureed chickpea dip*
kibbeh *meat or pumpkin fritters or pie*

212

koshary *Rice-A-Roni with lentils*
labni maa toum *thickened yogurt with garlic*
lahmajun *Middle Eastern pizza*
mekanek *lamb sausage*
milookhiya *mucilaginous Nile grass used in soup*
Moroccan cigars *pastry flutes*
mujadara *savory rice and lentils*
ouzy *individual phyllo pie*
salta *Yemeni bubbling brown gunk*
schwarma *lamb or poultry gyro*
shafota *Yemeni bread and yogurt porridge*
shakshuka *Israeli eggs with tomato sauce*
sujukh *Armenian sausage much admired in the
    Middle East*
tabbouleh *bulgur and parsley salad*
tawook *spice-dusted chicken*
zoug *green Yemeni hot sauce*

Egyptian

BAHRY FISH MARKET AND RESTAURANT ☆ ☆ 🐟
484 Bay Ridge Avenue, Brooklyn, 718-680-8135 Taking a cue
from Greek restaurants, this Egyptian fish market allows you to
make a whole-fish selection from a bed of ice in the window, and
then see it borne to the grill or deep fryer for cooking — at a fraction of the price of the Greek joints. A baba ghanoush laced with
pickle juice and the merguez sandwich are enthusiastically recommended, as are the "chips." If these were chips in the English
sense, you might pick rice instead. However, they turn out to be potato chips, some cut thick and some thin, fried to absolute perfection and dusted with finely powdered cumin, red pepper, and salt.

ELWADY ☆ 🐪
24-25 Steinway Street, Queens, 718-545-7705 Located on a
shady stretch of Steinway that boasts an Egyptian coffeehouse,
grocery, and halal butcher, this café offers a Middle Eastern menu
with Egyptian flourishes. From the dozen dishes we tasted, best
were a plate of fava beans in a rich gravy dotted with tomatoes
and streaked with tahini ("foul"), smoky kebabs of chopped lamb
and onions ("kefta"), and a pita sandwich of spice-dusted chicken
breast ("tawook"). Desserts are also a strong point, including a
creamy rice pudding sprinkled with toasted coconut, and a honey
cake of biblical antiquity served warm from the oven.

KABAB CAFÉ ★ ★ ⏀

35-12 Steinway Street, Queens, 718-728-9858 This Astorian stalwart is run by an Egyptian chef, who cooks in various European styles as well as dishes from the Egyptian countryside. If his wonderful gnocchi are on the menu, which changes daily according to whim, grab 'em! Other favorites of mine are a slimy green soup made from milookhiya that would make okra jealous, and a garlicky stew of fresh fava beans. Fried fish and kebabs always available.

SAHARA EAST ★ ⏀

184 1st Avenue, Manhattan, 212-353-9000 Right next door to the mosque, this narrow eatery with its picturesque tenement garden is also one of the best places in town to get couscous, the semolina bathed in a broth of root vegetables. It's served in a tajine, an earthenware platter with a pointed cover that keeps the good smells in, until the waitress removes it with a flourish. Another gem is moussaka, a baked preparation of eggplant, tomatoes, onions, and herbs that improves on the Greek version of the dish.

Israeli

BISSALEH ★ ⏀

1922 Coney Island Avenue, Brooklyn, 718-998-8811 This late night kosher dairy café is decorated in an oddball rustic style, and features a pan-Israeli menu, including pizza, hummus with mushrooms, feta cheese salad, and Yemenite specialties. Among the latter is malawach, a tasty Frisbee of oily puff pastry topped with a variety of goodies — in a biblical mood, we picked the version featuring honey, dates, and sesame seeds. Bissaleh means "a little something" in Hebrew, but also designates a serpentine pastry stuffed with cheese, spinach, mushrooms, or potatoes and sided with a tea-boiled egg.

CHESKEL'S SHWARMA KING ★

3715 13th Avenue, Brooklyn, 718-435-9542 This Borough Park kosher schwarma outfit overstuffs the pita in the usual fashion, but you can get twice as much chicken by ordering a "laff" for $1 more. Either format provides a chance to fill up a small Styrofoam plate with items from the more-expansive-than-usual salad bar. The baba ghanoush is charming, the fried eggplant and peppers welcome, while the various pickled items and slaws are monumentally fresh and tasty. Kebabs are another specialty. One afternoon a pile of spicy barbecued short ribs appeared, slathered with sauce. It was some of the most flavorful beef I'd had in a while.

D. ZION BURGER ☆ ☆
4102 18th Avenue, Brooоklyn, 718-871-9467 This is one of Brooklyn's busiest Sephardic restaurants, cooking the fare of Yemen, Morocco, the Middle East, Eastern Europe, and other areas from which Jews emigrated. The mainly Orthodox clientele is a cosmopolitan crowd speaking several modern and ancient languages. There's shakshuka, a Moroccan dish that's a close cousin of huevos rancheros. On the edge of the plate is a dab of pale tahini so smooth that it could pass for sour cream. Mixed with smoky eggplant, this tahini serves as the basis of supremely light and fluffy baba ghanoush. Jachnoon is a pastry cylinder composed of thick layers wound tight, damp but not sweet; better is malawach — many-layered, deep-fried, and amorphous in shape, it has a buttery taste, and is better dipped in baba ghanoush than in the pureed tomato that is the traditional accompaniment. Even more popular are the hearty and typically Yemeni soups. One sports an entire shank of lamb surrounded by potatoes in a dense, cumin-scented broth. Note: the name of this place changes from time to time, don't be alarmed if it's different when you get there.

HOOMOOS ASLI ☆ ⊘
100 Kenmare Street, Manhattan, 212-966-0022 Like the name says, this Sephardic Israeli grill is particularly proud of its hummus, which is fluffy and richly flavored with cumin. Have it ringed around tahini and roasted pignoli, tabbouleh, or, best of all, cradling an "Israel mixed grill" — a sauté of meat and poultry tidbits that can also contain organ meats like liver, at your request. Yemenite, Middle Eastern, Turkish, and North African dishes complete the menu, but whatever you order, make sure you get plenty of the homemade pitas. Other interesting offerings include the house malawach, a Yemenite pizza topped with feta, olives, and zaatar. The sunny room is relentlessly decorated with color photos of flower beds, and the air scented with rosewater.

JERUSALEM STEAK HOUSE ☆
533 Kings Highway, Brooklyn, 718-336-5115 This lively kosher meatery poised between Midwood and Gravesend is a hangout for Israeli immigrants, and offers some of the best charcoal-grilled meats in a neighborhood that dotes on kebabs: spicy merguez sausage, kofta made from flavorful ground lamb, and fatty veal chops — a belt-busting five per order. The best appetizer is a plate of six "Moroccan cigars," meat-stuffed pastry flutes swamped with tahini and tomato. The blinding fluorescent light, portraits of the late Lubavicher rebbe, and inspirational art will make you feel like you're halfway to heaven.

KOSHER DELIGHT ☆ ☆ 🐦

1365 Broadway, Manhattan, 212-563-3366 The chicken schwarma turning in the front window is divine. Cumin-dusted and moist, it's hacked off the cylinder at just the right moment and served on a pita. A paper basket on the side lets you load up with purple cabbage slaw, grilled eggplant, two kinds of peppers, pickles, onions, and baby falafel squeezed out of a scary machine. Three sauces are available to smother the chicken: tahini, a Yemenite cilantro chutney, and, my favorite, a very tart mango dressing. Also available: kosher Chinese that's not half bad.

RECTANGLES ☆ ☆ ⏰

159 2nd Avenue, Manhattan, 212-677-8410 This East Village Israeli standby with a Sephardic bent purveys good shish kebabs of lamb, chicken, and fish (try Nile trout), decent couscous, and exceptional meze like baba ghanoush, hummus, falafel, and tabbouleh, including an unusual Turkish salad featuring chopped tomatoes in a spicy chile puree. Even more compelling are the Yemenite specialties like malawach, a multilayer oily pancake served with fresh tomato sauce, fiery zhoug relish, and a tea-boiled egg — how you eat it is up to you. If your grumpy waiter forgets to give you the free plate of the turnip, cucumber, and olive pickles, remind her.

VILLAGE SCHAWARMA ☆ ☆

321 6th Avenue, Manhattan, 212-924-8700 While most of the schwarma joints in midtown have converted their spinners to chicken or turkey, V.S. sticks with lamb — strongly flavored and saturated with fat, the way it should be. The schwarma sandwich assembles a giant wad of warm meat, fiery and cooling condiments, and as much salad as you can spoon into the puffy and expansive pita from the Israeli-style salad bar. Added bonus: outdoor seating in a tenement backyard, the perfect setting to savor your schwarma. Open 24 hours.

Jordanian

TABOULEH ☆ ☆ ⏰

136 Smith Street, Brooklyn, 718-797-3313 Among all the pricey bistros blossoming in Cobble and Carroll, a few humble eateries linger. Tabouleh is a Jordanian café that excels at bulging pita sandwiches and hearty main courses like kebabs and roast chicken that are plopped on rice garnished with toasted almonds. Try kafta mechewi, a flavorful amalgam of beef and lamb laced with onions and peppers. There's also a killer foul madamas, a slurry of fava beans laked with tahini and olive oil, served with a tangy green relish. Every day there's an off-menu special — Monday it's mansef, a tart stew of lamb shoulder cooked in yogurt and clarified butter.

TANOREEN ☆ ◌

7704 3rd Avenue, Brooklyn, 718-748-5600 When asked for a brunch recommendation, I often suggest Tanoreen. The menu offers traditional Levantine breakfasts like vegetable fritters, hummus with meat, and foul madamas — tender fava beans dressed with olive oil, lemon, and garlic. Also brunch-worthy are two dozen hot and cold meze, including a pungent olive spread flavored with capers, the dried Armenian sausage sojuk, and sambusek — little braided turnovers filled with potatoes and peas and served with a homemade cilantro relish. Sandwiches, grilled meats, and desserts broaden the culinary terrain. And don't miss the Arabic coffee, ceremoniously served in a shiny brass pot.

Lebanese, Syrian, and Palestinian

ALSALAM RESTAURANT & MEAT MARKET ☆ ☆

7206 5th Avenue, Brooklyn, 718-921-1076 The chicken schwarma sandwich is the best in town — fresh cut from the homemade rotating cylinder, jammed in a pocketless pita with lettuce, tomatoes, sumac-dusted onions, and a powerful garlic sauce, with the surprise addition of split cornichons. It's then rolled in butcher paper and zapped in a Cuban-style sandwich press. This Middle Eastern lunch counter cum market — where you can get replacement supplies for your hookah, in addition to staple groceries (but no hash) — also features rotisserie chicken and vegetarian meze like spinach cooked with pine nuts and mujadara, rice tossed with lentils and frizzled onions. For superadventuresome diners there's a boiled brain salad that a brain-obsessed friend pronounced excellent.

BEDOUIN TENT ☆ ◌

47 Hicks Street, Brooklyn, 718-722-7777 Don't expect camels, belly dancers, or blowing sand; instead, find some of the best inexpensive food in Brooklyn Heights in a laid-back setting with plenty of sidewalk tables. Homemade pitas form the basis for "green pizza," lushly topped with leeks, scallions, fenugreek, and mozzarella. Also commendable are the pureed lentil soup flavored with garlic and caramelized onions, the vegetarian stuffed grape leaves, and a particularly creamy hummus. Finish up with basbousa, a honey-semolina cake, and a Turkish coffee with a hint of mint.

BREAD FROM BEIRUT ☆ ⏱

24 West 45th Street, Manhattan, 212-764-1588 Fabricated from pita dough, the baby pizzas are spectacular — luscious four-slice pies that shoot from the brick oven bearing Middle Eastern toppings ranging from pine nuts to ikawi cheese to zaatar, an herbal cousin of oregano and marjoram. The flat crispy falafel and colorful vegetable selections — like string beans stewed with tomatoes, olive-dotted vinegar potato salad, and spicy carrots, to name just three — are similarly commendable, and so are the miniature pies called sambusek, but beware the grilled meat selections, which are often reheated or served just plain tepid.

CAFE RAKKA ☆

81 St. Marks Place, Manhattan, 212-982-9166; 38 Avenue B, Manhattan, 212-982-9166 Attracting little attention, Cafe Rakka has been near the corner of St. Marks and 1st Avenue for nearly two decades, and to sit at one of its tables with the ceiling fan lazily revolving overhead is to feel like you're in Aleppo. The renditions of Syrian peasant food are convincing and cheap. Mujadara is usually my first choice, an earthy salad of cracked wheat and lentils garnished with heavenly caramelized onions, frizzled almost dry. My second choice is moussaka, a casserole of eggplant, tomatoes, and onions. The combination generates a sweetness greater than you'd expect from the constituents. In addition, I pick lemony stuffed grape leaves and fava beans, redolent of strong-tasting olive oil with just a hint of cumin and garlic. Turkish coffee is particularly good at the Avenue B location.

FOUNTAIN CAFÉ ☆

183 Atlantic Avenue, Brooooklyn, 718-624-6764 The vittles are unfailingly fresh at this bright and spacious Middle Eastern café: the stuffed grape leaves homemade and served warm in a tart tomato sauce, the baba ghanoush airy and properly smoky tasting, the kebabs cooked from scratch with lean meat and chicken. I particularly liked the kibbeh saneeya, which is a Lebanese pie of lamb and pine nuts with a cracked-wheat crust, served with minty yogurt sauce; a friend swears their lentil soup is the best in town.

KARAM ☆ ☆ ☆ ⏱

8519 4th Avenue, Brooklyn, 718-745-5227 For a small joint, Karam has a marvelously ambitious Lebanese menu, central to which is a series of pita sandwiches made by rolling a pita around the ingredients, rather than trying to wedge them into a pocket. Two excellent schwarma cylinders are always rotating, or select grilled mekanek (a cinnamony cousin of merguez), or one of the variety meats that includes a vinegary veal tongue that may be the best thing on the menu. The pistachio-strewn rice pudding is a superb end to a meal. Only the baba ghanoush proved disappointing.

KING SHAWARMA ☆

110 MacDougal Street, Manhattan, 212-387-0541 With their shabby furnishings and patina of grease, the falafel shacks of MacDougal — many of which date to the mid-1970s — are not much to look at. On the other hand, you can pretend you're eating in Damascus. One recent day, I tried all the schwarma on the block, and this place won, tendering a pita overstuffed with pungent lamb and dressed with yogurt, tahini, hot sauce, green chiles, brine pickles, and loads of other stuff.

LAILA ☆ ⟁

440 7th Avenue, Brooklyn, 718-788-0268 This sturdy Lebanese excels at meze like labni, a thickened yogurt laden with mint, chile powder, and garlic; smoky baba ghanoush; and airy falafel. The appetizer combo for two, containing all of the above, makes a perfect entrée. Main courses must be selected more carefully, since items like couscous and stuffed chicken are too damn bland. Instead go with stuffed grape leaves (ask for them hot) or ouzy, a phyllo pie stuffed with everything but the kitchen sink. Or try mulokhia, a Middle Eastern vegetable with the mucilaginous properties of okra.

MAZZA PLAZA ☆

8002 5th Avenue, Brooklyn, 718-238-9576 Not sure of the significance of the sign — "Now Cooking Here Is The Famous Chef J. Karam of Bay Ridge" — but the Plaza produces some of the best rotisserie chicken in the borough. Not only because of a perfectly cooked and spice-crusted bird, but because of the thick, knock-your-head-off garlic dipping sauce with so much raw garlic that hot sauce would be redundant. Other salad and smearing items, such as tabbouleh and baba ghanoush, are also fab, but I found that the grillables like kebab orfaly and sojouk — a chopped meat cylinder and spicy stubby sausage, respectively — arrived too charred for my taste at this nominally Palestinian joint.

MOUSTACHE ☆ ☆ ⟁

90 Bedford Street, Manhattan, 212-229-2220; 265 East 10th Street, Manhattan, 212-228-2022 The specialty of these sunny restaurants owned by an Iraqi expatriate is freshly baked pita, which must be eaten within five seconds or it turns into the dry, flat variety you buy in the supermarket. Moustache uses these to make sandwiches, the best featuring cumin-laced lamb merguez. They also make "pitzas." These are eight inches in diameter and the deep brown crust — a little more brittle and oily than regular pizza crust — is topped with cheese and tomato sauce. Optional ingredients include capers, olives, eggplant, artichokes, or mushrooms. Ask for the one featuring parsley and garlic, even though it's no longer on the menu.

SALAM CAFE & RESTAURANT ☆ $
104 West 13th Street, Manhattan, 212-741-0277 In spite of the uninspired decor at this rare upscale Syrian, the left-hand side of the menu is a near-perfect collection of meze, prepared with delicacy and invention. Take the fetoush — the standard iceberg lettuce has been replaced by baby lettuces, of course, and the traditional lemon dressing has been supplemented with balsamic vinegar. There are meat meze, as well: mekanek, a nutmeg-flavored lamb sausage that has a coarse texture that contrasts nicely with its diminutive size; and kibbee, a torpedo-shaped pie with a cracked-wheat crust, remarkably light considering its lamb and pignoli-nut filling. A traditional meal of meze is available in vegetarian and meat versions, and is highly recommended.

Yemeni

ALIBABA ☆ ⏀
515 Amsterdam Avenue, Manhattan, 212-787-6008 This new Yemenite café — closet, really — mounts one of the best schwarmas in town, made from turkey and piled high in a pita; as a bonus the sandwich is cushioned with good baba ghanoush. Supersize it by requesting lafah, a huge homemade flatbread. Either way, you're entitled to visit the salad bar, loaded with appealing pickled things. Unfortunately, most of the Yemenite selections on the large menu are only intermittently available, although we were able to sample malawach, a deep-fried pancake served with a boiled egg, and the less delectable habis, a combo of hummus and smashed fava beans.

HAPINA ☆ ☆ 🌶 ⏀
69-54 Main Street, Queens, 718-544-6262 The Cornish hen schwarma is a wonder at this kosher Yemenite restaurant, way downstream from Flushing's Chinatown. But even better are the fries, and the 10-foot help-yourself salad bar featuring cole slaw, hot chiles, sauerkraut, crunchy turnip and beet salad, grilled bell peppers, and plenty of other roughage, in addition to the three incredible hot sauces (red, green, and mango-based yellow) that characterize the Yemenite way with condiments. Among the typical Middle Eastern offerings, the chunky, creamy, smoky baba rules, with a surprisingly tomatoey Turkish salad a close second. Ignore the gruff service and skip the sickening kibbeh soup.

145 LUNCHEONETTE ☆ ☆

145 Court Street, Brooklyn, 718-624-9325 Don't be scared off by the Arabic-only menu posted on the wall — there's really only one meal available anyway. It begins with a pungent lamb bouillon, progresses to a sprightly green salad, then concludes spectacularly with a giant communal tray of rice pilaf festively festooned with various grilled meats, all halal, and little piles of curried potatoes. Meats vary, but often include roast lamb shank, roast lamb kebab, roast chicken, and sometimes, roast variety meats like kidneys, brains, and liver. A terrific place for a group of six or seven. Just sit down and say "Feed me."

YEMEN CAFÉ ☆ ☆

176 Atlantic Avenue, Brooklyn, 718-834-9533 On a night of high winds and pelting rains, our inundated ride wouldn't start and an expedition to a far-flung corner of Brooklyn had to be scuttled. Drenched, we dropped by Yemen Café and received a warm welcome, and dined sumptuously on a cumin-laced lamb bouillon, a salad of fresh greens bathed in spicy red dressing, a cauldron of bubbling salta topped with the foaming fenugreek jelly called hilbeh and sided with enormous flatbreads, and, finally, a festive communal platter of roasted halal lamb on a platter of fragrant white rice. We disappeared into the stormy evening happy and well stuffed.

Moroccan and Tunisian

Despite the ease of travel between Morocco and New York (a six-hour flight from Casablanca), there just aren't many Moroccans hanging out here, or Algerians, Tunisians, or Libyans for that matter. Ten years ago, our Moroccan restaurants were generally awful, but now the quality has improved, even though I can't say there's a really great Moroccan restaurant out there, with the possible exception of Aya's and Maison du Couscous. The cuisine of Tunisia, though it overlaps Moroccan in several key areas, offers distinctive dishes. On home turf, for example, the presence of vigorous tuna-canning and chicken-farming industries means that Tunisians put tuna and eggs on nearly everything. This combo is the most popular pizza topping along Tunis's grand Avenue de France, and it forms the basis of the national pastry, known as brik. North African cooking is among the most subtly spiced and adeptly executed in the world, and, now that we're passingly acquainted with it, we'd love to have lots more.

LOOK FOR:

bessara *pureed fava bean soup*
boulettes *lamb or fish balls*
boulfaf *lamb liver shish kebab*
braewat *flaky triangular turnover*
brik *flaky egg-and-tuna pastry*
b'stilla *warkha pigeon pie*
chebakia *pastry ribbons*
chermoula *green Moroccan spice paste*
cornes de gazelle *pastry crescents with almond filling*
couscous *semolina moistened with broth*

douara *tripe tajine*
harira *fast-breaking Ramadan lamb soup*
kaab ghozal *gazelle horn pastry*
merguez *spicy lamb sausage*
m'hanncha *serpent pastry*
mischouia *Spicy Tuisian red-pepper relish*
pates farcies *meat-filled pastries*
shebbakia *deep-fried pastry ribbons*
tajine *stews braised in a conical tajine*
tangia *soupy stew cooked in an amphora*
Tunisian salad *cubed raw vegetables in vinaigrette*
Tunisian sandwich *Niçoise-style tuna salad on a roll*
warkha *thick pastry leaves*

Moroccan

AL BARAKA ☆ $
1613 2nd Avenue, Manhattan, 212-396-9787 Penetrate deep into the interior, and discover a perfect imitation of a restaurant in Marrakech hidden deep within the souk, with low-slung settees and fabric-strewn sofas. Ferried on ornate metal trays, the food duplicates the pungency and style of Moroccan cooking better than any other place in town. Notable appetizers include moist and violently red merguez, and zaalouk — an eggplant puree closer to Sicilian caponata than Middle Eastern baba ghanoush. And even though the b'stilla is available in the authentic pigeon formulation ("farm raised" says the menu), I'd rather have any of the intense tajines.

AYA'S CAFÉ RESTAURANT ☆ ☆ ☆
25-60 Steinway Street, Queens, 718-204-6040 You might as well be in Morocco, in this well-lit lounge furnished with couches and handsome inlaid tables, with an area in the front window for ostentatiously smoking a hookah, in a manner that's become de rigueur on this stretch of Steinway, but may now be in danger due to Mayor Bloomberg's ban on smoking in restaurants. The exemplary food is also emphatically North African in its subtle use of sweet spices and typical selection of tajines, couscous, and kebabs. Best dish is chicken b'stilla, a round pie of flaky warkha pastry interleaved with chicken and almonds and sweetened with a crisscross of cinnamon and powdered sugar topside.

BAR SIX ☆

502 6th Avenue, Manhattan, 212-691-1363 This Village stalwart, one of the first modern attempts at a French-style bistro, offers a wonderful vegetable couscous at lunch and dinner, and a larger menu of Franco-Moroccan specialties on Friday evening.

CHEZ ES SAADA ☆ ⏰ $

42 East 1st Street, Manhattan, 212-777-5617 Just down the block from the Catholic Worker, a mysterious and unmarked entrance is darkened except for a pair of tin lamps that allow light to escape through narrow slits. But through the iron-barred door one is surprised to find a barroom with a homey aura — if your home is Marrakech, that is. The bar is clad in ceramic tile with geometric designs; on top a wide bowl brims with assorted olives smeared with chiles and herbs. Inevitably you are drawn through a portal in the rear and down a winding and clammy stairway strewn with rose petals. As is the rule in many glamorous and overhyped restaurants, the appetizers are great, while the entrées are just so-so. We especially enjoyed the Marrakech salad — nine stunning mounds including spicy diced beets, caramelized onions with chickpeas and raisins, herby cakes, planked carrots with lemon, and a fluffy hummus. The rather daring choice of tajine is lamb, prunes, and ginger, and the sauce is so rich that most of it gets left behind. Which is probably fortunate, since few could gauge the effects of so many prunes on the human digestive system.

GALIL ☆ $

1252 Lexington Avenue, Manhattan, 212-439-6203 This glatt kosher restaurant has an intriguing Moroccan bent. The lamb tajine is particularly good, featuring a huge shank sweetened with prunes and raisins served in a painted ceramic tajine on a bed of couscous (the serving is enough for two), while fish balls, a quintessential Sephardic dish, are bathed in a cumin-inflected tomato sauce and sided with good fries. The fish of choice is mushat, or St. Peter's fish — firm fleshed and nicely charred from the grill. Also dig the vegetable-stuffed pastries known as Moroccan cigars (fingers of Fatima in some Muslim countries), and the excellent mint tea.

LA MAISON DU COUSCOUS ☆ ☆ ☆ ⏰

484 77th Street, Brooklyn, 718-921-2400 This gem replaces the late lamented Casablanca as the city's premier working-class Moroccan restaurant. As the brown ceramic cone is doffed, the inexpensive tajines explode with flavor, and the choices are breathtaking, too: lamb with peas and artichokes, chicken with raisins and caramelized onions, and the vegetable-heavy tajine tafrawatt, featuring chicken or lamb matched with a bounty of summer squashes, pumpkins, eggplant, carrots, and potatoes. Don't miss the North African pastries displayed on the glass counter; wash them down with a pot of sugary mint tea.

MOGADOR ★ ⚲

101 St. Marks Place, Manhattan, 212-677-2226 Go after 5 p.m. when, to begin, they bring a lovely tray of small dishes and let you take your pick. Try the cumin-laced beet salad, the verdant tabbouleh, or the carrot salad, doused with olive oil and lemon juice. The menu at Mogador is mainly Moroccan, at a price that beats the other joints in town. The best entrée choice is the tajine, a thick stew made with lamb or chicken in six variations. My favorite is made with chermoula — a powerful paste of garlic, cilantro, and chiles.

L'ORANGE BLEUE ★ $

430 Broome Street, Manhattan, 212-226-4999 A single tajine du jour heads up the menu at L'Orange Bleue, a French-Moroccan bistro. Though not served in a tajine, it was as good in its own way: a half chicken simply flavored with lemon rind, fennel, and a handful of black olives. As added improvements, the skin was crisp and herby, and caramelized strips of fennel kept the underlying couscous moist. A similar technique was used with the cod, wherein diced beets kept the semolina damp and colored it a lurid red. The fish is baked in parchment with a slices of lime and a smear of chermoula, a Moroccan spice paste of onions, garlic, flat-leaf parsley, cilantro, and a touch of red pepper.

ZITOUNE ★ ★ ⚓ $

46 Gansevoort Street, Manhattan, 212-675-5224 Central to the menu at this meat market Moroccan is a series of innovative tajines — slow cooked and subtly flavored stews served in a distinctive ceramic vessel. One mixes Cornish hen with preserved lemon — an improvement on an old favorite — while others are more off-the-wall: one matches salmon forcemeat with tomatoes and olives, while another deposits a tajine of lamb and quince over bulky Israeli couscous. Best of all is a beef rib tangia, a bachelor's supper of rich meat cooked with lemon served in a Roman-style amphora. Also recommended: duck b'stilla. Chill in the sedate dining room and watch the hordes descend on Pastis, just across cobbled Gansevoort Square.

Tunisian

LA BARAKA ★ $

255-09 Northern Boulevard, Queens, 718-428-1461 This elegant French restaurant is a favorite of the stodgy burghers of Little Neck, a dating spot for aging couples. The proprietors, however, are Tunisian, and manage to slip a Tunisian specialty or two onto the menu. The couscous, indeed, are exceptional, and this obscure corner of Queens is definitely worth visiting for that reason.

EPICES DU TRAITEUR ☆
103 West 70th Street, Manhattan, 212-579-5904 This French bistro has an intriguing sideline: Tunisian food, including a few specialties you won't find elsewhere. Foremost is brik, a curious fan-shaped pastry featuring canned tuna and a runny egg that remains hemmed in until you bite down and the yolk squirts all over your shirt. Hey, it's good! There's also a spicy onion, tomato, and red pepper relish called mischouia, and an abundant mixed grill matching four merguez sausages with four fork-tender baby lamb chops. Be warned: The Moroccan specialties, like the lamb-and-lemon tagine, bomb.

TUNISIAN CREPES

The French part of Tunis begins at the shallow, salt-water Lac de Tunis and extends west to the Sea Gate, the monumental arch where the much older Arab town begins. From the lake to the arch is a distance of two kilometers, and is all landfill created by French engineers, who also laid out the streets in a predictable grid. Standing at the current shoreline and looking over your shoulder, you may see the commuter train to the wealthy suburbs and ruins of Carthage chugging along the narrow causeway across the lake. First stop: the city's rough-and-tumble seaport, La Goulette. Directly in front of you, neatly bisecting the French town, is Avenue Bourguiba, a boulevard with a tree-lined esplanade in the middle. The esplanade is dotted with kiosks that sell domestic and foreign periodicals, cigarettes, and cassette tapes, which run the gamut from traditional Tunisian, to Algerian rai, to the latest Madonna, and all for a buck sixty. Either side of the boulevard is colonial architecture, including the old French theater with its unexpected frieze of bare-breasted maidens, the cathedral, hotels, banks, and government buildings. At street level, the most notable feature is a string of cafés with names like Café Paris, Venezia, and Chez Max. A couple of these have tables on the street where Tunisian men linger for hours over glasses of sweet mint tea. Most have no tables at all, and the diners eat at crowded counters, or take their food away wrapped in pieces of butcher paper.

The most interesting offerings are the crepes, which are made evenings only at a portable workstation that is wheeled out onto sidewalks thronged with office workers on their way home. The booth contains two round griddles and a pile of premade crepe wrappers, and the list of ingredients that go into them is limited to tuna, cheese, and egg, which you can have in any combination for about $1 per crepe. Most diners pick all three. The crepe artist puts a wrapper on the griddle, slaps on the harissa, throws on a generous handful of tuna and grated cheese, and finally breaks two eggs over the filling. Using a spatula, he neatly folds the wrapper into a square, pats it a few times and flips it a few times. Remarkably, nothing leaks out. When the crepe puffs, it's ready, and the cook wraps it in a piece of paper, carefully turned back at one edge to expose the crepe for easy eating. The taste is hot, salty, and satisfying. It's hard to imagine eating more than one, although two with "the works" is the standard order.

LE SOUK ☆

47 Avenue B, Manhattan, 212-777-5454 You might as well be sitting in Tunis's Old Medina once you dig into ajar merguez, a delicious poach of lamb sausages in a fragrant, brick-red sauce subtly laced with cumin. In the middle floats a runny egg like the sun rising over the ruins of Carthage. I was disappointed with Le Souk's brik. While the original is a meal-size phyllo box stuffed with potato, tuna, and undercooked egg, this version is, alas, a trio of dainty pita triangles enclosing a niggling smear of spuds and capers. I was disappointed with the chicken tajine, while the kitchen got high marks for its lamb tajine, perfumed with prunes and boasting a strongly flavored shank, and an Egyptian vegetable stew called bourma, which charms with its odd collection of vegetables like bamia — baby dried okras that you can find threaded on long strings at Middle Eastern markets.

Persian
and Afghani

Though the Turks popularized the mainly vegetarian snacks called meze, this style of eating originated with the Persians, who invented many of the constituent dishes as finger foods to go with wine. The shish kebab itself was probably also invented in Persia, allowing the unmessy eating of grilled meat with the fingers. The kebab proved so popular that its range is now nearly worldwide. But Persian food is so much more, as the national dish of fesanjan demonstrates, with its wild combination of poultry

LOOK FOR:

albaloo palow *sour cherry pilaf*

ash mash *lentil and turnip stew*

ash reshteh *vegetarian bean soup*

asheh kishida *noodles in yogurt sauce*

ashi lobya *noodles with kidney beans*

baghali polo *green rice*

bolani kadu *pumpkin turnover*

borani bademjan *eggplant slices with yogurt*

dugg *salty yogurt drink*

fesanjan *walnut-and-pomegranate sauced chicken*

gheimeh *yellow split-pea stew*

ghourmeh sabzi *beef, kidney bean, and herb stew*

jujeh *Cornish hen kebab*

kalbi *raisin and carrot pilaf*

kobideh *minced-meat kebab*

maste *shallot-flecked yogurt dip*

morgh palow *pistachio and orange-rind pilaf*

torshi *vinegary vegetable pickle*

and pomegranates. Also unique to the cuisine is the series of stews called koresht, mixing ingredients like spinach, kidney beans, and dried limes into a pungent swamp.

Afghanis share the Iranian obsession with kebabs, and sometimes scarf meat stews and pastas similar to Persian ones (though the pastas in both countries probably originated in Central Asia, where Marco Polo reported finding them). Unfortunately, most Afghani restaurants in town limit their menus mainly to kebabs and pilafs. Brooklyn's **Bahar** hints at the broader range of Afghani food that's largely missing from the kebab houses, and their crackly pumpkin turnover is certainly among the city's best dishes. As New York police harass religious Pakistanis and Afghanis, it's likely that our small collection of Afghan restaurants will dwindle.

Afghani

AFGHAN KABAB PALACE ☆
75-07 Parsons Boulevard, Queens, 718-591-8700 While I wouldn't exactly describe it as a palace, the decor is admittedly handsome, with rustic log wainscoting, broad tables flanked by comfortable chairs, plenty of woven decorations in rich colors, and wooden niches displaying samovars, kerosene lamps, and other reminders of a desert and mountain culture. Dine on savory kebabs, berry-laced rice palows, dumplings well-stuffed with onions and meat, vinegary pickles, and the yogurt drink known as dugg. Right next door in this neighborhood we might as well call Little Kabul (though a section of Flushing's Main Street also vies for the title) is the wonderful New Kouchi Super Market — where you can get a color postcard of Westerners lounging by a motel pool in Kabul.

ALI BABA ☆ ☆
183-10 Horace Harding Expressway, Queens, 718-463-7362 It wasn't enough that this Afghani newcomer — hovering over the Long Island Expressway on the access road — had charcoal-grilled kebabs, luscious fried eggplant topped with yogurt, and miraculously good green rice, they've added a section of American food like Philly cheese steaks, hamburgers, and buffalo wings, and they're damn good! The baba ghanoush is the most garlicky I've ever tasted and utterly admirable; it's a shame it comes with pitas rather than one of the locally made Central Asian breads. At least the pitas are warm, and they wrap nicely around the borani bademjan, slices of eggplant splotched like a Pollock

painting with meaty-tasting red oil and herb-flecked yogurt. Evenings, they turn on the giant waterfall in the dining room, where a set of brocade chairs and a tea service sits forlornly on a dais, as if waiting for the shah and his family to return.

BAHAR SHISHKEBAB HOUSE ☆ ☆ ☆ ✆
984 Coney Island Avenue, Brooklyn, 718-434-8088 I dream about the pumpkin turnovers seeping a thick orange filling — one

---

MANHATTAN AFGHANI

Manhattan has a collection of bargain Afghanis centered on 9th Avenue in Hell's Kitchen. Compared with similar establishments in Brooklyn and Queens, they're not that good. However, they're a convenient stopover for decent grilled shish kebabs on the way to a movie or Lincoln Center.

ARIANA AFGHAN KEBAB ☆
787 9th Avenue, Manhattan, 212-262-2323 This is my fave of the Manhattan Afghanis, though it may be an Uzbeki restaurant under deep cover. In addition to Afghan standards or homemade noodles and lamb shish kebab, there are fish kebabs and sambosa, Afghani samosa.

AFGHAN KEBAB HOUSE ☆
764 9th Avenue, Manhattan, 212-307-1612; 155 West 46th Street, Manhattan, 212-768-3875; 2680 Broadway, Manhattan, 212-280-3500; 74-16 37th Avenue, Queens, 718-565-0471 The first branch listed was the progenitor of the chain, and it's still the best. Lamb, fish, and kofta kebabs rule.

Here are a couple of lace-curtain East Side Afghanis that can be counted on to grill a decent kebab and boil up some tasty pastas:

PAMIR ☆
1437 2nd Avenue, Manhattan, 212-734-3791 Perfectly OK, with good lamb shish kebabs, but nothing spectacular.

PERSEPOLIS ☆
1423 2nd Avenue, Manhattan, 212-535-1100 Time your visit to take advantage of the lunch specials. For some reason, the *Zagat Survey* is particularly fond of this place.

of several unexpected vegetarian choices at this Afghani meatery. But there are more surprises in store, including a savory dish of homemade noodles dressed with yogurt and red beans, and a multiple-choice approach to rice pilaf. There are inexpensive kebabs, too, of course — but the balance of the menu is much more interesting in this Pakistani neighborhood that hops 24 hours a day.

Persian

NADER ☆ ☆ ☾
48 East 29th Street, Manhattan, 212-683-4833 For appetizers, skip the too-familiar hummus, baba, and tabbouleh in favor of "dry yogurt and eggplant" — grilled slices smeared with kashk, made from a dehydrated yogurt whey that imparts a wonderful mushroomy flavor. Also don't miss torshi, a complicated pickle that makes even the boring pitas taste good. The heart of Iranian cooking is koresht — stews that mix lentils, fruit, meat, and herbs to spectacular effect. The superior choice is gheimeh, yellow split peas and beef in a gravy tinged with tomato and flavored with dried limes and sweet spices. For an additional 50 cents, you can add baby eggplant to this tasty concoction. Inevitably, there are the kebabs, offered in 16 combinations ($9.90–$19.90). The best (and cheapest) are the plain brochettes of buttery Cornish game hen and koobideh — beef ground with plenty of onions. Don't miss the rice cooked with zereshk, a tiny native berry that's like a miniature cranberry. Known in Europe as barberry, it is said in Thomas Culpeper's *Complete Herbal* (1649) to "get a man a good stomach to his victuals." I couldn't agree more.

PATOUG ☆ ☆ ☾
220-06 Horace Harding Expressway, Queens, 718-279-3500 Glowing like a saffron sun, chelo rice commands the center of the table. Served on a plate the size of a small yacht, each glistening grain tastes individually buttered. At Patoug the rice arsenal also includes plain basmati mingled with currants and tart barberries, and a dilled rice flecked with tender baby limas smaller than a fingernail. The single best dish we had, though, was ash reshteh, a humble vegetarian soup crammed with wholesome ingredients — green lentils, kidney beans, chickpeas, noodles, scallions, fenugreek leaves, and mint.

Regional and Vernacular American

Barbecue; Cajun and Creole; Hamburgers; Hot Dogs; Lunch Counters, Diners, and Ice Cream Parlors; New American; Philly Cheese Steaks; Sandwiches and Comfort Food; Seafood; Southwestern; and Tex-Mex and Burritos

Soul Food and Jewish-American have their own chapters, but here are some additional regional American stylings that have left their mark on Gotham. I'm happy to report that barbecue has improved 100 percent since the last edition of this book, and that we now have a portfolio of Philly cheese steaks at our disposal. It's no longer necessary to drive up to Massachusetts or Maine for a great shore dinner, and Harlem now has a Cajun Creole joint started by a real New Orleans chef (now departed) that would probably get over in the Big Easy. Meanwhile, we are riding the crest of a hamburger and hot dog revival, probably as a result of the continued economic downturn.

If you get tired of our tiny collection of good barbecue joints, you can find some of the same smoky flavors in Indian tandoori, Jamaican jerk chicken, Argentine parrillada and, perhaps best of all, Uzbekistani charcoal-grilled kebabs in the Central Asian and Caucasian chapter. See also Pizza and the box on Hot Italian Roast Beef Heroes, both in the Italian chapter.

Barbecue

BLUE SMOKE ☆ ☆ ✒ $
116 East 27th Street, Manhattan, 212-447-7733 Uniquely yoked to a jazz club, this Danny Meyer project began disappoint-

ingly with distinctly unsmoky 'cue, but constant tinkering with the system — which, I contend, still doesn't feature enough actual wood — has improved the product by about 500 percent. The brisket is now quite good, especially if you ask for the fatty type (lean is also available). The ribs remain all over the map, referencing 'cue from Memphis, Texas, St. Louis (Meyers's hometown), Kansas City, Oklahoma, and elsewhere, but are not quite yet on the money — maybe that will change by the time you read this, since there's a tendency to constantly attempt to make it better. At a recent revisit, the sausage appetizer was great, and save room for the killer chocolate cake.

DAISY MAY'S BBQ USA ☆
46th Street and 11th Avenue, Manhattan, 212-977-1500 When I saw the color picture and read the hype about this place in the *Times* Wednesday food section, I thought, "This has got to suck." Nevertheless, I ran right up there to check it out. Was I ever full of it — the barbecue runs from mediocre to quite good, depending on the cut. Unpredictable fave was an "Oklahoma" barbecued beef rib the size of a hatchet, gobbed with a sweet and spicy sauce. The pulled pork was pretty good, too, heaped on a bun in conventional Carolina style with cole slaw, though the brisket sandwich was awful. Service is confused, but the conversations you'll have with other line standers make up for it.

PEARSON'S TEXAS BBQ ☆ ☆ ✐
71-04 35th Avenue, Queens, 718-779-7715 Formerly known as Stick To Your Ribs, the city's best barbecue moved from Long Island City to Jackson Heights three years ago, and has since been prey to rumors that it's going downhill. Despite understandable variations — wood and meat are always somewhat unpredictable — the barbecue maintains the same high standards. The pork ribs are luscious, sloughing tender, smoke-pink meat, and the two kinds of sausage, pepper-dotted hot links and Polish sausage (founder Robert Pearson's innovation), were irresistible in their greasy saltiness. The brisket they're currently using is a little too lean, and hence not quite so tender. That's the way the patrons like it, according to the current proprietor.

PEARSON'S TEXAS BARBECUE ☆ ☆ ✐ $
170 East 81st Street, Manhattan, 212-288-2700 Robert Pearson's new Texas-style barbecue evokes its inspiration in color photos — the smiling pitmaster at Cooper's, the old Kreuz Market (now Smitty's), and so forth, and the 'cue tries hard to live up to those pictures. The crowd is mainly aging neighborhood types, since the place has been written off by barbecue purists. The pork shoulder — white and moist and fairly smoky — is a surprise fa-

vorite, but for an authentic taste of Texas, go for the wonderful hot links, with brisket and pork ribs close runners-up. Sandwiches are the best deal, sided with the shareable $3 pickle platter. The crisp and greasy onion rings rule!

UNCLE SAL'S RIBS AND BIBS ☆
1770 East Tremont Avenue, Bronx, 718-892-8181 This closet-sized eatery crams more types of fast food into its tiny and well-organized premises than you could imagine. Moistened with a kicky red sauce and falling apart the minute you touch them, the baby-back made me think a smoker was concealed somewhere on the premises.

VIRGIL'S REAL BARBECUE ☆
152 West 42nd Street, Manhattan, 212-921-9494 This OK place tries to cover all the bases, serving several regional types of barbecue, as well as Southern cooking, grilled seafood, and even raw shellfish. Dinners are expensive; the sandwich platters are more affordable. Pick the red-edged, machine-sliced, and somewhat smoky brisket. Memphis pork ribs platter comes a close second. Five good sauces are provided on the table: three traditional sweet tomato sauces, a North Carolina vinegar-based sauce, and a Mexican hot sauce made in Jalisco. This place's big trick is blowing smoke into the dining room so you think you're eating real barbecue. You know what? It works.

Also see the Soul Food chapter for Carolina-style oven barbecue.

Cajun and Creole

BAYOU ☆ ☆ 🐟 $
308 Malcolm X Boulevard, Manhattan, 212-426-3800 Returning great New Orleans–style food to Harlem after an absence of several decades, Bayou concentrates on food presentations that range from earthy to elegant. From the former category comes a catfish platter outfitted with hush puppies and excellent fries, and the mud-swilling Mississippi denizen has never tasted better. In the latter category find an "ensemble" of shrimp and crab in a saffron cream sauce. Somewhere in between is a perfect rendition of okra-thickened gumbo loaded with shrimp and smoky tasso ham. Downside: you may find the sweeping view of the revamped 125th Street depressing.

HARGLO'S CAFÉ ☆
974 2nd Avenue, Manhattan, 212-759-9820 This East Side bar tried to surf the popularity of Cajun food in the early 1980s, serving up gumbos, étouffées, jambalayas, and blackened redfish

(and, occasionally, alligator) as if they knew what they were doing. The chicken jambalaya's not half bad — made with the whole chicken and not just breast meat, rife with sausage (OK, it's Italian fennel and not andouille), and pleasingly spicy and tasting of celery and onions. The seafood étouffée, however, is a train wreck, bobbing with bizarrely incongruous elements like canned baby corn, frozen peas, and other things that make it seem more like a Chinese stir-fry.

Hamburgers

BIG NICK'S ☆
2175 Broadway, Manhattan, 212-362-9238 Since 1962 Big Nick has been turning out a superior product in a chaotic space on the Upper West Side lined with smeary pictures of near-celebrities. Frantically innovating, it offers dozens of choices. Skip the ostrich, buffalo, sumo (one pound), Texas (topped with an egg?), Port Cheddar (ahoy, mate!), vegetable, and veal, in favor of the simple six-ouncer, a moist beef patty grilled over a 100 percent natural gas flame by someone who is paying attention.

BLUE 9 BURGER ☆
92 3rd Avenue, Manhattan, 212-979-0053 Zenlike in its simplicity, this bare-bones burger joint — probably inspired by Los Angeles's In And Out Burger — looks like a franchise waiting to happen. The menu is so small, it can be listed on a business card: hamburger, cheeseburger, Blue 9 burger, fries, soft drinks, and three kinds of shakes. The burger bedevils Ronald and his pals by being made with fresh meat and cooked to order, and not covered with glop. Shakes are of the thick variety that's hard to find in these parts

BURGER JOINT ☆ ☆
119 West 56th Street, Manhattan, 212-245-5000 Originally, this space concealed behind a curtain adjacent to the main desk of the Parker Meridien Hotel wanted to exist without a name, but Burger Joint soon stuck. Like an off-off-off-Broadway show, the crew struggles at the grill behind the small counter, generating a menu confined to burgers (get "the works"), cheeseburgers, fries, sodas, bad lemonade, milkshakes (only after 2:30), and a decent brownie. The burgers are great in their own way, made with never-frozen beef with plenty of fat.

DB BISTRO ☆ ☆ ☆ $
55 West 44th Street, Manhattan, 212-391-2400 It used to be that Patroon served the most expensive burger in town, and at $23, it failed to justify the price. Now along comes Daniel Boulud,

235

who applies his playful artistic sensibilities to America's favorite meal. With a well-browned exterior, and a rare interior of exemplary beef, the burger ($29) at DB Bistro is further stuffed with foie gras and shredded short ribs. Hitting this mother lode is like winning the lottery.

JUMBO HAMBURGERS ☆

274 West 145th Street, Manhattan, 212-491-5444 The yellow lean-to known as Willie's Burgers has been transformed into a gleaming metal-clad shed that looks positively bombproof. The structure seems perennially closed, but just to the east Jumbo Burgers has moved into the storefront, flipping the standard half-steamed, half-fried Harlem burgers, made with fresh meat with plenty of fat that cooks down into a moist diffuse lump, shaped by the poking and prodding of the cook. You're making a big mistake if you don't heap on the fried onions, cheese, bacon, and anything else that strikes your fancy. Fries are completely forgettable; the regulars never order them.

KARAVAS ☆ ☆

108 7th Avenue South, Manhattan, 212-807-6892 This is going to get a little kinky, but bear with me. Go to Greek stalwart Karavas and order the burger, and don't be discouraged when the cook pulls the large patty from the freezer and plops it on the griddle. Request fried onions and the so-called "white sauce" usually used on the gyro, which is really Hellenic tzatziki. The burger is made with good meat and remains moist despite the cook's constant fiddling.

ON THE PARK ☆ ☆

103 West 110th Street, Manhattan, 212-222-2306 Harlem's hamburger specialist recently moved to more luxurious digs on Central Park, bringing along their breathtaking 29-burger array, of which my fave is the breakfast burger, a half pound of good ground beef topped with bacon, two fried eggs, and yellow cheese-food product. Yum, and not just for breakfast!

PETER LUGER ☆ ☆ ☆

78 Broadway, Brooklyn, 718-387-7400; 255 Northern Boulevard, Great Neck, 516-487-8800 When it arrives, it doesn't look too impressive — the seeded bun, barely big enough to contain the meat, is squished, and when you lift the lid, the burger is dressed with a single slice of raw onion. No lettuce, no tomato. But when you bite into the lunch-only burger at Luger's, the rush of flavor is like you've just injected 500 mikes of premium LSD. It's surprisingly cheap, one of the best deals in town. Ask for mashed potatoes instead of fries. And hey, the steaks aren't bad, either.

POP BURGER ☆ 🐟

58-60 9th Avenue, Manhattan, 212-414-8686 You'll either love 'em or hate 'em — miniature burgers, sold in pairs for $5, topped with a tiny swatch of cheese and a slice of plum tomato on a picture-perfect brown bun, smeared with Russian dressing. The ground beef is fresh, but I thought the patty came out too dry, though my dining companion thought these sliders were just fine. I preferred the fried shrimp sandwich, while we both agreed that the fries were not very good. This place, which has a cocktail lounge lurking behind it, is more about design than food, with handsome curvy metal chairs and a space-station aura.

RARE ☆

303 Lexington Avenue, Manhattan, 212-481-1999 Though Rare gives itself hipster airs, it's really just a dining room in a re-vamped traveling-salesman hotel. The specialty is burgers, ranging from the standard flame-grilled "classic" with multiple topping choices to theme burgers like the surprisingly delicious "The Mexican," topped with great guacamole and spicy bean paste. Others feature a seed-crusted salmon fillet that can be topped with a fried egg, and a lentil vegetarian patty that didn't do anything for me. Appetizers are skippable; instead concentrate on sides and the double-size desserts. Hey, please bake the apple cobbler another 20 minutes or so!

TONY'S BURGERS ☆ ☆ ☆

34 East 32nd Street, Manhattan, 212-779-7191 Afraid that the neighborhood burger joint is being bullied out of town by Ronald McDonald, Dave, and their evil pals? Here's their fiercest foe — a hamburger specialist capable of flame-grilling a juicy six-ounce patty to a perfect medium rare. Grab the bacon cheeseburger, festooned with four rashers and planted in a mountain of fries and foliage.

Also see Petite Abeille in the French and Belgian chapter.

Hot Dogs

More surely than the Dow Jones, hot dogs mirror the ups and downs of the economy. During flush times, we're too good for tube steaks. When times are hard, we're prone to consider them an entire meal. And these are hard times, sister. Hipster hot dog hangs like **Crif Dogs** and **Sparky's** are proliferating, making the enjoyment of these treats a tribe-defining communal event. Meanwhile, such bastions as **Nathan's**, **Coney Island Joe's**, and **Papaya King** persist and flourish, not to mention the army of **Sabrett's** and **Hebrew National** vendors. How many zillions of franks are sold in New York each summer? Don't ask me. Here are some of the city's best hot dog vendors.

CONEY ISLAND JOE'S ☆ ☆
1572 Linden Boulevard, Brooklyn, 718-342-5959 Wishing it were at the beach, this garish red-and-yellow-striped blockhouse's peculiar innovation is the double dog — a pair of crisp-skinned franks lolling on a length of French baguette. The extensive condiments bar permits you to concoct your own fantasy frank.

CRIF DOGS ☆ ☆ ☆ ☼
113 St. Marks Place, Manhattan, 212-614-2728 Central to a menu that swings wildly from one crazy idea to another is the Crif dog, a beef-pork ballparker fried in emulation of Rutt's Hut, but for such a brief time that it might be called a "creaser." There's also a natural-skin New York dog, a tofu frank so good it could be mistaken for meat, and a corn dog using any of the above made from fresh batter rather than pulled out of the freezer case. Crif's greatest invention, though, is the bacon wrap, a rasher carefully wrapped around a New York dog and deep-fried to crispness.

DAWGS ON PARK ☆ ☼
178 East 7th Street, Manhattan, 212-598-0667 Picturesquely located right on Tompkins Square Park, D.O.P. also offers a good deep-fried hot dog and a corn dog, too, and a decor plastered with dog photos, creating confusion as to what your hot dog is really made of.

F & B ☆ ☼
269 West 23rd Street, Manhattan, 646-486-4441 F & B (stands for "frites and beignets") affects a European air and mounts a strange and diverse menu. There are nine kinds of franks, including salmon, chicken, and tofu, sporting names like hot diggity dog, bare bones, and prairie dog. My favorite is the great dane, a Milwaukee pork dog topped with Danish mustard, French remoulade, Middle Eastern frizzled onions, apple ketchup, and sweet pickles.

FRANK-N-FRITE ☆ ☆
31 Victory Boulevard, Staten Island, 718-448-8073 Staten Island finally has its own upscale hot dog parlor, innovatively offering a "frite dog" that features a natural-skin frank piled high with french fries. Any sandwich with the fries inside is fine with me — certain New Orleans po' boys come to mind — and this version is tasty, even though the fries are not the twice-fried Belgian variety the name might lead you to expect.

238

HOT DOG HISTORY

The sausage originated in Frankfurt, Germany ("frankfurter"), or Vienna, Austria ("wiener"), depending on who you talk to. In 1880 Antoine Feuchtwanger sold them in the streets of St. Louis sans bun, passing out white gloves so consumers wouldn't soil their hands. Thereafter some genius replaced the gloves with a bun. Dispensed by strolling sidewalk vendors, frankfurters were the hit of Chicago's 1893 World's Columbian Exposition, and by 1900 they'd become a fixture at Coney Island, the nation's preeminent beach resort. At about the same time, Tad Dorgan heard the vendors hawking "dachshund sausages" during a Giants game at the Polo Grounds in Harlem. Not knowing how to spell dachshund, he wrote "hot dog" in the balloon over his cartoon of a canine cradled in a bun, coining a new term. Later, someone would notice how much dachshunds resemble frankfurters, and begin calling them wiener dogs.

GRAY'S PAPAYA ☆ ☆
402 6th Avenue, Manhattan, 212-260-3532; 2090 Broadway, Manhattan, 212-799-0243 Beginning life as a Papaya King, these 24-hour dog stands feature a Recession Special that features a pair of excellent franks washed down with a choice of jumbo fruit drinks, most of which suffer from dilution and grittiness. Comically, the papaya allegedly possesses medicinal properties.

KATZ'S ☆ ☆ ☆
205 East Houston Street, Manhattan, 212-254-2246 They've been making hot dogs on the premises since before they were called hot dogs. Founded in 1888 by the Iceland brothers, the store was taken over by partner Willy Katz in 1903. The thick-skinned dogs are slender, dark, and unexpectedly subtle in flavor and texture.

NATHAN'S FAMOUS ☆ ☆ ☆
1310 Surf Avenue, Brooklyn, 718-946-2202 Foremost among old-timers is Nathan's Coney Island branch, founded in 1916, not the myriad strip-mall evocations around town. Though the natural-skinned all-beef frank is pricey, the thunderous pop when you bite into it and the saline tang of the pink flesh are partial justification.

NEDICK'S ☆

Grand Central Station, LIRR level New York's baseball-themed hot dog and orange drink joint — with its distinctive buns, like a mutant piece of white bread — had gone the way of the dodo in the 1980s. Now it's been resurrected, as a place offering hot dogs in several regional styles. Mmmmm, the Chicago red hot is not bad, topped with grainy mustard, chopped tomato, slivers of sour pickle, tiny green chiles, fluorescent sweet relish, and skanky raw onions in a poppy seed bun.

PAPAYA KING ☆ ☆

1161 2nd Avenue, Manhattan, 212-665-5732 This is the mother ship of a Manhattan cut-rate hot dog empire, but beware that the dogs are almost twice the price of the Gray's Papaya off-shoot. Papaya King devotees claim theirs are much better, though nobody I know has ever eaten both side by side.

RUTT'S HUT ☆ ☆ ☆

417 River Road, Clifton, New Jersey, 973-779-8615 The father of all antique doggeries is included here, not only because of its proximity to the Lincoln Tunnel, but because of its unique cooking method: the franks are immersed in bubbling fat till they rip up the side, hence the nickname "ripper." A specimen fried even further is called a "cremator." The mustard-pickle relish is homemade, the perfect accompaniment to these deliciously mutilated franks.

SCHNACK ☆

122 Union Street, Brooklyn, 718-855-2879 Red Hook's latest dive utilizes sumptuous Stahl-Meyer franks, pink and moist and salty and fresh tasting, more aggressively flavored than most. Their tiny hamburgers — the same size as White Castle but much better tasting — are also worth checking out.

SPARKY'S ☆

135A North 5th Street, Brooklyn, 718-302-5151 This former garage in industrial Williamsburg prides itself in still looking like a garage, but it trumps other nouveau-chien establishments by offering effete Niman Ranch franks, which fail in the artificial color department, but are extralong as compensation.

Lunch Counters, Diners, and Ice Cream Parlors

LA BONBONNIERE ★ ⌔

26 8th Avenue, Manhattan, 212-741-9266 For hundreds of years La Bonbonniere has been serving the breakfast needs of Villagers, though there's nothing French about it but the name. A diner-style breakfast menu features sunny-side up eggs, sodden but tasty bacon, griddle cakes, and French toast (oops! another French thing). The biggest decision: white or whole-wheat toast. On fine days, the tables spill out onto the sidewalk and the aroma drifts northward towards Chelsea.

DINER ★

85 Broadway, Brooklyn, 718-486-3077 Located under the Williamsburg Bridge, the decrepit premises of Diner really did once contain a diner. Now it's Williamsburg's hippest eatery, with a limited menu of crowd pleasers like steak frites and hamburgers, both memorable. All of the culinary action, however, is on the ever-changing specials menu, which might include an eggplant sandwich one day at lunch, and an ambitious special of something French, say, duck confit, in the evening.

EDDIE'S SWEET SHOP ★ ★ ★ ⌔

105-29 Metropolitan Avenue, Queens, 718-520-8514 One of the chief summer pleasures of Queens lies in discovering and investigating antiquarian ice cream parlors. Founded in 1909, Eddie's seems untouched by modernity. The hardwood stools at the long counter were not designed to accommodate the tender adult butt — kids won't mind. In several flavors, the Cokes are concocted from syrup and soda, the 22 flavors of ice cream are made on the premises, and the soda jerk is well versed in the arcana of freezes, floats, sundaes, and malts, for which he spoons powder from a tin marked "Horlicks." Very highly recommended.

HINSCH'S ★

8518 5th Avenue, Brooklyn, 718-748-2854 It's something of a minor miracle that this ancient Teutonic ice cream parlor cum candy shop and luncheonette still exists just off the painfully modern 86th Street shopping strip. The sandwiches and breakfasts that were once standard shopper's fare still comprise much of the menu, complemented by good homemade ice cream that can be

241

enjoyed at a real soda fountain replete with spinning green Naugahyde stools. Waffles are a more modern addition, a bit dry on their own, but brought to life with a range of gloppy toppings. My favorite item: scrambled-egg-and-sausage sandwich on toasted whole wheat washed down with a refillable cup of great retro coffee.

JAHN'S ☆ ☆

117-03 Hillside Avenue, Queens, 718-847-2800 This 80-year-old ice cream parlor stands across the street from the shuttered Triangle Hofbrau, once the largest German restaurant in town and favorite spot of Babe Ruth and Mae West. The interior makes me think I'm in Green Bay, Wisconsin: dark polished woods, dim tulip lamps, red-upholstered booths, and plenty of carved wood. The butterscotch sundae is a thing of beauty — salty, buttery, and served in a giant goblet topped with clouds of whipped cream, and there are a couple dozen more sundaes, shakes, and egg creams to choose from. The food is strictly diner-style, useful only as a prelude to the ice cream.

LEXINGTON CANDY SHOP ☆ ⏱

1226 Lexington Avenue, Manhattan, 212-288-0057 For an unforgettable taste of the indigenous haute cuisine of the Upper East Side, including foamy chocolate egg creams and oozing grape-jelly omelets, there's no better place than the handsomely retrograde Lexington Candy Shop. Swivel on a stool or sprawl in a booth and ponder, Why is this place still here? (Hint: frequent movie and fashion shoots.)

SHAIKH'S PLACE ☆ ☆ ⏱

1503 Avenue U, Brooklyn, 718-375-2572 Positioned to snare weary travelers as they tumble down the steps from the elevated Q station, this donut shop and breakfast counter fries the best glazed donuts in town, and I'm including Krispy Kreme in that assessment. As the clerk assembles your order, you can admire the autographed photo of Joe Franklin.

TIBBETT DINER ☆ 🐟

3033 Tibbett Avenue, Bronx, 718-549-8893 Talk about obscure locations! Just try to find Tibbett Avenue. When you do, you'll be on top of Tibbett Diner. The eclectic menu goes from whole broiled fish (impressively fresh) to Italian to Greek to Irish, all better than average. From the final category comes a savory chicken pot pie, loaded with poultry and hand-hewn vegetables. The pebbly chrome exterior is a paradigm of 1960s architectural flash.

TOM'S ☆ ⏱

782 Washington Avenue, Brooklyn, 718-636-9738 Whisk yourself back to the 1930s at this Prospect Heights soda fountain, which prides itself on the antiquarian normalcy of its food. Brisket sandwich with gravy? Meat loaf and lumpy mashed potatoes? Tuna melt? Of course, though many wise patrons opt for the breakfast-all-day approach, which includes a distinguished version of challah French toast. Closes at 4 p.m.

WAVERLY RESTAURANT ☆ ⍟

385 6th Avenue, Manhattan, 212-675-3181 Nobody's tried the breakfasts at all of the hundreds of diners in town. I find myself returning here consistently for the two eggs sunny-side up, two fat sausage links, two pieces of buttered whole-wheat toast, shredded hash browns, fresh orange juice, and coffee at Village stalwart Waverly Restaurant. The serenity-amid-hubbub of the premises, and relentless efficiency of the staff (you never have to wait for more coffee) don't hurt, either.

New American

ANGELICA KITCHEN ☆ ☆ ⍟

300 East 12th Street, Manhattan, 212-228-2909 Be sure to wear some flowers in your hair when you dine at Angelica, a throwback to San Francisco circa 1968. Lucky for us the cuisine has evolved considerably since then. A pair of ambitious specials is offered each day: on one visit, a memorable pair of curried grain croquettes topped with homemade chutney and napped with dal, with a side of roast beets ramping up the plate's earthy flavors. Soups are a particular strong point, with great depth of flavor achieved without resort to meat stocks.

FIVE FRONT ☆ ☆ ⍟ $

5 Front Street, Brooklyn, 718-625-5559 It was slim pickin's as far as dinner was concerned during the recent Dumbo studio crawl, with Superfine and the new Bubby's East jammed with scenesters. We hesitated at the door of Five Front, having heard mixed reviews, but once inside were charmed by the relaxing decor of this small house dwarfed by the Brooklyn Bridge. The lush and perfectly dressed salads — one featuring endive, baby arugula, walnuts, red grapes, and blue cheese — impressed us, but the highlights of the evening were the smokey chipotle short ribs and the chocolate cake served with mint chocolate chip ice cream.

PRUNE ☆ ☆ $

54 East 1st Street, Manhattan, 212-677-6221 This joint has got personality to spare, a small dining room filled with fiercely loyal regulars, and a quirky menu that runs from the inspired to the merely insane. Forgo the canned sardines and Triscuits in favor of the coriander-crusted smoked duck breast, sided with a strangely irresistible omelet filled with rye groats, or the humongous prawns dressed with anchovy butter — the crunchy heads are the best part. And though the osso bucco swamped in purple cabbage didn't quite kick ass (salt helps), the steamed and grilled artichoke strewn with fried fava beans did.

Philly Cheese Steaks

BB SANDWICH BAR ☆
120 West 3rd Street, Manhattan, 212-473-7500 In response to an urgent call from a friend, I hopped on my bike and pedaled over, only to find a line snaking out the door, down the stairs, and up 3rd Street. The sole production of this narrow storefront is Philly cheese steaks, but not a doctrinaire version. The sandwich piles sliced rib eye on a poppy-seeded kaiser roll that's already been plied with white American cheese, red-pepper relish, and caramelized onions. There's also the slightest hint of Worcestershire in there somewhere.

CARL'S STEAKS ☆ ☆
507 3rd Avenue, Manhattan, 212-696-5338 Chalk up another attempt to recreate Philadelphia's foremost vernacular culinary attraction, the cheese steak. Doomed to failure? Only partly. This project has been undertaken by a real cheese-steak scholar, and the formula features thin-sliced beefsteak worried on the griddle with a pair of long spatulas, then heaped with fried onions and one of the doctrinaire collection of cheeses: American, provolone, Swiss, and — perhaps most authentic — Cheez Whiz. Though the Whiz is applied with a timid hand, the sandwich comes as close to the original as anyone ever will on the East Side of New York. Which is about 70 percent of the way there.

PHILLY'S CHEESE STEAKS ☆ ☆
724A 7th Avenue, Manhattan, 212-974-0524 Rooted in the hardscrabble soil of South Philadelphia, the cheese steak's terroir has proved impossible to duplicate here — though resourceful folks keep trying. Latest attempt is Philly's, a window on Times Square that, around lunchtime, hosts a circle of supplicants who stand gamely waiting on the sidewalk. Though forgoing the bubbling can of Cheez Whiz, this carryout does provide a choice of cheeses, with provolone holding down the high end and American cheese the low. The sirloin's cut a little thick, and fried onions are oddly deemphasized. Still, it's a formidable tuck-in.

PHILLY STEAK & SUB ☆
South Street Seaport Pier, 3rd-floor food court The cheese steak at this fast-food stall ain't bad, especially if you pick provolone for your cheese and have them top it with fried onions and peppers.

Sandwiches and Comfort Food

COWGIRL HALL OF FAME ☆
519 Hudson Street, Manhattan, 212-633-1133 The barbecue menu here is limited to brisket and beef ribs. The brisket, although copious, is a bit dry. But the ribs are great. You get five huge ones, plenty meaty, with sides of potato salad and coleslaw for $11.95. While this is not cheap, ribs rarely are. A couple more good things are the honey-dipped fried chicken and fried catfish. Portions are uniformly enormous, and the sides frequently outshine the entrées. They also offer a few weirdo dishes — like chili served in a ripped-open bag of Fritos, said to have originated in Texas. The displays of rodeo paraphernalia are diverting, and help to make this one of the best eateries for kids in town.

EISENBERG'S SANDWICH SHOP ☆ ☆
174 5th Avenue, Manhattan, 212-675-5096 Step into the past, when sandwiches weren't made with faddish ingredients like arugula, pesto, and ciabattas. In 1929 when Eisenberg's was founded, New York City was paved with these places. A lonely presence on this stretch of 5th Avenue among fast-food emporia and pita palaces, it steadfastly retains the standard lunch menu of soups, sandwiches, and sour pickles. Their egg salad is creamy and clean tasting, and only slightly salty. Order it on rye, and strike a blow for heirloom eating. Add bacon and find nirvana.

MAMA'S FOOD SHOP ☆ ☆ ⍟
200 East 3rd Street, Manhattan, 212-777-4425; 222 Sullivan Street, Manhattan, 212-505-8123 This downtown stalwart cooks up some of the best — and healthiest — standard American fare in New York. Entrées are limited to a few choices, including above-average fried chicken, roast chicken, salmon, and mac and cheese, often elbowed out of the way behind the sneeze guard by the profusion of room-temperature vegetable selections, mostly cooked in a convection oven. Tradition meets innovation in this comfy den lined with pix of moms.

TINY'S GIANT SANDWICH SHOP ☆ ⍟
127 Rivington Street, Manhattan, 212-982-1690 Though this hip Loisaida sandwich shop is called Tiny's, the sandwiches are gigantic. In addition to innovative hot and cold heroes based on ham, turkey, roast beef, and chicken cutlets, each sandwich also exists in a vegetarian version in the same multilayered presentation. My fave is the hot turkey hero, plied with sautéed onions,

245

chopped hot peppers, and melted mozzarella, which, for an extra dollar, can be made with "unturkey." Frozen smoothies, salads, and great soups — such as kale and kidney beans with smoky Portuguese sausage — round out the menu.

Seafood

CLEMENTE'S MARYLAND CRABHOUSE ☆ 🐟 $
3939 Emmons Avenue, Brooklyn, 718-646-7373 Thwack, thwack, thwack! The wooden mallet arcs downward, shooting shell, crabmeat, roe, grease, and Old Bay seasoning in every direction. The tiny plastic bib barely covers you. Welcome to the city's reasonable facsimile of a Maryland crab house, though the view is of parked Skidoos rather than baymen picturesquely trolling for crab traps. All you can eat: $24.95, with fries and corn. Another worthwhile splurge is the lobster fra diavolo, split and smothered in spicy red sauce and dumped on a mess of linguine. Warning — nearly impossible to find without your Hagstrom map.

JORDAN'S LOBSTER DOCK ☆ ☆ ☆ 🐟
Knapp Street and Harkness Avenue, Brooklyn, 800-404-CLAW This reasonable facsimile of a Maine lobster pound is located in a white saltbox house right on Shellbank Creek, with a lighthouse and lobster skiffs out back. The whole steamed lobsters are excellent, served with drawn butter and decent fries. For duffers, there's a lobster roll for which you should request extra packets of mayo, and freshly shucked oysters and clams that can match Grand Central's Oyster Bar for freshness, if not for breadth of selection.

MARY'S FISH CAMP ☆ ☆ ☆ 🐟 $
64 Charles Street, Manhattan, 646-486-2185 A bust-up between the partners of Pearl Oyster Bar has left happy Villagers with two excellent seafood cafés. Mary's offers mild twists on Yankee classics like creamy clam chowder zapped with bacon, scintillatingly fresh oysters opened as you watch, and a bulging lobster roll with homemade mayo and a sprinkling of chives. New to the formula is a salad with gorgonzola (replacing Pearl's Caesar), and an appetizer of cold lobster "knuckles" — the joint in the leg, with the sweetest meat. Cracking them is a test of dexterity and perseverance.

NICK'S LOBSTER RESTAURANT ☆ ☆ 🐟
2777 Flatbush Avenue, Brooklyn, 718-253-7117 Located on an estuary off of Jamaica Bay, it mimics a great lobster pound Down East. The lobsters are right before you in a tank as you enter, and there are extensive outdoor seating areas, including one

right on the water. Stick with the whole lobsters or king crab legs, and you'll have a great meal. Side it with a baked potato, rather than french fries or spaghetti marinara, if you know what's good for you.

PEARL OYSTER BAR ☆ ☆ ☆ 🐟 $
18 Cornelia Street, Manhattan, 212-691-8211 Though the premises recently doubled in size, Pearl's menu has been kept elemental, with an emphasis on amazingly fresh oysters, clams, lobster, and one or two catches of the day. The signature Caesar salad with anchovy dressing is celebrated, while the lobster roll is a perfect reproduction of the item found in Maine's pounds, only more luxuriantly stuffed. Another triumph is an oyster po' boy that would be good enough to serve at Uglesich's in New Orleans, sided, like the lobster roll, with a haystack of ultraskinny fries.

RENCHER'S CRAB INN ☆ ☆ 🐟
407 Myrtle Avenue, Brooklyn, 718-403-0944 Though not particularly large, the shrimp at Rencher's — an old and forgotten institution in Clinton Hill — stand with the best of 'em. Sold by the pound, they've been lovingly cooked in a Maryland-style red seafood boil, which means they taste of celery, cayenne, and brine, in that order. Miraculously, Rencher's hangs on through succeeding waves of gentrification and fast-foodization in the neighborhood.

SHORE ☆ 🐟
41 Murray Street, Manhattan, 212-962-3750 This offshoot of the pricey and excellent seafood restaurant Fresh features pristine raw clams and oysters, decent chowders (though avoid the underoystered pan fry), diverting seafood pot pies, a world-class lobster roll, and a crappy clam roll. The location in an old bar near City Hall is one of the best features of this intentionally divey seafood place.

Southwestern

LOS DOS MOLINOS ☆ ☆ 🌶
119 East 18th Street, Manhattan, 212-505-1574 Named after the grinding stones that turn corn into cornmeal, this offspring of a Phoenix establishment offers a New Mexico spin on Mexican cooking. There are fresh green chiles galore — go, in particular, for the chiles relleno topped with a fried egg. Enchiladas are stacked rather than rolled, and this time the fried egg's on the side. Other oddities include deep-fried burritos, red-chile-smeared adovada pork ribs, and sopapillas — puffy damp pillows like Indian pooris drizzled with honey. They were more leaden than they should have been.

KITCHEN MARKET ☆ 🌮 🕐

218 8th Avenue, Manhattan, 212-243-4433 This offshoot of the weird-ass Bright Food Shop is the city's most dependable gringo seller of Southwestern and Mexican groceries, including dried and fresh chiles, south-of-the-border sodas, hot sauces, and kitschy gift items. Their San Francisco–style customized burritos are top-notch (Yucatan pork and green-chile pozole are my favorites), but skip the salady Los Angeles burritos.

Tex-Mex and Burritos

EL CANTINERO ☆

86 University Place, Manhattan, 212-255-9378 Even though we now have many fine examples of real Mexican cooking around town, there's no reason why you shouldn't continue to enjoy the chili gravy magnificence of El Cantinero, which was once a Pancho Villa's. Dig the sizzling steak fajitas and combo platter of chile relleno and beef enchilada (#8). Their cheap margaritas have been lunchtime salvation for generations of office workers.

COSMIC CANTINA ☆ 🌮 🕐

105 3rd Avenue, Manhattan, 212-420-0975 Though wraps have come and gone, burritos, apparently, are here to stay. While the traditional chains like Burritoville have overextended themselves and become flaccid, Cosmic remains independent, with a novel approach that includes organic ingredients and sticking to burrito basics. My fave: "Old school chicken" with plenty of fresh jalapeño puree.

MEXICO LINDO ☆

459 2nd Avenue, Manhattan, 212-679-3665 Lined with autographed photos of Latino celebrities whose names your parents would recognize, this old standby serves versions of Mexican food from the days before the cuisine was gourmetized and reduced to regions. Not a bad thing, considering the care they put into these ancient Tex-Mex renditions. Stick with the combos, which permute the raw materials of taco, enchilada, chile relleno, and tamale into the maximum number of pairings, but begin with the excellent garlic soup.

PANCHO MAGICO ☆ 🕐

213 Pearl Street, Manhattan, 212-344-1992 Big steaming plates of Tex-Mex is the forte of this financial district loft, where abundant chips and piquant salsa precede entrées like enchiladas suizas, huevos rancheros, and "magic burritos." Best of all is a steak tampiqueño bathed in chipotle sauce, Tuesday and Wednesday only.

SAN LOCO ★ ★ 🌶️ 🍅

124 2nd Avenue, Manhattan, 212-260-7948; 151 Avenue A, Manhattan, 212-982-5653; 111 Stanton Street, Manhattan, 212-253-7580 There's nothing "authentic" about this East Village favorite, like a hippie dreaming of Mexican food. Corn and flour tortillas met for the first time in their taco loco, married by re-fried beans, inspiring Taco Bell's rip-off. The beef enchiladas and fish tacos are also great, especially swabbed with Stupid, the very very hottest salsa.

See the International chapter for restaurants serving wraps.

Russian and Ukrainian

majority of Brighton Beach's residents hail from the Ukraine, a country that was only recently separated from Mother Russia by the dissolution of the Soviet Union. Yet the language that you hear, except among a few fanatics, is Russian, not Ukrainian, as is the menu served at most of the eateries in this delightful seaside region, which resembles the Black Sea in the minds of the residents. Like our own cuisine, Russian food is a melting pot, and many of the favorite dishes originated in far-flung parts of the empire, like the soup kharcho (from Georgia), pelmeni dumplings (from Siberia), and chicken Kiev (from Ukraine). We concen-

LOOK FOR:

basturma *air-dried beef*

blini *pancakes served with caviar*

chicken Kiev *breast wrapped around butter*

escargot *snails served with garlic and butter*

henkali *Georgian-style puckered dumplings*

kasha *steamed buckwheat*

kulesh *mushroom-barley soup*

letcho *Ukrainian goulash*

manti *Uzbeki meat-filled dough purses*

midnight in Moscow *plum-sauced pork cutlet*

pelmeni *little Siberian dumplings*

pierogi *noodle dumplings stuffed with meat, cheese, or fruit*

pirozhki *flaky turnovers*

red borscht *beet soup*

vareniki *potato ravioli*

trate below on modest establishments with minimal emphasis on bad entertainment.

Just as successive waves of German and German-Jewish immigrants made the East Village their home base before and after 1900, respectively, the Ukrainians, fleeing Soviet domination after the collapse of the Third Reich, thronged the neighborhood in the late 1940s. Many of their institutions remain, like the Ukrainian American Youth Association and the Ukrainian Orthodox Federal Credit Union, even though the community has declined. In fact, Ukrainian eateries used to dominate the East Village; now Polish places, boasting a similar Slavic menu, are more common.

Russian

ANYWAY CAFE CLUB ☆
34 East 2nd Street, Manhattan, 212-533-3412 It's Brighton Beach meets the East Village at this Russian trattoria, which fills up with Russian hipsters every evening about nine. Many come just to drink, smoke, and chat, but there's also a list of eats like big doughy dumplings called pelmeni, intense smoked herring sided with potatoes, an herbed Russian burger with no bun, and, best of all, blintzes oozing cheese and not even slightly sweet. Skip the misconceived eggplant appetizer, but don't miss the bizarre garlic-flavored vodka.

CAFE GLECHIK ☆ ☆ ☆
3159 Coney Island Avenue, Brooklyn, 718-616-0494 Cafe Glechik goes out of its way to distinguish itself from the other Russian joints in Brighton Beach. There's no Casio, no attempt to lure you into a big splurge featuring bad caviar, free-flowing vodka, and endless courses of desiccated smoked fish and imitation French cuisine. The menu offers simple, freshly prepared peasant fare from all corners of the former Soviet Union, with a penchant for Ukrainian and Central Asian dishes, including a delicious rabbit in sour-cream sauce and braised lamb shank. An elongated clay plate schleps kebabs to table, sided with parsley fries and sumac onions. Lamb is king — gorgeous smoky cubes still pink in the middle, though the fattier pork has its polysaturated appeal. A lidded pot houses kulesh, a dilled mushroom-barley soup way better than you expect from Jewish delis or Polish cafés. Maybe it's the handful of crushed garlic thrown on top of this Lenten standard at the last minute. A decidedly nonvegetarian version called "kulesh in the meadow" is also offered; the English translation notes it contains "chicken bowels." We dutifully ordered it every visit, but it was never available.

BIG BLOWOUT

Each and every Russian émigré who lives in Brighton Beach has a friend or relative who works at one of the dozen or so nightclubs that line Brighton Beach Avenue and the adjacent streets (though some have now strayed to Bensonhurst and Mill Basin). No matter whether your restaurant of choice is the best or the most expensive or has some other distinguishing feature, your allegiance is a matter of community ties and not preference. These glitzy palaces are intended to verify the perceived opulence of the new land — with their huge chandeliers, brocade fabrics, towering ceilings, sweeping stairways, and endless carpeting — even if they sometimes look shabby and tasteless to outsiders. They are also fabulously expensive, as well, the more so since Russians vie with each other to demonstrate their own status as New World high-rollers by flagrant overtipping (you're expected to do the same), as the Casio orchestra pumps out peasant tunes and disco standards at earsplitting volume and the vodka flows as freely as the Volga River. Places like **National** (273 Brighton Beach Avenue, Brooklyn, 718-646-1225), **Odessa** (1113 Brighton Beach Avenue, Brooklyn, 718-332-3223), and **Rasputin** (2670 Coney Island Avenue, Brooklyn, 718-332-8111), with their cream-sauced retro-French food and questionable caviar, are wretched places to dine. Still, I wouldn't blame you if you went just once just to savor the scene.

CAFE PARIS ☆ 🐟

3178 Coney Island Avenue, Brooklyn, 718-646-0800 When I first spotted this place from the elevated tracks above Brighton Beach, I figured it was a Haitian restaurant. But then a couple of Russian friends from the neighborhood recommended it enthusiastically. Russian food is not exactly light fare — in fact, it's difficult to imagine enjoying it unless there's a chill in the air. Take the escargots swamped with a garlicky mixture of white cheese and cream, garnished with chopped fresh dill. Only slightly lighter were the vareniki, pillow-shaped dumplings filled with potatoes and garnished with masses of mushrooms. Chicken Kiev bears little resemblance to the puny version served at the Russian Tea Room, a giant double-breast of chicken wrapped around a stick of butter, bread-crumbed and deep-fried, with a single bone left sticking out the end. The chicken has been rolled so tight that when you cut into it, the butter squirts out and soaks your shirt. I asked one of those Russian friends what the protruding bone was for and she replied, "To pick it up and suck the butter out."

HARCHEVNYA ✯ ✯
2568 86th Street, Brooklyn, 718-714-4525 This is one of a new flock of Russian fast-food places in Brighton Beach, Gravesend, and Bensonhurst that offer the full range of former-Soviet specialities from Russia, Georgia, Uzbekistan, Siberia, and the Ukraine at bargain prices with none of the nightclub baggage of the opulent Brighton Beach palaces. Harchevnya is diminutive for harcho, the verdant Georgian beef soup loaded with dill and cilantro. Half of Harchevnya's menu is devoted to dumplings, served in massive platters for less than $5, including Ukrainian vareniki, Russian pelmeni, Uzbekistani manti, and Georgian henkali, the latter shaped like a round coin purse with a pucker at the top. Heart of the menu is a series of big single-plate feeds, offered at bizarrely low prices, including a wonderful roast rabbit; pork chop Moldavian-style, thick and oddly butchered with a wobbly collar of fat; and the Georgian classic chicken tabaka — which we affectionately dubbed "roadkill chicken."

PASTORALE ✯ 🐟
410 Brighton Beach Avenue, Brooklyn, 718-648-5484 Autumn sees the Brighton Beach dining action move indoors from the sidewalk cafés on the boardwalk to the more formal joints inland. Under the elevated D train, Pastorale is one of the more stranger-friendly, slinging pan-Soviet cuisine as banquetteers dance to the throbbing oratorio of Saint Casio. The cold platter of smoked and pickled fish is the compulsory starter, but don't miss the excellent red borscht. Among main courses, chicken tabaka and chicken Kiev are budget-wise choices; for a few dollars more there's "midnight in Moscow," a huge pork cutlet topped with plum sauce.

POP'S PIEROGI ✯ 🚲
190 Bleecker Street, Manhattan, 212-505-0055 Brighton Beach comes to Bleecker Street in this narrow fast-food stall, which features the soups and dumplings of Russia, the Ukraine, the Transcaucasus, and Central Asia. Best of all is the little clay pot of Siberian pelmeni — fragrant greasy meat dumplings shaped like tortellini and heaped with fresh dill. These excellent sinkers are also available in a light broth as pelmeni soup. There are a bewildering variety of fruit, vegetable, and meat blintzes and pierogi, which tend to be a little too sweet for me, and flaky pastries called pirozhki of the type that are often sold from carts in Brooklyn's Little Odessa.

BOARDWALK BONANZA

Summer weekends and evenings on the Brighton Beach boardwalk are a trip, as throngs of Russian immigrants promenade in their dress-up best. Bringing a welcome chill to the air, sunset reddens the faces of the promenaders. Wearing a sound system strapped to his chest, a sallow-faced trumpeter launches a melancholy air, sending a black poodle with red toenails scurrying. Five establishments spill their tables onto the boardwalk. Though they're expensive and the food is often mediocre, you may want to sit in one for a while and enjoy this evocation of a Black Sea resort at the height of the season. The southernmost, **Caffe Volna** (3145 Brighton Street (the boardwalk), Brooklyn, 718-332-0341), is the one I usually recommend, since the food seems a shade better there. First to arrive are plums soaked in red wine, each pit replaced by a whole walnut. "Russian pancakes with red caviar" is, of course, blini, six with a tiny dish of salty salmon roe. Basturma generates nearly as much excitement: thin slices of air-dried beef generously veined with fat, with the funk of Italian soppressata. As the heat of the day dissipates, chicken tabaka becomes more appealing. Moist inside and glistening without, it would bring fans of Southern fried chicken to their knees. Equally admirable is sturgeon shish kebab, but the favorite seafood is flounder, an entire critter lightly floured and crisply fried.

Ukrainian

KIEV ☆
117 2nd Avenue, Manhattan, 212-674-4040 In the early 1980s rock musicians used to hang out here, when it was the only café in the East Village open late into the night. Every couple of years, the place would expand into another adjacent tenement storefront; now it's one of the most oddly configured restaurants in the neighborhood. The chicken cutlets are legendary, but many opt for blintzes or other breakfast items.

VESELKA ★ ★ 🍑

144 2nd Avenue, Manhattan, 212-228-9682 Veselka is a breakfast hangout beloved of East Villagers. Sit below the funky mural and watch the world wake up, as artists drift in for their first espresso of the day, then furtively head off to their day jobs. The muffins, lush and large, are among the best in town, especially the whole-wheat blueberry. Also order anything made with buttermilk, such as the well-browned waffles dusted with powdered sugar and served with a chunky raspberry puree. The cheese blintzes are fab, too; other selections that reflect the restaurant's Ukrainian heritage include kielbasa and kasha — steamed buckwheat with a nutty flavor.

South Asian

Anglo-Indian, Bangladeshi, Gujarati, Hyderabadi, Northern Indian, Pakistani, Southern Indian, Sri Lankan, and Tibetan

This culinary category is bursting at the seams, and I was sorely tempted to break it into separate chapters. But the overlapping nature of these cuisines — Sri Lankan and South Indian share many dishes, for example, as do Northern Indian and Pakistani — and my own delight in the plenitude of choices they represent prompted me to leave this sprawling chapter intact. You can go upscale at places like the Upper East Side's **Chola**, where haute regional Indian has been carried to new heights, or go next door to **Dawat**, which presents a competing roster of regional specialties. Eating has never been cheaper at the tiny Pakistani cafés that cater to cabbies — though the federal government's deplorable treatment of Pakistanis, and Muslims in general, has caused many to leave, effectuating a consequent decrease in meaty dining opportunities. Perhaps the largest surge in new places is South Indian. While most fancy Indian places of whatever stripe now dabble in dosas, a plethora of purer joints have appeared in the wake of the fabulous **Dosa Hutt**, and now you can even get dosas from a cart in Washington Square. In Queens's newest Little India, along the easternmost stretch of Hillside Avenue in Floral Park, restaurants dedicated to Keralan and other Southern Indian regional cuisines are now popping up, and Jersey is holding its own in regional southern fare, at places like Edison's wonderful Hyderabadi restaurant **Deccani**.

Though Staten Island rarely receives plaudits for its restaurants, the plucky island leads the way in Sri Lankan cooking thanks to a thriving immigrant community that demands great food. Catering to the culinary needs of Buddhists, Muslims, Hindus, and even Christians, these places concoct "black curries" made with complex toasted spice mixtures, proffered with wonderful homemade breads such as bowl-shaped hoppers (known as appam in South India) and potato-stuffed thosai (their spelling of dosa). While Tibetan food constituted a minifad when the last edition of this book was published, the number has decreased by half — leaving the better places, I'm convinced. Increasingly, neighborhood Indian restaurants have appeared, often offering a lunchtime fixed-price buffet. Though this institution invites a physique-destroying pig-out, it gives you a good idea of the potential of the kitchen. A restaurant that scrimps on its buffet warns you that its more expensive dishes are probably not too great, either.

Other Indian-style food can be found in the Trinidadian, Guyanese, and Surinamese chapter.

LOOK FOR:

achaari murgh *chicken cooked with mixed pickle*
alu chat *tamarind-dressed potatoes*
appam *South Indian hopper*
baghar baigan *Hyderabadi stuffed eggplant in tamarind-peanut sauce*
Balti *Anglo-Pakistani cooking style*
bhale *round flatbread*
bhortas *Bangladeshi veggie mashes*
bindi dopiaza *okra in tomato-onion sauce*
biryani *spice-dotted fried rice*
black curry *lamb in toasted coconut sauce*
bocha *Tibetan butter tea*
Ceylani naan *tandoori flatbread baked in a spiral shape*
Chettinar chicken *fiery chicken curry*
chicken jalfrazi *with onions and green peppers*
chicken karahi *Pakistani stew thickened with yellow split peas*
chili chicken *Indo-Chinese sweet, sour, and hot stir-fry*
haleem *Pakistani beef-and-cornmeal pudding*
hopper *bowl-shaped pancake*
iddly *South Indian vegetarian dumplings*
kacchi biryani *mutton fried rice*
kachori *smooshed-pea fritters*

kadi pakora *vegetable fritters in yogurt sauce*
karahi gosht *thick Hyderabadi goat stew*
khaman dhokla *Gujarati cake of lentil and chickpea flours*
kos kariya *Sri Lankan jackfruit curry*
lampries *Sri Lankan banquet of many small dishes*
loofah *ridged green squash*
luksha shamdy *curried lamb soup*
machi ka saalan *catfish in yogurt sauce*
masala *spice mixture*
masala dosa *potato-filled crepe*
momo *Tibetan dumplings*
mukmara *lemon chicken*
mulligatawny *Anglo-Indian tomato and dal soup*
mutton champ *grilled lamb chops*
palak paneer *Mughal spinach and cheese*
paper dosa *unfilled crepe*
paya *braised cow feet*
phaal *Anglo-Indian lamb in tomato sauce*
poori *deep-fried flatbread*
rava dosa *stuffed wheat and rice crepe*
roshgulla *sweetened homemade cheese*
roti *whole-wheat flatbread*
sambar *lentil soup*
sambol *onion relish*
samosa *potato turnover*
sarsoka sag *Bengali mustard greens served with corn bread*
smore *fish cooked in spicy coconut paste*
string hopper *rice-noodle pancake*
uppma *nutted and spiced cream of wheat*
utthappam *vegetarian stuffed pancake*
vindaloo *hottest Goan curry*

Anglo-Indian

BRICK LANE CURRY HOUSE ★ ✎
342 East 6th Street, Manhattan, 212-979-2900 Named after a curry-crammed London street, this newcomer presents English-style Balti cooking, plus other regional Indian specialties. It offers

what might be the city's hottest dish: phaal — choose chicken, lamb, shrimp, or mixed vegetables. The thick brick-red sauce delivers an alarming and lingering burn. Though the menu brags "we will require you to sign a disclaimer not holding us liable for any physical or emotional damage after eating this curry," it's a disappointing bluff. What they will do if you finish is give you a free bottle of beer and inscribe your name on a chalkboard over the bar.

CURRY SHOP ☆

381 5th Avenue, Brooklyn, 718-832-7701 This English curry shop shares space with Chipshop, offering a separate menu with a handful of Balti-style curries, making curries seem Brit. Mulligatawny soup and samosas are a couple of the best things there, and the curry list features a mix and match approach that allows to you deposit meat in a variety of sauces, which have a slightly bottled taste. Choices run from a somewhat tepid vindaloo (the best, as far as I'm concerned) to Balti curry. Balti refers to a wok-like cooking vessel and a spice mixture, both native to Baltistan in Pakistan.

Bangladeshi

BOMBAY HARBOUR ☆ ☆ ⌀

72-32 Broadway, Queens, 718-898-5500 Offering dramatic views of the intersection of Broadway and Roosevelt Avenue from its second-floor dining room, Bombay Harbour has revitalized Indian food in Jackson Heights. In addition to the standard Mughal menu, it dabbles in Goan cuisine — via the marvelous chicken xacuti — and other southern-leaning cooking styles, deploying bales of curry leaves and shotgunning dishes with black mustard seed. Dhaka Hazi's biryani, dotted with chewy bits of goat, reprises a Bangladeshi street-food favorite. Though chicken chettinad is described as a specialty of Madras, it really originated with the Chettinars, one of the few nonvegetarian groups in the south. Their cooking has become notorious in the north for its awesome hotness, achieved at Bombay Harbour through use of both chiles and crushed black peppercorns, producing a lingering spectrum of burn. Avoid the appetizers, with the exception of samosa chat and tandoori mixed grill.

DHAKA CAFE JHILL ☆ ☆ 🐟 🐟

35-55 33rd Street, Astoria, Queens, 718-786-8484 This spacious Bangladeshi café offers plenty of surprises — a wealth of aquatic choices including buffalo fish, a pink-fleshed salmon cousin served in a piquant tomato sauce. There's also more beef than you'll find in a typical Indian café. Choices run to handi kebab, which arrives stickless in a yogurt-laced sauce with plenty of fire. Vegetables are scarce, generally appearing as mashed mixtures called singara, and in a wonderful lentil-based sauce flavored with mustard oil that comes with most of the main courses.

GRAMEEN ☆ ⏿

75-18 37th Avenue, Queens, 718-505-4083 You've probably inadvertently eaten Indian food made by Bangladeshis plenty of times, but have you ever eaten real Bangladeshi food? Heavy on the heat and the mustard oil, it's an unforgettable experience. At Grameen, instead of the usual overcooked Punjabi vegetables, we have bhortas: coarse vegetable mashes of zucchini and eggplant, in which the rich colors and textures still predominate.

LITTLE BANGLADESH RESTAURANT & KEBAB HOUSE ☆ ☆ ✑

483 McDonald Avenue, Brooklyn, 718-871-7080 What's the difference between Bangladeshi food and that of India and Pakistan? Hit this gleaming cafeteria and find out. Though many of the choices of meats, vegetables, and dals are nearly identical, you'll

---

CURRY ROW

Twenty-six years ago three Indian restaurants appeared on the south side of East 6th Street between 1st and 2nd Avenues, owned by immigrants from a single town in Bangladesh, but offering a straight-arrow Mughal menu from northern India. At one time, 26 of these joints ran along both sides of the block and spilled onto adjacent avenues. While the old rumor that the curries flow underground in pipes connected to a common kitchen has never been verified, a glance at the menus posted outside indicates a frustrating sameness to the food. Indeed, for 20 years there wasn't much culinary innovation, except for the introduction of tandoori chicken halfway through that epoch. Meanwhile, resourceful restaurateurs in other parts of town added South Indian iddly and dosai, fiery Chettinar chicken, and otherworldly Indian vegetables like ashgourd and snake squash to their menus. On 6th Street, iddly never meant diddly. Eventually, the facade cracked, and now your choices on the slowly revamping street include a couple of Balti places, a couple of vegetarian South Indian places, and **Banjara**, a generalist in Indian cuisine. Give Curry Row another try.

find a lavish use of mustard oil — which embraces some dishes in a yellow haze and produces a mild delayed burn — simpler palette of flavors, increased use of cardamom and other sweet spices, admiration of fish, and great reverence toward veggies. Biryani is a given, decorated with a boiled egg and mild in flavor — till you bite down on one of the tiny peppers. Lamb curry is spicy, and elementally simple in composition. Best of all is the okra stewed with tomatoes, peppers, and a huge quantity of garlic.

Gujarati

CHOWPATTY ☆ ☆ ☆ 🌶 🔔

809 Newark Avenue, Jersey City, New Jersey, 201-222-1818; 1349 Oak Tree Road, Edison, New Jersey, 732-283-90200 Jersey City's Little Gujarat is three solid blocks of Indian businesses with names like Patel's Video, Patel's Cash and Carry, and Patel Snacks. In their midst is Chowpatty, a restaurant that features three vegetarian cuisines of the subcontinent: Mughal, South Indian, and Gujarati, the latter unlike either North or South Indian. The selection of vegetables, for example, includes choices unknown to Westerners — like tindora, a small, cucumber-shaped gourd that grows on a vine, and tori, which looks like a dildo with spiny ridges. These are prepared by a dry-cooking method that involves very slow frying in oil with spices. One dish cooked this way is tindora bataka, strips of gourd and sweet potato flavored with cumin and asafetida, which has a pleasing leathery texture. Another choice is undhiyu, a wild mélange of 10 vegetables that demonstrates the full range of Gujarati flavors.

VATAN ☆ ☆ 🔔

409 3rd Avenue, Manhattan, 212-689-5666 The dining room is like the stage set from a 1930s movie, with a spreading banyan tree, town square, and a miniature colonial building with tables on the roof. The fare is the strictly vegetarian provender of Gujarat, India's westernmost state, and the arrangement is all-you-can-eat for $19.95. Enjoy vegetables prepared by the "dry cooked" method, pea-stuffed fritters, and kedgeree, the dish that inspired a British breakfast favorite.

See Chennai Garden in the Southern Indian section for additional Gujarati fare.

Hyderabadi

DECCANI ☆ ☆ ☆ 🖎 ♨

691 Route 1 South and Wooding Avenue, Edison, New Jersey, 732-819-9110 Among Southern Indian cuisines, Hyderabadi is odd man out. The population includes a substantial number of meat-eating Muslims, among the vegetarian Hindus of surrounding states. The fare is fascinating as a result, and Deccani ably demonstrates the mixture of fiery, flesh-heavy Northern Indian fare of the sort we associate with Pakistan and the Punjab, with plenty of South Indian spices and techniques thrown in. Bell peppers come stuffed with the minced meat called keema, ramified with tiny green chiles that blow the roof off your mouth, while catfish lounge in a mellow sauce driven with coconut milk and spiced, in the southern fashion, with curry leaves and black mustard seeds. Biryani is Deccani's proudest dish, festooned with onions, tomatoes, and boiled eggs, and oddly accompanied by a mild peanut sauce. The breads are a particularly good bet, especially the spiral Ceyloni naan, and the kulcha filled with fresh herbs. Located in a Califonia-style strip shopping mall, the restaurant also features a menu of regular vegetarian South Indian fare.

Northern Indian

BANGAL CURRY ☆ ♨

111 Church Street, Manhattan, 212-267-8342 Open 24 hours, 7 days in a neighborhood just north of the former Twin Towers where most eateries close on the weekends, this tiny Indian features noticeably fresh vegetarian and meat-bearing entrées at bargain-basement prices. We dined lavishly on chicken makhani, cauliflower curry, and, best of all, potatoes cut like french fries and sautéed with gira (cumin seed) and hot pepper pods — a home-style treat rarely seen in restaurants. These dishes over rice with papadam, mixed pickle, and soda came to just over $5. Dig the mural of tea-leaf pickers on a hillside.

BANJARA ☆ ☆

97 1st Avenue, Manhattan, 212-477-5956 When the dishes begin to arrive, the most surprising is dumpakht, a pie with a naan-like crust stretched over the mouth of a copper vessel. Underneath lies a bed of boneless chicken blanketed with a nutfragrant beige sauce. Its resemblance to an English meat pie is no coincidence — while the name is Persian, the dish is Anglo-Indian, popularized by British military officers. The Banjara are Indian gypsies who weave the mirrored fabric familiar to any patron of Pier 1. Though the restaurant uses their wayfaring as a metaphor for its own culinary adventuresomeness, the menu varies from neighboring establishments not in its breadth, but in its improved versions of 6th Street classics. The usually dry alu gobi (potatoes and cauliflower) is transformed into phool aur aloo ki subzi through addition of peas and a pungent red sauce, while lamb vindaloo arrives smirched with a thick gravy more fiery than usual.

BAY LEAF ☆ ☆ 🍃 $

49 West 56th Street, Manhattan, 212-957-1818 The food is a magical mystery tour of the subcontinent, focusing mainly on Northern India. From Lucknow comes murgh zaffrani, chicken in a saffron sauce thickened with cashews and almonds. Another good choice is from Madras: kodi mellagu, chicken in a fragrant sludge of black pepper and curry leaves. From the vegetarian section of the menu comes baghar baigan, a spectacular dish of tiny purple eggplants from the city of Hyderabad. The sauce is made with coconut milk and lemon juice, and the aubergines are cooked firm. The appetizers are largely forgettable. An exception is khaman dhokla, delectable spongy cakes from Gujarat sprinkled with black mustard seed and shredded coconut.

CHICKEN CITY ☆

112-11 Jamaica Avenue, Queens, 718-850-7342 Cruising through Richmond Hill on the way to Lester Young's grave, we were drawn into this darkling establishment by a sign advertising fried chicken, which turned out to be a vestige of a previous joint. Instead, there were a couple of gals frying up fresh potato samosa, and if you've never had one hot out of the fat, you've never lived. Though the meaty goat curry and cauliflower and potato curry were a little on the bland side, the situation was easily remedied with the homemade yogurt hot sauce.

CURRY LEAF ☆ ☆ 🍃

99 Lexington Avenue, Manhattan, 212-725-5558 This offspring of Kalustyan's grocery, and sibling of Curry in a Hurry, charges into Lexington Avenue with the some of the best Indian food on the Curry Hill strip, featuring a range of dishes that covers most of the subcontinent (though Mughal prevails, as usual). Favorites on a first visit were a Malabar fish curry in a pungent, gingery coconut sauce and aloo dum, half potatoes with a semicrunchy stuffing and mellow gravy. Another delight was a light and ungreasy shrimp biryani with a flavor dominated by fresh mint.

CURRY IN A HURRY ☆ 🕙

119 Lexington Avenue, Manhattan, 212-683-0900 Those who remember the cramped quarters of the original on 29th Street — the first Indian fast-food on Curry Hill — will be impressed by these spacious corner digs. The food still rates a solid "B" — whether it's Mughal stuff like alu gobi and saag paneer, tandoori specialties like chicken tikka and lamb kufta, or South Indian masala dosa and iddly. Best part is the second-floor dining room with its big picture windows. Dig the unique chutney bar — fresh green chiles; raw onions; rice pudding; chutneys of cilantro, coconut, and tamarind; salad fixin's; lemon wedges; and an astringent pickle of green olives, chile pepper, and lime.

DARBAR EAST ☆
239 1st Avenue, Manhattan, 212-677-0005 Not to be confused with the expensive place in midtown called Darbar, this small and cheap place in the hospital district nevertheless excels at fresh and carefully prepared Indian food, with a few Nepalese dishes thrown in for good measure. Particularly tasty are chicken makhani, with torn pieces of tandoori chicken immersed in a mellow yogurt sauce, and lamb pasand, thickly gravied with sweet-spice accents. Unless you're in a hurry, skip the steam table offerings in favor of the wider-ranging menu.

DESI VILLAGE ☆ ☆
2812 Ocean Avenue, Brooklyn, 718-648-3200 Into the dry gulch of Brooklyn Indian food falls this obscurely located institution. Skip the free Russian-leaning appetizer salads, which are uniformly awful, and dive into a menu that includes excellent chicken methi and the tangy stewed mustard greens called sarsoka sag. Instead of white rice, order any of the carefully cooked biryanis, especially gosht dum, filled with tender lamb chunks and flavored with acerbic citrus pickle. The bread list is one of the best in the city, including a couple of surprises: Afghan Kabuli naan, chock full of fruit and nuts, and "village naan," topped with garlic, onions, and hot chiles.

DIWAN-E-KHAAS ☆ ⚘
53 Nassau Street, Manhattan, 212-571-6369 Ever wonder what fenugreek tastes like? Chicken methi — a frequent special at this Wall Street Indian — features poultry morsels hosed with fenugreek leaves, imparting a mellow toasty flavor. You'll probably never again find the spice used with such directness. Lamb vindaloo is long on spice and short on potatoes, palak paneer a spinach puree with less homemade cheese than you might like. As the number of Indian steam tables south of Canal Street has skyrocketed, it is now possible to be rather picky about your Mughal (or is that Muggle?) food.

5 STARS PUNJABI INDIAN CUISINE ☆ ☆
13-15 43rd Avenue, Queens, 718-784-7444 You've never had biryani like this before, fragrant with citrus peel, studded with whole spices and chunks of rich goat. Tandoori-cooked breads

shine, too, especially the one stuffed with cauliflower and fennel. Dining in this architecturally distinguished diner is loads of fun, and there's always a table of hipsters or two digging the food, in addition to the usual in-a-hurry cabbies.

INDIA HOUSE ✫
139 Court Street, Brooklyn, 718-852-3486 Everyone knows of an old chop suey parlor that has pointedly ignored newfangled ideas about Chinese food. Well, this is the Indian equivalent. The Northern Indian food at this antique establishment just off Atlantic Avenue is dark, mellow, and well-spiced, and even vegetarian dishes have a meaty aura. The green chutney is spicier than most, and the samosa and bhajia are generous, economical, and well-fried. Reflecting a stint making Indian food in Flatbush, the proprietor serves up his variation on the Trinidadian roti, a thick flatbread filled with potatoes and goat. It's gr-r-r-eat!

INDIAN TAJ ✫ ♨
37-25 74th Street, Queens, 718-651-4187 What's the best Indian buffet in Jackson Heights? Of the four, Indian Taj offers the most sumptuous of the all-you-can-eat lunches, then outdoes itself by providing dinner at only a dollar more. Highlights include a stark-red vegetarian biryani, mattar paneer that actually contains large quantities of homemade cheese, the yogurt-sauced vegetable fritters of kadi pakora, and a powerfully flavored goat curry (most buffets offer chicken, but no other meat). There's also a chat stand where fried noodles called papri can be festooned with various condiments, including homemade carrot chutney.

JACKSON DINER ✫ ♨
37-47 74th Street, Queens, 718-672-1232 OK, this Little India mainstay is never again going to be what it once was. The charming earlier location, which really was a diner, slung perfect, if

---

NEW TANDOORI

The name originally comes from the Babylonian word for fire, but similar Turkish, Hebrew, Arabic, and Persian words have been used for millennia to designate a beehive-shaped clay oven used to cook bread and meat. Surprisingly, the tandoor wasn't introduced into India until 1948, when an Old Delhi hot spot called Moti Mahal began brandishing one for an admiring crowd of politicians and celebrities. The restaurant is still there, and the trend it started has snowballed in India, and in the United States as well.

265

modest, Indian food to hordes of demanding Indian shoppers. Now it's a yuppie joint with all the charm of an airline terminal. A goat curry lacked flash, while a lamb saag that used to be a friend's favorite dish was way too salty. Several subsequent visits to see if the kitchen had settled into a groove found that it hadn't. Your best bet is to go for the still-glorious luncheon buffet from 11 a.m. to 4 p.m. on weekdays.

MINAR ☆ 🍴

5 West 31st Street, Manhattan, 212-684-2199; 138 West 46th Street, Manhattan, 212-398-4600 When a second branch of this proletarian Indian restaurant opened near Times Square, it was an instant hit with its low prices, well-stocked steam table, vegetarian options, and made-to-order dosas (go Wednesday for the special butter dosa). It now exceeds the original branch in quality, maybe 'cause they shuffled their best cooks to the new store. Because the meat and poultry is not halal, Minar is cut off from much of its potential cabby constituency. Instead, it encourages the patronage of South Indian vegetarians by offering iddly, utthappam, and masala dosa.

PUNJABI KEBAB HOUSE ☆

91-52 Lefferts Boulevard, Queens, 718-846-2800 Is Richmond Hill becoming, foodwise, the new Jackson Heights? The corner of Lefferts and Atlantic now boasts four Indian restaurants, each with its own attractions. This modest kebab house, with gleaming pink and white decor, is the retail operation of a much larger catering hall. It mounts a magnificent $5 buffet each day from 11 a.m. to 4 p.m., long on sharply spiced vegetable purees, well-sauced stews, and desserts of a quality seldom seen at steam table joints, sometimes including both rice pudding and warm carrot halwah, cousin to Middle Eastern halvah.

QUALITY FOOD PALACE ☆ ☆ $

184-22 Horace Harding Expressway, Queens, 718-353-3804 The Horace Harding Expressway, which shadows the LIE through most of eastern Queens, hosts some of the borough's most interesting white-tablecloth restaurants. The ethnic origin of the oddly named Quality Food Palace is undiscernible until you step inside and smell the delicious curry spices. The broad-ranging menu goes from well-seasoned biryanis, to succulent whole-fish tandoori, to meaty incendiary lamb vindaloo, to a bread roster that would be the envy of East 6th Street. Go for the buttery multilayered lacha paratha.

RAJ MAHAL ☆ 🥢 🍴

248-08 Union Turnpike, Queens, 718-831-0200 This slightly overblown restaurant welcomes guests with an ornate cloisonné door, a samovar the size of a small car, and a stadium-size dining room. In addition to standard Mughal fare, tandooris, and biryanis, the menu offers a handful of regional specialties, including a Kerala goat fry of flavorful meat with a piquant masala, and a wonderful bindi masala featuring lemony baby okra. As we downed our excellent chicken tandoori, a wide-screen television presented colorfully turbaned Sikhs confronting Brit colonialists on the cricket pitch. Not the way I remember it.

SIRTAJ ☆ ⊘
36 West 26th Street, Manhattan, 212-989-3766 In contrast to your typical Indian steam table joint, this two-decade-old mainly lunchtime greasy spoon assembles the dishes to order, making them significantly fresher tasting. Recommended: onion kulcha, vegetable kofta, tandoori chicken, and Manhattan's best samosa.

TANDOORI HUT ☆ ☆ ☆ ✎
119-04 94th Avenue, Queens, 718-850-8919 As in any new culinary art form, there's plenty of room for innovation, and at the head of the local vanguard stands Tandoori Hut. Adjoining a Hindu temple, there's no decor to speak of apart from a wall-mounted thermometer you should take as a warning. The standard red tandoori chicken is excellent, with a coating spicier than usual and a rare moistness. A yellow version is also offered, coated with lemon pickle that rivals the red for shock value. Chicken tikka is given a reprieve from its usual boring incarnation. Of four flavors, I especially dig the hariyali tikka, thickly coated with mint chutney, adding bright green to the restaurant's color palette. In exuberant pursuit of the tandoori lifestyle, the Hut doesn't content itself with merely cooking great tandoori. It goes on to use tandoori as as a point of departure for fanciful culinary excursions. Named after a shrine to the goddess of fire, chicken jawalamukhi is a sputtering mountain of poultry in a sweet sauce flecked with fenugreek. The best of these creations is chicken katakat, a julienne of chicken strips bathed in a light lemon sauce. I had to reassure a timid friend that it didn't contain any cat.

THALI ☆ ⊘
28 Greenwich Avenue, Manhattan, 212-367-7411 This narrow establishment, decorated in eye-searing tones of red, orange, and yellow, offers a single tray of food (a "thali") at lunch and dinner. The tray contains a series of small dishes such as, at a recent lunch, dal, yellow rice, savory potatoes and cauliflower, a paratha, tangy carrot salad, and a milk-based sweet. Dinner is double the food at double the price. Sometimes the dishes are prepared in Gujarati fashion: slowly dry-cooked with a little oil, no water, and mild spices. I can't wait to go back. Finally, vegetarian food served the way most Indians eat it.

Pakistani

BUKHARA ☆
1095 Coney Island Avenue, Brooklyn, 718-859-8033 Jog past the big-screen TV, where mooning lovers cavort and sing, to the outsized L-shaped steam table. Pick earthy goat stew, loaded with potatoes in a chocolate-brown gravy, or, even more intense, a fricassee of kidneys and long green chiles. Don't neglect the snacks on the glass shelf, like samosa, pakora, and the A1 potato fritters: fried rounds of mashed spuds flecked with red chiles. This restaurant, a cabby favorite, is Pakistani — not Uzbekistani, as the name would suggest.

FIZA DINER ☆ 🌶
259-07 Hillside Avenue, Queens, 718-347-3100 This gleaming Floral Park diner, now a Pakistani establishment, immodestly proclaims on the marquee: "America's Best Grilled Kebabs," and I'd be the last to contradict them. The range of tandoori-cooked meats is indeed impressive, from the outsize lamb chops well-rubbed with a fragrant masala, to the quail which cower on the glass shelf, to the $10 whole chicken, glowing red and looking like it wants to jump onto your plate. Kissed with cinnamon, the samosa bulge with filling, while the biryani is nut-brown and heaped with jagged chunks of lamb. The cornmeal-thickened beef pudding called haleem comes festively strewn with frizzled onions.

HAANDI ☆ ☆ ☆ 🌶
113 Lexington Avenue, Manhattan, 212-685-5200 Follow the swarm of cabs to this restaurant, where vegetables are forsaken in favor of one of the meatiest and most highly flavored cuisines on the planet. Ignore the illuminated menu, and carefully scan the steam table and the glass shelf above it before ordering. Nearly always in evidence is chicken karahi, a mellow yellow stew thickened with split peas, and paya, a screwy gluey braise of cow feet that's often enjoyed at breakfast. One day a flock of succulent tandoori quail landed on the counter, to be succeeded by the damper masala quail on the steam table the next day. The best steam table dish after many visits was an orange slurry of lamb and rutabagas, the mashed turnips furnishing a concentrated sweetness. Propelled by whole camphor pods that look like small shriveled prunes, the flavor is amazing, as if Mom had rubbed the lamb's chest with Vapo-Rub.

HALAL INDO-PAK RESTAURANT ☆
1750 1st Avenue, Manhattan, 212-987-8150 Don't be misled by this no-nonsense thimble of a place — the food is prepared

EAST VILLAGE TRUCK STOPS

For a cheap meal on the run, it's hard to beat the East Village's Pakistani truck stops. Bread, rice, and two steam table dishes run around $5 in most cases. They're hard to spot — many masquerade as the grocery stores they once were. Made to address the 24-hour dining needs of cabdrivers, anyone is welcome.

PUNJABI
114 East 1st Street, Manhattan, 212-533-9048 A couple of narrow wooden counters invite you to stand up and nosh. The fare is strictly vegetarian, and the starch component is provided by whole-wheat rotis. My favorite dish is saag, a puree of spinach dotted with onions and laced with hot chiles.

PAK STAR DELI
78 East 1st Street, Manhattan, 212-260-5884 The sunny disposition of the Bengali counter guy almost makes up for inferior chow. His hot tea, however, is wonderful: prepared by immersing a tea bag in hot water with plenty of milk and sugar, then dipping a jet from an espresso maker and blowing bubbles till the whole beverage is a creamy froth.

PAK PUNJAB
40 East 3rd Street, Manhattan, 212-614-0107 The underachieving cousin of defunct Swad in Brooklyn, this joint offers a lot more selection than the other places. Especially good are the bulging potato samosas and the chicken-ball and boiled-egg stew.

LAHORE DELI
132 Crosby Street, Manhattan, no phone The food is every bit as good as the other three despite its abject condition. Order not from the refrigerator case, but from the plastic tubs on top, used for dishes that have just been created. My potato and eggplant curry rocked on a recent visit.

with great care and affection. Check out karahi gosht, a thick stew of goat attributed to the city of Hyderabad. Skip the tandoori items, which may be a little old and tired, and concentrate on what's on the steam table. Vegetarians will find an array of selections in a Mughal vein, like the tasty palak paneer. Open 24 hours, this restaurant is a resource in a food-challenged neighborhood.

KHYBER KEBAB ☆

207 10th Avenue, Manhattan, 212-727-0144 Don't believe the sign that says Chelsea Big Wok; persevere into the dilapidated premises that serves some of the best Pakistani food in Manhattan. You need go no further than the fish cakes that sit on the counter, deep-fried hockey pucks of kingfish laced with onions, scallions, and a touch of fennel seed. Request the homemade cilantro chutney for dipping. Also estimable is a meatless curry of pumpkin and cabbage with the bright taste of cardamom and cumin. No kebabs in sight, though. Open till 4 a.m.

QASIM ☆

338 9th Avenue, Manhattan, 212-695-6556 "Halal Fried Chicken" screams the awning at Qasim, and the advertised product is quite good — with a crackling skin barely dusted with flour, and a damp, flavorful interior. You might have gotten it at Mary Mac's Tearoom in Atlanta. But look to the chicken biryani for a dish closer to the hearts of the cooks. The tumbled yellow and white rice is dotted with orange peel, black peppercorns, and fenugreek leaves, and big empty pan leaves have dumped their perfumes into the rice. Though this feast will set your mouth on fire, the goat curry's even hotter.

PAKISTAN TEA HOUSE ☆ ☆ 🍎

176 Church Street, Manhattan, 212-240-9800 Don't miss the tandoori fish at this gently named eatery, mobbed at lunch with a diverse crowd of businesspeople, artists, and cabdrivers. Also, don't confuse this location with several imitators that have sprung up in the immediate neighborhood with similar names. Accept no substitutes! The broad range of breads, many cooked in the tandoor just inches from your face, would be reason enough to visit, but also try the chicken jalfrazi, made with fresh onions and green peppers that miraculously retain their character in the thick stew. Open 24 hours.

PEARL PALACE ☆ 🍎

60 Pearl Street, Manhattan, 212-482-0771 Not quite as good as Pakistan Tea House, this way-downtown 24-hour eatery may be perfect if you're making your yearly pilgrimage to the Statue of Liberty, or visiting a rich uncle on Wall Street. The all-you-can-eat lunch buffet is the ideal way to experience the Pakistan-oriented menu. Especially recommended: okra masala, onion kulcha (a stuffed bread), and the splendid ginger chicken, aromatic with sweet spices.

RAWAL RAVAIL RESTAURANT ☆ ☆ ☆ 🥢

641 Lydig Avenue, Bronx, 212-319-1500 This grandly alliterative new Pakistani place has its work cut out for it at the Bronx's best food corner, which features everything from Albanian bureks to Russian-Jewish baked goods to vegan Jamaican. Luckily, the 3Rs is up to the task, proffering moist spicy chicken biryani, glistening lacha paratha, perfect goat curry mellowed with a light gravy, a braise of potatoes and cauliflower swimming in mustard oil, and urad dal — miniature white lozenges with a creamy flavor and slight crackle, like Rice Krispies. The highlight of one meal was the Pakistani favorite haleem. Though this name can be applied to a range of dishes, in this case it was a saucer of beef that had been pulled and smashed almost into a paste. Our host revealed the secret of the quivering puddinglike consistency: corn flour.

Southern Indian

CHENNAI GARDEN ☆ ☆ ☆ ⏻
129 East 27th Street, Manhattan, 212-689-1999 There are now plenty of places in Curry Hill where you can get a masala dosa, the delicious potato-filled crepe of South India, but Chennai Garden has carried the obsession further than most other establishments, offering manifold variations like rava dosa (with a supple cream-of-wheat batter), paper dosa (an ultrathin unfilled crepe), and, my fave, a "gunpowder" masala dosa hosed with hot pepper. In addition to such southern snacks as iddly and utthappam, the menu goes exploring in the Punjab and Gujarat, respectively, for specialties like okra masala and undhiyu, an unusual stew of yam, snow peas, and eggplant.

CHOLA ☆ ☆ 🌶 🐟 ⏻ $
232 East 58th Street, Manhattan, 212-688-0464 Never in New York has the neglected food of South India received so much attention. Look in the Dakshin Specials section to find "more kozhambu," a stew of baby okra and spongy dumplings in a thick buttermilk sauce redolent of mustard, onions, and curry leaves. These leaves (pronounced "kari") are central to southern cooking, imparting a pungent fragrance somewhere between lemongrass and bay leaf. Find them also in avial malabar, a favorite of Cochin, a former Dutch colony on the Malabar coast. A cumin-laced mélange of carrots, zucchini, and eggplant thickened with coconut and yogurt, it's pleasingly mellow and tart at the same time. Other estimable oddities include three dishes from the Jewish community of Calcutta. Their Middle Eastern origins are reflected in the lemon, slivered almonds, and yellow raisins of chicken makmura.

DOSA HUTT ☆ ☆ ☆ 🌱 ⏻
45-63 Bowne Street, Queens, 718-961-6228 Right next to a baroque Hindu temple, the Hutt is a plain white box with a menu limited to the luncheon dishes of South India. The strictly vegetar-

ian bill of fare includes perfect made-from-scratch renditions of dosa, utthappam, vada, and iddly, each served with a Styrofoam cup of sambar and a green puddle of homemade coconut chutney. The standard masala dosa is not particularly large, but the wrapper is crisp and well browned, and the filling more complex than most, featuring dal and cashews tossed with a potato mixture accented with cumin, onions, and curry leaves. The best is the "special butter masala dosa," so drenched in ghee that you can smell its nutty fragrance anywhere in the neighborhood.

INDIAN COFFEE HOUSE ☆ ☆ ☆ 🍂 🐚

260-07 Hillside Avenue, Queens, 718-347-4797 Far out in Floral Park's new Little India, just steps from the Long Island border, this humble Keralan establishment hides a small café with checkered tablecloths behind a store hawking coconut oil and masalas. Don't let the humble presentation fool you: the food is brilliant, and this could be the new Jackson Diner, though the cuisine originates in Southern rather than Northern India. Witness the profoundly pungent mutton curry dotted with black mustard seeds and curry leaves; the seasonal fish fry, featuring a delicate pomfret rubbed thickly with spices; or the vegetarian specialties, which include dosas filled with eggs and spongy flatbreads called appams which mop up everything else.

MADRAS CAFE ☆ 🐚

79 2nd Avenue, Manhattan, 212-254-8002 This strictly vegetarian café is a breath of fresh air in the East Village's Curry Corridor, the first in this zone to specialize in Southern Indian cooking.

DOSAS À LA CART

One of the most unusual food carts in the city is pushed to the corner of West 4th and Sullivan Streets on weekdays by Thiru Kumar, a Sri Lankan immigrant who used to flip dosas at the sainted **Dosa Hutt**. The menu is simple: 10 kinds of homemade dosas, plus Singapore noodles and a handful of South Indian snacks, and the line frequently snakes down the block. Everything is efficiently made to order as you watch, and he'll apply just the right amount of hot sauce to the interior of the pancake. The accompanying coconut chutney, with little flecks of red in it, is homemade, and the sambar has a touch of heat. Dig in the soda cooler and you'll sometimes find a can of Sri Lankan ginger beer. His cell number, in case you wonder about the actual hours: 917-710-2092.

We especially liked the lentil soup laced with lemon and cilantro, spongy iddly dumplings, and lemon rice studded with cashews and toasted dal. Dosa are available in seven variations, but even better are the utthappam, spongy fermented rice-and-lentil pancakes. The menu is rounded out with breads and curries of eggplant, green beans, cauliflower, and homemade cheese.

MADRAS MAHAL ☆ ☆ ⏾

104 Lexington Avenue, Manhattan, 212-684-4010 This progenitor of the current kosher Indian vegetarian fad, which claims five restaurants in Curry Hill alone, drifted into mediocrity a few years back, but has returned to top form with a refurbished dining room and amplified service. The $5.95 lunch buffet is the best in the city, and the crispy masala dosa is huge enough to justify its higher Manhattan price.

MAHARAJA QUALITY ☆ ☆ ⏾

73-10 37th Avenue, Queens, 718-505-2680 Anybody who thinks the Jackson Heights Indian restaurant scene is moribund better pay another visit. There are several relatively new joints, among them this chat shop, specializing in shopper's snacks like nuts, sweets, masala tea, and "chats," elaborate concoctions that begin with a samosa or potato patty and pile on all sorts of chutneys, chopped onions, fried noodles, and yogurt, making for a tasty inexpensive mess. Dosas are good, too, filled with several types of dal swirled with potatoes and onions, shotgunned with black mustard seed.

SANTOOR ☆ ☆ 🐟

257-05 Union Turnpike, Queens, 718-343-3939 Named after a 100-string instrument played with tiny hammers, Santoor recalls Jackson Diner in its heyday. Like its template, the restaurant is owned by Sikhs who have contrived a menu to satisfy diners from several parts of India, from the meat-loving curry consumers of the north, to the cow-worshipping vegetarians of the south, to the continuum of omnivores in between. A couple of the best selections hail from Malabar, the southwestern coastal region that glories in the freshness of its seafood and the pungency of its spices. Foremost is malabar fish curry, chunks of firm white fish in a dark brown gravy speckled with black mustard seeds and floating limpid curry leaves that shimmer in the dim light. The coconut-laced gravy is sweet and pungent, the perfect foil for the bland chunks of fish. To go with it, order malabari paratha — it pulls apart into floppy buttery layers.

Sri Lankan

BOWNIE ☆ ☆
143-05 45th Avenue, Queens, 718-463-8621 Sri Lankan food debuts in Queens with this new luncheonette, serving the brooding, spice-laced "black curries" (pick lamb); mellow, coconut-laced fish curries (pick kingfish), and the range of breads like appams (weekends only) and outsize rotis that make Ceylonese cooking delightfully unique. The dosas are particularly good (referred to as "thosas" in Sri Lanka). Outflanking its Staten Island brethren, Bownie also serves additional vegetarian South Indian specialties like curd rice — a glorious tart sludge flavored with black mustard seed and curry leaf. Also don't miss puttu, a loaf of crumbled brown rice snowed with dried coconut.

LAKRUWANA ☆
358 West 44th Street, Manhattan, 212-957-4480 One of the best items at this Sri Lankan restaurant (one of only two in Manhattan, the other is Taprobane) is the hopper — a bowl-shaped lentil pancake cradling a poached egg, served with a zippy onion relish.

LAKSHMI'S ☆ ☆ ☉
324 Victory Boulevard, Staten Island, 718-876-5560 Like its neighbor New Asha Café, this Sri Lankan hash house is located across the street from the picturesque Albanian mosque. Surprisingly, there are a number of unique dishes, including roast bread, a mind-bogglingly big slice of white bread that's been toasted like zwieback, making you want to see the loaf it came from, and a dish of shredded beets that does a good imitation of steak tartare. Commonplaces like the cylindrical mutton roll coated with toasted coconut, and goat curry — a delicate dice of boneless meat — are rendered with special flair.

NEW ASHA CAFÉ ☆ ☆ ☆ ⬥ ☉
322 Victory Boulevard, Staten Island, 718-420-0649 The bread's the thing at working-class Sri Lankan joints like Staten Island's New Asha Café. Mottled brown on top, gloriously gummy underneath, rectangular rotis stand atop the counter folded and stacked like diapers. Next to them totter amazing bowl-shaped breads called hoppers — some with a still-jiggy steamed egg melded to the bottom. The Sri Lankan rendition of dosas, called thosas, are also available. Breads can be paired with relishes called sambols (no charge), or with one of the fragrant curries. An inky eggplant stew is knocked for a loop by a spice mixture known as suwunda kudu, featuring cumin, black cumin, cloves, fenugreek, and, especially, cinnamon. Kingfish steaks loll in a banana-

colored coconut broth dancing with droplets of red oil, while chicken curry boasts a chocolate-brown broth tangled with so many flavor-bearing twigs and leaves it looks like a beaver dam. This is one of Sri Lanka's notorious black curries, powdered spice mixtures given deep and rich flavor by pan-toasting.

TAPROBANE ☆

234 West 56th Street, Manhattan, 212-333-4203 Try the strange-sounding black curry — chunks of tender lamb in a midnight brown sauce powerfully flavored with toasted fennel, coriander seed, coconut, and fenugreek. The spice combinations for most of the dishes, like pork red curry and beef smore (no graham crackers or chocolate involved), are novel enough that you'll know you're not eating Indian food.

Tibetan

TIBETAN YAK ☆ ☆ ☆ 🌶 ♨

72-20 Roosevelt Avenue, Queens, 718-779-1119 The year-old Yak has settled into a groove, purveying the best Tibetan food in town with a menu twice the length of the lackluster East Village places. Thrill to la phing, a dome of cryptic white jelly mantled in hot sauce and laked in soy sauce, or tsel thinthuk, homemade pasta in a rich vegetarian broth with white radish and baby bok choy (vegetable selection varies). Meat selections are also well spiced, including chile-sautéed tongue and a thick lamb curry with plenty of cardamom and cinnamon. Perversely, the signature dumplings called momo are below par. You can do fine without them.

TIBET SHAMBALA ☆ ☆ ♨

488 Amsterdam Avenue, Manhattan, 212-721-1270 The fried dumplings called kothey are exquisite, especially when lathered with the killer homemade hot sauce. This long-running Upper West Side gem is second only to Tibetan Yak in the excellence of its Himalayan food. Biggest surprise: the butter-slicked tea called bocha grows on you.

See Darbar East in the Northern Indian section above for an introduction to Nepalese food.

Senegalese, Guinean, Ivory Coastal, and Malian

Thirteen years ago, when African bistros began lining West 116th Street and popping up on the avenues, the Senegalese ruled, offering cheap and abundant one-dish meals like cheb, yassa, and mafe. Gradually, coffee-drinking and baguette-wielding immigrants from Côte d'Ivoire infiltrated, and within six years their establishments came to dominate the area, while Malians and Guineans continued as a minor presence. But gradually, though the Senegalese remained a major presence in Harlem, the anglophone Nigerians and Ghanaians and their cafés became the most important African presence in other parts of town, like Williamsbridge and College Point in the Bronx and Flatbush and New Lots in Brooklyn. There is even an entirely above-ground Nigerian restaurant in Staten Island, one that makes a special attempt to make all diners feel welcome and at ease. The Guineans continue to live in the Soundview section of the Bronx, even though one of their number, Amadou Diallo, was murdered by cops as he reached for his wallet, discouraging West Africans from moving here and causing others to move away, leaving the Senegalese, Côte d'Ivoire, and Guinean dining scene somewhat diminished.

I have seen the African cuisines change as they've absorbed American influences. While mashes and fufus were formerly made with a whole range of raw materials, today instant potato flakes have come to dominate the fufu market, although the Africans have made the product their own, and created a distinct and wonderful version of mashed potatoes. Less wonderfully, the Maggi seasoning omnipresent in Senegalese restaurants has been replaced by ketchup as the favored condiment — or maybe the Africans switch the bottles when they see us coming. And, saddest of all, palm oil — an oil made in heaven, tastewise — has all but disappeared from the food.

Although the African restaurants in New York feature an abundance of meat, chicken, fresh seafood, and vegetables, the vast majority of people living in Africa see a piece of meat or chicken once a month or less, and eat almost nothing but rice or porridge smothered in piquant sauces, called "soups." For an idea of what some of the raw materials look like, visit the **West African Grocery** at 40th Street and 9th Avenue, which sells an astounding assortment of African food products — dried fish, palm oil, herbs and spices, even African beer. The smell alone is like a quick vacation to West Africa.

LOOK FOR:

aloko *Ivoirian fried plantain*

athieke *Ivoirian cassava meal porridge*

bissap *sorrel beverage*

boisson au gingembre *very intense homemade ginger drink*

boulettes *Senegalese fish balls*

cassava *starchy root vegetable also called manioc or yuca*

cheb *Senegalese fish paella*

claire viande *beef stew*

dakhine *Senegalese peanut-sauced lamb and cowpeas*

diby *grilled lamb chops*

epinards *spinach-and-peanut sauce*

la firie *Malian rice cooked with okra*

foutout *Ivoirian okra, peanut, and lamb stew with starch balls*

joloff rice *dirty rice, sometimes with meat and veggies*

mafe *Senegalese lamb in peanut sauce*

netetou *African turmeric, used in Senegalese soupikandia and curries*

poisson *roast or grilled whole fish, usually red snapper*

ragout *Ivoirian lamb stew*

rissoles *meat-filled turnovers*

sauce de feuilles *Guinean sweet-potato-leaf sauce*

soup *any sauce that goes over rice or mash*

soupikandia *lamb in okra sauce*

tô *millet porridge*

yassa *Senegalese fish with onions in mustard sauce*

Guinean

KALOUM ☆ 🐚
126 West 116th Street, Manhattan, 212-864-2845
Kaloum's interior is a symphony of Formica, dominated by contoured cream benches and maroon tables. There's a delightful mural of a West African village with chickens and goats in the foreground and citizens staring toward an empty village square. Maybe they're awaiting the arrival of fast-food franchises. The menu includes Senegalese as well as Guinean fare, which is remarkable for its leaf-based sauces. Typical is sauce de feuilles, a stew of beef thickened with sweet-potato leaves that generate a deep-green sludge with a faint oxalic tang. Served in a soup bowl, it accompanies a huge plate of rice that lets you know that the meal is fundamentally rice with a little sauce on the side, rather than the other way around. Kaloum's version of Senegalese cheb features bluefish, cabbage, carrots, and eggplant over brownish rice, perfectly adequate. As we looked around, we noticed that most of the diners — all male, dressed in black leather jackets or three-piece suits — were eating delicious-looking whole roasted chickens, presented on a bed of salad. Up yours, Colonel Sanders!

SOKOBOLIE ☆ ☆ 🐚
2529 8th Avenue, Manhattan, 212-491-3969 While most West African restaurants offer only three or four set meals at a time, this convivial Harlem establishment mounts a daily menu that features a dozen or so Guinean and Senegalese specialties. There's always one leaf-based sauce ("sauce de feuilles" — the national dish of Guinea), made with either spinach or sweet-potato leaf, and often there's a fricassee of chicken in palm sauce, and a peanut-laced stew of smoked fish that has the intriguing texture of driftwood. Less challenging Senegalese staples like grilled lamb chops ("diby") and steak with onions are also available. Open 24 hours!

See also African and American Family Restaurant in the Senegalese section, below.

Ivory Coastal

AFRICAN GRILL ☆ ☆ 🐟
496 5th Avenue, Manhattan, 212-987-3836 Tucked under the chin of the verdant and mountainous Marcus Garvey Park, African Grill occupies the former premises of a Harlem dive known as the Fifth Avenue Hideaway. Inside, java makers replace the usual booze bottles — including a percolator, an espresso machine, and

the redoubtable Mr. Coffee — a tip-off that the proprietors hail from the Côte d'Ivoire, where the brown brew is a ruling passion. A chalkboard broadcasts the daily bill of fare, which might be mistaken for that of a French bistro. The biggest surprise is ragout, a savory lamb gravy jotted with finely ground meat and poured over hunks of creamy white yam, more filling than potato. Another delight is kidneys sautéed with plenty of garlic and onions, sided with petits pois and a Gallic gob of mayonnaise. We also enjoyed an expertly fried kingfish steak, rubbed with salt, pepper, and herbs, and served on a bed of athieke (pronounced "ah-check-aye"), the national dish of grated cassava stodge. The fish was heaped with a warm mustardy relish of onions, bell peppers, and tomatoes, a delicious accompaniment. One of the cooks is Senegalese, so expect some stuff from that country.

FARFINA COFFEE SHOP ☆

219B West 116th Street, Manhattan, 212-856-8408 They don't get around to making athieke at Farfina until five in the afternoon, so I was out of luck when I arrived around noon. In spite of an awning that rather comically advertises hot and cold sandwiches, two hot dishes are what's usually available. One is sous, a serviceable lamb stew with a thick brown gravy that the waitress, who is from Burkina Faso, referred to rather disparagingly — maybe because its meat-intensive blandness didn't seem particularly African. Then I asked about la firie, a dish advertised on a scrap of paper in the window. She nodded approvingly, lifting the lid to reveal a pot of rice cooked with dried okra, observing "Now this is really African."

LE WORODOUGOU ☆ 🐟

2192 8th Avenue, Manhattan, 212-864-6339 This restaurant replaces a previous Senegalese establishment that tried to go upscale with exposed-brick walls and a public relations firm. The trendy walls, at least, remain. The current Ivory Coast scarf is light-years different: a plate of perfect rice topped with a choice of okra or spinach sauces, the former dotted with bits of lean lamb and properly viscous, the latter loaded with fish and beef and mellowed with palm oil. Or get a fried red snapper napped with African tomato salsa and strewn with onions.

Malian

MALI-BO ☆ ☆ 🍤

218 West 116th Street, Manhattan, 212-665-4481 Travel posters decorate the spare interior of Mali-Bo, the most prominent depicting the Grande Mosque at Djenné, a magnificent adobe structure with protruding beams that keep the mud in place. An ostrich egg tops each of the soaring towers. There is no printed menu, but the waitress gladly recites the offerings in English, French, or Bambara. We asked for tô, a millet porridge eaten in many Sahel countries. Mali-Bo's version substitutes the readily available cornmeal for millet. The "soup" that goes with it features big chunks of beef in a thin tomato and palm-oil sauce. Floating atop the soup is a wonderful fishy puree of okra flavored with sun-dried stockfish. Most entrées come with salad and aloko, slices of sweet fried plantain that are a West African staple.

Senegalese

AFRICAN AND AMERICAN FAMILY RESTAURANT
☆ ☆ 🐟

2535 3rd Avenue, Bronx, 718-742-4797 This pit stop for car service drivers among the gas stations and tire-change palaces of Mott Haven was formerly a Guinean café. Now it's a Senegalese joint with a formidably talented cook, whose lamb mafe is thick and tasty, while her cheb is a marvel of veggies, stuffed bluefish, and rice so rich it puts Cajun dirty rice to shame. To satisfy the old constituency, there is usually a Guinean dish on the steam table. Today it was soupe de touré, a thick and pleasantly spicy sauce of beef and dried fish thickened with okra. Open daytime only.

AFRICA RESTAURANT #1 ☆ 🐟 🐟
247 West 116th Street, Manhattan, 212-666-9400 Don't believe the sign that says Kine Restaurant. The Senegalese mainstays at Africa #1 have been shuffled onto a lunch menu, while dinner reflects an Africanized take on French cuisine. A heap of tasty charcoal-grilled lamb chops called diby arrives with a vinaigrette salad and choice of french fries, couscous, or rice; an immense bluefish comes smeared with an unforgettable mustard-and-onion relish. One recent evening, though, between conversations on their cell phones, most diners seemed to be enjoying chebu yap, a mound of mahogany broken rice surmounted by an outsize lamb shank inundated with oily natural gravy. New to Senegalese menus is a selection of soups. Cow foot features a dense and fiery broth, from which you can dredge pieces of rubbery, jelly-sloughing foot.

AFRICA RESTAURANT #2 ☆ ☆ 🐟 🐟
346 West 53rd Street, Manhattan, 212-399-7166 The downtown branch of Africa Restaurant #1 aspires to nightclub elegance, and has a devoted clientele who seem more like businesspeople than cabdrivers. One day I stumbled on a special of soupikandia, a real rarity in New York. It contained several big pieces of lamb in a chile-sharpened gravy thickened with dried okra and enriched with a couple of fragments of stockfish — the sun-dried fish used

as a flavoring agent. I can never resist cheb in a Senegalese restaurant, and was pleasantly surprised at this rendition. Instead of the usual bluefish, there was a big hunk of kingfish stuffed with pureed parsley and garlic. The cheb was subtly flavored and fragrant, the rice deep brown with Maggi, the Swiss answer to soy sauce. A surprise inclusion was a handful of dried snails, the kind you often see in African markets threaded on sticks.

DABAKH-MALIK ☆

1194 Fulton Street, Brooklyn, 718-789-2888 Located in the midst of the multimosque strip that's become Brooklyn's premier Muslim neighborhood (a sign in the window promises "No Pork"), this Senegalese café offers views of the Slave #1 Theatre. The cheb is rich and complex, a mountain of red rice dotted with bluefish, cabbage, cassava, carrot, and wisps of dark stockfish. We also dug a dish of lamb in an olive-colored cassava-leaf sauce — the national dish of neighboring Guinea. Ask for a dab of the Scotch bonnet hot sauce, then use it carefully. Unfortunately, this place has taken to mounting a steam table buffet during most of the day, with your plate weighed to determine the cost. I like the idea, but somehow the food is not as good after it's languished on the steam table, and the tendency is to present parts of dishes rather than full-blown West African masterpieces.

HARLEM'S LITTLE AFRICA

West 116th Street is the original African outpost in town, spawned by the presence of the Malcolm Shabazz Mosque and a halal butcher shop. The mosque sponsors an African market on 116th Street between Frederick Douglass Boulevard and 5th Avenue, with about 50 stalls selling mud cloth, cowries, drums, batik fabric, and bootleg designer merchandise — the cops look the other way. A slew of eateries — eight at last count — radiate from the corner of Adam Clayton Powell Boulevard and 116th. The African presence on 116th is not limited to eateries, however. A couple of doors east of **Africa Restaurant** is Touba Khassayitt, a store that sells Senegalese religious articles and curios. The smell of incense wafts out the door, and the prerecorded chant of the muezzin calls the faithful to prayer. There are also hair braiding salons, convenience stores selling African products, and a real Ivory Coast coffee shop. We leave it to your peregrinations to discover the latest mix of African businesses on the block.

KEUR N' DEYE ✮ ✮ ⌀

737 Fulton Street, Brooklyn, 718-875-4937 This restaurant restricts itself to "Senegalese Traditional Home Cooking," according to its business card. Senegalese cuisine is among the best in Africa, featuring fresh seafood and lots of vegetables including okra, yuca, yams, sweet potatoes, cabbage, calabaza, eggplant, and carrots. The seafood and vegetables are essential elements of tiebou dienn, the national dish, affectionately referred to as "cheb." The cheb here is nicely prepared, though presented nontraditionally in individual servings. This place is the longest-running Senegalese restaurant in town, and a real hangout for Fort Greene bohos. Other typical Senegalese dishes include chicken or beef mafe and fish yassa. Don't miss the homemade bissap and ginger drinks.

KEUR SOKHNA ✮ ✮ ⬿

225 West 116th Street, Manhattan, 212-864-0081 A hand-scrawled sign offering lamb head made me think Keur Sokhna might be Ivoirian, even though "keur" is Wolof for village. Ivoirian, too, seemed the table of dark-skinned men eagerly downing sandwiches loaded with chunks of lamb. I'd never seen sandwiches in a Senegalese restaurant before, but when I tried to order one, the waitress explained that the men had brought the baguettes in themselves. We ordered the unfamiliar suluxu, lamb in a powerful gravy that pits sun-dried stockfish against pureed peanuts: two powerful flavors in combat. The fish wins. Skipping the French-leaning dinner menu, we asked for the Senegalese national dish of paella-derived cheb, and were told a batch would be ready in 15 minutes. Proving to be well worth the wait, it was the best cheb ever tasted in New York, with five vegetables instead of the usual three, several hunks of fish — each slitted and stuffed with green onion and cilantro, an improvement often skipped in America — and a hump of savory rice tinted chocolate brown.

LA MARMITE ✮ ✮ ✮ ✮ ⬿

2264 8th Avenue, Manhattan, 212-666-0653 Supplanting an earlier Ivory Coast spot called Le Grenier ("the granary") is La Marmite ("the stew pot"), a Senegalese restaurant that also offers a Guinean dish or two on its traditional African lunch menu. Less is newfangled here than at some other Senegalese spots — the cheb, for example, has five vegetables instead of the usual three, and bits of tamarind flavor the rice (though there's no palm oil. Damn!). The lamb mafe, bathed in peanut sauce, is probably the best I've ever tasted, with bits of okra giving gluey body to the gravy. Dinners lean more toward the French: roast guinea fowl, grilled fish, and braised lamb shank. A very comfortable and friendly place to eat.

Soul Food

What we call soul food, or, sometimes, Southern cooking, is one of America's proudest inventions, a compilation of West African and Native American cooking styles, with some French, Spanish, and English practices thrown in. The quintessential dishes are so tasty and cost effective that they've made their way into the mainstream American cuisine, after being carried northward by countless individuals over the last century and a half. Maybe brought by Portuguese to the west coast of Africa, Southern fried chicken is a thing of beauty, and who can deny the universal appeal of soupy red beans, cornbread, or collards dotted with smoked meat? The list below is heavy on old-time places that have remained virtually unchanged since Carolina and Georgia immigrants first arrived in Harlem and Bedford-Stuyvesant nearly a century ago.

As 125th Street clogs with franchises like Starbucks, Old Navy, and the Disney Store — making this sainted precinct feel like any other tacky commercial strip on the East Coast — the heart of Harlem has drifted elsewhere. My favorite backward-leaning locale is the corner of 135th Street and Malcolm X Boulevard, where the New York Public Library's Schomburg Center for Black Culture gazes disdainfully down on street action that could have been scripted from a Chester Himes novel. Newspapers are hawked from a wooden shipping flat as if they'd just fallen off a truck, while enterprising street vendors hustle everything from phone cards to pomade to hats of Niger River mud cloth. Bandaged patients emerge from Harlem Hospital rubbing their eyes in the bright winter sunlight, then go across the street to the bar called the **Recovery Room** for a stiff belt, while the serpentine orange counter at **Pan Pan** is just beginning to fill with people forking down the Harlem-invented soul food standard — fried chicken and waffles.

LOOK FOR:

biscuits *baking-powder-risen wheat flour pastry*

chitterlings *pork small intestines*

chow chow *multivegetable sweet pickle relish flavored with mustard*

collard greens *dark leafy vegetable of the cabbage family*

country ham *salt-cured raw pork, must be cooked*

deviled eggs *boiled eggs, the yolk mashed with spices and reinserted*

dirty rice *cooked with ground meat or chicken liver and gizzards*

grits *ground hominy*

Harvard beets *in a thick sweet-sour syrup*

hoe cake *flat Georgia corn cake originally cooked on a hoe over a fire*

hominy *corn slaked with lye, forming giant bloated kernels*

hoppin' john *African dish of rice and field peas*

red eye gravy *coffee and pork fat*

red velvet cake *red chocolate cake with white frosting*

salmon croquettes *canned-fish fritters*

smothered chicken *in brown gravy*

succotash *lima beans and corn*

trotters *pig feet*

CARMICHAEL'S DINER ☆

117-08 Guy Brewer Boulevard, Queens, 718-723-6908 After a pilgrimage to drummer Milford Graves's amazing decorated house at 106th Street and 110th Avenue, we dropped by this establishment, pride of the Baisley Pond neighborhood just north of Kennedy Airport. A museum of Naugahyde and linoleum, Carmichael's doesn't aspire to be anything more than a diner, although its menu combining diner standards and soul food is unique. The salmon croquettes — patties, really — are top-notch, and you can side them with other Southern faves like succotash, black-eyed peas, and Harvard beets. Breakfast is available all day. Served with grits, of course.

CHARLES SOUTHERN STYLE KITCHEN ☆ ☆

2839 8th Avenue, Manhattan, 212-926-4313 This double storefront — one side carryout, the other all-you-can-eat café — is the successor to Charles Mobile Soulfood Kitchen, a wonderful van that Jim Leff and I used to chase as it made stops all over Harlem with the some of the best African-American cooking around. Some say the carryout side is better, but in the café there's nothing like eating your fill of turkey-dotted collards, vinegary barbecue ribs, crunchy fried chicken, and macaroni and cheese made fluffy with a bit of egg. The tariff (half price for kids) includes beverage and a slice of melon for dessert. Note: In an odd corner of Harlem, this place is difficult to get to.

CAROLINA VS. GEORGIA

Clad in dark weathered woods, **North Carolina Country Store** (1991 Atlantic Avenue, Brooklyn, 718-498-8033) features classic products like Peanut Patch brand green boiled peanuts, Jolly Aid lemon soda concentrate, and Red Bird assorted candies. There are 15 varieties in the 12-ounce box, including peppermint, lemon, horehound, cinnamon, clove, pineapple, wintergreen, strawberry, peanut butter, cream penny, orange, sassafras, banana, cherry, and grape. This down-home store also sells pig parts, including bags of fried pig skin, red (hot) or beige (not). The opposing wing of the horseshoe-shaped store is devoted to a steam table that features decent renditions of Southern favorites, in addition to a trio of wonderful grilled sausages concocted on the premises and presented on two slices of white bread with mustard, two sausages to an order for $2.75. There's a beef sausage that tastes like a large hot dog, a hot beef sausage that's also red and large, and a sage sausage that tastes like Jimmy Dean's, only thicker and coarser. The steam table was hauled from the **North Carolina Country Kitchen** across the street when that institution went belly-up last year.

Re: the name. It was John T. Edge who first observed, though it was there for all to see, I guess, that Carolina immigrants tended to settle in Bed-Stuy, while Georgians made for Harlem (see Georgia Sausage, below). Throwing down the gauntlet, a Georgia-related store has opened across Atlantic Avenue from North Carolina Country Store, selling jams, pecans, watermelons, and other comestibles. The proprietor's real business, though, is moving households back to Georgia in a reverse migration. On the way back, rather than running the trucks empty, he carries groceries.

COPELAND'S TAKE-OUT AND CATERING ☆
549 West 145th Street, Manhattan, 212-234-2357 Successor to a doomed establishment that operated a decade ago on 125th Street, and next-door neighbor to the pricier Copeland's Restaurant, this steam table joint offers excellent soul food, with plenty of comfortable seating in spite of the name. Go for any of the chicken concoctions, including a rib-sticking and livid-yellow chicken and dumplings, fried chicken, smothered chicken, and, on a recent afternoon, a special of Dutch chicken. "It's coated in Dutch spices," the counter guy explained. Best sides: tomato-sauced okra, finely minced coleslaw with plenty of sweet white dressing, and a particularly cheesy mac and cheese.

DEVINS FISH & CHIPS ☆ ☆ 🐟
747 St. Nicholas Avenue, Manhattan, 212-491-5518 Descend into this narrow carryout, decorated in Gay '90s style in red and black, featuring a grainy photo of a Harlem civil rights demonstration of nearly 100 years ago. The humble-sounding fish sandwich ($3.50) is a wonder, three substantial whiting fillets freshly breaded and fried and heaped on two slices of bread, with tartar and hot sauces at the ready. Larger appetites will seek out the porgie special ($8.50), which includes two whole fish and a couple of sides. I chose the skin-on french fries and the Dominican-style rice with pigeon peas and green olives, turning the porgies into dinner for two.

MARGIE'S RED ROSE ☆
267 West 144th Street, Manhattan, 212-862-8110 Located midblock, this ancient Harlem eatery has been overlooked by all but the neighborhood regulars. The very good fried chicken, lightly coated with flour, salt, and pepper, is upstaged by the spectacular collard greens. Tart and sweet, ungreasy, and slow-cooked with a good quantity of chile pepper, they may be the best in town. Whiting was another hit at our table, four filets to an order and sided with potato salad and cole slaw. Look for your favorite 1960s and '70s soul and disco hits on the jukebox. Food is sometimes uneven, but you can't beat the warmth of the welcome.

MA'S SOUL FOOD CAFÉ ☆
1551 Fulton Street, Brooklyn, 718-221-0235 An evening's stroll down Bed-Stuy's Fulton Street reveals a culinary scene in decay, as franchise restaurants like McDonald's, Burger King, KFC, and Popeye's muscle out the family-run eateries that used to characterize this noble street. In defiance of the trend, Ma's offers a traditional menu of soul food staples. The fried chicken is particularly good — fresh and moist, with a modest coating of flour, letting the skin do the crispness work. The mac and cheese and corn

GEORGIA SAUSAGE

It all started out when I dropped by **Smoke's Seafood and Soul Food Haven** at 114th and **Fred Douglass**, one of my favorite Harlem hangs. I expected to cop their specialty, Georgia sausage, a blistering hot and large-circumference weenie that's plopped on a piece of white bread and extravagantly smeared with mustard. The smoky taste and grainy texture are unforgettable. One day I had asked if it really came from Georgia, and the guy behind the counter fished around in the trash and came up with a plastic wrapper that said "Tifton, Georgia" on it. Unfortunately, Smoke's closed soon thereafter.

Then I discovered where places like Smoke's and **Pan Pan** get their Georgia sausage — **Umoja's** (543 Lenox Avenue, Manhattan, 212-495-9413), a meat market that pushes a grill into the street in the afternoon and cooks hamburgers, Philly cheese steaks, and sausages. On sunny days, Umoja's is not the only place to offer this Southern treat — freelancers up and down the avenue push makeshift grills out onto the sidewalk, hoping to cop a little business from the nearby Harlem Hospital. Just the thing after your triple bypass! The sausage is made principally from beef hearts, according to the label, and reflects the great African-American migration from Georgia and the Carolinas 80 years ago that made Harlem the most rollicking musical and literary neighborhood in town.

muffins are also particularly fine, though the tepid and under-cooked ribs are a disappointment. Neighborhood kids flock to the ice cream counter.

M & G DINER ☆ ☆
383 West 125th Street, Manhattan, 212-864-7326 This Harlem old-timer will put almost anything between two slices of white bread. Try the short rib sandwich: four huge hunks of cow in a rich brown gravy with only a few bones to get in the way. The specialty of the house is Southern fried chicken, cooked fresh throughout the day with just a trace of breading on the crunchy skin, and tender throughout. Like it says on the neon sign out front, "Old Fashion But Good." Breakfast served till 1:00 p.m., and don't miss the salmon croquettes.

PAN PAN ☆ ☆ ☆ 🍎

500 Lenox Avenue, Manhattan, 212-926-4900 Every second diner at this old-fashioned snaking lunch counter is chowing down on waffles, which issue from a quartet of irons fuming in the corner. Available all day, these chestnut-colored beauties are simultaneously crunchy and spongy, with deep wells that trap plenty of syrup, and a mellow, toasty flavor. Have them naked, or paired with fried chicken in the manner that Harlem made famous, or sided with beef sausage that has a mule-kick of hot pepper. Out of curiosity, I chose the waffle sandwich one day, not knowing what to expect. Like other faux sandwiches of the Deep South — fried chicken and barbecued ribs come to mind — this creation is not a conventional sandwich at all. The waffle comes on one plate, while another holds a scrambled egg, folded like a napkin and snuggling a sage breakfast sausage. A yellow blob spreads over the waffle, confirming a sign that proclaims "We Serve Oleo." There are plenty of other goodies, too, like barbecued ribs done on a smoker in the basement, mac and cheese made with tons of real cheddar, and the cryptic "baloney burger."

PINK TEA CUP ☆

42 Grove Street, Manhattan, 212-807-6755 This longtime favorite bills itself as the "foremost soul food restaurant in the Village" — it's the only one as far as I know, although Greenwich Village has been a center of African-American culture since before the Civil War. In our own time, this neighborhood is home to prominent black writers like bell hooks, Stanley Crouch, and Walter Mosley, among others. The four-course lunch special is an unbelievable deal, but I'm more likely to make the scene at breakfast for their salmon croquettes, spicy sausage, and unassailable biscuits.

POOR FREDDIE'S RIB SHACK ☆

157-06 Linden Boulevard, Queens, 718-659-7000 The name induces pity, but it turns out "Poor Freddie" owns a few other businesses in the same South Jamaica neighborhood, where neatly kept houses, festooned with decorative ironwork and lushly landscaped, stand by roads the city seems to have neglected. The Rib Shack is an obvious source of local pride, a gleaming, built-from-the-ground-up business with giant plate glass windows, a stainless steel counter that meanders like a country road, even a wheelchair ramp at the front entrance. Indeed, the premises looks more like a newly built interstate diner than any kind of shack, real or metaphoric. It also turns out, as the song says, that "Freddie's Dead," since a funeral announcement is prominently displayed by the register, featuring an encomium by former congressman Floyd Flake. Freddie — who also owned a car repair shop and tire dealership — had a system, and it didn't die with him. The place is so clean you could eat off the floor, and the attendants stand like soldiers in the activity areas behind the counter. In addition to the demeanor of the counter guys, one is immediately struck by the ambiguous signs scattered on the walls, often duplicated at several spots: "Take Control of Your Health! Eat More Fish," for example. This is pale advice when most of the dishes for sale oink, but it does draw attention to Poor Freddie's picture on the funeral announcement — he weren't no stick, believe me.

ROSSCOE'S HOUSE OF CHICKEN AND WAFFLES ☆
3601 Church Avenue, Brooklyn, 718-826-1200 Look carefully at the spelling of "Rosscoe's" — otherwise you might think this spacious corner soul food spot is related to the famous Los Angeles institution of (almost) the same name. Still, the made-to-order fried chicken is top-notch, crisp-skinned and moist. And the waffles that come along with it in pairs are more delicate and malty tasting than the overgrown "Belgian" variety currently popular. Other choices — paralleling the menu of its L.A. prototype — include a chicken liver omelet, salty macaroni and cheese, and well-buttered grits.

ROYAL RIB HOUSE ☆ ☆
303 Halsey Street, Brooklyn, 718-453-9284 This wildly popular but obscurely located Bed-Stuy institution serves up the best Carolina 'cue in Brooklyn. The savory sauce — pick it mild or hot — makes up for the lack of smokiness with a startling combination of flavors. Chopped pork is best, and ribs are also fab; skip the dry barbecued chicken. My favorite side is the potato salad dotted with egg and spiked with sweet-pickle juice, but you can also get good collards, peas and rice, and meat-dotted lima beans. Like many places in Georgia and the Carolinas, Royal Rib is only open Thursday, Friday, and Saturday, carryout only.

S & V SOUL FOOD CASTLE ☆
106-50 Sutphin Avenue, Queens, 718-206-1484 Offering inspiring views of a funeral-home complex, this carryout specializes in Carolina-style soul food, and most of the pristine selections are visible on the long steam table: barbecue ribs, pulled pork, chitlins, candied yams, pig feet, and macaroni salad. We inhaled mac and cheese with a thick cheddar crust, a huge portion of fatty oxtails in a mellow brown gravy, and mayonnaise potato salad in which the potatoes retained their character. The collards, though, were way too sweet.

SOUL FIXIN'S ☆ 🐟
371 West 34th Street, Manhattan, 212-736-1345 Chicken is king at this soul food hang, whether you order it baked, barbecued, or deep-fried (my pick). Or you can make do with just the wings —

served Buffalo-style. Other mainstays include decent barbecued pork ribs and wonderful whiting, cornmeal-coated and fried to order with skin intact and a few spiny things sticking out here and there. Sides in order of preference: candied yams with a touch of nutmeg, vinegary collard greens, corn off the cob, and macaroni and cheese. Open weekdays till 7 p.m.

Spanish and Portuguese

Asturian, Basque, Catalan, Galician, Pan-Regional Spanish, Portuguese, and Tapas

A decade ago our collection of a dozen Spanish restaurants was concentrated in the West Village and Chelsea, with a few stragglers on the southern end of midtown. Dating to the 1960s, they projected a romantic Spanish ideal that seemed to date from the Spanish civil war or even before. Then the tapas craze hit. The oldsters were able to take advantage of the phenomenon, since they'd been serving tapas on a limited basis all along. Still, the fervor with which their new competitors chased the fad must have astonished the long-established Spanish places. And the tapas fad has not yet abated, as two or three new places are added each year. Sometimes these places expand their menus to include larger servings, and thus have become like the restaurants they first thumbed their noses at.

Don't expect much in the way of Portuguese restaurants in the five boroughs — for an abundance of them, one must sojourn to the Ironbound section of Newark. Why there are virtually no Portuguese places in the city is a matter of debate, but I think it has to do with the language barrier between Portuguese and Spanish immigrants, and the predominance of Spanish speakers here. I've included a couple of places from Ironbound, easily attainable by riding the PATH train to its Newark terminus and walking a few blocks down Ferry Street. And don't forget to hang out in a pastry shop (there are about 10) after your meal.

LOOK FOR:

albondigas *meatballs*
allioli *Catalan garlic mayonnaise*
bacalao *salt cod*
broa *dark cornmeal loaf*
cabrales *Asturian blue cheese*
caldo verde *Portuguese kale soup*
carne de porco a alentejana *pork and shellfish stew*
chorizo *wine-flavored sausage*
empanada *Galician pie*
ensalada de pulpito *baby octopus salad*
linguica *thick Portuguese garlic sausage*
merluza *Basque fish stew*
morcilla *blood sausage*
paella *yellow rice cooked with meat and seafood*
piri-piri *Portuguese-Angolan hot sauce*
sangria *wine punch*
Serrano ham *air-cured like prosciutto*
tapas *bar snacks*

Asturian

MESON ASTURIAS ☆ ☆
40-12 83rd Street, Queens, 718-446-9154 Meson Asturias is the grand dame of Queens's Spanish restaurants, named after the rugged maritime province east of Galicia, where wolves still roam and fierce sea breezes carry the sound of bagpipes. Undisturbed by the Moors, the residents of this isolated region have as much in common with the Irish and Breton French as they do with other Spaniards. Sit at the bar and check out the tapas, which reflect the

RUBOUT!

New York has had its share of restaurants, like **Umberto's Clam House**, that are more notable for gangland murders than for their chow. **Meson Asturias** is an exception to the rule — though it, too, boasts a famous rubout. One blustery evening in March 1992 the crusading former editor of *El Diario*, Manuel de Dios Unanue, was sitting at the small bar, when a man in a hooded gray sweatshirt drifted in from the street and blew his brains out with a 9 mm handgun. Speculation ran high as to whether the assassin was sent by Colombian drug lords, right-wing Cubans, or grifting Puerto Rican policemen, all of whom had been exposed by the muckraking journalist.

products and sensibilities of Asturias. Favorites include chorizo cooked in cider, blue-veined cabrales cheese, and plates of perfect hand-cut Serrano ham, which demand to be washed down with a Ribera del Duero red or a glass of sherry.

Basque

MARICHU ☆ ☆ ～ $
342 East 46th Street, Manhattan, 212-370-1866 You have to go upscale for the city's best Basque food, alas. Catering to patrons from the United Nations, Marichu is an informal space decorated with color photos of Spain. The food leaves a powerful impression, especially chiparones — baby squid coated with a thick black sauce made from ink, and a special soup that features potatoes and spicy chorizo in a paprika-red broth. Skip the lackluster paella, aimed at those who don't know Basque from basket. The eight-selection Spanish cheese plate performs equally well as appetizer or dessert.

OLIVA ☆
161 East Houston Street, Manhattan, 212-228-4143 I guess an authentically great Basque restaurant like they have in Boise, Idaho, and Bakersfield, California, would be too much to hope for. A place where even the humble red bean soup — fortified with a powerful lamb stock — is so delicious you could eat it forever. Instead, we have a cooking-school version of Basque food. Even though the bacalao-stuffed pimentos and the crispy roast chicken are admirable, merluza falls flat, a tepid fish stew that seems more concerned with the preening beauty of its ingredients than with delivering lusty Basque flavors.

PINTXOS ☆ ☆
510 Greenwich Street, Manhattan, 212-343-9923 This microscopic café on a quiet block offers a Basque take on tapas, including piquillo peppers stuffed with a light creamy salt-cod mousse, and octopus in a spicy paprika dressing, a dish that's unique in New York. Even though entrées tend to be on the pricey side, a meal of tapas comes in under $20.

Catalan

ALLIOLI ★ ★ ★ 🐟

291 Grand Street, Brooklyn, 718-218-7338 The grilled sardines at Catalan tapas bar Allioli come planted on a piece of toast, so no juices go to waste, and heaped with a zesty tomato relish that contrasts nicely with the dark flavor of Iberia's favorite fish. Order a glass of Rioja and side the sardines with the excellent bowl of mixed olives — laced with garlic, rosemary, and lemon rind — and you've got a perfect meal. The tenement garden out back is a wonderful place to fritter away a summer evening.

Galician

XUNTA ★ ★

174 1st Avenue, Manhattan, 212-614-0620 The East Village's favorite tapas bar got off to a slow start when it opened in the former Pete's Spice, but now it's jumping. A bit of luck gets us a table after a 20-minute wait. The 32 selections are pleasantly doctrinaire except for a few Galician twists, like tasty empanadas of tuna and salt cod cooked as massive pies instead of turnovers. Some of the simplest tapas are the best, like a slightly charred chorizo or a plate of dry-cured ham. More ambitious but equally delicious is a stew of scallops and white aparagus accented with wine and served in a big shell. A flaming bowl of mushrooms is brought to the table by a waiter who, we couldn't help but notice, had all the hair singed off his arm.

Also see Galicia in the Cuban, Dominican, and Puerto Rican chapter, a Dominican restaurant specializing in food from Galicia.

Pan-Regional Spanish

SEVILLA ★ 🐟

62 Charles Street, Manhattan, 212-929-3189 Does this place really have the best paella in town? Or is it just another excuse for Upper West Siders to cavort in the West Village? Search me. The paella is indeed abundant and tasty, presented in outsize servings sufficient for two or three diners, and the menu is filled out with the usual seafood in red or green sauce. The smell of garlic pouring out the kitchen door is often enough for me.

SPAIN ☆ 🐟

113 West 13th Street, Manhattan, 212-929-9580 Make the journey into the past by negotiating the dark sunken hallway into the skylit rear room, festooned with paintings like Van Gogh's *Sunflowers*, whose bright yellows have long since withered to dark browns. The pungent food is just as you remember it — a massive paella with more volume devoted to shrimp, clams, chicken, chorizo, and lobster tail than to rice, a bowl of mussels steamed in white wine with garlic, and — the perpetual amuse gueule — wonderful short ribs cooked to the texture of stiff rope, and brushed with a tarry sauce.

Portuguese

LUZIA'S ☆ 🐟

429 Amerrsterdam Avenue, Manhattan, 212-595-2000 Why aren't there any really cheap Portuguese places in town? Portugal, vying with Ireland and Spain as poorest country in Western Europe, might be expected to spawn budget eateries. Luzia's, unfortunately, is not cheap, but the food is well worth the splurge. If Portuguese fish stew is available — grab it! Also get anything made with shellfish, especially the dish of pork, clams, potatoes, and chorizo that's typical of the meat/shellfish combos of southern Portugal. Desserts also recommended, especially if you're there as they come right out of the oven in the afternoon.

PAO ☆ ☆ 🐟

322 Spring Street, Manhattan, 212-334-5464 Home is the sailor, home from the sea, and his table is set at Pao, New York's finest Portuguese restaurant, a cramped and dimly lit matchbox of a place in a neighborhood with no name. Marvel at carne de porco a alentejana, a novel combination of pork chunks and small clams that comes from the Alentejo region in the south. An appetizer enjoyed all over Portugal is a length of linguica flamed in brandy. The incineration of this thick garlic sausage takes place tableside in a ceramic barbecue shaped like a pig. Native to the Algarve region is a seafood combo steamed in white wine and garlic in a cataplana, a hinged pot that looks like a Valkyrie's brassiere. The extensive list of affordable Portuguese wines is another big plus.

PIC-NIC ☆

233 Ferry Street, Newark, New Jersey, 973-589-4630 At this Portuguese barbecue, a pitmeister presides over two coffin-shaped brick pits pushed against the wall. Over one is suspended a score of splayed chickens on a rotisserie that can be hand-cranked to turn them over. To a quarter of the birds he administers a dense red piri-piri sauce that mostly slides off into the fire. Every once in a while he picks up a bag of charcoal briquettes and dribbles them into the pit to keep the smoke going. I ordered a half chicken and a half order of pork ribs, which the cashier extracted from a holding area, cut up expertly, and dumped into a huge aluminum carryout tray. He filled the balance of the space with a volume of french fries sufficient to feed three people by itself, then crimped foil over the top, with a few holes punched to allow steam to escape.

SEABRAS MARRISQUIERA ☆ ☆ ☆ 🐟
87 Madison Street, Newark, New Jersey, 201-465-1250
Founded in 1989, this is Newark's only Portuguese seafood restaurant. Sure, every Ferry Street chow shack serves a substantial number of dragged-from-the-ocean specialties, but Seabras is typical of a style of Portuguese eatery that hasn't migrated here. In the rear is a formal dining room with a menu sporting dozens of pricey selections, in the front a well-tiled bar serving a handful of seasonal specialties prepared with tons of garlic and bargain priced. Tops on a recent visit was a plate of sardines which, astonishingly, included six large fish flamed so the skin was blackened in spots, ringed with boiled potatoes and sided with a small salad. I also had a cauldron of cockles, cooked with scads of garlic, cilantro, and olive oil, making a very thick and fragrant broth. Soon after we went for a seafood stew, containing more kinds of fish than I could identify. We also had beef Lavrador-style, cooked in an incredibly concentrated tomato sauce.

Tapas

1492 ☆ ☆
60 Clinton Street, Manhattan, 646-654-1114 High ceilings, minimalist decor, music that won't leave you with a headache, and a beguiling list of Spanish wines set the scene for one of Manhattan's best tapas bars. The small savory plates, mainly around $5, include baby asparagus spears wrapped in grilled piquillo peppers, french fries with three Spanish sauces, and, arriving with the bread, a fabulous garlic mayonnaise.

Ñ ☆
33 Crosby Street, Manhattan, 212-219-8856 Narrow as a pencil, Ñ (pronounced "enya") sports two copper-topped bars and little additional seating. After a steady diet of Spanish reds and headache-inducing sangria at other tapas bars, you'll welcome the list of 24 sherries. The companion vittles are admirably suited to the small size of the establishment. I like the little empanadas of

tuna, toasts smeared with olive puree and pimiento, and an incredible plate of spinach sautéed with ground almonds that has an exotic North African flavor.

PIPA ☆ ☆ ◔ $

39 East 19th Street, Manhattan, 212-677-2233 I wasn't prepared for Pipa to be so wonderful. Located in ABC Carpet, this younger sibling of the now-defunct Chicama is Douglas Rodriguez's flamboyant tribute to the Spanish tapas bar, and many of the best dishes are the simplest: a plate of killer Serrano ham sliced to just the right thickness, a pair of grilled sardines scattered with raisins and pine nuts in a sweet trickle of dark sauce, and a free bowl of herb-marinated green olives of wildly different sizes. The decor seems like a collaboration of Salvador Dalí and Miss Havisham, with dusty chandeliers and concrete pillars bearded with pebbles and shells.

TAPERIA MADRID ☆

1471 2nd Avenue, Manhattan, 212-794-2923 The facade's faded tiles will put you in a Spanish mood at this Upper East Side watering hole. The tapas themselves are way better than you'd expect, and a bargain in these latitudes: pickled mussels in their shells, chile-dusted fries with Catalan allioli and, especially, morcilla de la abuela ("grandma's blood sausage"), despite conjuring nightmare images of granny swinging a bloody ax. Poised on a slice of toast to collect all the stray crumbs, it's crusty on the outside, damp and cumin scented within, and dotted with cubes of fat. You've never tasted better.

Thai and Burmese

Historically, New York has been devoid of great Thai restaurants. Those that we had limited themselves to a tired formula of carved vegetables and gooey sauces sometimes known as Royal Thai. Gradually, superior Siamese began to appear along a great swath of Elmhurst and Woodside about five years ago, probably looking from the air like one of those Andean crop circles created by alien spacecraft. At these places less attention was lavished on presentation and more on conjuring sharp taste combinations. While the menus overlapped with those of the old-timers, the livelier newcomers presented fare of working-class bent, with lots of budget noodle dishes and salads, fewer color-coordinated curries, and interesting regional fare, especially from the north. These places were often thronged with Thais, who seemed to be relishing what they ate. Now, at places like **Pam Real Thai Food**, **Bennie's**, and **Olieng**, great Thai food has returned to Manhattan.

What are the elements of Siamese food? An emphasis on sharp, emphatic flavors like galangal, lemongrass, cilantro, and holy basil (a smaller cousin of the Italian leaf with more pungency), and a menu that runs from homely noodle dishes that use the everything-but-the-kitchen-sink approach, to soupy curries with plenty of burn, to savory stuffed omelets, to barely sauced stir-fries that depend on garlic, fish sauce, and a handful of basil leaves for flavor.

New York has trouble hanging onto its Burmese restaurants. Eight years ago there were 10 in town, four south of 14th Street. The number has sadly dwindled, and now I count only three citywide. The oldest is **Village Mingala**, located a beer bottle's throw from McSorley's. Burmese cooking incorporates the food of neighbors China, India, and Thailand. The influence of the first two is particularly profound — since the deposition of King Thibaw in 1885, there has been a massive migration from those countries, which explains why, until recently, most restaurants in

Myanmar were Chinese or Indian. Traditional Burmese fare was more likely to be found in the homes of private citizens and street-vendor stalls. To go to the heart of Myanmar cuisine, stick to the curries, noodles, and salads.

LOOK FOR:

bu du *fish-flavored sauce*

jungle curry *soupy pork-and-eggplant curry*

Massaman curry *creamy lamb-and-potato curry*

mee grob *sweet shrimp-and-noodle salad*

mohinga *Burmese angel-hair pasta in fish sauce*

nam sod *pork salad*

nems *pork sausage*

pad kee mao *Northern Thai rice noodles with Chinese veggies*

panthy kow swear *wheat noodles with tofu and curry paste*

pla chu chee *fish in peanut sauce*

Rangoon night market noodles *thin noodles with duck*

thokes *Burmese salads with crunchy split peas*

thousand-layer pancake *buttery Burmese paratha*

tom yam *sour shrimp soup*

yum *composed salad*

yum ped *salad of duck, tempeh, and fresh fruit*

Burmese

VILLAGE MINGALA ★ ★ ☺
21 East 7th Street, Manhattan, 212-529-3656 This East Village chestnut is one of only three Burmese joints remaining in the city, and it's pretty damn good. Go for the curries, made from a paste of onions, ginger, garlic, turmeric, and chile powder rather than a welter of powdered spices in the Indian fashion. Best is beef, and it can be ordered with a buttery flatbread known hyperbolically as "thousand-layer pancake." Other stunners include an astringent salad featuring tea leaves, a sweeter salad highlighting tender ginger shoots (both of these belong to a family of Burmese salads known as "thokes"), and a savory noodle dish with the disturbing name of panthy kow swear.

Thai

AMARIN ☆
617 Manhattan Avenue, Brooklyn, 718-349-2788 A renegade staffer from Planet Thailand established this joint in Polish Greenpoint, and the food has some of the same sparkling qualities. "Naked shrimp salad" features six perfectly grilled crustaceans, ringing baby lettuces with a light chile dressing; even the house salad is a revelation, decorated with lattice potato chips and bathed in a peanut sauce not even slightly sweet. Look to the specials list, though, for the best choices, such as a delightful red curry of rubbery homemade fish cake with green beans and eggplant. Surprisingly, some of the dishes poach on Italian territory.

ARUNEE THAI ☆ ☆ ☆ 🌶
37-68 79th Street, Queens, 718-205-5559 Only steps away from the hurly-burly of Roosevelt Avenue, this serene spots offers bargain renditions of the full range of Siamese food. There's a long list of noodle concoctions; fried and steamed appetizers that arrive in ceramic boats; spicy red, green, and panang curries; and an assortment of braises and stir-fries. Don't miss the pig leg in spicy sauce, or the salad of crispy fried catfish with plenty of greenery in a mild fish sauce. You've never tasted yum this good before. Planted on a bed of unblemished Boston lettuce, the other ingredients of the amazing yum hnam sod are equally pristine: shreds of purple onion and sweet red pepper, cilantro fronds, crunchy roast peanuts, tiny rings of scorching green chile, and pale clumps of mellow boiled pork that, in its grainy grayness, reads like an antique photo against the lush green frame of the lettuce. A shower of lime juice and little swatches of lime peel knock the flavor into orbit. No dish was a bigger hit on several visits than a pair of quails, fried to a deep mahogany and gobbed with crunchy nuggets of caramelized garlic.

BANGKOK CAFÉ ☆
27 East 20th Street, Manhattan, 212-228-7681 A particularly fine concoction is crispy duck salad — boneless pieces of crunchy-skinned mallard with red and green onions, cashews, baby lettuces, roasted chiles, and fresh pineapple dressed with lime juice. It works, believe it or not. Any dish on the menu with the first word "basil" is also top-notch. At most Thai eateries, the holy basil leaves are tossed in with the stir-fry, so their pungency is enjoyed only when you chomp down on the actual leaf. At Bangkok Café the leaves are chopped fine and fried in the oil before other ingredients are added, resulting in a flavor that permeates the dish. Basil fried rice and basil noodles are particularly good show-

300

cases for this technique. Also recommended is anything made with the green curry paste, which packs a greater wallop than usual.

BENNIE'S ☆

88 Fulton Street, Manhattan, 212-587-8930 The windows of the subterranean Bennie's face a cityscape mural, as if you needed something to look at besides the excellent Thai fare — multiple yums and noodle dishes with flavors sharper and prices lower than you'd expect. The avid clientele is mainly Wall Streeters, disproving the old rule that a Thai restaurant can't be good unless it has a Thai constituency.

CHEERS ☆

612 Metropolitan Avenue, Brooklyn, 718-599-4311 This unfortunately named café took over from Moondog, the local ice cream chain that overextended itself, then vanished overnight. The current occupant offers Siamese with a few Malaysian twists, and bohos fleeing the tourist crush of Planet Thailand have filtered in. Appetizers of steamed mussels and mee grob, a sweet salad of fried noodles and shrimp, are excellent, especially if you spoon on the homemade hot sauce which tastes like Hong Kong XO. And while pad thai flounders, the green and red curries are delicious, served with plenty of rice-soaking gravy.

JAI-YA ☆

396 3rd Avenue, Manhattan, 212-889-1330 This is the second branch of a popular Elmhurst Thai spot — it appealed mainly to Indians — that picked up and moved to Hicksville a year ago. At the Manhattan offspring, which has managed remain intact, you can't go wrong ordering shrimp: start with the provocatively named naked shrimp, barely cooked and tossed with lemongrass and green onion in a sharp lemon dressing, then proceed to an entrée of shrimp with ground pepper and garlic — six jumbos deep-fried with a coating that's mainly garlic. Although the Thai food reaches a consistently high level, crowded tables and frantic service discourage frequent visits. The weekday lunch specials are a particularly good deal.

JOYA ☆ ☆

215 Court Street, Brooklyn, 718-222-3484 Fleeing an atrociously bad meal at the now-defunct Uncle Pho, we landed here, a café that resembles a garage, a concrete box with a bustling open kitchen. The entrées are mainly priced at $8.50 or less, making it an instant hit with neighborhood residents who hesitate to pay $50 or more for a dinner of uncertain quality in other local spots. Maybe the pad thai is a little too sweet, and it's difficult to distinguish one curry from another, but the flavors are loud and lusty, and the portions huge enough so you can order one dish for each diner, and walk away stuffed.

KHAO HOMM ★ ★ ☺

39-28 61st Street, Queens, 718-205-0080 A stone's throw from Sripraphai, this new establishment gives that venerable Thai hash house a run for its money, with noodle dishes like pad kee mao, a tour de force of broad rice noodles laced with onions, Chinese greens, basil leaves fried crisp, and delicate red chiles, with deep red oil oozing around the edges. Emulating the great Siamese noodle houses of east Hollywood, the soups are also fab, especially the prosaic-sounding beef noodle soup, which turns out to be a fragrant mahogany broth rife with rice noodles and big chunks of meat, an emulation of Vietnamese pho. Don't miss the sweet snacks on the counter for dessert.

BROOKLYN THAI

It all started with **Thai Café**, a corner store in the middle of Polish Greenpoint that hesitatingly began offering a nuts-and-bolts Siamese menu, together with a handful of Italian dishes, as if they weren't sure the Thai part would work. But soon, hipsters were migrating northward from Williamsburg to enjoy hot and sweet Thai food that was a thrill, though it minimized some of the skanky goodness of more authentic Thai food. There was a tendency to quiet the chile burn, add more sugar, and throw away the fish sauce. We loved it.

Thai Café begat **Planet Thailand**, which in turn spun off places like **Cheers**, **Amarin**, and **Moon Shadow**; these in turn generated about a dozen more places, along upper Manhattan Avenue in Greenpoint, Smith Street in Carroll Gardens and Cobble Hill, and all across the map in Williamsburg itself. The final step was the establishment of giant halls, such as **Joya** and **SEA**, which, following the lead of the newest Planet Thailand, added aspects of nightclub and cocktail lounge to the concept. There are now about a score of these places in the borough, and the idea has spread to Manhattan. It now merits designation as a separate cuisine: I dub thee Brooklyn Thai.

MOON SHADOW ★ ☺

843 Manhattan Avenue, Brooklyn, 718-609-1841 There are now at least 10 Siamese cafés in Williamsburg and its northern suburb of Greenpoint, and in the latter locale we find Moon Shadow. Prepared for disappointment, I was impressed with the sharpness of its flavors and the freshness of the fixin's, even at offpeak hours. The luncheon special (served until 4 p.m.) is a particularly good deal, featuring an egg roll and peanut-dressed salad in addition to a choice of main dishes. Otherwise, entrées like Massaman curry and red snapper filet with tamarind sauce, sided with rice, run less than $10.

MY THAI ✳ ✳ 🦐 🍎

83-47 Dongan Avenue, Queens, 718-476-6743 The larb is the best I've ever tasted: served warm, this ground pork salad is sharply seasoned with lime, mint, green onions, and a touch of fish sauce, and served on a bed of onions and greenery. Other salads and stir-fries display the same potent and well-balanced spicing, including pad prik moo grob, a toss of crispy pork fragments with lots of herbs and green chiles. When you ask for spicy, you can be sure your food will arrive scaldingly hot. My Thai is successor to Kway Tiow, another excellent Siamese restaurant on the same spot.

OLIENG ✳ ✳ 🍎

644 10th Avenue, Manhattan, 212-307-9388 Manhattan's wild, wild west is accumulating Thai restaurants good enough to give Queens a run for its money. Joining Pam Real Thai Food west of 9th Avenue is Olieng, a shoebox of a place that, in contrast to Pam, boasts a decor charming enough to qualify it as a date spot. The chicken satays are pristine, well-browned, and as delicate as they should be, with a peanut sauce clearly not out of a can. Other favorites on a first visit included jungle curry and the ground-pork salad known as nam sod, both hot enough to scald your mouth. The name refers to Thai iced coffee.

PAM REAL THAI FOOD ✳ ✳ 🦐 🍎

404 West 49th Street, Manhattan, 212-333-7500 And they're not kidding! In contrast to the disappointing Siameses up and down 9th Avenue, this newcomer's cooking is closer to the vernacular cuisine of modern Thailand, with a zestiness lacking in its neighbors. The papaya salad is spicier, with miniature dried shrimp and peanuts providing crunch, and there are plenty of northern-leaning noodle dishes and salads. Another favorite is duck with chile sauce, flavored with lime leaf and featuring plenty of crisp skin. Pam, who hails from Chiang Mai in northwest Thailand, will emerge halfway through the meal to see how you like the food.

PATTAYA ✳ ✳ 🦐

1069 1st Avenue, Manhattan, 212-752-9277 Named after a freewheeling beach resort, recently renovated Pattaya is a cut or two above the usual neighborhood Thai, with more piquant and complex spicing and a handful of unusual dishes. Foremost is Pattaya duck: roasted, deboned, flattened like chicken tabaka, and deep-fried to perfect crispness. On the side, rendered juices are deployed in a soup — thick with vegetables and heaped with roasted cashews — that doubles as a dipping sauce. A lunch special served until 4 p.m. includes rice, main dish, and soup.

ROYAL SIAM ☆

240 8th Avenue, Manhattan, 212-741-1732 The "royal" cuisine of Thailand was a 19th-century invention of a gourmet king. This is one of my favorite places to enjoy it, with a broad range of carefully prepared dishes accented with ginger, garlic, and holy basil, and swimming in rich coconut milk. Check out the ethereal duck salad — nuggets of crunchy-skinned Daffy tossed with purple onion, roasted cashews, oranges, red peppers, and tempeh in a tangy tamarind dressing. Or pick any of the whole-fish preparations like pla chu chee — sea bass smothered in a unique curried peanut sauce that will leave you licking the plate after the last morsel is gone.

SEA ☆ ⚲

114 North 6th Street, Brooklyn, 718-384-8850 This barnlike space features several activity areas, including a reflecting pool with a small boat (don't try it), giant statuary, novel bathrooms, diverse seating galore, and an illuminated bar that shines like the face of heaven from the back of the restaurant. Though it's more about design and cocktails than food, the food is just fine, and the price is right. Brooklyn Thai at its most ebullient and festive.

SUGUNYA ☆

87-19 Atlantic Avenue, Queens, 718-849-6076 This fascinating establishment is the city's only Muslim Thai restaurant, founded by a family from Bangkok. On a practical level, this means that all meat is halal and no pork is served, and this may be the only Thai in town serving goat. There are also several dishes you won't find elsewhere, including a delectable sweet-and-sour curry called sma go reng, probably Malaysian in origin. Not everything accrues to the positive side of the ledger, however — red curry could be mistaken for bottled French dressing, and the menu is too big for the cook to do everything well. Noodles particularly recommended.

SRIPRAPHAI ☆ ☆ ☆ ✐

64-13 39th Avenue, Queens, 718-899-9599 The decor is so plain here that the high points are a pair of large television monitors. The proprietor flashes a crooked smile and warns us that jungle curry is way hot, putting us on notice that he doesn't intend to pull his punches. Entering in a clay pot, it bobs with tiny Thai eggplants streaked red and green, pork strips, lime leaves, string beans, bamboo, and basil, with plenty of liquid to soak the accompanying plate of rice. The awesome and lingering hotness comes from both red and black pepper, with a tiny dish of fresh green chiles in vinegar offering a third vector for the seriously deranged. Our favorite not-hot selection is rice with vegetables and bu du sauce — a spunky, fish-flavored dressing. Highly recommended is crispy catfish in spicy sauce, the flesh pounded into a lattice and then fried, producing a texture like loofah or cruller. It's served with plenty of vegetables in a hot and tart sauce.

THAI CAFÉ ☆
925 Manhattan Avenue, Brooklyn, 718-383-3562 Greenpoint and Williamsburg are loaded with Siamese eateries, but when this favorite first opened 13 years ago on Manhattan Avenue, it was an extreme anomaly on the Polish strip. Though pared down and rendered on the menu only in English, the food remains piquant and freshly prepared, and where else can you eat your fill of shrimp for $10? This café was progenitor to Planet Thailand (141 North 7th Street, Brooklyn, 718-599-5758), the wildly popular Williamsburg eatery that expanded into a giant L-shaped premises, becoming more bar and sushi bar than Thai restaurant. Make the hike and hang with the parent. This is where Brooklyn Thai originated.

YUM ☆
129 West 44th Street, Manhattan, 212-819-0554 You'll be disappointed if you expect carved vegetable garnishes or ethnographic geegaws at this no-frills, weekdays-only lunch counter — but the food is more surely and subtly spiced than the city's more pretentious Thai eateries. Best summer choice is yum ped, nuggets of crunchy duck tossed with apple, orange, pineapple, and tempeh in a delicious tart dressing. We also fought over a pad thai that was not the usual circus of discarded meat and seafood, but a barely dressed heap of noodles and big shrimp with clear, sharp flavors. The place could use more ventilation, so you may want to take the food to Bryant Park.

Trinidadian, Guyanese, and Surinamese

W ending its way northward through Crown Heights and Bed-Stuy, Nostrand Avenue rocks to an island beat. The busy thoroughfare is lined with bakeries offering cassava pone and pine tart; fish stands hawking croakers, porgies, grunts, and jacks; and beauty parlors where locks, twists, braids, and dreads are the preferred styles. A rasta in a puffy leather cap wields a machete outside a vegetable stand, hacking green coconuts to free the juice. Above the tumult rises the bright red sign of **A & A Bake and Doubles**. Even though it's late Saturday afternoon and the shopping crowds have ebbed, a long line of patrons still snakes out the door eager for doubles.

Crown Heights and Flatbush are the premier Guyanese and Trinidadian neighborhoods in town, and rotis are as common there as, say, sushi is in the East Village. Islanders are inveterate snackers, too, eating little fried tidbits like pholourie and crummer that originated in India. African contributions to these cuisines are harder to put your finger on, but stewed leaves like callaloo and the love of the funky flavor of dried fish products are two important African features. And don't underestimate the influence of the British, especially when it comes to baked goods.

Like a lock of hair on the forehead of Brazil, Surinam clings to the northeast coast of South America. The food of this former Dutch colony, 90 percent roadless rain forest, is among the most diverse in the world, reflecting an amazing ethnic mix of Amerindians, East Indians, Javanese, Chinese, Europeans, and Africans, among whom are the Bushnegroes — descendants of 18th-century slaves who disappeared into the outback, only to return in the 1980s as a revolutionary movement called Jungle Commando. Another surprising component is the Indonesians, who came

306

to South America as indentured plantation workers in the late 19th century and still retain many of their folkways, including gamelan music and a love of street-food vendors called warungs.

LOOK FOR:

aloo pie *potato turnover*

bake *bread slit and stuffed with smoked fish salad*

bust-up shot *curry with dahl poorie on the side*

channa *fried or boiled chickpeas*

chicken cook-up *weekend Guyanese stew with black-eyed peas*

crummer *fingers of fried dough*

dahl poorie *flatbread filled with crushed yellow peas*

doubles *chickpea sandwich*

mauby *bittersweet carob-tree bark beverage*

mittai *sweet fritters*

pholourie *crunchy Trinidadian snack*

roti *curry wrapped in flatbread*

sadhu bake *sandwich of fish-stuffed wheat-flour flatbread*

sauto *Surinamese chicken soup*

sea moss *seaweed beverage*

telo *Surinamese fried yuca with fish gravy*

toolum *Guyanese coconut balls*

Guyanese

ALICE'S PALACE ☆ ☆

3148 Fulton Street, Brooklyn, 718-277-5023 "Palace" is a bit of an exaggeration, but this comfy Guyanese manages to be lots more than a roti shop. Island-style Chinese food occupies a major portion of the menu, principally fried rice and lo mein, and Alice's also functions as a snack shop, selling bags of crunchy pholourie, fried plantain chips, patties, and channa — fried or boiled chickpeas. The goat roti is the best in town, deploying a subtle goat curry and a minimum of potatoes. The weekend special chicken cook-up is similarly delectable, coated with a dark tangy sauce enfolding miniature black-eyed peas. Pork curry is another special at this nonhalal eatery.

FLAVORED WITH ONE LOVE ☆

1941 Madison Avenue, Manhattan, 212-426-4446 Like it says on the menu: "Dishes bursting with flavor served in a warm and delightful atmosphere." This modest East Harlem Guyanese cooks up a wonderful chicken soup, laced with oregano and powerfully fortified with potatoes and starchy finger dumplings. Any of several savory stews and curries (think oxtail, goat, chicken, or vegetable) can be loaded into a dahl poori to make a roti, or served with a more fragile Indian flatbread to make a "bust-up shot." The rice and peas are also fab, especially with a little beef gravy poured on. Just the thing for a cold winter's afternoon.

GUYANA ROTI HOUSE ☆

3021 Church Avenue, Brooklyn, 718-940-9413 This modest Flatbush lunch counter cum bakery has a roti selection that always includes shrimp, chickpeas, chicken, goat, and beef. Also check out the Guyanese snacks, like the East Indian–inspired mittai and crummer — little fingers of fried dough — or the more familiar cod cakes and tamarind balls, all priced at $1 per package. Beverage selection includes Caribbean standards of mauby, sea moss, and ginger beer even though Guyana, of course, is located on the South American continent.

SYBIL'S ☆

2210 Church Avenue, Brooklyn, 718-469-9049 This Flatbush institution, with its genteel tearoom atmosphere, is the premiere Guyanese restaurant in town, serving a pan-Caribbean menu that often includes jerk chicken and curry goat, in addition to Indian-leaning national specialties like dal and channa, and the colonial legacy of effete British pastries like tennis rolls.

Surinamese

SORRENTO BAKERY ☆ ☆

88-17 Jamaica Avenue, Queens, 718-846-0313 Don't be fooled by the Italian name: although it's also still a bakery, Sorrento is the city's sole Surinamese eatery. Glass cases filled with biscotti, cream puffs, and sfogliatelle dominate a room whose decor is limited to a framed Lord's Prayer and a pair of ebony cranes, whose heads incline toward the ceiling as if looking for a speck in the spotless interior. The expansive menu offers West Indian standards you'd expect to find in Jamaica, Trinidad, or Guyana. The turkey roti features big gobbets of bony poultry with potatoes and chickpeas in a thick curry gravy, so soupy it must be eaten by breaking off little bits of the bread and dipping it in the sauce. The menu also includes Hispano-Caribbean favorites like arroz con pollo and pernil. A version of nasi goreng, Indonesian fried rice, comes topped with an appealing stewed chicken tasting of palm sugar, soy sauce, and garlic. Briny cucumber pickles on one side support a fiery homemade relish of shredded habanero peppers. Also Javanese is sauto, a variation on Mom's chicken soup featuring a triple starch whammy: noodles, rice, and match-sticks of fried potato. In a distinctly African vein is telo, jagged yuca chunks fried till the interior is pillowy soft, then inundated with a funky dried-fish gravy.

Trinidadian

A & A BAKE AND DOUBLES ☆ ☆ ☆ 🐟 🐟 ⊘
481 Nostrand Avenue, Brooklyn, 718-230-0753 Both singular and plural, doubles is the Trinidadian weekend delight, a pair of glistening flatbreads drawn from a red soda cooler, smeared with a thick chickpea curry, sliced with mango and pepper sauces, then twisted into a bit of tissue paper to make a rather gooey sandwich, all for $1 apiece. A doubles is delicious, with an eggy taste and a spicy kick that leaves a warm glow in your stomach. To take a single bite is to wolf down the entire thing and get back into line for a re-peat. A & A is a Trinidadian breakfast and lunch stall invariably thronged with admirers willing to stand in line for 20 minutes to get a doubles, a bake, or a sadhu bake, the latter a fish sandwich made with a larger and less greasy bread cut into quarters, and recom-mended only if you insist on keeping your mitts clean. Closes at 4 p.m., or when the doubles run out, which is sometimes as early as 2 p.m. Open Tuesday through Saturday only.

ALI'S TRINIDAD ROTI SHOP ☆ ☆ 🌶
1267 Fulton Street, Brooklyn, 718-783-0316 There's often a line out the door at this popular Bed-Stuy roti shack, where the marquee invites "Hurry, Hurry, Come for Curry." Of the rotis, my fave is conch — a plenitude of tender gastropod vying with potato for domination of the brown, thyme-inflected gravy. Or pick from cur-ries of shrimp, goat, oxtail, and beef, any of which can also be poured over peas and rice. A particular favorite is the vegetarian corn chowder, mobbed with okra, taro, carrots, and micro-dumplings, and thickened Chinese-style with cornstarch. The sweet and frothy peanut punch is better as a dessert.

BAKE & THINGS ☆ 🐟
184 East 35th Street, Brooklyn, 718-826-1807 The long red storefront — with a nifty flagstone terrace alongside the street for dining, though there are no tables inside — does an expansive Trinidadian menu with some Bajan specialties like souse and coo coo thrown in. The selection of bakes is spectacular, especially the

roast bake, a giant rectangle of soda bread halved horizontally and smeared with herring, saltfish, shark, or whatever kind of fish salad they happen to have hanging around. Rotis can be in the "bust-up shot" configuration, with the wadded flatbread presented on the side. The goat curry rules, but the promised green banana pie was nowhere to be found.

GLENDA'S HOME COOKING ☆ 🐟

854 St. Johns Place, Brooklyn, 718-778-1997 The yellow awning that promised more dishes than I can list dragged me in, even though the view in the window was eclipsed by a forest of potted cacti. Paneled rec-room style, the interior is lined with care-free pictures of life in the islands. The stew fish is wonderful — a big slab of fried kingfish smeared with tangy tomato gravy and plumped down on a bed of well-oiled rice and peas. Also fantastic is the goat roti, crammed with halal meat and curried potatoes, so carefully constructed — as one regular pointed out to me — that you can pick it up and eat it like a sandwich. If you dare, wash it down with mauby, a beverage that tastes like a cross between bubble gum and quinine.

HALAL ROTI ☆ ☆ 🐟 🐟

2345 8th Avenue, Manhattan, 212-749-8758 Even though this older-timer pressed behind a shoe repair stall (formerly known as A & R West Indian Restaurant and Roti Shop) underwent a

---

GET YOUR HOT DOUBLES

On Saturday Brooklyn's Nostrand Avenue comes alive. A couple of blocks south of Atlantic Avenue is a food stand called **Carl's Hot Doubles,** where a small boy (Carl?) stands behind a series of makeshift counters displaying snacks. In addition to carefully preparing doubles (a small flatbread sandwich with a curried chickpea filling), he also dispenses aloo pies and pholourie, the former a makeshift and somewhat misshapen empanada stuffed with potato curry, the latter a cousin of the donut hole tasting of lentils. Also vended — from an ancient, belt-driven contraption that looks like it was borrowed from a county fair — are snow cones in a variety of tropical flavors. The guava is particularly recommended, made from a thin red syrup that tastes homemade, or at least acquired from a supplier who really cares about the taste and not just the color.

change of ownership a couple of years ago, the conch roti remains a thing of beauty, the roti wrapper enfolding plenty of conch, potatoes, and peregrine green herbs. Little black specks encountered in a recent devouring turned out to be dried shrimp, amping up the seafood flavor and summoning a picture of Port of Spain, Trinidad, in the process. Besides the usual menu, look for Bajan specialties like flying fish and coo coo.

MOLLY'S BAKERY ☆

820 Nostrand Avenue, Brooklyn, 718-773-8691 Catty-corner from Glenda's Home Cooking is Molly's Bakery, a modest establishment with a couple of very cluttered counters and a few stools looking out the smeary picture window. The pay phone, in constant use, is the center of the establishment, and Molly herself seemed to always be on it. They make great cheap rotis here — chicken, vegetarian, oxtail, and goat. The dahl poori wrapper is a little thicker and less yielding than most, but the potato filler is particularly savory and dense. The counter guy, who has a dish towel wrapped haphazardly around his noggin (not a religious turban, just a dish towel), ladles on lots of chickpeas.

ROTI SHACK ☆ ☆

738 Flatbush Avenue, Brooklyn, 718-856-5956 Pungent chunks of lean and nearly boneless goat, a rather soupy potato curry, and a flatbread layered with crushed yellow split peas (sold separately as a "skin") are assembled into what may be Flatbush's best roti — you've got to order the chickpeas separately. Also available are dinners of smoked herring, duck stew, kingfish, and oxtail, and snack-size sandwiches known as bakes. Best to come on the weekend, when specials include conch roti, kingfish, coo coo Bajan style, and "shark and bake," which sounds like a certain boxed supermarket product.

SINGH'S ROTI SHOP #3 ☆ ☆ 🐟 🐠 🐂

18-06 Liberty Avenue, Queens, 718-835-7255 Located on a stretch of Liberty Avenue that caters to ethnic Indians from Trinidad and Guyana, Singh's features a wonderful L-shaped steam table and a counter filled with all sorts of goodies like toolum — coconut balls flavored with ginger and molasses. You can have a goat or conch roti rolled up in the usual fashion, or presented with a flatbread on the side as a "bust-up shot" (dialect for "busted-up shirt," referring to the crumpled bread). In addition to fish-bearing bakes, there are also vegetarian dishes like bhaggie, bodie, and pumpkin.

Turkish

Turkish cuisine is a house divided. There's the vegetarian side of the menu, said to have been inspired by the Persians. This cuisine was promulgated around a good part of the Mediterranean by the Ottoman Empire. Now many nations claim baba ghanoush and hummus as their own, but you'll often find the best versions in Turkish joints. The other side of the menu, of course, is the meat, and the favored flesh is lamb. The Turks have dozens of ways to butcher it, mince up, mix it, and grill it. Over the last few years, many places have begun to deploy chicken, Cornish hen, or even turkey in their kebabs, rather than lamb, but this seems to be more an economic measure than a knee-jerk to the laughable and sorely misplaced health consciousness of our age. At any rate, not only will a Turkish restaurant satisfy your vegetarian friends, it will allow you to simultaneously indulge in some of the most toothsome grilled meat around.

LOOK FOR:

adana kebab *lamb or beef chopped with peppers*

arnavut cigeri *Albanian-style cubed lamb's liver*

barbunya *kidney bean stew*

beyti kebab *ground lamb laced with chile*

borek *flaky pastry*

cigara bureka *feta-filled pastry flutes*

cig kofte *steak tartare*

doner *twirling mystery meat*

guvec kebabi *lamb stew in a crock-baked pie*

iman bayildi *stuffed and braised eggplant*

iskembe corbasi *tripe soup, a hangover remedy*

Iskender kebab *sliced doner heaped on pita with yogurt and tomato sauces*

Istanbul pilavi *pilaf with almonds, pistachios, saffron, and chicken*

kadayif *shredded wheat pastry*
kavurma *griddle-fried lamb*
kisir *bulgur salad, like tabbouleh*
lahmacum *street pizzas topped with minced meat
paste*
menemen *green-pepper omelette*
pasturma *air-dried beef*
patlican salatasi *eggplant puree flavored with
olive oil and lemon juice*
piyaz *white bean salad*
shepherd's salad *diced vegetable salad*
soslu patlican *chunky eggplant stew*
uskumru lakerda *Turkish sashimi*

ANATOLIAN GYRO ☆

1605 Sheepshead Bay Road, Brooklyn, 718-769-4754 This
narrow den near the Q station displays its specialty right in the
window: a lumpy cylinder of lamb revolving slowly, with a fat wad
perched on top that continuously bastes the meat. The doner
sandwich is a full meal, loaded with roughage and drizzled with
both chile and garlic-yogurt sauces. Full Turkish menu also available.

BAY SHISH KEBAB ☆ ☆ ⓒ

2255 Emmons Avenue, Brooklyn, 718-769-5396 An expanded appetizer list features five eggplant choices alone, ranging
from the too-familiar baba ghanoush to the more obscure soslu
patlican — the Barneylike vegetable cubed and stewed with tomatoes, green chiles, and chunky garlic. The olive-oil ooze was quickly
staunched with freshly made pide bread flecked with nigella and
sesame seeds. The menu also offers obscure kebabs like calf liver,
garlicky and peppery beyti, and the criminal's nemesis, cop
shish — chunklets of baby lamb. All were distinguished by tasty
meat and plenty of smoke. But there are also a handful of Uzbeki
dishes on the menu. The reason: there's a large Turkic population
in that former Soviet republic; in fact, one of the cooks grew up
there. Manti dumplings are massive doughy pouches more flavorful than their simple filling of lamb, parsley, and onions suggests.
Samsa loads a similar filling into a pastry crust. The best choice,
however, is the national dish: palav, a deliriously oily entrée of rice
simmered with carrots, onions, chickpeas, and lamb. As it cooks,
rice anneals to the bottom of the pan; scraped off and strewn, it
becomes a crunchy topping.

BEREKET ☆ ⊘

187 East Houston Street, Manhattan, 212-475-7700 Never fabulous but always solidly good, Bereket has been the midnight salvation of rock fans who go to clubs that ring it like a Krispy Kreme donut. Open 24 hours, the premises wouldn't be recognized by the café's earliest advocates, who remember it as a mere closet. Nowadays, there's a big bright open dining room, and a steam table that does best in a vegetarian vein. If the baba rocks, then so does the kisir, a cracked wheat concoction leaking red oil like a damaged spaceship. The best kebab has always been the adana, made with coarsely chopped and rich meat that drips fat continuously into the fire, generating clouds of flavorful smoke.

BEYOGLU ☆ ☆ ⊘

1431 3rd Avenue, Manhattan, 570-5666 Dispensing with entrées almost entirely, this walkup Turk attempts to reproduce a type of restaurant common in Istanbul's Beyoglu neighborhood that features appetizers exclusively. Assembling a meal in this rollicking warren has a pleasure all its own. Begin with crunchy pastry flutes filled with feta called boreks, then proceed to uskumru lakerda — a bowl of barely pickled mackerel that might remind you of sashimi. Next, down a formidable Greek salad (Greek salad?) boasting stuffed grape leaves and artichokes around its circumference. Finally, dive into a bowl of hummus, subtly flavored with cumin and dribbled with olive oil.

BEYTI KEBAB ☆

4105 Park Avenue, Union City, New Jersey, 201-865-6281 When 20 of us celebrated a birthday here, our ravenous party ate plate after plate of meze and mixed kebabs piled high on platters, and drank glass after glass of raki for a bargain price of less than $25 per person. The hummus was one of the best I've ever tasted, coarsely textured but light, with a restrained touch to the garlic. It's served with fine Turkish bread, a round, yeasty loaf with a wrinkled brown crust. Chicken shish kebabs, marinated in yogurt and moister than most, are especially good. Don't miss kisir, a salad of bulgur with a thick, peppery tomato dressing.

CAFE ISTANBUL ☆ ☆ ☆ ⊘

1715 Emmons Avenue, Brooklyn, 718-368-3587 Since the last time I dropped in years ago, this tiny has Turk morphed into a complex of dining rooms, so jammed with curios that you feel like you're in a tourist kiosk in Constantinople. The menu has expanded, too, and the food is as pristine and lovely as it always was, as is the view of the concrete trough that is Sheepshead Bay. Whole fish are now available, though the wonderful homemade pide bread — served plain or stuffed like a calzone — is still the heart of the menu.

FINCAN TURKISH CUISINE ☆ ☆ ⓒ
95-36 Queens Boulevard, Queens, 718-897-1509 The eight-item vegetarian appetizer plate at this Rego Park restaurant (pronounced "fin-john," formerly known as Kazan) is spectacular, including smoky hummus, labni (thickened yogurt zapped with garlic and walnuts), a sweet and savory stew of eggplant and tomatoes called patlican soslu, and a bulging grape leaf stuffed with rice and pine nuts. Cigara bureka, thin pastry flutes stuffed with dilled cheese, are also fab. With starters like these, the more predictable kebabs come as a slight disappointment. My fave is kasarli kofte, little grilled cheeseburgers with the feta cheese inside. Another plus: the staff is particularly friendly and accommodating.

SAHARA ☆ ☆ ⓒ
2337 Coney Island Avenue, Brooklyn, 718-376-8594 Even if the food wasn't first-rate, the fact that Sahara bakes its own bread would be enough to make you check it out. That bread is a flat oblong loaf generously sprinkled with yellow and black sesame, well browned and crusty. The interior is white, porous, resilient — perfect bread, fit to be compared with any bread on earth — especially good with the excellent meze. Arnavut cigeri is cubes of baby calves liver lightly dusted with flour and sautéed in paprika-laced oil. The version of patlican salatasi varies the usual plainish puree of eggplant and garlic with fragments of tomato and sweet red pepper. King of the entrées is the mixed grill, with four different preparations of lamb: doner kebab, shish kebab, lamb chops, and adana kebab. Ask to substitute beyti kebab for adana, because it contains hot red chiles and lots more garlic. The vine-festooned rear garden is one of the best places to hang in Brooklyn.

SAHARA GRILL ☆
558 7th Avenue, Manhattan, 212-391-6554 The gang from the late lamented Ali Baba has made a dramatic return in this corner-located shoebox in the garment center, open 24 hours. Gyros of chicken or lamb are the preferred flesh, with the poultry so fresh it almost jumps off the cylinder and into the sandwich. Pick the yogurt sauce over the tahini, and ask for an additional dab of chile sauce. Among meze, the baba ghanoush is best, with enough raw garlic to blow the top of your head off. Also look for a pot of non-menu provender bubbling on the burner — it's often what the staff are making for themselves. On a recent afternoon, it was a scram-

ble of eggs and long green chiles. Though it's mainly carryout, there are a handful of tables where you can sit and ponder why a Turkish place is named Sahara Grill.

SAHARA'S TURKISH CUISINE ☆ ☆ ౘ
513 2nd Avenue, Manhattan, 212-532-7589 Owned by the same folks as Sahara Grill, a distinguished carryout in the garment center, Sahara's is a sit-down restaurant with comfortable tables and minimal decor. The extensive menu lacks the seafood of nearby Turkish Kitchen, but there are plenty of other interesting anomalies. One is "special beyti sarma," a kebab of chopped lamb that's been cooked over charcoal, wrapped in a thin pastry, and cooked again, with a drizzle of yogurt on top — fantastic! Best of all was the elongated, homemade, seed-studded bread brought to the table hot, perfect with the smoky baba ghanoush.

SULTANA ☆ ⬗
2085 Coney Island Avenue, Brooklyn, 718-336-7500 Joining three other Turkish restaurants in the vicinity of the intersection of Coney Island Avenue and Kings Highway, Sultana seeks to distinguish itself with an intriguing list of seafood, running from mullets, snappers, and trout to imported fish that don't have English names, like izmir cupra. Unfortunately, they don't always have them. Instead, there's the standard list of charcoal-grilled kebabs (the chile-laced beyti is best), and plenty of composed salads. The red-tinged tabbouleh is especially good, as is a garlicky hummus. For hot appetizers, pick the calves liver cubes or "cigarette" burekas. Open till 3 a.m.!

TURKUAZ ☆ ౘ $
2637 Broadway, Manhattan, 212-665-9541 The narrow entranceway doesn't hint at the humongous dining room, wrapped in fabrics like a sultan's tent, and dimly lit for the benefit of dating couples who hold hands in the flickering candlelight. Perhaps for them also, the food is blander than it usually is in a Turkish restaurant, and the signature grilled green chile is missing from the ensembles. Nevertheless, the shepherd's salad is abundant and well oiled, and the fingers of Fatima (cigara burekas) are well fried, with good feta oozing out both ends. Contrary to form, the chicken breast kebab is superb, arriving moist in the interior and slicked with orangish oil.

YATAGAN ☆ ☆ ☆
104 MacDougal Street, Manhattan, 212-677-0952 If you crave doner kebab, that amalgam of twirling mystery meat known to the Greeks as gyro and Middle Easterners as schwarma, go to

Yatagan, a long-running Turkish stand that serves the best in town. Ask for both the yogurt and hot sauce on your overstuffed sandwich, and check out the interesting range of Turkish soft beverages, like sour cherry. There is a pint-sized dining room, but most folks step up to the window.

Vietnamese and Cambodian

Twelve years ago Vietnamese cafés were springing up everywhere in Manhattan's Chinatown, offering over-rice meals cheaper than anyone else. The delicate charcoal-grilled pork chops, lemongrass chicken, and steaming bowls of pho (pronounced "ffffuh!") became an obsession with many diners, and the bright-tasting palate of flavors — which included fresh mint, cilantro, Asian basil, and the vinegary fish sauce called nuoc cham — influenced chefs all over the city. Pricewise, these cafés were eventually undersold by newer Malaysian and Fuzhou places, and most descended into mediocrity or simply disappeared.

But great Vietnamese food didn't vanish completely. Like many Manhattanites, it simply moved to Brooklyn. Sunset Park's Chinatown is becoming a haven for Vietnamese eating establishments, numbering five at last count, including the city's foremost purveyor of banh mi, the French-Vietnamese hero. But Vietnamese expansion was not limited to Chinatowns — Viet places began to appear in mainly occidental neighborhoods like Bensonhurst and Bath Beach, offering a more sophisticated menu than their Manhattan counterparts had done, but one that also featured Chinese dishes. Still, Vietnamese fare in Gotham lags behind Thai in a manner that only a fresh infusion of Vietnamese refugees can redress — hence the lack of any three-star establishments.

Cambodian food presents an interesting twist on the flavors you'll recognize from other Southeast Asian cuisines — lemongrass, galangal, garlic, cilantro, and sweet spices. Unfortunately, there's only one restaurant that serves it, a very friendly Fort Greene spot that lards the menu with other countries' cooking, just to confuse you. Don't miss chicken ahmok, a light mousse sparkling with tart flavors.

LOOK FOR:

ahmok *Cambodian coconut-milk chicken pudding*
banh cuon *Vietnamese crepe*
banh trang *rice-paper wrapper*
bo la nho *beef charred in grape leaves*
bo luc loc *buttered beef on a bed of salad*
bo nhung dam *Vietnamese beef fondue*
cha gio *deep-fried vermicelli-filled egg rolls*
chao tom *minced shrimp on sugarcane skewer*
goi bo *astringent beef salad*
goi tom cang *shrimp and cucumber salad*
nataing *ground meat dip for vegetables*
norm lahong *Cambodian green-papaya salad*
nuoc cham *clear dipping sauce with shredded vegetables flavored with nuoc mam*
nuoc mam *fermented fish sauce*
nuong *charcoal grilled*
pho *beef and noodle soup flavored with sweet spices*
samlor *any thick Cambodian soup*
samlor kaw co *thick Cambodian catfish soup*
samlor mchoo srae *tart Cambodian chicken soup*
tchruok spey koaob *Cambodian pickled veggies*
tom *shrimp*

Cambodian

SOUTH EAST ASIAN CUISINE ☆ ☆

87 South Elliot Place, Brooklyn, 718-858-3262 In Phnom Penh when people go out to eat, the choices are mainly French and Chinese, which means that Khmer chefs do most of their Cambodian cooking at home. This convention has continued in this country, with many Cambodian immigrants in Los Angeles and New York preferring to eat Chinese, which is plentiful, cheap, and familiar. But New York has one Cambodian restaurant — South East Asian Cuisine. Its slogan: "Less fat — better than Chinese food." S.E.A. Cuisine is located on a sunny square in Fort Greene. The dining room is strikingly utilitarian, with no embellishment except the obligatory Heimlich maneuver poster. The first thing to order is tchruok spey koaob, a lovely dish of sweet-and-sour pickled vegetables good for nibbling. Next get chicken ahmok, surely one of the strangest and most delicious dishes available in New York. Looking like a small white Frisbee with a fluted edge, it perchs on a kale island in a dense lemongrass broth with shredded leaves in the center, a musty herb called lamb leaf. The mousselike texture is achieved by beating raw chicken breast with coconut milk. Other estimable selections include mekong fish, a two-pound tilapia in a subtle chile sauce; and samlor mchoo srae, reminiscent of the Thai soup tom yum. Cambodian meals often begin like an American cocktail party, with chips and dips, only instead of chips they use slices of French bread or slivers of raw vegetable. There are a couple of typical dips on the S.E.A. menu, including "hot and spicy ground beef appetizer," which is a small bowl of fiery ground meat.

Vietnamese

GIA LAM ✺ ✺
5402 8th Avenue, Brooklyn, 718-854-8818 At the southern end of Sunset Park's Chinatown, this restaurant is thronged with Vietnamese families eating spring rolls and big bowls of soup. One such soup is pho dac biet, described on the menu as "special rice noodles soup w. beef, brisket, navel, flank and tendon." To the uninitiated, these various forms of beef are indistinguishable. But each has a unique character and they are mixed and matched in eight different soups that are made with a thin but flavorful meat broth and contain flat rice noodles and a sprinkling of chopped green onions. Each is served with a plate of sprouts and basil leaves. The unusually large spring rolls contain ground pork and vermicelli in a superthin wrapper. A small plate with romaine lettuce leaves and fresh mint comes on the side. I always thought you were supposed to wrap each roll in a lettuce with some mint before downing it, but Vietnamese diners nearby wolfed them down straight and reserved the lettuce for bites between mouthfuls of soup.

LITTLE SAIGON CAFE ✺
374 West 46th Street, Manhattan, 212-956-0639 When they say little, they mean little. This café in the theater district has only 12 seats at four tables and a kitchen so small that you couldn't lie down in it. But the food is a bargain and quantities are generous. The highlight of the meal is the chef's special kim-ting shrimp, six good-sized shrimp wrapped in rice paper and stuffed with vermicelli and ground pork. End your meal with "French black condensed milk coffee" or one of the other slow-dripping varieties made at your table. During the summer, the café puts a couple of tables out on the sidewalk.

MISS SAIGON ✺
1425 3rd Avenue, Manhattan, 212-988-8828 In an era when many restaurants are festooned with kitsch, the functionality of the

interior at Miss Saigon is one of its chief attractions, and the cheap prices don't hurt either. High points of a meal include a wonderful salad of grilled beef and green papaya in an astringent dressing, and barbecued pork chops marinated in lemongrass and garlic — the volume of meat so abundant, it nearly fed three. Conversely, a Chinese-style plate of spare ribs was rather dull and fatty. This is a real cheap dining resource for the neighborhood, but not to be confused with much better places. Not to be confused with the Broadway musical of the same name, either.

NEW PASTEUR ☆ ☆

85 Baxter Street, Manhattan, 212-608-3656 This now somewhat shabby shop was the place that first taught New Yorkers to love real Vietnamese food, and their over-rice dishes are still toothsome classics. Com xuon bi cha is one great plate of food: a mesa of rice topped with a charcoal-grilled pork chop, a dusty julienne of gelatinous pork skin, and a mysterious vermicelli omelet — yellow on top, brown below, with a faint taste of crab. With the usual Vietnamese garnish of cucumber and mint leaves, and a pour-over sauce containing vinegar, sugar, carrots, and the funky Vietnamese fish sauce, nuoc mam, the plate is enormous for the money, and can't be called boring. The pork chop in particular is unforgettable — sliced razor thin, with a sweet glaze that complements the smoky flavor. New Pasteur is named after one of Saigon's main drags, not a comment on the general hygienic conditions in the restaurant.

PHO CONG LY ☆ ☆

124 Hester Street, Manhattan, 212-343-1111 Hearing rumors that Pho Cong Ly had closed, I rode my bike by the venerable greasy spoon, only to find it — renovated! The new decor doesn't improve much on the old spare café, still geared to cabdrivers and other working-class folk. The food remains spicier than average for Viet fare, with no concessions to make it more acceptable to Western tastes. Unfortunately, while the new menu is expanded somewhat, it eliminated my favorite offering, the rice-starch-wrapper crepe called banh cuon. Please ask for it! A great dish that remains is chao long, a rice soup that the waitress, the soul of hospitality, warned me away from. How could I resist? It turned out to contain pig intestines, organ meats, delicious rounds of very French sausage studded with peppercorns, and crisp dried shrimp. Every bite was heavenly.

PHO NAM BO ☆ ☆

7524 18th Avenue, Brooklyn, 718-331-9259 Most of the Vietnamese action has long since moved out of Chinatowns, and this spanking new Bensonhurst restaurant is proof, offering excellent pho with a cinnamon-scented broth, chicken curry thickened with coconut milk and authentically sided with a Gallic baguette, and a wonderful appetizer platter that provides seven Vietnamese favorites for only $10.

PHO TAY HOY ✮ ✮

2351 86th Street, Brooklyn, 718-449-0199 At this great Bath Beach establishment, patrons run from Russian immigrants to Italian homeys to Chinese Brooklynites looking for exotic fare. As the name implies, the noodle soups called pho are the heart of the menu. Pho Tay Ho has a special predilection for beef. We spotted bo luc loc on nearly every table, hunks of coarse-textured meat sautéed in butter and piled on a salad that becomes deliciously sodden with juices. If this sounds French-influenced, be assured it is. Similarly Gallic are banh mi bo kho, a rich ragout of beef, potatoes, and carrots served with an entire baguette, and bo nhung dam, a vat of vinegary boiling water that invites you to cook slices of thin-shaved beef in its depths by swooshing them with your chopsticks. Fondue!

PHO VIET HUONG ✮ ✮

73 Mulberry Street, Manhattan, 212-233-8988 The most ambitious Viet restaurant in town – decorated like a Southeast Asian village – has a menu featuring a bewildering array of dishes. Skip the legendary seven-course beef dinner that prefaces the menu and cherry-pick the constituent dishes that excel, including a warm salad of tender beef strips in a citrus dressing (goi bo), a delectable beef congee made with broken rice, and nuggets of beef charcoal-charred inside grape leaves (bo la lop). The menu is bewildering in its length, encompassing lots of dishes pitched toward Chinese tastes, as well as nicely prepared Viet standards. Grilled pork chops are especially good, and so is duck with peanut sauce.

TI-AN VIETNAMESE RESTAURANT ✮ ✮

5604 8th Avenue, Brooklyn, 718-492-1592 Though it pretends to be a merely a pho palace, Ti-An's menu places it among the most ambitious Vietnamese restaurants in town. Included are such French-Viet staples as banh mi sandwiches and dense beef stews, as well as grilled beef and pork dishes, and all sorts of Chinese-leaning soups and stir-fries. The rice-noodle crepes are exceptional, and so is the pho, concocted of a long-boiled stock laced with sweet spices that turn it a particularly dark color.

MEATBALL HERO

Ask somebody on the street "Who invented the hero?" and chances are the respondent will credit Italian-American immigrants, who modified a torpedo-shaped French loaf, freighted it with cold cuts or leftover meatballs, crammed it into a lunch pail, and carried it off to work. But wait a minute! Halfway around the world the hero was simultaneously being invented by the Vietnamese. Also deploying a modified baguette — one that combined rice and wheat flours — they piled on rubbery pâté, sliced pork, and anisey Chinese sausage. Then they garnished it with sweet-pickled vegetables and cilantro, and smeared it with chile paste. Known as banh mi, the resulting clash of cultures and flavors represents an invention as formidable as the Italian-American hero. Banh mi have been popular around area China-towns for more than a decade. They first attracted attention when a sign, now gone, appeared at **Tan Phong Supermarket** at 85 Bowery bearing the pink neon come-on: "Vietnam Sandwich French Sandwich." That sign has long been extinguished, but these delicious sandwiches live on. To be completely authentic, wash them down with a can of pennyroyal drink or young green coconut milk.

BA XUYEN ☆ ☆ ⟋⟍

4222 8th Avenue, Brooklyn, 718-633-6601 Everybody's favorite Vietnamese sandwich shop has moved around the corner into more spacious digs, expanded the menu, and decorated the premises in the style of a Chinese bakery. The sandwiches preserve their excellence and cheapness ($2.75), with meatball (#8) proving a surprise favorite. Ask for hot peppers. Other choices: sardine, grilled pork, and the traditional pâté, pork roll, and barbecued pork.

BANH MI SO 1 ☆

369 Broome Street, Manhattan, 212-219-8341 As you enter, a woman peels long stalks of sugarcane by the front door to make fresh juice, and further inside a fascinating collection of snacks are displayed: sticky rice in lurid shades of green, yellow, and red; thick jackfruit chips; chewy mung bean cakes and crunchy mung bean cookies; cans of pâté; and nems, garlic-cured pork sausages usually eaten raw. Banh mi selection includes a delicious chicken version.

Neighborhood

Index

BROOKLYN

BAY RIDGE

Alsalam Restaurant & Meat Market (Lebanese), 217
Bahry Fish Market and Restaurant (Egyptian), 213
Casa Calamari (Italian), 130–31
Chianti (Italian), 131
Hinsch's (Regional American), 241–42
Karam (Lebanese), 218–19
La Maison du Couscous (Moroccan), 224–25
Mazza Plaza (Lebanese), 219
Mykonos (Greek), 107
Tanoreen (Jordanian), 217

BEDFORD-STUYVESANT

A & A Bake and Doubles (Trinidadian), 306, 309
Ali's Trinidad Roti Shop (Trinidadian), 309
Bis Milalh (International), 117
Dabakh-Malik (Senegalese), 281
House of Jerk (Jamaican), 161
Ma's Soul Food Café (Soul Food), 286–87
North Carolina Country Store (Soul Food), 285
Royal Rib House (Soul Food), 289
Sylvia's Restaurant (Jamaican), 165

BENSONHURST/DYKER HEIGHTS

Caravello's (Italian), 135
Casa Calamari (Italian), 130–31
Clemente's (Italian), 127, 128
Krispy Pizzeria (Italian), 145, 149
Mona Lisa (Italian), 143
Monte's (Italian), 129
Pho Nam Bo (Vietnamese), 321–22
Pho Tay Hoy (Vietnamese), 322
Romano Restaurant (Italian), xii, 124, 134
Tasty Pizza and Pasta Ristorante (Italian), 141
Tony's & Elena Ristorante (Italian), 136

BOROUGH PARK

Cheskel's Shwarma King (Israeli), 214
D. Zion Burger (Israeli), 215
DiFara Pizzeria (Italian), 146, 148

BRIGHTON BEACH

Cafe Glechik (Russian), 251
Café Kashkar (Uighur Chinese), 23, 43
Cafe Paris (Russian), 252–53
Cafe Shish-kebab (Uzbekistani), 21

Caffe Volna (Russian), 254
Chio Pio (Uzbekistani), 21
Eastern Feast (Uzbekistani), 21–22
National (Russian), 252
Odessa (Russian), 252
Pastorale (Russian), 253

BROOKLYN HEIGHTS

Bedouin Tent (Lebanese), 217
Brawta (Jamaican), 158
Fountain Café (Lebanese), 218

BROWNSVILLE/EAST NEW YORK

Blue Mountain Café (Jamaican), 158
Coney Island Joe's (Regional American), 237, 238
El Pulgarcito de America (Salvadoran), 16
Eve's Restaurant (Haitian), 113
Lams Kitchen & Sports Bar (Nigerian), 103
Louise's (Vincentian), 166
Ricky's Eat-Well (Jamaican), 164
Rose's Restaurant (Haitian), 115

BUSHWICK

Alex Aguinaga—aka Fanny (Ecuadorian), 65
El Salvador (Salvadoran), 17
Estrabar (Italian), 143
La Guadalupana (Mexican), 204
Tacos La Hacienda (Mexican), 208–9
Taqueria La Asuncion (Mexican), 210

CARROLL GARDENS/ COBBLE HILL/ RED HOOK

Defonte's Sandwich Shop (Italian), 127
El Cibao (Dominican), 50
Ferdinando's (Italian), 135

India House (Northern Indian), 265
Joya (International and Thai), 120, 301, 302
145 Luncheonette (Yemeni), 221
Schnack (Regional American), 240
Sur (Argentinian), 4
Tabouleh (Jordanian), 216–17
Yemen Café (Yemeni), 221

CONEY ISLAND

Nathan's Famous (Regional American), 237, 239
Totonno Pizzeria Napolitano (Italian), 124, 144, 151

CROWN HEIGHTS/ PROSPECT HEIGHTS

Carl's Hot Doubles (Trinidadian), 310
Cock's (Bajan), 157
Culpepper's (Bajan), 157
Fi Wih Kitchen (Jamaican), 160–61
Glenda's Home Cooking (Trinidadian), 310, 311
Kelso Diner (Panamanian), 13, 15
Molly's Bakery (Trinidadian), 311
Pysne's (Grenadian), 157
St. John's Café and Restaurant (Jamaican), 164
TCB's (Grenadian), 158
Tom's (Regional American), 242–43

FLATBUSH

Baje's P & T Eatery (Bajan), 156–57
Bake & Things (Trinidadian), 309–10
Danny and Pepper (Jamaican), 160
Finger Likin's "R" Us (Jamaican), 160
Frittaile Lacaye (Haitian), 113–14

326

Guyana Roti House (Guyanese), 308

Icons Afro-West (Nigerian), 101-3

Marcus Island Deli (Jamaican), 162

Mirage (Nigerian), 103

New Combination (Nigerian), 103

Pearly's (Jamaican), 164

Rosscoe's House of Chicken and Waffles (Soul Food), 289

Roti Shack (Trinidadian), 157, 311

Sybil's (Guyanese), 308

Tummy Paradise (Jamaican), 165

Yoyo Fritaille (Haitian), 115-16

FORT GREENE/ CLINTON HILL

À Table (French), 84

Castro's (Mexican), 201

Chez Oscar (French), 85-86

Demu Café (Nigerian), 101

Hall Street Kosher Café (Jewish-American), 180

Keur n' Deye (Senegalese), 282

Locanda Vini & Olii (Italian), 139

Madiba (South African), 80

Mo-Bay (Jamaican), 163

Palava Hut (Nigerian), 104

Rencher's Crab Inn (Regional American), 247

South East Asian Cuisine (Cambodian), 319-20

FULTON FERRY/DUMBO

Five Front (Regional American), 243

Jacques Torres Chocolate (French), 86

GREENPOINT

Amarin (Thai), 300, 302

Happy End (Polish), 61-62

Moon Shadow (Thai), 302-3

Old Poland Bakery and Restaurant (Polish), 62

Thai Café (Thai), 302, 305

ValDiano (Italian), 136

HOMECREST/ GRAVESEND/ MARINE PARK

Adelman's (Jewish-American), 181

Brennan & Carr (Irish), 75

Deli Corner (Jewish-American), 180

Desi Village (Northern Indian), 264

Harchevnya (Russian), 253

Jackie's Delicatessen (Italian), 127-28

Jay & Lloyd's (Jewish-American), 181

Joe's of Avenue U (Italian), 124, 135

John's Deli (Italian), 128

L & B Spumoni Gardens (Italian), 132, 145

Nick's Lobster Restaurant (Regional American), 246-47

Pirosmani (Georgian), 20

Rocky's (Italian), 128

Sahara (Turkish), 315

Shaikh's Place (Regional American), 242

Sultana (Turkish), 316

Tblisi (Georgian), 20

Win Sing (Cantonese), 30-31

KENSINGTON

E & R (Haitian), 113

Joe & Joe's Restaurant (Italian), 132

Little Bangladesh Restaurant & Kebab House (Bangladeshi), 260-61

Los Mariachis (Mexican), 204

MIDWOOD

Bahar Shishkebab House (Afghani), 229, 230-31

Bissaleh (Israeli), 214

Bukhara (Pakistani), 268

327

Jerusalem Steak House (Israeli), 215
Sarmish (Azerbaijani), 19-20

PARK SLOPE

Catene Deli (Italian), 126
Chipshop (English), 74, 259
Coco Roco (Peruvian), 64, 69, 70
Curry Shop (Anglo-Indian), 75, 259
Elora's (International), 118
Java Indonesian Rijsttafel (Indonesian), 191, 194
La Villa (Italian), 146, 151
Laila (Lebanese), 219
Los Chorros (Salvadoran), 16
Salinas (Ecuadorian), 68
Tacos Nuevo Mexico (Mexican), 210
Trattoria Mulino (Italian), 136

SHEEPSHEAD BAY

Anatolian Gyro (Turkish), 313
Bay Shish Kebab (Turkish), 23, 313
Cafe Istanbul (Turkish), 314-15
Clemente's Maryland Crabhouse (Regional American), 246
Jordan's Lobster Dock (Regional American), 246
Mrs. Stahl's Knishes (Jewish-American), 21
Randazzo's (Italian), 134
Roll N Roaster (Italian), 128

SUNSET PARK

Ba Xuyen (Vietnamese), 323
El Tesoro (Ecuadorian), 69
Eva Restaurante (Ecuadorian), 66-67
Gia Lam (Vietnamese), 320
Honduras Maya (Honduran), 15
Kikiriki (Peruvian), 70
Las Antillas (Dominican), 49
Los Compadres (Mexican), 202
Los Pollitos (International), 121
Monika (Polish), 62

North Mai Xiang Cun Dumpling House (Northern Chinese), 27
Nyonya (Malaysian), 194-95
Restaurant Milan's (Czech), 59
Rico's Tamales Oaxaqueños (Mexican), 207-8
Ricos Tacos (Mexican), 207
Ti-An Vietnamese Restaurant (Vietnamese), 322
Usuluteco (Salvadoran), 17

WILLIAMSBURG

Allioli (Spanish), 294
Bamonte's Restaurant (Italian), 124, 130
Black Betty (International), 117
Brick Oven Gallery (Italian), 147
Caffe Capri (Italian), 133, 143
Cheers (Thai), 301, 302
D.O.C. Wine Bar (Italian), 126, 153
Diner (Regional American), 241
Driggs Pizzeria (Italian), 148
El Chile Verde (Mexican), 201-2
Fada (French), 86
Giando (Italian), 131-32
Gottlieb's Restaurant (Jewish-American), 180
Krezo 2 (Lithuanian), 61
La Locanda (Italian), 132-33
La Piazzetta (Italian), 134
Matamoros Puebla Grocery (Mexican), 205
Peter Luger (Regional American), 236
Planet Thailand (Thai), 300, 302, 305
Raymund's Place (Polish), 63
SEA (Thai), 302, 304
Sparky's (Regional American), 237, 240

BRONX

African American Restaurant (Ghanian), 99
African and American Family Restaurant (Senegalese), 278, 280

All Star Café Restaurant (Albanian), 55–56, 97

Aziza (Nigerian), 101

Brook Luncheonette (International), 118

Burektorja Dukagjini (Albanian), 56

Café al Mercato (Italian), 133

Caribbean Taste Inc. (Jamaican), 159–60

Ebe Ye Yie (Ghanian), 99

El Economica (Dominican), 50–51

El Nuevo Bohio (Puerto Rican), 53

Giovanni's (Italian), 149

Gurra Cafe (Albanian), 56

H.I.M. (Jamaican), 161

In God We Trust (Ghanian), 99–100

Jerk Center (Jamaican), 161

Joey's Cold Heroes (Italian), 129

La Fondita (Puerto Rican), 53

La Orquidea (Honduran), 15

Lechonera El Coqui (Puerto Rican), 53

Madonia Brothers Bakery (Italian), 143

Mister Taco (Mexican), 205–6

Motherland Cuisine (Ghanian), 101

Patricia's (Italian), 133–34

Rambling House (Irish), 76

Rawal Ravail Restaurant (Pakistani), 270–71

Restorant Shqiptar (Albanian), 56–57

Roberto's (Italian), 141

Royal Bake Shop (Jamaican), 164

Sabrosura (Dominican-Chinese), 49

Schlitz Inn (German), 95

Tibbett Diner (Regional American), 242

Uncle Sal's Ribs and Bibs (Regional American), 234

Venice Restaurant (Italian), 137

Vernon's New Jerk House (Jamaican), 165–66

MANHATTAN

CHELSEA

Calidad Latina (International), 118

F & B (Regional American), 238

Grand Sichuan (Sichuan and Hunan), 40

Havana Chelsea Luncheonette (Cuban), 47

Khyber Kebab (Pakistani), 270

Kitchen Market (Regional American), 248

La Chinita Linda (Cuban-Chinese), 48

La Taza de Oro (Puerto Rican), 53

Le Gamin (French), 86

Le Singe Vert (French), 91

Le Zie (Italian), 142

Markt (Belgian), 81, 82

Maroons (Jamaican), 162–63

Matsuri (Japanese), 176

Negril (Jamaican), 163

Pepe Giallo (Italian), 140–41

Pizza Supreme (Italian), 145, 150

Pop Burger (Regional American), 237

Qasim (Pakistani), 270

Royal Siam (Thai), 304

Rue des Crepes (French), 90

Sirtaj (Northern Indian), 267

Soul Fixin's (Soul Food), 289–90

Wild Lily Tea Room (International), 123

CHINATOWN

American East Fuzhou Restaurant (Fujianese Chinese), 32

Banh Mi So 1 (Vietnamese), 323

Big Eat (Hong Kong Chinese), 34

C & F Restaurant (Hong Kong Chinese), 34

Chanoodle (Chiu Chow Chinese), 31

329

Chao Zhou (Chiu Chow Chinese), 31

Congee (Cantonese), 27–28

Congee Village (Cantonese), 27, 28

East Broadway Gourmet (Fujianese Chinese), 32–33

18 Aharns (Vegetarian Chinese), 44

88 Reach House (Fujianese Chinese), 33

Excellent Dumpling House (Cantonese), 28–29

Family Noodle (Cantonese), 29

416 B.C. (Bulgarian), 58

Fried Dumpling (Northern Chinese), 26–27

Fu Chow Restaurant (Fujianese Chinese), 33

Funky Broome (Hong Kong Chinese), 34–35

Good World (Swedish), 97

Grand Sichuan (Sichuan and Hunan), 40

Happy Shabu Shabu (Chinese), 37

Joe's Ginger (Chinese), 31

Joe's Shanghai (Chinese), 31, 37–38, 39

N.Y. Noodle Town (Cantonese), 30

Natural Restaurant (Cantonese), 30

New Bai Wei Gourmet Food Inc. (Fujianese Chinese), 33–34

New Chao Chow (Chiu Chow Chinese), 31–32

New Green Bo (Shanghai Chinese), 38

New Pasteur (Vietnamese), 321

Nyonya (Malaysian), 194–95

Peking Duck House (Northern Chinese), 26

Pho Cong Ly (Vietnamese), 321

Pho Viet Huong (Vietnamese), 322

Ping's (Hong Kong Chinese), 36

Proton Saga (Malaysian), 195

Shanghai Cuisine (Shanghai Chinese), 38–39

Singapore Café (Singaporean), 197

Sogo (Taiwanese), 42–43

Spring Boy Fuzhou Food (Fujianese Chinese), 34

Sun Golden Island (Chiu Chow Chinese), 32

Sun Hop Shing Tea House (Cantonese), 28, 30

Sweet-N-Tart (Taiwanese), 28, 43

Taste Good (Malaysian), 195–96

Tasty Dumpling (Northern Chinese), 27

Ten Pell (Shanghai Chinese), 39

Wong's Rice and Noodle Shoppe (Cantonese), 31

X.O. Kitchen (Hong Kong Chinese), 36

Yeah Shanghai Deluxe (Shanghai Chinese), 39–40

EAST VILLAGE

Angelica Kitchen (Regional American), 243

Anyway Cafe Club (Russian), 251

Assenzio (Italian), 126, 152

B & H Dairy Restaurant (Jewish-American), 62, 179, 181

Banjara (Northern Indian), 262–63

Bar Veloce (Italian), 152–53

Basso Est (Italian), 137

Bereket (Turkish), 314

Blue 9 Burger (Regional American), 235

Boca Chica (International), 117–18

Bond Street (Japanese), 175, 177

Borobudur (Indonesian), 193

Brick Lane Curry House (Anglo-Indian), 75, 258–59

Café Deville (French), 85

Cafe Rakka (Lebanese), 218

330

Caracas Arepa Bar (Venezuelan), 11

Casa Adela (Puerto Rican), 52–53

Casimir (French), 87

Chez Es Saada (Moroccan), 224

Cosmic Cantina (Regional American), 248

Creperie (French), 90

Crif Dogs (Regional American), 237, 238

Crosby Connection (Italian), 129

Darbar East (Northern Indian), 264, 276

Dawgs on Park (Regional American), 238

Dok Suni (Korean), 185

El Maguey y La Tuna (Mexican), 203

Elvie's Turo-Turo (Philippine), 196

Emerald Planet (International), 119

Emilio's Ballato (Italian), 131

Flea Market (French), 87

Flor's Kitchen (Venezuelan), 12

1492 (Spanish), 296

Ghenet (Ethiopian), 79

Hasaki (Japanese), 173–75

Il Bagato (Italian), 124

'inoteca (Italian), 154

Jeoladdo (Japanese), 175

Jewel Bako (Japanese), 175

Katz's (Jewish-American and Regional American), 180, 182, 239

Kiev (Ukrainian), 254

Komodo (International), 120

La Focacceria (Italian), 135–36

Lahore Deli (Pakistani), 269

Le Souk (Tunisian), 227

Le Zoccole (Italian), 142

Lil' Frankie's (Italian), 148

Lima's Taste (Peruvian), 64, 70

Little Poland (Polish), 62

Luca Lounge (Italian), 149

Lucien (French), 87

Madras Cafe (Southern Indian), 272-73

Mama's Food Shop (Regional American), 245

Max (Italian), 140

Mie (Japanese), 174, 176

Mogador (Moroccan), 225

Moustache (Lebanese), 219–20

New Manila Food Mart (Philippine), 196

Oliva (Spanish), 293

Otafuku (Japanese), 170

Pak Punjab (Pakistani), 269

Pak Star Deli (Pakistani), 269

Pie (Italian), 150

Pomme-Pomme (Belgian), 84

Pommes Frites Authentic Belgian Fries (Belgian), 84

Prune (Regional American), 243–44

Puebla Mexican Food (Mexican), 207

Punjabi (Pakistani), 269

Pylos (Greek), 108

Radio Perfecto (International), 122

Rai Rai Ken (Japanese), 169

Rectangles (Israeli), 216

Resto Léon (French), 87

Rice (International), 122

Sahara East (Egyptian), 214

Saint's Alp Teahouse (Hong Kong Chinese), 36

San Loco (Regional American), 249

Sapporo East (Japanese), 172

Second Avenue Deli (Jewish-American), 180, 181, 182

Soby-ya (Japanese), 169

Spanish American Food (Dominican), 52

Stromboli (Italian), 145, 151

Teresa's (Polish), 63

Tiny's Giant Food Shop (Regional American), 245-46

Trattoria Paolina (Italian), 142

Veniero's Pasticceria (Italian), 143–44

Veselka (Ukrainian), 255

Village Mingala (Burmese), 298, 299

Viva Herbal Pizzeria (Italian), 152

Win49 (Japanese), 170–71

331

Xunta (Spanish), 294
Yakiniku West (Japanese), 171
Zaragoza Grocery (Mexican), 211

FLATIRON

Bangkok Café (Thai), 300–1
Eisenberg's Sandwich Shop (Regional American), 245
Havana Central (Cuban), 46–47
La Pizza Fresca (Italian), 146, 150
Le Pain Quotidien (Belgian), 81, 83
Los Dos Molinos (Regional American), 247
Periyali (Greek), 108
Pipa (Spanish), 297
Republic (International), 122
Silver Swan (German), 92, 96
Via Emilia (Italian), 142

HARLEM

Africa Restaurant #1 (Senegalese), 280, 281
African Grill (Ivory Coastal), 278–79
Bayou (Regional American), 234
Charles Southern Style Kitchen (Soul Food), 284–85
Copeland's Take-Out and Catering (Soul Food), 286
Devins Fish & Chips (Soul Food), 286
El Despertar (Dominican), 50, 294
El Rincon Boricua (Puerto Rican), 53
El Vaquero (Mexican), 210–11
Farfina Coffee Shop (Ivory Coastal), 279
Flavored with One Love (Guyanese), 308
Food Hut (Jamaican), 161
Halal Roti (Trinidadian), 157, 312–13
Jumbo Hamburgers (Regional American), 236

Kaloum (Guinean), 278
Keur Sokhna (Senegalese), 282
La Casa de los Tacos (Mexican), 201
La Hacienda (Mexican), 201, 203
La Marmite (Senegalese), 282
Le Worodougou (Ivory Coastal), 279
Lechonera Sandy (Dominican), 51
M & G Diner (Soul Food), 287
Mali-Bo (Malian), 279–80
Margie's Red Rose (Soul Food), 286
Massawa (Eritrean), 78–79
Mexico Dos (Mexican) 205
Mi Mexico Lindo Panaderia (Mexican), 205
New Caporal Fried Chicken (Dominican), 52
On the Park (Regional American), 236
One Stop Patty Shop (Jamaican), 163
Pan Pan (Soul Food), 283, 287, 288
Patsy's (Italian), 144, 149
Saji's (Japanese), 172
Sokobolie (Guinean), 278
Strictly Roots (Jamaican), 164–65
Sun Shine Kitchen (Jamaican), 165
The Mill (Korean), 188
Umoja's (Soul Food), 287

HELL'S KITCHEN

Afghan Kebab House (Afghani), 230
Africa Restaurant #2 (Senegalese), 280–81
Ariana Afghan Kebab (Afghani), 230
Bali Nusa Indah (Indonesian), 193
Brazil Grill (Brazilian), 8
Chimichurri Grill (Argentinian), 3
Churrascaria Plataforma (Brazilian), 10

Daisy May's BBQ USA (Regional American), 233
Dalquis Restaurant (Dominican), 50
Esca (Italian), 174
Grand Sichuan (Sichuan and Hunan), 40
Hallo Berlin (German), 92, 94, 96
Island Spice (Jamaican), 163
Lakruwana (Sri Lankan), 274
Le Soleil (Haitian), 115
Little Saigon Cafe (Vietnamese), 320
Marseille (French), 88
Meskerem (Ethiopian), 77, 79–80
Market Café (International), 120–21
Olieng (Thai), 298, 303
Pam Real Thai Food (Thai), 298, 303
Pigalle (French), 89
Pomaire (Chilean), 5
Queen of Sheba (Ethiopian), 77, 80
Rinconcito Peruano (Peruvian), 72
Salon Mexico (Mexican), 208
Soup Kitchen International (International), 123
Tacocina (Mexican), 208
Taprobane (Sri Lankan), 274, 275
Uncle Nick's Greek Cuisine (Greek), 110
West African Grocery, 277

MIDTOWN

Afghan Kebab House (Afghani), 230
Argentine Pavilion (Argentinian), 2
B. Frites (Belgian), 83
Bay Leaf (Northern Indian), 263
Bella Napoli (Italian), 145, 147
Bread from Beirut (Lebanese), 218
Burger Joint (Regional American), 235
Cabana Carioca (Brazilian), 8

Carnegie Deli (Jewish-American), 180
Chikubu (Japanese), 170
DB Bistro (Regional American), 235–36
Diamond Dairy Restaurant (Jewish-American), 178, 179
Djerdan #3 (Bosnian), 58
Estiatorio Milos (Greek), 105, 110
Felidia (Italian), 138
Gan Eden (Uzbekistani), 22–23
Genki Sushi (Japanese), 173
Haru (Japanese), 173
Hatsuhana (Japanese), 174, 175
Ishihama (Korean), 188
Katsuhama (Japanese), 169, 170
Kosher Delight (Israeli), 216
Kuruma Sushi (Japanese), 174, 175–76
Mandoo (Korean), 186
Margon (Cuban), xii, 45, 47
Marichu (Spanish), 293
Menchanko-Tei (Japanese), 168–69
Mezze (International), 121
Minar (Northern Indian), 266
Molyvos (Greek), 105, 110
Nedick's (Regional American), 240
New York Kom Tang Soot Bul House (Korean), 189
Nick's Place (Greek), 107–8
Philly's Cheese Steaks (Regional American), 244
Rare (Regional American), 237
Restaurant Nippon (Japanese), 169
Sahara Grill (Turkish), 315–16
Sapporo (Japanese), 172
St. Andrews (Scottish), 76
Sushi Yasuda (Japanese), 174, 176–77
Sushisay (Japanese), 174, 176
Taam Tov (Uzbekistani), 23
Ulrika's (Swedish), 97
Veronica Ristorante Italiano (Italian), 137

Victor's (Cuban), 48
Virgil's Real Barbecue (Regional American), 234
Wu Liang Ye (Sichuan and Hunan), 41
Yoshinoya (Japanese), 171
Yum (Thai), 305

MURRAY HILL

Artisanal (German), xi, 92
Blue Smoke (Regional American), 232–33
Caridad (Dominican), 49
Carl's Steaks (Regional American), 244
Chennai Garden (Southern Indian), 261, 271
Curry in a Hurry (Northern Indian), 263–64
Curry Leaf (Northern Indian), 263
Enoteca I Trulli (Italian), 153
Grand Sichuan (Sichuan and Hunan), 40
Haandi (Pakistani), 268
Haru (Japanese), 173
Havana Pies (International), 120
Jai-Ya (Thai), 301
Koko (Japanese), 175
Madras Mahal (Southern Indian), 273
Mexico Lindo (Regional American), 248
Mosaico (International), 121
Nader (Persian), 231
Persepolis (Afghani), 230
Rolf's (German), 92
Sahara's Turkish Cuisine (Turkish), 316
Sarge's (Jewish-American), 182
Tony's Burgers (Regional American), 237
Vatan (Gujarati), 261
Wu Liang Ye (Sichuan and Hunan), 41

SOHO

Aquiloni (Italian), 152
Balthazar (French), 84–85
Giorgione (Italian), 126, 153
Honmura An (Japanese), 168

Hoomoos Asli (Israeli), 215
La Conquita (Dominican), 50
Le Pain Quotidien (Belgian), 81, 83
Lombardi's (Italian), 144, 149
L'Orange Bleue (Moroccan), 225
Mooncake Foods (International), 121
Ñ (Spanish), 296–97
Palacinka (French), 90
Pao (Portuguese), 295
Pepe Rosso (Italian), 140–41
Pintxos (Spanish), 293
Provence (French), 89–91
Snack (Greek), 109
Sullivan Street Bakery (Italian), 151
The Yoghurt Place II (Greek), 110–11
12 Chairs (International), 123

TRIBECA

Bread Tribeca (Italian), 137–38
Danube (Austrian), 92
Next Door Nobu (Japanese), 177
Nobu (Japanese), 174, 175, 176, 177
Pakistan Tea House (Pakistani), 270
Pepolino (Italian), 141
Petite Abeille (Belgian), 81, 83, 237
Shore (Regional American), 247
Sophie's (Cuban), 47
Thalassa (Greek), 110

UPPER EAST SIDE

Al Baraka (Moroccan), 223
Beyoglu (Turkish), 314
Café Sabarsky (Austrian), 93
Chicky's on 86 (Greek), 106
Chola (Southern Indian), 256, 271
Dawat (Regional Indian), 256
Emo's (Korean), 186
Galil (Moroccan), 224
Halal Indo-Pak Restaurant (Pakistani), 268–69

Harglo's Café (Regional American), 234–35
Haru (Japanese), 173
Heidelberg (German), 92
Jubilee (French), 87–88
Le Pain Quotidien (Belgian), 81, 83
Lexington Candy Shop (Regional American), 242
Miss Saigon (Vietnamese), 320–21
Mocca Hungarian (Hungarian), 60
Pamir (Afghani), 230
Papaya King (Regional American), 237, 238, 240
Pastrami Queen (Jewish-American), 182
Pattaya (Thai), 303–4
Payard Patisserie and Bistro (French), 89
Pearson's Texas Barbecue (Regional American), 233–34
Serafina Fabulous Pizza (Italian), 150–51
Siegel's Kosher Delicatessen (Jewish-American), 182–83
Taperia Madrid (Spanish), 297
Wu Liang Ye (Sichuan and Hunan), 41

UPPER WEST SIDE

Afghan Kebab House (Afghani), 230
Alibaba (Yemeni), 220
Awash (Ethiopian), 79
Barney Greengrass (Jewish-American), 179
Big Nick's (Regional American), 235
Caridad La Original (Dominican), 49
Celeste (Italian), 138
Epices du Traiteur (Tunisian), 226
Gabriela's (Mexican), 202–3
Gray's Papaya (Regional American), 239
Haru (Japanese), 173
Krik Krak (Haitian), 114–15
Los Paisas (Mexican), 206
Luzia's (Portuguese), 295

Nice Matin (French), 88
Pampa (Argentinian), 4
Tibet Shambala (Tibetan), 275
Turkuaz (Turkish), 316

WALL STREET

Bangal Curry (Northern Indian), 262
Bennie's (Thai), 298, 301
Diwan-E-Khaas (Northern Indian), 264
Nikoniko (Japanese), 172
Pancho Magico (Regional American), 248
Pearl Palace (Pakistani), 270
Philly Steak & Sub (Regional American), 244

WASHINGTON HEIGHTS/ INWOOD

El Conde (Dominican), 50
El Lina (Dominican), 51
El Malecon (Dominican), 51
El Mambi (Dominican), 51–52
El Mundo Fried Chicken (Dominican), 52
El Taxista Ecuatoriano (Ecuadorian), 68–69
Galicia (Dominican), 51
La Cabana Salvadoreña (Salvadoran), 15–16

WEST VILLAGE

A Salt and Battery (English), 74, 75
Babbo (Italian), 136
Bar Six (Moroccan), 224
BB Sandwich Bar (Regional American), 244
Beatrice Inn (Italian), 130
Bouchon (French), 85
Café Asean (International), 118
Cafe de Bruxelles (Belgian), 81, 83, 84
Café Topsy (English), 73, 74
Chez Brigitte (French), 85
Cowgirl Hall of Fame (Regional American), 245
Crepes to Go (French), 90
Da Andrea (Italian), 138

Delícia (Brazilian), 8–9
Do Hwa (Korean), 185
DoSirak (Korean), 185–86
El Cantinero (Regional American), 248
Faicco's (Italian), 129
Flor's Kitchen (Venezuelan), 12
Gallo Nero (Italian), 138–39
Gobo (International), 119–20
Grano (Italian), 139
Gray's Papaya (Regional American), 239
Hanamai (Japanese), 171
'ino (Italian), 126, 153
Joe Jr. (Greek), 106
John's (Italian), 144, 145
Karavas (Regional American), 236
King Shawarma (Lebanese), 219
Kumar cart (Southern Indian), 272
La Bonbonniere (Regional American), 241
La Metairie (French), 81
La Ripaille (French), 81
Le Frite Kote (Belgian), 84
Le Gigot (French), 86
Lupa (Italian), 139–40
Maletesta Trattoria (Italian), 140
Mama's Food Shop (Regional American), 245
Manna (Korean), 186–88
Marquet Patisserie (French), 88
Mary's Fish Camp (Regional American), 246
Meskerem (Ethiopian), 77, 79–80
Mi Cocina (Mexican), 205
Moustache (Lebanese), 219–20
Myers of Keswick (English), 74
Negril (Jamaican), 163
NL (Dutch), 92, 93–94
Ony (Japanese), 169
Otto (Italian), 140, 146
Paradou (French), 88–89
Pastis (French), 81, 89, 225
Pearl Oyster Bar (Regional American), 246, 247

Pepe Verde (Italian), 140–41
Petite Abeille (Belgian), 81, 83, 237
Pink Tea Cup (Soul Food), 288
Pop's Pierogi (Russian), 253
Saint's Alp Teahouse (Hong Kong Chinese), 36
Salam Cafe & Restaurant (Lebanese), 220
Sevilla (Spanish), 294
Snack Taverna (Greek), 109
Spain (Spanish), 295
Tea and Sympathy (English), 75
Thali (Northern Indian), 267
Thiru Kumar cart (Southern Indian), 272
Tokyo La Men (Japanese), 169–70
Village Schawarma (Israeli), 216
Wallsé (Austrian), 93
Waverly Restaurant (Regional American), 243
Yatagan (Turkish), 316–17
Yujin (Japanese), 177
Zitoune (Moroccan), 225

QUEENS

ASTORIA

Atlixco Deli (Mexican), 201
Aya's Café Restaurant (Moroccan), 223
Bascarsija (Bosnian), 57
Cantina de Lina (Brazilian), 8
Cevabdzinica Sarjevo (Bosnian), 57
Christos Hasapo-Taverna (Greek), 106
Costal Colombiana (Colombian), 10
Dhaka Cafe Jhill (Bangladeshi), 259–60
Elwady (Egyptian), 213
Girassol (Brazilian), 10
House of Pizza (Bosnian), 58
Istria Sports Club (Istrian), 60–61
Kabab Café (Egyptian), 214
Koliba (Czech), 59

La Espiga II (Mexican), 202
Rose & Joe's Italian Bakery
    (Italian), 145, 150, 151
S'Agapo (Greek), 108
San Antonio Bakery #2
    (Chilean), 5–6
Scouna Taverna (Greek),
    108–9
Stamatis (Greek), 109–10
Terra Brasil (Brazilian), 9
Tierras Colombianas (Colom-
    bian), 11
Uncle George's (Greek), 110
Zenon (Greek), 111
Zlata Praha (Czech), 59–60
Zodiac (Greek), 111

BAYSIDE/DOUGLASTON

Akida (Japanese), 173
La Baraka (Tunisian), 225–26
Laterna (Greek), 107
Patoug (Persian), 231
Santoor (Southern Indian),
    273

CORONA

Corona Pizza (Italian), 147
Don Pepe (Ecuadorian), 66
El Arrayan (Chilean), 1, 5
El Gauchita (Argentinian), 4
El Tio Julio (Peruvian), 72
Green Field (Brazilian), 10
La Espiga (Mexican), 202
La Esquina Criolla
    (Uruguayan), 6
La Union (Peruvian-Chinese),
    72

ELMHURST

Captain King (Taiwanese), 41
David's Taiwanese Gourmet
    (Taiwanese), 41
Dee's West Indian Bakery
    (Jamaican), 160
La Fusta (Argentinian), 3–4
Malaysian Rasa Sayang
    (Malaysian), 194
Meson Asturias (Spanish),
    292–93
My Thai (Thai), 303

Olympic Garden (Korean), 189
Taste Good (Malaysian), 195–
    96

FLORAL PARK

Fiza Diner (Pakistani),
    268
Indian Coffee House (South-
    ern Indian), xii, 272
Raj Mahal (Northern Indian),
    266–67

FLUSHING/COLLEGE
POINT/MURRAY HILL

A Touch of Hungary (Hungar-
    ian), 60
ABC American Cooking (Hong
    Kong Chinese), 35
Afghan Kabab Palace
    (Afghani), 229
Bownie (Sri Lankan), 274
Buddha Bodai (Vegetarian
    Chinese), 44
Dosa Hutt (Southern Indian),
    xii, 256, 271–72
Dumpling Stall (Northern
    Chinese), 26
Flushing Mall Food Court
    (International), 119
Gum Fung (Cantonese), 28,
    29
Haejo (Korean), 187
Hong Kong Seafood (Hong
    Kong Chinese), 35
Laifood (Taiwanese), 42
Lee Park Sa (Korean),
    186
Master Grill (Brazilian), 10
No. 1 People's and People
    (Shanghai Chinese),
    38
Nolbu Sushi (Korean), 188
Satay Hut (Malaysian), 195
Seoul King Dumplings
    (Korean), 189
Shin Jung (Korean), 189–90
Sichuan Dynasty (Sichuan and
    Hunan), 40, 41
Sol Bawoo (Korean), 190
Spicy & Tasty (Sichuan and
    Hunan), 40–41

Sweet-N-Tart (Taiwanese), 28, 43

Yang Tze River (Shanghai Chinese), 39

FOREST HILLS

Eddie's Sweet Shop (Regional American), 241

Fincan Turkish Cuisine (Turkish), 315

Mickey's Place (Japanese), 171

Tadjikistan (Tajikistani), 20–21

FRESH MEADOWS

Ali Baba (Afghani), 229–30

Deli Masters (Jewish-American), 180

Quality Food Palace (Northern Indian), 266

HOWARD BEACH

Lenny's Clam Bar (Italian), 132

JACKSON HEIGHTS

Afghan Kebab House (Afghani), 230

Arunee Thai (Thai), 300

Bombay Harbour (Bangladeshi), 259

El Grano de Oro 2000 (Mexican), 203

El Sitio (Cuban), 47

Famous Pizza (Italian), 146–47, 148

Grameen (Bangladeshi), 260

Hornado Ecuatoriano (Ecuadorian), 67

Indian Taj (Northern Indian), 265

Inti Raymi (Peruvian), 69

Jackson Diner (Northern Indian), xii, 265–266, 272

La Cabana (Argentinian), 3

La Picada Azuaya (Ecuadorian), 67–68

La Pollada de Laura (Peruvian), 71–72

La Portena (Argentinian), 3, 4

Maharaja Quality (Southern Indian), 273

Pearson's Texas BBQ (Regional American), 233–34

Pio Pio (Peruvian), 71

Taqueria Coatzingo (Mexican), 210

Tibetan Yak (Tibetan), 275

Tierras Colombianas (Colombian), 11

Tierras Salvadoreñas (Salvadoran), 17

JAMAICA

El Comal (Salvadoran), 16

La Xelaju (Guatemalan), 14

Norman's Jerk Chicken Restaurant (Jamaican), 163

Poor Freddie's Rib Shack (Soul Food), 288–89

S & V Soul Food Castle (Soul Food), 289

KEW GARDENS/KEW GARDENS HILLS

Hapina (Yemeni), 220

Inca's (Peruvian), 69

Uzbekistan Community Center (Uzbekistani), 22, 23

LONG ISLAND CITY

El Sitio (Cuban), 47

5 Stars Punjabi Indian Cuisine (Northern Indian), 264–65

Flor de Luna (Mexican), 202

Malagueta (Brazilian), 9

Rincon Colombiano (Colombian), 11

Tulcingo #4 (Mexican), 210

REGO PARK

Cheburechnaya (Uzbekistani), 21

Pio Pio (Peruvian), 71

Registan (Uzbekistani), 23

Salut (Uzbekistani), 23

Tangra Masala (Indian-Chinese), 37

RICHMOND HILL

Alice's Palace (Guyanese), 307

Chicken City (Northern Indian), 263
Jahn's (Regional American), 242
King of Latvia II (Latvian), 61
Pio Rico (Peruvian), 71
Pique y Pase (Ecuadorian), 68
Punjabi Kebab House (Northern Indian), 266
Singh's Roti Shop #3 (Trinidadian), 311
Sorrento Bakery (Surinamese), 308–9
Sugunya (Thai), 304
Tandoori Hut (Northern Indian), 267
Zum Stammtisch (German), 63, 96

RIDGEWOOD/ MASPETH/MIDDLE VILLAGE

Bosna-Express (Bosnian), 57
Forest Pork Store (German), 96
Fortunata's (Italian), 148
Niederstein's (German), 92, 94–95
O'Neill's (Italian), 146, 149–50
Tikki Masala (International), 122

ROCKAWAY BEACH

El Refugio (Salvadoran), 17

ST. ALBANS/CAMBRIA HEIGHTS

Boston Jerk Palace (Jamaican), 158
Carmichael's Diner (Soul Food), 284
Halal Kitchen (Cantonese), 29

SUNNYSIDE

La Pollera Colorado (Colombian), 11
Mi Bolivia (Bolivian), 65
Natural Bean Curd (Korean), 188–89
Yerevan (Armenian), 18–19

WOODSIDE

Braulio's and Familia (Ecuadorian), 66
Donovan's (Irish), 75–76
Ihawan (Philippine), 197
Izalco (Salvadoran), 16
Khao Homm (Thai), 302
La Uruguaya y Paraguayita Bakery (Uruguayan), 6
Las Gaviotas (Chilean), 5
Sripraphai (Thai), 302, 304–5
Warteg Fortuna (Indonesian), 194

STATEN ISLAND

Denino's (Italian), 145–46, 147, 149
Fortune Garden (Cantonese), 29
Frank-N-Frite (Regional American), 238
Go-Go Souvlaki King (International), 120
Joe and Pat's (Italian), 144, 149
Killmeyer's Old Bavarian Inn (German), 94
Lakshmi's (Sri Lankan), 274
New Asha Café (Sri Lankan), 274–75
Nunzio's (Italian), 146
Skippers (Ghanian), 104
Taco Azteca (Mexican), 208
The Polish Place (Polish), 63
Tomo (Japanese), 172–73
West Brighton Italian Grocery (Italian), 129–30

NEW JERSEY

Beyti Kebab (Turkish), 314
Chowpatty (Gujarati), 261
Deccani (Hyderabadi), 256, 262
Pic-Nic (Portuguese), 295–96
Restaurant Oaxaqueño #2 (Mexican), 209
Rutt's Hut (Regional American), 238, 240
Seabras Marrisquiera (Portuguese), 296
Tapajos River Steak House (Brazilian), 9

Restaurant Index

Restaurants are alphabetized under the initial article, if there is one.

A & A Bake and Doubles (Trinidadian), 306, 309

A & R West Indian Restaurant and Roti Shop (Trinidadian). See Halal Roti

A Salt and Battery (English), 74, 75

À Table (French), 84

A Touch of Hungary (Hungarian), 60

ABC American Cooking (Hong Kong Chinese), 35

Adelman's (Jewish-American), 181

Afghan Kabab Palace (Afghani), 229

Afghan Kebab House (Afghani), 230

Africa Restaurant #1 (Senegalese), 280, 281

Africa Restaurant #2 (Senegalese), 280–81

African American Restaurant (Ghanian), 99

African and American Family Restaurant (Senegalese), 278, 280

African Grill (Ivory Coastal), 278–79

African Restaurant. See African American Restaurant

Akida (Japanese), 173

Al Baraka (Moroccan), 223

Alex Aguinaga—aka Fanny (Ecuadorian), 65

Ali Baba (Afghani), 229–30

Alibaba (Yemeni), 220

Alice's Palace (Guyanese), 307

Ali's Trinidad Roti Shop (Trinidadian), 309

All Star Café Restaurant (Albanian), 55–56, 97

Allioli (Spanish), 294

Alsalam Restaurant & Meat Market (Lebanese), 217

Amarin (Thai), 300, 302

American East Fuzhou Restaurant (Fujianese Chinese), 32

Anatolian Gyro (Turkish), 313

Angelica Kitchen (Regional American), 243

Anyway Cafe Club (Russian), 251

Aquiloni (Italian), 152

Argentine Pavilion (Argentinian), 2

Ariana Afghan Kebab (Afghani), 230

Artisinal (German), xi, 92

Arunee Thai (Thai), 300

Assenzio (Italian), 126, 152

Atlixco Deli (Mexican), 201

Awash (Ethiopian), 79

Aya's Café Restaurant (Moroccan), 223

Aziza (Nigerian), 101

B. Frites (Belgian), 83

B & H Dairy Restaurant (Jewish-American), 62, 179, 181

Ba Xuyen (Vietnamese), 323

Babbo (Italian), 136

341

Bahar Shishkebab House (Afghani), 229, 230–31

Bahry Fish Market and Restaurant (Egyptian), 213

Baje's P & T Eatery (Bajan), 156–57

Bake & Things (Trinidadian), 309–10

Bali Nusa Indah (Indonesian), 193

Ballato (Italian). *See* Emilio's Ballato

Balthazar (French), 84–85

Bamonte's Restaurant (Italian), 124, 130

Bangal Curry (Northern Indian), 262

Bangkok Café (Thai), 300–1

Banh Mi So 1 (Vietnamese), 323

Banjara (Northern Indian), 262–63

Bar Six (Moroccan), 224

Bar Veloce (Italian), 152–53

Barney Greengrass (Jewish-American), 179

Bascarsija (Bosnian), 57

Basso Est (Italian), 137

Bay Leaf (Northern Indian), 263

Bay Shish Kebab (Turkish), 23, 313

Bayou (Regional American), 234

BB Sandwich Bar (Regional American), 244

Beatrice Inn (Italian), 130

Bedouin Tent (Lebanese), 217

Belgo (Belgian), 81–82

Bella Napoli (Italian), 145, 147

Bennie's (Thai), 298, 301

Bereket (Turkish), 314

Beyoglu (Turkish), 314

Beyti Kebab (Turkish), 314

Big Eat (Hong Kong Chinese), 34

Big Nick's (Regional American), 235

Bis Milalh (International), 117

Bissaleh (Israeli), 214

Black Betty (International), 117

Blue Mountain Café (Jamaican), 158

Blue 9 Burger (Regional American), 235

Blue Smoke (Regional American), 232–33

Boca Chica (International), 117–18

Bombay Harbour (Bangladeshi), 259

Bond Street (Japanese), 175, 177

Borobudur (Indonesian), 193

Bosna-Express (Bosnian), 57

Boston Jerk Palace (Jamaican), 158

Bouchon (French), 85

Bownie (Sri Lankan), 274

Braulio's and Familia (Ecuadorian), 66

Brawta (Jamaican), 158

Brazil Grill (Brazilian), 8

Bread from Beirut (Lebanese), 218

Bread Tribeca (Italian), 137–38

Brennan & Carr (Irish), 75

Brick Lane Curry House (Anglo-Indian), 75, 258–59

Brick Oven Gallery (Italian), 147

Brook Luncheonette (International), 118

Buddha Bodai (Vegetarian Chinese), 44

Bukhara (Pakistani), 268

Burektorja Dukagjini (Albanian), 56

Burger Joint (Regional American), 235

C & F Restaurant (Hong Kong Chinese), 34

Cabana Carioca (Brazilian), 8

Café al Mercato (Italian), 133

Café Asean (International), 118

Cafe de Bruxelles (Belgian), 81, 83, 84

Café Deville (French), 85

Cafe Glechik (Russian), 251

Cafe Istanbul (Turkish), 314–15

342

Café Kashkar (Uighur Chinese), 23, 43
Cafe Paris (Russian), 252–53
Cafe Rakka (Lebanese), 218
Café Sabarsky (Austrian), 93
Cafe Shish-kebab (Uzbekistani), 21
Café Topsy (English), 73, 74
Caffe Capri (Italian), 133, 143
Caffe Volna (Russian), 254
Calidad Latina (International), 118
Cantina de Lina (Brazilian), 8
Captain King (Taiwanese), 41
Caracas Arepa Bar (Venezuelan), 11
Caravello's (Italian), 135
Caribbean Taste Inc. (Jamaican), 159–60
Caridad (Dominican), 49
Caridad La Original (Dominican), 49
Carl's Hot Doubles (Trinidadian), 310
Carl's Steaks (Regional American), 244
Carmichael's Diner (Soul Food), 284
Carnegie Deli (Jewish-American), 180
Casa Adela (Puerto Rican), 52–53
Casa Calamari (Italian), 130–31
Casimir (French), 87
Castro's (Mexican), 201
Catene Deli (Italian), 126
Celeste (Italian), 138
Cevabdzinica Sarjevo (Bosnian), 57
Chanoodle (Chiu Chow Chinese), 31
Chao Zhou (Chiu Chow Chinese), 31
Charles Southern Style Kitchen (Soul Food), 284–85
Cheburechnaya (Uzbekistani), 21
Cheers (Thai), 301, 302
Chennai Garden (Southern Indian), 261, 271

Cheskel's Shwarma King (Israeli), 214
Chez Brigitte (French), 85
Chez Es Saada (Moroccan), 224
Chez Oscar (French), 85–86
Chianti (Italian), 131
Chicken City (Northern Indian), 263
Chicky's on 86 (Greek), 106
Chikubu (Japanese), 170
Chimichurri Grill (Argentinian), 3
Chio Pio (Uzbekistani), 21
Chipshop (English), 74, 259
Chola (Southern Indian), 256, 271
Chowpatty (Gujarati), 261
Christos Hasapo-Taverna (Greek), 106
Churrascaria Plataforma (Brazilian), 10
Clemente's (Italian), 127, 128
Clemente's Maryland Crabhouse (Regional American), 246
Cock's (Bajan), 157
Coco Roco (Peruvian), 64, 69, 70
Coney Island Joe's (Regional American), 237, 238
Congee (Cantonese), 27–28
Congee Village (Cantonese), 27, 28
Copeland's Take-Out and Catering (Soul Food), 286
Corona Pizza (Italian), 147
Cosmic Cantina (Regional American), 248
Costal Colombiana (Colombian), 10
Cowgirl Hall of Fame (Regional American), 245
Creperie (French), 90
Crepes to Go (French), 90
Crif Dogs (Regional American), 237, 238
Crosby Connection (Italian), 129
Cuchifritos 2000 (Puerto Rican). See La Fondita
Culpepper's (Bajan), 157

343

Curry in a Hurry (Northern Indian), 263–64

Curry Leaf (Northern Indian), 263

Curry Shop (Anglo-Indian), 75, 259

D.O.C. Wine Bar (Italian), 126, 153

D. Zion Burger (Israeli), 215

Da Andrea (Italian), 138

Dabakh-Malik (Senegalese), 281

Daisy May's BBQ USA (Regional American), 233

Dalquis Restaurant (Dominican), 50

Danny and Pepper (Jamaican), 160

Danube (Austrian), 92

Darbar East (Northern Indian), 264, 276

David's Taiwanese Gourmet (Taiwanese), 41

Dawat (Regional Indian), 256

Dawgs on Park (Regional American), 238

DB Bistro (Regional American), 235–36

Deccani (Hyderabadi), 256, 262

Dee's West Indian Bakery (Jamaican), 160

Defonte's Sandwich Shop (Italian), 127

Deli Corner (Jewish-American), 180

Deli Masters (Jewish-American), 180

Delícia (Brazilian), 8–9

Demu Café (Nigerian), 101–3

Denino's (Italian), 145–46, 147, 149

Denise Pizza (Italian), 145

Desi Village (Northern Indian), 264

Devins Fish & Chips (Soul Food), 286

Dhaka Cafe Jhill (Bangladeshi), 259–60

Diamond Dairy Restaurant (Jewish-American), 178, 179

DiFara Pizzeria (Italian), 146, 148

Diner (Regional American), 241

Diwan-E-Khaas (Northern Indian), 264

Djerdan #3 (Bosnian), 58

Do Hwa (Korean), 185

Dok Suni (Korean), 185

Don Pepe (Ecuadorian), 66

Donovan's (Irish), 75–76

Dosa Hutt (Southern Indian), xii, 256, 271–72

DoSirak (Korean), 185–86

Driggs Pizzeria (Italian), 148

Dumpling House (Northern Chinese), 26, 27

Dumpling Stall (Northern Chinese), 26

E & R (Haitian), 113

East Broadway Gourmet (Fujianese Chinese), 32–33

Eastern Feast (Uzbekistani), 21–22

Ebe Ye Yie (Ghanian), 99

Eddie's Sweet Shop (Regional American), 241

Efendi (Turkish), 315

18 Aharns (Vegetarian Chinese), 44

88 Reach House (Fujianese Chinese), 33

Eisenberg's Sandwich Shop (Regional American), 245

El Arrayan (Chilean), 1, 5

El Cantinero (Regional American), 248

El Chile Verde (Mexican), 201–2

El Cibao (Dominican), 50

El Comal (Salvadoran), 16

El Conde (Dominican), 50

El Despertar (Dominican), 50, 294

El Economica (Dominican), 50–51

El Gauchita (Argentinian), 4

El Grano de Oro 2000 (Mexican), 203
El Lina (Dominican), 51
El Maguey y La Tuna (Mexican), 203
El Malecon (Dominican), 51
El Mambi (Dominican), 51–52
El Mundo Fried Chicken (Dominican), 52
El Nuevo Bohio (Puerto Rican), 53
El Pulgarcito de America (Salvadoran), 16
El Refugio (Salvadoran), 17
El Rincon Boricua (Puerto Rican), 53
El Salvador (Salvadoran), 17
El Sitio (Cuban), 47
El Taxista Ecuatoriano (Ecuadorian), 68–69
El Tesoro (Ecuadorian), 69
El Tio Julio (Peruvian), 72
El Vaquero (Mexican), 210–11
Elora's (International), 118
Elvie's Turo-Turo (Philippine), 196
Elwady (Egyptian), 213
Emerald Planet (International), 119
Emilio's Ballato (Italian), 131
Emo's (Korean), 186
Enoteca I Trulli (Italian), 153
Epices du Traiteur (Tunisian), 226
Esca (Italian), 174
Estiatorio Milos (Greek), 105, 110
Estrabar (Italian), 143
Eva Restaurante (Ecuadorian), 66–67
Eve's Restaurant (Haitian), 113
Excellent Dumpling House (Cantonese), 28–29

F & B (Regional American), 238
Fada (French), 86
Faicco's (Italian), 129
Family Noodle (Cantonese), 29
Famous Pizza (Italian), 146–47, 148

Famous Ray's (Italian), 148
Fanny (Ecuadorian). See Alex Aguinaga
Farfina Coffee Shop (Ivory Coastal), 279
Felidia (Italian), 138
Ferdinando's (Italian), 135
Fi Wih Kitchen (Jamaican), 160–61
Fincan Turkish Cuisine (Turkish), 315
Finger Linkin's "R" Us (Jamaican), 160
Five Front (Regional American), 243
5 Stars Punjabi Indian Cuisine (Northern Indian), 264–65
Fiza Diner (Pakistani), 268
Flavored with One Love (Guyanese), 308
Flea Market (French), 87
Flor de Luna (Mexican), 202
Flor's Kitchen (Venezuelan), 12
Flushing Mall Food Court (International), 119
Food Hut (Jamaican), 161
Forest Pork Store (German), 96
Fortunata's (Italian), 148
Fortune Garden (Cantonese), 29
Fountain Café (Lebanese), 218
416 B.C. (Bulgarian), 58
1492 (Spanish), 296
Frank-N-Frite (Regional American), 238
Fried Dumpling (Northern Chinese), 26–27
Frittaile Lacaye (Haitian), 113–14
Fu Chow Restaurant (Fujianese Chinese), 33
Funky Broome (Hong Kong Chinese), 34–35

Gabriela's (Mexican), 202–3
Galicia (Dominican), 51
Galil (Moroccan), 224
Gallo Nero (Italian), 138–39
Gan Eden (Uzbekistani), 22–23

Genki Sushi (Japanese), 173
Ghenet (Ethiopian), 79
Gia Lam (Vietnamese), 320
Giando (Italian), 131–32
Gino's Focacceria (Italian), 135
Giorgione (Italian), 126, 153
Giovanni's (Italian), 149
Girassol (Brazilian), 10
Glenda's Home Cooking (Trinidadian), 310, 311
Gobo (International), 119–20
Go-Go Souvlaki King (International), 120
Good World (Swedish), 97
Gottlieb's Restaurant (Jewish-American), 180
Grameen (Bangladeshi), 260
Grand Sichuan (Sichuan and Hunan), 40
Grano (Italian), 139
Gray's Papaya (Regional American), 239
Green Field (Brazilian), 10
Gum Fung (Cantonese), 28, 29
Gurra Cafe (Albanian), 56
Guyana Roti House (Guyanese), 308

H.I.M. (Jamaican), 161
Haandi (Pakistani), 268
Haejo (Korean), 187
Halal Indo-Pak Restaurant (Pakistani), 268–69
Halal Kitchen (Cantonese), 29
Halal Roti (Trinidadian), 157, 312–13
Hall Street Kosher Café (Jewish-American), 180
Hallo Berlin (German), 92, 94, 96
Hanamai (Japanese), 171
Hapina (Yemeni), 220
Happy End (Polish), 61–62
Happy Shabu Shabu (Chinese), 37
Harchevnya (Russian), 253
Harglo's Café (Regional American), 234–35
Haru (Japanese), 173
Hasaki (Japanese), 173–75

Hatsuhana (Japanese), 174, 175
Havana Central (Cuban), 46–47
Havana Chelsea Luncheonette (Cuban), 47
Havana Pies (International), 120
Heidelberg (German), 92
Hinsch's (Regional American), 241–42
Honduras Maya (Honduran), 15
Hong Kong Seafood (Hong Kong Chinese), 35
Honmura An (Japanese), 168
Hoomoos Asli (Israeli), 215
Hornado Ecuatoriano (Ecuadorian), 67
House of Jerk (Jamaican), 161
House of Pizza (Bosnian), 58

Icons Afro-West (Nigerian), 101–3
Ihawan (Philippine), 197
Il Bagato (Italian), 124
In God We Trust (Ghanian), 99–100
Inca's (Peruvian), 69
India House (Northern Indian), 265
Indian Coffee House (Southern Indian), xii, 272
Indian Taj (Northern Indian), 265
'ino (Italian), 126, 153
'inoteca (Italian), 154
Inti Raymi (Peruvian), 69
Ishihama (Korean), 188
Island Spice (Jamaican), 163
Istria Sports Club (Istrian), 60–61
Ithaka (Greek), 109
Izalco (Salvadoran), 16

Jackie's Delicatessen (Italian), 127–28
Jackson Diner (Northern Indian), xii, 265–66, 272
Jacques Torres Chocolate (French), 86
Jahn's (Regional American), 242

Jai-Ya (Thai), 301

Java Indonesian Rijsttafel (Indonesian), 191, 194

Jay & Lloyd's (Jewish-American), 181

Jeoladdo (Japanese), 175

Jerk Center (Jamaican), 161

Jerusalem Steak House (Israeli), 215

Jewel Bako (Japanese), 175

Joe & Joe's Restaurant (Italian), 132

Joe and Pat's (Italian), 144, 149

Joe Jr. (Greek), 106

Joe's Ginger (Chinese), 31

Joe's of Avenue U (Italian), 124, 135

Joe's Shanghai (Chinese), 31, 37–38, 39

Joey's Cold Heroes (Italian), 129

John's (Italian), 144, 145

John's Deli (Italian), 128

Jordan's Lobster Dock (Regional American), 246

Joya (International and Thai), 120, 301, 302

Jubilee (French), 87–88

Jumbo Hamburgers (Regional American), 236

Kabab Café (Egyptian), 214

Kaloum (Guinean), 278

Karam (Lebanese), 218–19

Karavas (Regional American), 236

Karl Ehmer (German), 96

Katsuhama (Japanese), 169, 170

Katz's (Jewish-American and Regional American), 180, 182, 239

Kazan (Turkish). See Fincan Turkish Cuisine

Kelso Diner (Panamanian), 13, 15

Keur n' Deye (Senegalese), 282

Keur Sokhna (Senegalese), 282

Khao Homm (Thai), 302

Khyber Kebab (Pakistani), 270

Kiev (Ukrainian), 254

Kikiriki (Peruvian), 70

Killmeyer's Old Bavarian Inn (German), 94

Kine Restaurant (Senegalese). See Africa Restaurant #1

King of Latvia II (Latvian), 61

King Shawarma (Lebanese), 219

Kitchen Market (Regional American), 248

Koko (Japanese), 175

Koliba (Czech), 59

Komodo (International), 120

Kosher Delight (Israeli), 216

Krezo 2 (Lithuanian), 61

Krik Krak (Haitian), 114–15

Krispy Pizzeria (Italian), 145, 149

Kumar cart (Southern Indian), 272

Kuruma Sushi (Japanese), 174, 175–76

Kway Tiow (Thai). See My Thai

L & B Spumoni Gardens (Italian), 132, 145

La Baraka (Tunisian), 225–26

La Bonbonniere (Regional American), 241

La Cabana (Argentinian), 3

La Cabana Salvadoreña (Salvadoran), 15–16

La Caravelle (French), 176

La Casa de los Tacos (Mexican), 201

La Chinita Linda (Cuban-Chinese), 48

La Conquita (Dominican), 50

La Espiga (Mexican), 202

La Espiga II (Mexican), 202

La Esquina Criolla (Uruguayan), 6

La Focacceria (Italian), 135–36

La Fondita (Puerto Rican), 53

La Fusta (Argentinian), 3–4

La Guadalupana (Mexican), 204

La Hacienda (Mexican), 201, 203

La Locanda (Italian), 132–33

La Maison du Couscous (Moroccan), 224–25

347

La Marmite (Senegalese), 282
La Metarie (French), 81
La Orquidea (Honduran), 15
La Piazzetta (Italian), 134
La Picada Azuaya (Ecuadorian), 67–68
La Pizza Fresca (Italian), 146, 150
La Pollada de Laura (Peruvian), 71–72
La Pollera Colorado (Colombian), 11
La Portena (Argentinian), 3, 4
La Ripaille (French), 81
La Taza de Oro (Puerto Rican), 53
La Union (Peruvian), 72
La Uruguaya y Paraguayita Bakery (Uruguayan), 6
La Villa (Italian), 146, 151
La Xelaju (Guatemalan), 14
Lahore Deli (Pakistani), 269
Laifood (Taiwanese), 42
Laila (Lebanese), 219
Lakruwana (Sri Lankan), 274
Lakshmi's (Sri Lankan), 274
Lams Kitchen & Sports Bar (Nigerian), 103
Las Antillas (Dominican), 49
Las Gaviotas (Chilean), 5
Laterna (Greek), 107
Le Frite Kote (Belgian), 84
Le Gamin (French), 86
Le Gigot (French), 86
Le Pain Quotidien (Belgian), 81, 83
Le Singe Vert (French), 91
Le Soleil (Haitian), 115
Le Souk (Tunisian), 227
Le Worodougou (Ivory Coastal), 279
Le Zie (Italian), 142
Le Zoccole (Italian), 142
Lechonera El Coqui (Puerto Rican), 53
Lechonera Sandy (Dominican), 51
Lee Park Sa (Korean), 186
Lenny's Clam Bar (Italian), 132
Lexington Candy Shop (Regional American), 242

Lil' Frankie's (Italian), 148
Lima's Taste (Peruvian), 64, 70
Little Bangladesh Restaurant & Kebab House (Bangladeshi), 260–61
Little Poland (Polish), 62
Little Saigon Cafe (Vietnamese), 320
Locanda Vini & Olii (Italian), 139
Lombardi's (Italian), 144, 149
L'Orange Bleue (Moroccan), 225
Los Chorros (Salvadoran), 16
Los Compadres (Mexican), 202
Los Dos Molinos (Regional American), 247
Los Dos Rancheros Mexicanos (Mexican). See Salon Mexico
Los Mariachis (Mexican), 204
Los Paisas (Mexican), 206
Los Pollitos (International), 121
Louis G.'s (Italian), 143
Louise's (Vincentian), 166
Luca Lounge (Italian), 149
Lucien (French), 87
Lupa (Italian), 139–40
Luzia's (Portuguese), 295

M & G Diner (Soul Food), 287
Madiba (South African), 80
Madonia Brothers Bakery (Italian), 143
Madras Cafe (Southern Indian), 272–73
Madras Mahal (Southern Indian), 273
Maharaja Quality (Southern Indian), 273
Malagueta (Brazilian), 9
Malaysian Rasa Sayang (Malaysian), 194
Maletesta Trattoria (Italian), 140
Mali-Bo (Malian), 279–80
Mama's Food Shop (Regional American), 245
Mandoo (Korean), 186
Manna (Korean), 186–88

Marcus Island Deli (Jamaican), 162
Margie's Red Rose (Soul Food), 286
Margon (Cuban), xii, 45, 47
Marichu (Spanish), 293
Market Café (International), 120–21
Markt (Belgian), 81, 82
Maroons (Jamaican), 162–63
Marquet Patisserie (French), 88
Marseille (French), 88
Mary's Fish Camp (Regional American), 246
Massawa (Eritrean), 78–79
Ma's Soul Food Café (Soul Food), 286–87
Master Grill (Brazilian), 10
Matamoros Puebla Grocery (Mexican), 205
Matsuri (Japanese), 176
Max (Italian), 140
Max Café (Italian), 140
Mazza Plaza (Lebanese), 219
Menchanko-Tei (Japanese), 168–69
Meskerem (Ethiopian), 77, 79–80
Meson Asturias (Spanish), 292–93
Mexico Dos (Mexican) 205
Mexico Lindo (Regional American), 248
Mezze (International), 121
Mi Bolivia (Bolivian), 65
Mi Cocina (Mexican), 205
Mi Mexico Lindo Panaderia (Mexican), 205
Mickey's Place (Japanese), 171
Mie (Japanese), 174, 176
Minar (Northern Indian), 266
Mirage (Nigerian), 103
Miss Saigon (Vietnamese), 320–21
Mister Taco (Mexican), 205–6
Mo-Bay (Jamaican), 163
Mocca Hungarian (Hungarian), 60
Mogador (Moroccan), 225
Molly's Bakery (Trinidadian), 311
Molyvos (Greek), 105, 110

Mona Lisa (Italian), 143
Monika (Polish), 62
Monte's (Italian), 129
Moon Shadow (Thai), 302-3
Mooncake Foods (International), 121
Mosaico (International), 121
Motherland Cuisine (Ghanian), 101
Moustache (Lebanese), 219–20
Mrs. Stahl's Knishes (Jewish-American), 21
My Thai (Thai), 303
Myers of Keswick (English), 74
Mykonos (Greek), 107

Ñ (Spanish), 296–97
N.Y. Noodle Town (Cantonese), 30
Nader (Persian), 231
Nathan's Famous (Regional American), 237, 239
National (Russian), 252
Natural Bean Curd (Korean), 188–89
Natural Restaurant (Cantonese), 30
Nedick's (Regional American), 240
Negril (Jamaican), 163
New Asha Café (Sri Lankan), 274–75
New Bai Wei Gourmet Food Inc. (Fujianese Chinese), 33–34
New Caporal Fried Chicken (Dominican), 52
New Chao Chow (Chiu Chow Chinese), 31–32
New Combination (Nigerian), 103
New Green Bo (Shanghai Chinese), 38
New Manila Food Mart (Philippine), 196
New Pasteur (Vietnamese), 321
New York Kom Tang Soot Bul House (Korean), 189
Next Door Nobu (Japanese), 177

349

Nice Matin (French), 88

Nick's Lobster Restaurant (Regional American), 246-47

Nick's Place (Greek), 107-8

Niederstein's (German), 92, 94-95

Nikoniko (Japanese), 172

NL (Dutch), 92, 93-94

No. 1 People's and People (Shanghai Chinese), 38

Nobu (Japanese), 174, 175, 176, 177

Nolbu Sushi (Korean), 188

Norman's Jerk Chicken Restaurant (Jamaican), 163

North Carolina Country Store (Soul Food), 285

North Mai Xiang Cun Dumpling House (Northern Chinese), 27

Nunzio's (Italian), 146

Nyonya (Malaysian), 194-95

Odessa (Russian), 252

Old Poland Bakery and Restaurant (Polish), 62

Olieng (Thai), 298, 303

Oliva (Spanish), 293

Olympic Garden (Korean), 189

On the Park (Regional American), 236

145 Luncheonette (Yemeni), 221

One Stop Patty Shop (Jamaican), 163

O'Neill's (Italian), 146, 149-50

Ony (Japanese), 169

Otafuku (Japanese), 170

Otto (Italian), 140, 146

Pak Punjab (Pakistani), 269

Pak Star Deli (Pakistani), 269

Pakistan Tea House (Pakistani), 270

Palacinka (French), 90

Palava Hut (Nigerian), 104

Pam Real Thai Food (Thai), 298, 303

Pamir (Afghani), 230

Pampa (Argentinian), 4

Pan Pan (Soul Food), 283, 287, 288

Pancho Magico (Regional American), 248

Pao (Portuguese), 295

Papaya King (Regional American), 237, 238, 240

Paradou (French), 88-89

Pastis (French), 81, 89, 225

Pastorale (Russian), 253

Pastrami Queen (Jewish-American), 182

Patoug (Persian), 231

Patricia's (Italian), 133-34

Patroon (American), 235

Patsy's (Italian), 144, 149

Pattaya (Thai), 303-4

Payard Patisserie and Bistro (French), 89

Pearl Oyster Bar (Regional American), 246, 247

Pearl Palace (Pakistani), 270

Pearly's (Jamaican), 164

Pearson's Texas Barbecue (Regional American), 233-34

Pearson's Texas BBQ (Regional American), 233

Peking Duck House (Northern Chinese), 26

Pepe Giallo (Italian), 140-41

Pepe Rosso (Italian), 140-41

Pepe Verde (Italian), 140-41

Pepolino (Italian), 141

Periyali (Greek), 108

Persepolis (Afghani), 230

Peter Luger (Regional American), 236

Petite Abeille (Belgian), 81, 83, 237

Philly's Cheese Steaks (Regional American), 244

Philly Steak & Sub (Regional American), 244

Pho Cong Ly (Vietnamese), 321

Pho Nam Bo (Vietnamese), 321-22

Pho Tay Hoy (Vietnamese), 322

Pho Viet Huong (Vietnamese), 322

Pic-Nic (Portuguese), 295–96
Pie (Italian), 150
Pigalle (French), 89
Ping's (Hong Kong Chinese), 36
Pink Tea Cup (Soul Food), 288
Pintxos (Spanish), 293
Pio Pio (Peruvian), 71
Pio Rico (Peruvian), 71
Pipa (Spanish), 297
Pique y Pase (Ecuadorian), 68
Pirosmani (Georgian), 20
Pizza Supreme (Italian), 145, 150
Planet Thailand (Thai), 300, 302, 305
Pomaire (Chilean), 5
Pomme-Pomme (Belgian), 84
Pommes Frites Authentic Belgian Fries (Belgian), 84
Poor Freddie's Rib Shack (Soul Food), 288–89
Pop Burger (Regional American), 237
Pop's Pierogi (Russian), 253
Proton Saga (Malaysian), 195
Provence (French), 89–91
Prune (Regional American), 243–44
Puebla Mexican Food (Mexican), 207
Punjabi (Pakistani), 269
Punjabi Kebab House (Northern Indian), 266
Pylos (Greek), 108
Pysne's (Grenadian), 157

Qasim (Pakistani), 270
Quality Food Palace (Northern Indian), 266
Queen of Sheba (Ethiopian), 77, 80

Radio Perfecto (International), 122
Rai Rai Ken (Japanese), 169
Raj Mahal (Northern Indian), 266–67
Rambling House (Irish), 76
Randazzo's (Italian), 134
Rare (Regional American), 237

Rasputin (Russian), 252
Rawal Ravail Restaurant (Pakistani), 270–71
Raymund's Place (Polish), 63
Rectangles (Israeli), 216
Registan (Uzbekistani), 23
Rencher's Crab Inn (Regional American), 247
Republic (International), 122
Restaurant Milan's (Czech), 59
Restaurant Nippon (Japanese), 169
Restaurant Oaxaqueño #2 (Mexican), 209
Resto Léon (French), 87
Restorant Shqiptar (Albanian), 56–57
Rice (International), 122
Ricky's Eat-Well (Jamaican), 164
Rico's Tamales Oaxaqueños (Mexican), 207–8
Ricos Tacos (Mexican), 207
Rincon Colombiano (Colombian), 11
Rinconcito Peruano (Peruvian), 72
Roberto's (Italian), 141
Rocky's (Italian), 128
Rolf's (German), 92
Roll N Roaster (Italian), 128
Romano Restaurant (Italian), xii, 124, 134
Rose & Joe's Italian Bakery (Italian), 145, 150, 151
Rose's Restaurant (Haitian), 115
Rosscoe's House of Chicken and Waffles (Soul Food), 289
Roti Shack (Trinidadian), 157, 311
Royal Bake Shop (Jamaican), 164
Royal Rib House (Soul Food), 289
Royal Siam (Thai), 304
Rue des Crepes (French), 90
Rutt's Hut (Regional American), 238, 240

S & V Soul Food Castle (Soul Food), 289

Sabrosura (Dominican-Chinese), 49

S'Agapo (Greek), 108

Sahara (Turkish), 315

Sahara East (Egyptian), 214

Sahara Grill (Turkish), 315–16

Sahara's Turkish Cuisine (Turkish), 316

Saint's Alp Teahouse (Hong Kong Chinese), 36

Saji's (Japanese), 172

Salam Cafe & Restaurant (Lebanese), 220

Salinas (Ecuadorian), 68

Salon Mexico (Mexican), 208

Salut (Uzbekistani), 23

Sam Won Gahk (Korean), 187

San Antonio Bakery #2 (Chilean), 5–6

San Loco (Regional American), 249

Santoor (Southern Indian), 273

Sapporo (Japanese), 172

Sapporo East (Japanese), 172

Sarge's (Jewish-American), 182

Sarmish (Azerbaijani), 19–20

Satay Hut (Malaysian), 195

Schlitz Inn (German), 95

Schnack (Regional American), 240

Scouna Taverna (Greek), 108–9

SEA (Thai), 302, 304

Seabras Marrisquiera (Portuguese), 296

Second Avenue Deli (Jewish-American), 180, 181, 182

Seoul King Dumplings (Korean), 189

Serafina Fabulous Pizza (Italian), 150–51

Sevilla (Spanish), 294

Shaikh's Place (Regional American), 242

Shanghai Cuisine (Shanghai Chinese), 38–39

Shanghai Gourmet (Shanghai Chinese), 39

Shin Jung (Korean), 189–90

Shore (Regional American), 247

Shopsins (American), 109

Sichuan Dynasty (Sichuan and Hunan), 40, 41

Siegel's Kosher Delicatessen (Jewish-American), 182–83

Silver Swan (German), 92, 96

Singapore Café (Singaporean), 197

Singh's Roti Shop #3 (Trinidadian), 311

Sirtaj (Northern Indian), 267

Skippers (Ghanian), 104

Snack (Greek), 109

Snack Taverna (Greek), 109

Soby-ya (Japanese), 169

Sogo (Taiwanese), 42–43

Sokobolie (Guinean), 278

Sol Bawoo (Korean), 190

Sophie's (Cuban), 47

Sorrento Bakery (Surinamese), 308–9

Soul Fixin's (Soul Food), 289–90

Soup Kitchen International (International), 123

South East Asian Cuisine (Cambodian), 319–20

Spain (Spanish), 295

Spanish American Food (Dominican), 52

Sparky's (Regional American), 237, 240

Spicy & Tasty (Sichuan and Hunan), 40–41

Spring Boy Fuzhou Food (Fujianese Chinese), 34

Sripraphai (Thai), 302, 304–5

St. Andrews (Scottish), 76

St. John's Café and Restaurant (Jamaican), 164

Stamatis (Greek), 109–10

Stick to Your Ribs (American Regional). See Pearson's Texas BBQ

Strictly Roots (Jamaican), 164–65

Stromboli (Italian), 145, 151

Sugunya (Thai), 304

Sullivan Street Bakery (Italian), 151

Sultana (Turkish), 316

Sun Golden Island (Chiu Chow Chinese), 32

Sun Hop Shing Tea House (Cantonese), 28, 30

Sun Shine Kitchen (Jamaican), 165

Sur (Argentinian), 4

Sushi Yasuda (Japanese), 174, 176–77

Sushisay (Japanese), 174, 176

Sweet-N-Tart (Taiwanese), 28, 43

Sybil's (Guyanese), 308

Sylvia's Restaurant (Jamaican), 165

Taam Tov (Uzbekistani), 23

Tabouleh (Jordanian), 216–17

Taco Azteca (Mexican), 208

Tacocina (Mexican), 208

Tacos La Hacienda (Mexican), 208–9

Tacos Nuevo Mexico (Mexican), 210

Tadjikistan (Tajikistani), 20–21

Tandoori Hut (Northern Indian), 267

Tangra Masala (Indian-Chinese), 37

Tanoreen (Jordanian), 217

Tan Phong Supermarket (Vietnamese), 323

Tapajos River Steak House (Brazilian), 9

Taperia Madrid (Spanish), 297

Taprobane (Sri Lankan), 274, 275

Taqueria Coatzingo (Mexican), 210

Taqueria La Asuncion (Mexican), 210

Taste Good (Malaysian), 195–96

Tasty Dumpling (Northern Chinese), 27

Tasty Pizza and Pasta Ristorante (Italian), 141

Tblisi (Georgian), 20

TCB's (Grenadian), 158

Tea and Sympathy (English), 75

Ten Pell (Shanghai Chinese), 39

Teresa's (Polish), 63

Terra Brasil (Brazilian), 9

Thai Café (Thai), 302, 305

Thalassa (Greek), 110

Thali (Northern Indian), 267

The Mill (Korean), 188

The Polish Place (Polish), 63

The Yoghurt Place II (Greek), 110–11

Thiru Kumar cart (Southern Indian), 272

Ti-An Vietnamese Restaurant (Vietnamese), 322

Tibbett Diner (Regional American), 242

Tibet Shambala (Tibetan), 275

Tibetan Yak (Tibetan), 275

Tierras Colombianas (Colombian), 11

Tierras Salvadoreñas (Salvadoran), 17

Tikki Masala (International), 122

Tiny's Giant Food Shop (Regional American), 245–46

Tokyo La Men (Japanese), 169–70

Tom's (Regional American), 242–43

Tomo (Japanese), 172–73

Tontonno Pizzeria Napolitano (Italian), 124, 151

Tony's & Elena Ristorante (Italian), 136

Tony's Burgers (Regional American), 237

Totonno Pizzeria Napolitano (Italian), 124, 144, 151

Toyamadel (Jamaican). See Food Hut

Trattoria Mulino (Italian), 136

Trattoria Paolina (Italian), 142

Tulcingo #4 (Mexican), 210

Tummy Paradise (Jamaican), 165

Turkish Kitchen (Turkish), 316

Turkuaz (Turkish), 316

12 Chairs (International), 123

Ulrika's (Swedish), 97

Umberto's Clam House (Italian), 292

(Soul Food), 287
..eorge's (Greek), 110
..e Nick's Greek Cuisine
    (Greek), 110
Uncle Sal's Ribs and Bibs
    (Regional American), 234
Usuluteco (Salvadoran), 17
Uzbekistan Community Center
    (Uzbekistani), 22, 23
Uzbekistan Tandoori Bread
    (Uzbekistani). *See* Uzbek-
    istan Community Center

ValDiano (Italian), 136
Vatan (Gujarati), 261
Venice Restaurant (Italian),
    137
Veniero's Pasticceria (Italian),
    143-44
Vernon's New Jerk House
    (Jamaican), 165-66
Veronica Ristorante Italiano
    (Italian), 137
Veselka (Ukrainian), 255
Via Emilia (Italian), 142
Victor's (Cuban), 48
Village Mingala (Burmese),
    298, 299
Village Schawarma (Israeli),
    216
Virgil's Real Barbecue (Re-
    gional American), 234
Viva Herbal Pizzeria (Italian),
    152

Wallsé (Austrian), 93
Warteg Fortuna (Indonesian),
    194
Waverly Restaurant (Regional
    American), 243

West African Grocery, 277
West Brighton Italian Grocery
    (Italian), 129-30
Wild Lily Tea Room (Interna-
    tional), 123
Win Sing (Cantonese), 30-
    31
Win49 (Japanese), 170-71
Wong's Rice and Noodle
    Shoppe (Cantonese), 31
Wu Liang Ye (Sichuan and
    Hunan), 41

X.O. Kitchen (Hong Kong
    Chinese), 36
Xunta (Spanish), 294

Yakiniku West (Japanese),
    171
Yang Tze River (Shanghai
    Chinese), 39
Yatagan (Turkish), 316-17
Yeah Shanghai Deluxe (Shang-
    hai Chinese), 39-40
Yemen Café (Yemeni), 221
Yerevan (Armenian), 18-19
Yoshinoya (Japanese), 171
Yoyo Fritaille (Haitian), 115-
    16
Yujin (Japanese), 177
Yum (Thai), 305

Zaragoza Grocery (Mexican),
    211
Zenon (Greek), 111
Zitoune (Moroccan), 225
Zlata Praha (Czech), 59-60
Zodiac (Greek), 111
Zum Stammtisch (German),
    63, 96